12/98

MIDLOTHIAN
PUBLIC LIBRARY

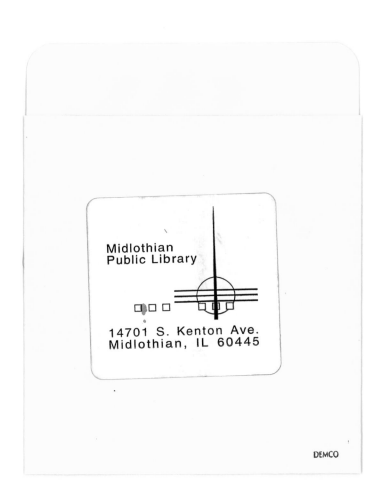

The World
Encyclopedia
of Comics

Edited by Maurice Horn

VOLUME 2

THE CONTRIBUTORS

Manuel Auad (M.A.), *The Philippines*
Bill Blackbeard (B.B.), *U.S.*
Gianni Bono (G.B.), *Italy*
Joe Brancatelli (J.B.), *U.S.*
MaryBeth Calhoun (M.B.C.), *U.S.*
Javier Coma (J.C.), *Spain*
Bill Crouch (B.C.), *U.S.*
Giulio Cesare Cuccolini (G.C.C.), *Italy*
Mark Evanier (M.E.), *U.S.*
Wolfgang Fuchs (W.F.), *Germany*
Luis Gasca (L.G.), *Spain*
Robert Gerson (R.G.), *U.S.*
Denis Gifford (D.G.), *Great Britain*
Paul Gravett (P.G.), *Great Britain*
Peter Harris (P.H.), *Canada*
Hongying Liu-Lengyel (H.Y.L.L.), *China*
Maurice Horn (M.H.), *France/U.S.*
Pierre L. Horn (P.L.H.), *U.S.*
Slobodan Ivkov (S.I.), *Yugoslavia (Serbia)*
Bill Janocha (B.J.), *U.S.*
Orvy Jundis (O.J.), *The Philippines*
Hisao Kato (H.K.), *Japan*
John A. Lent (J.A.L.), *Asia*
Richard Marschall (R.M.), *U.S.*
Alvaro de Moya (A.M.), *Brazil*
Kalmán Rubovszky (K.R.), *Hungary/Poland*
Ervin Rustemagić (E.R.), *Yugoslavia*
John Ryan (J.R.), *Australia*
Matthew A. Thorn (M.A.T.), *Japan*
Dennis Wepman (D.W.), *U.S.*

The World Encyclopedia of Comics

Edited by Maurice Horn

VOLUME 2

Chelsea House Publishers
Philadelphia

Acknowledgments

The editors of *The World Encyclopedia of Comics* wish to extend their sincere thanks to the following persons: Bill Anderson, Jerry Bails, Larry Brill, Mary Beth Calhoun, Frank Clark, Bill Crouch, Leonard Darvin, Tony Dispoto, Jacques Glénat-Guttin, Ron Goulart, George Henderson, Pierre Horn, Pierre Huet, S. M. "Jerry" Iger, Jessie Kahles Straut, Rolf Kauka, Heikki Kaukoranta, Roland Kohlsaat, Maria-M. Lamm, Mort Leav, Vane Lindesay, Ernie McGee, Jacques Marcovitch, Victor Margolin, Doug Murray, Pascal Nadon, Harry Neigher, Walter Neugebauer, Syd Nicholls, Tom Peoples, Rainer Schwarz, Silvano Scotto, Luciano Secchi, David Smith, Manfred Soder, Jim Steranko, Ernesto Traverso, Miguel Urrutía, Jim Vadeboncoeur, Jr., Wendell Washer, Peter Wiechmann, Mrs. John Wheeler and Joe Willicombe.

We would also like to thank the following collectors who donated reproductions of art from their collections: Wendy Gaines Bucci, Mike Burkey, Tony Christopher, Russ Cochran, Robert Gerson, Roger Hill, Bill Leach, Eric Sack, and Jim Steranko.

Special thanks also to Michel Mandry, Bernard Trout, José Maria Conget of Instituto Cervantes in New York, Four-Color Images Gallery, Frederik Schodt, David Astor, Alain Beyrand, Manuel Halffter, Dominique Petitfaux, Annie Baron-Carvais, Janice Silverman.

Our appreciation also to the following organizations: Associated Newspapers Ltd., Bastei Verlag, Bulls Pressedienst, Comics Magazine Association of America, Editions Dupuis, ERB Inc., Field Newspaper Syndicate, Globi Verlag, The Herald and Weekly Times Ltd., Kauka Comic Akademie, King Features Syndicate, Marvel Comics Group, San Francisco Academy of Comic Art, Strip Art Features, Walt Disney Archives and Walt Disney Productions.

Finally, we wish to thank Don Manza for his photographic work.

Chelsea House Publishers
1974 Sproul Road, Suite 400
P.O. Box 914
Broomall PA 19008-0914

Typeset by Alexander Graphics, Indianapolis IN

Library of Congress Cataloging-in-Publication Data

The world encyclopedia of comics / edited by Maurice Horn.
    p. cm.
    Includes bibliographical references and index.
    ISBN 0-7910-4854-3 (set). — ISBN 0-7910-4857-8 (v. 1). — ISBN
0-7910-4858-6 (v. 2). — ISBN 0-7910-4859-4 (v. 3). — ISBN
0-7910-4860-8 (v. 4). — ISBN 0-7910-4861-6 (v. 5). — ISBN
0-7910-4862-4 (v. 6). — ISBN 0-7910-4863-2 (v. 7)
    1. Comic books, strips, etc.—Dictionaries.   I. Horn, Maurice.
PN6710.W6   1998
741.5'03—dc21   97-50448
                                                                      CIP

CAESAR, KURT (1906-1974) Italian cartoonist and illustrator of German origin, born in 1906 in Montigny, Lorraine, when it was part of the German Empire. After starting his career as a journalist for the Ulman News Agency in Germany, Kurt Caesar decided to settle in Italy in the mid-1930s. There he began his new activity as an illustrator, signing his pages with the pen name "Caesar Away" (or "Avai"). His first published works appeared in the weekly *La Risata*, which in 1936 published *I Due Tamburini* ("The Two Drummer-Boys") and *Cristoforo Colombo*. Now and then he would contribute to other big-circulation weeklies, such as *Topolino* and *L'Intrepido*, with illustration work and comic features. In 1938 he produced his most famous creation, *Romano il Legionario* ("Romano the Legionary"), about an Italian pilot whose adventures took place during the Spanish Civil War. (Later, Romano would be able to contribute to a bigger conflict, World War II.)

Although heavily influenced by Alex Raymond as far as his characterization was concerned, Caesar cast a new and very personal element, which is apparent in the perfect technical rendering of machines and flight scenes. The intricate detail of his drawings has earned him the appellation of "master craftsman of the comics," a very apt description. Caesar's ability to faithfully reproduce machines and aircraft led him into more war stories, all widely popular at the time, such as *I Moschettieri del Aeroporto Z* ("The Musketeers of Airport Z"), *Will Sparrow*, and *Il Mozzo del Sommergibile* ("The Cabin-Boy of the Submarine"). Caesar's favorite fields of operation were the pages of the Catholic weekly *Il Vittorioso*, where his big illustrations of war machines were always well received.

After the war, Caesar published a few more stories in *Il Vittorioso* and in *Il Giornalino*, but devoted most of his time to illustration work, producing a good number of covers for *Urania* (a monthly science-fiction magazine published by Mondadori) and drawing many pages for Fleetway Publications in Britain, all of them with a war or science-fiction angle. In the 1960s Caesar drew the first episodes of the new science-fiction strip *Perry Rhodan* for a German publisher, and he also contributed grandiose and intricate double-page spreads for the *Messaggero dei Ragazzi* of Padua.

Kurt Caesar died at Bracciano, where he had been living and working for the previous two decades, on July 12, 1974.

G.B.

CALKINS, RICHARD (1895-1962) American artist and writer, born in 1895 in Grand Rapids, Michigan. Richard (Dick) Calkins studied at the Chicago Art Institute and soon became a cartoonist for the *Detroit Free Press*. In 1917 he joined Hearst's *Chicago Examiner* as a sports cartoonist and illustrator. During World War I he was commissioned a lieutenant in the U.S. Air Force

but the war ended before he saw any action (for a long time afterwards he would sign "Lt. Dick Calkins").

Discharged from service in 1919, Calkins went back to the *Chicago Examiner*, where, in addition to his other duties, he originated a weekly panel, *Amateur Etiquette*; later he joined the John F. Dille Co. When Dille decided to launch a daily science-fiction strip based on a Phil Nowlan novel that he had retitled *Buck Rogers 2429 A.D.*, Calkins became the first artist on the feature, which debuted on January 7, 1929. That same year Calkins created, in collaboration with another former pilot, Lieutenant Lester J. Maitland (who did the writing), *Skyroads*, an aviation strip.

Calkins was to draw *Buck Rogers* till November 29, 1947; after Nowlan's death in 1940 he also assumed the writing duties. (On the other hand, the Sunday feature, while credited to Calkins, was actually ghosted by his assistants, Russell Keaton and Rick Yager.) In 1947 Calkins left *Buck Rogers* after a bitter dispute with his employers.

In the latter part of his life, Calkins worked mostly in comic books, chiefly in a writing capacity. He scripted a good many stories for the *Red Ryder* comic books published by Western in the late 1940s and early 1950s. Calkins died on May 13, 1962, in Tucson, Arizona.

Calkins' work as an illustrator looks outmoded and clumsy today, but he had a flair for depicting spaceships and other far-out gadgets in a detailed and almost naturalistic fashion. His visual inventiveness never flagged, his drawings and compositions fired the imagination of his adolescent readers, and (as Ray Bradbury, among others, has testified) his influence on future science-fiction writers proved decisive and enduring.

M.H.

CALVIN AND HOBBES (U.S.) The most innovative and delightful comic strip to come out in the last decade was sprung on an unsuspecting public on November 19, 1985. Distributed by Universal Press Syndicate, it was called *Calvin and Hobbes*, and the perpetrator was a 27-year-old cartoonist named Bill Watterson.

The keynote was struck in the very first daily with the introduction of six-year-old Calvin and his pet tiger Hobbes, whom he had captured with the lure of a tuna sandwich. From the outset the relationship between the crabby, querulous, manic Calvin and the suave, laid-back Hobbes proved to be the heart of the matter. The good-natured tiger added a dash of sophistication and a whiff of wisdom as a willing participant in Calvin's many escapades. These adventures took place unbeknownst to the boy's parents and to the world at large, for whom Hobbes appeared to be a normal, stuffed toy tiger.

"I don't think of Hobbes as a doll that miraculously comes to life when Calvin's around. Neither do I think of Hobbes as the product of Calvin's imagination," Watterson once declared, suggesting that Hobbes, the

"Calvin and Hobbes," Bill Watterson. © Bill Watterson/UPS.

flesh-and-blood tiger, might have been the secret identity of Hobbes, the stuffed animal (a kind of ironic twist on the Superman/Clark Kent gambit). In any case, the tiger soon became Calvin's favorite—and often only—companion, accomplice, and alibi. When the boy came back with his clothes filthy and in tatters from a wild ride through the woods in his wagon, he would blame it on Hobbes' lack of driving skill; and when asked by his parents for his school report card, he could announce with a straight face that his "tiger ate it."

The strip's main protagonists were given a very limited cast of characters with whom to interact. There were Calvin's unnamed parents—Dad, a sarcastic, somewhat remote figure; Mom, the disciplinarian and nurturer whom Calvin imagined in his more resentful moments as his "evil arch-enemy—Mom-Lady." At school his nemesis was Moe, the schoolyard bully who periodically shook down the cowering Calvin for his lunch money; and his persistent suitor, the straight-A student Susie Derkins, with whom he entertained a love-hate relationship. (He once kidnapped her doll, Binky Betsey, for ransom, but he also sent her hate-mail valentines every year.) Miss Wormwood, his much put-upon teacher, and Rosalyn, the tough (and justifiably well-paid) babysitter, rounded out the strip's list of characters.

To relieve the tedium of school or the routine of home life, the hyperactive Calvin would cast himself as "Spaceman Spiff," the interplanetary pioneer; "Tracer Bullet," the unflappable private eye; or "Safari Al," the indomitable jungle explorer. His more sedate pursuits led him to found the "Get Rid of Slimy Girls" Club, or GROSS for short, and he declared himself its Supreme Ruler and Dictator for Life; in most instances a sarcastic Hobbes would bring his high-flying companion back to earth with some barbed remark. The interplay between boy and tiger, in turn joyful and introspective, complicitous and antagonistic, gave the strip its peculiar charm along with undertones of pathos and poignancy.

Calvin and Hobbes represented a welcome oasis of superlative (if understated) draftsmanship, luminous composition, and graceful design. Watterson often returned to the wellspring of the form, drawing inspiration from the medium's greats—George Herriman, Winsor McCay, Walt Kelly—whom he emulated but never copied. This painstaking attention to detail produced inevitable burnouts for Watterson, during which times the strip would go into reruns. (These elicited almost no protest from the readers, since *Calvin and*

Hobbes reprints were still wittier and better drawn than many other comics.)

Calvin and Hobbes enjoyed unprecedented popularity from the start. The strip ran in every major newspaper market to great acclaim, and its many book reprints invariably topped the *New York Times* best-seller lists. Amid all this adulation Watterson abruptly decided to discontinue the 10-year-old feature, citing a variety of reasons (fatigue, disgust at the ever-shrinking space allotted to comics on the newspaper page, disputes with his syndicate over the artist's adamant refusal to allow merchandising of his characters). The last release appeared on December 31, 1995.

Calvin and Hobbes was to its multitude of fans an endless freshet of inspiration and charm, and its passing was felt by many like a death in the family. Watterson is still young, and the advent of the new millenium may well bring the second coming of *Calvin and Hobbes*.

M.H.

Edmond-François Calvo, *"Le Centaure Vezelay."* © SPE.

CALVO, EDMOND-FRANÇOIS (1892-1958) A French cartoonist and illustrator born in 1892 in Fleury-sur-Andelle, a little town in Normandy, Calvo, who liked to draw even in early childhood, had the usual cartoonist's training, working on one publication after another. After World War I (when he saw service) his career stabilized somewhat and he started contributing cartoons and illustrations to nationally distributed publications.

Calvo came into the comic strip field late in life. His earliest recorded work in this area is *La Vengeance du Corsaire* ("The Privateer's Revenge," for the comic weekly *Junior* (1938), followed in 1939 by the excellent *Le Centaure Vezelay* ("The Vezelay Centaur") on a script by Robert Mazières, a historical strip set at the time of the French Revolution. Then came the flood: an adaptation of the Errol Flynn movie *Robin Hood* (also 1939), the Western *Tom Mix* (1940-1942), and the gag strip *Croquemulot*, only a few of the many titles contributed by Calvo from 1939 to 1943. Then in 1944-1945 he produced what many consider his masterwork: a two-volume comic strip allegory of World War II, *La Bête Est Morte* ("The Beast Is Dead"). In this animal transposition closely paralleling historical events as they were then known, the Germans were presented as wolves, the British were bulldogs, the Russians bears, the Japanese monkeys, etc. Calvo followed this with another excellent creation in 1946, *Rosalie*, about the comic tribulations of an old jalopy.

Aside from a few forays into advertising art and illustration, Calvo devoted the rest of his life to comic strip work. Among the innumerable features he created or worked on, the most worthy of mention are *King Kong* (1948); *Cricri Souris d'Appartement* ("Cricri Apartment Mouse"), a charming animal strip written by Marijac and drawn by Calvo from 1948 to 1955 (his most popular series, it was reprinted *ad nauseam* long after the cartoonist's death); *Babou* (1952); *Captain Gin* and *Moustache et Trotinette* (started in 1957, this seems to be Calvo's last creation).

In the mid-1950s Calvo (while continuing with his drawing) retired to his native town of Fleury. There he opened a hostelry where, as his friend Marijac stated, "he was the best customer." Calvo died in 1958, almost without notice.

Calvo's position is difficult to assess: his talent is indisputable but he never created—aside, perhaps, from the offbeat *La Bête Est Morte*—any enduring work. He remains, however, an important figure in the French comic strip field of the 1940s and 1950s.

M.H.

CANALE, ANTONIO (1915-1991) Antonio Canale was born in 1915 in Monza but grew up in Milan, where he lived all his life. He started his career in the early 1930s as an illustrator; but only the comic strip gave him the opportunity to fully realize his talents. Before World War II Canale drew some beautiful stories for the comic weeklies *L'Audace* and *Il Vittorioso*. Between 1939 and 1940 he produced several comic features, first for *L'Audace*, then for *Topolino*, where he

Antonio Canale, "Vecchia America." © Canale.

created his first recognized masterpiece, *Il Solitario dei Sakya* ("The Long One of the Sakya"), on a text by Federico Pedrocchi. Unfortunately Canale was drafted into service before he could complete the story, which was continued by Bernardo Leporini.

Immediately after the end of the war, in 1945, Canale reached an important stage in his artistic development with a relatively short-lived feature, *I Dominatori dell'Abisso* ("The Rulers of the Abyss"): by eschewing etch marks and relying chiefly on contrasting masses of blacks and whites, he was able to renew and refresh his drawing style. His new comic strip style was further emphasized in such works as *Yorga* (1945) and in the series *Amok, il Gigante Mascherato* ("Amok, the Masked Giant," 1946). Also in 1946, for *Topolino*, Canale drew one of the best episodes of *Virus*, "Il Signore del Buio" ("The Master of Darkness").

Then, after many years of drawing uncounted war and espionage stories for London's Fleetways Publications, Canale made a comeback on the Italian comic strip scene around 1960 with his drawing of Hiawatha's adventures in the *Corriere dei Piccoli*, on a text by R. D'Ami. In these stories Canale succeeds in blending a subtle mixture of the grotesque and the realistic, an approach perfectly suited to old legends and ballads. This stylistic innovation is further refined in his "Stories of Old America," which Canale did in 1963 but which were only recently published.

Canale seemed to be going more and more in that direction, and his next venture was being awaited with much anticipation. In his later years, however, he turned more and more to illustration. He died on October 15, 1991.

G.B.

CANIFF, MILTON (1907-1988) American cartoonist and writer, born February 28, 1907, in Hillsboro, Ohio. He attended high school in Stivers, Ohio, and graduated from Ohio State University in 1930. While still in school Caniff successively worked on the *Dayton Journal*, the *Miami Daily News*, and the *Columbus Dispatch*. In 1932 he moved to New York City and joined the Associated Press, for which he created in 1932 *The Gay Thirties*, a weekly panel; and *Dickie Dare*, a daily adventure strip, in 1933. In 1934 his work was brought to the attention of Captain Joseph Patterson, publisher of the *New York News*, who was then looking for a feature "based on a blood-and-thunder formula, carrying a juvenile angle, and packed with plenty of suspense." The answer to the captain's prayer turned out to be *Terry and the Pirates*, which Caniff debuted as a daily strip on October 22, 1934, and as a Sunday page a few weeks later.

During the war, while continuing *Terry*, Caniff created *Male Call*, a strip especially designed for the G.I.s. Due to contractual difficulties, Caniff abandoned *Terry* in December of 1946 (it was taken over by George Wunder) to start his own strip, *Steve Canyon*, for Field Enterprises (January 1947).

A cartoonist of unequalled qualities (who has often been referred to as "the Rembrandt of the comic strip") and a first-rate storyteller, Milton Caniff is one of a small group of artists who succeeded in raising the comic strip to the level of art. Caniff's mastery of drawing, his subtle sense of composition, his skillful use of characterization and dialogue, have all made him justly famous in and out of his profession. He has influenced a whole school of cartoonists who have heavily borrowed from his techniques.

In addition to his comic strip work Caniff also did book and magazine illustration, wrote many articles about his work and comic art in general, and lectured extensively on the subject. His awards, civil and military, are too numerous to mention. He was one of the original founders of the National Cartoonists Society in 1946, and served as its president in 1948-49.

A man fiercely devoted to his work, Caniff continued to write *Steve Canyon* in its entirety and to draw it with the assistance of Norman Rockwell's nephew Dick Rockwell; not even ill health and advancing age could keep him away from the drawing board. He died in New York City of lung cancer on April 3, 1988; his strip survived him only by a few weeks.

M.H.

CAPITAINE FANTÔME, LE (France) This highly unusual comic strip was created by writer Jacques François (actually Jacques Dumas, better known as Marijac) and artist Raymond Cazanave in issue number 10 of the French illustrated magazine *Coq Hardi* (April 1946). Set in the 18th century, *Le Capitaine Fantôme* ("Captain Phantom") is a story of violence and horror the likes of which were rarely (if ever) seen in the pages of European comic papers of the time. Murder, torture, and rape are among its more subdued moments, and its mood of unrelieved psychological terror is a far cry from the wholesome fun offered by the rest of the *Coq Hardi* pages.

During an ocean crossing to Europe from South America, Don Juan Cavaloros' ship is attacked by pirates. Don Juan is left for dead and his daughter Juanita is abducted. A young Frenchman, De Vyrac, swears to deliver Juanita, who is to be sold as a slave. He joins the pirates, led by a peg-legged, mysterious figure known as "Captain Phantom" and his sinister henchman, Pater Noster, a hunchbacked monster. After many fights, plunders, and other pleasantries, De Vyrac saves Juanita and Pater Noster (who turns out to be the girl's lost father, whose body and spirit have broken down under Indian torture). Mad with rage, Captain Phantom sets fire to his own ship and massacres the entire crew before he is himself stabbed to death by the demented Pater Noster. At the end of the episode (June 1947) only Juanita, Pater Noster, and De Vyrac are left alive.

The authors had probably planned to conclude on this note, but the insistence of their readers forced them to hastily concoct a sequel, which started appearing in *Coq Hardi* 88 (November 1947). In this episode, titled "Le Vampire des Caraïbes" ("The Vampire of the Caribbean"), Captain Phantom reappears as a specter who must drink human blood in order to keep his human appearance (shades of Dracula!), and there is the usual quota of mayhem and mischief going on before De Vyrac and Juanita are finally allowed to marry each other. A third episode, "Les Boucaniers" ("The Buccaneers"), has the couple battling to save their estate from Juanita's greedy uncles, but Captain Phantom does not appear in this one. The series finally ended on something of an anticlimax on September 26, 1948.

Le Capitaine Fantôme seems to have been inspired largely by Russell Thorndyke's *Dr. Syn* novels, with which it shares its black mood, supernatural happenings, ghoulish characters, and unruly passions. The nar-

"Le Capitaine Fantôme," Raymond Cazanave. © Coq Hardi.

rative is well served by Cazanave's style, sinister and brooding, and his compositions of ominous black splashes and blinding whites, unrelieved by any shade of gray. As it is, *Le Capitaine Fantôme* is an oddity in the French comic strip, like one of those black monoliths sometimes found in sunny Southern landscapes.

M.H.

CAPITAN L'AUDACE (Italy) *Capitan l'Audace* ("Captain Fearless") was the longest-running Italian costume adventure strip. Its chief character was a corsair clearly derived from Salgari's novels, and a worthy successor to that author's Black Corsair. Written by the prolific Federico Pedrocchi and drawn by the brilliant Walter Molino, *Capitan l'Audace* made its first appearance in the pages of the comic weekly *L'Audace* on April 20, 1939.

With his faithful lieutenants Barbanera ("Blackbeard") and Spaccateste ("Headbreaker"), Capitan l'Audace fights against the sinister Baron Armando di Torrerossa, who plans to marry his attractive cousin, the Countess Vera, in order to lay hands on the young girl's estate, which had been willed to her by her father, Count Stefano di Coldrago. Of course, after innumerable bloody battles, hairbreadth escapes, and suspenseful chases, victory finally belongs to the bold captain, who marries the beautiful Vera.

After the Captain's wedding, unfortunately, the story loses its incisiveness and originality, a fact further precipitated by Molino's departure from the strip and his replacement by Edgardo dell'Acqua and Bernardo Leporini. (At the same time as it changed artists, *Capitan l'Audace* also changed magazines, while still remaining in Mondadori's fold—transferring first to *Paperino* and then to *Topolino*, where it remained until its demise in 1946.)

A few episodes of *Capitan l'Audace* were reprinted in the series "Albi d'Oro" (1948).

G.B.

CAPITAN MIKI (Italy) In the 1950s the teenage hero (usually no more than 16 years of age) was a popular staple of Italian comic books, with titles numbering in the dozens. *Capitan Miki* was different from other such

"Capitan Miki," Essegesse. © Editrice Dardo.

"El Capitan Misterio," Emilio Freixas. © Freixas.

features because it presented less-tangled plots and combined mystery with adventure and humor.

Capitan Miki was produced by Essegesse (a collective label combining the names of authors Sinchetto, Sartoris, and Guzzon) and appeared for the first time in publisher Dardo's *Collana Scudo* on July 1, 1951. Miki is a 16-year-old boy whose guardian, Clem, was killed by a band of outlaws; along with his loyal companion Doppio Rum ("Double Rum"), he enlists in the "Nevada Rangers." After he has unmasked the killer and accomplished a multitude of other hair-raising exploits, Miki rises to the rank of captain (thus justifying the title of the strip).

The daughter of the fort commandant, Susy, is Miki's girlfriend. She leads a lonely life, with her fiancé always away on dangerous missions in the company of his two sidekicks, Doppio Rum and Dr. Salasso ("Bloodletting"), a pair of characters cut out of a different cloth from the hero. While Miki is a teetotaler with a brave and honest heart, his companions are inveterate drinkers, troublemakers, and swindlers, and no paragons of courage either. They often disrupt the hero's earnest undertakings with their uninhibited shenanigans. (*Capitan Miki*'s straight narratives are also often enlivened by freckle-faced Susy's scenes of jealousy.)

With *Miki* the authors hit on a winning formula that they later utilized in other titles such as *Grande Blek* ("Big Blek"), *Alan Mistero,* and *Commandante Mark.* After Essegesse left the strip in the early 1960s, the feature was continued by artists Franco Bignotti and Nicolino Del Principe on scripts by Amilcare Medici. *Capitan Miki* was published in two of Dardo's comic books, *Collana Prateria* and *Collana Freccia.* It came to an end in the 1980s.

G.B.

CAPITAN MISTERIO, EL (Spain) *El Capitan Misterio* was created by the illustrator Emilio Freixas on an idea and script by Angel Puigmiquel. The first episode was published in the comic book collection *Mosquito* in 1944; the following year the feature transferred to the magazine *Gran Chicos*, where it ran uninterruptedly from October 1945 to July 1948. In 1949 it was being published in the magazine *Historietas* and in the comic weekly *Chicos*, where it ended its career later in July of that year.

Capitan Misterio was a masked justice-fighter of the Far East, with strong athletic and hypnotic powers and indomitable spirit and courage. In his most imaginative adventure he discovered the lost city of Tanit located on one of the Pacific islands, where Queen Nerea fell in love with him. Misterio's companions, the gigantic mulatto Pancho Tonelada and the youthful Balin, helped him in his fights against mad scientists with exotic names and Nazi faces who were always trying to conquer the world. To conceal his real identity (of which nothing is known except that the hero is blond and is named John), Misterio covers his face with a purple hood decorated with a skull—a sign with which he marks his enemies. As one can easily see, *El Capitan Misterio* has more than a passing resemblance to *The Phantom* (with elements of *Jungle Jim* and *Mandrake* thrown in).

In this feature, which unfolded in the course of four episodes, Emilio Freixas had recourse to his usual technique made of a conventional panel layout and a line at once fine and powerful, to emphasize his main strengths: the drawing of animals—in which he is a master—and the skillful depiction of the human body. A talented anatomist, Freixas made Capitan Misterio into his most perfect hero, while giving us at the same time a model of feminine beauty in the person of the queen of Tanit.

L.G.

CAPITAN TERROR (Germany) *Capitan Terror*, as the name suggests, is a pirate captain born on Spanish soil. He was created by Peter Wiechmann, editorial director of the Kauka comic book line, in cooperation with the Bardon Art Studios of Barcelona, Spain. The first adventure was drawn by noted comic artist Esteban Maroto in a somewhat restricted style that helps tell the story and avoids drowning it in graphic experimentation. *Capitan Terror* first appeared in *primo* number

"Capitan Terror," Sola. © Rolf Kauka.

9/1974. As expected, readers liked this additional entry to the line of Kauka adventure comics.

Capitan Terror is the story of Captain Javier Aguirre, who, after refusing to enter the military services of the dictatorial Catalonian governor, finds his ship attacked and sunk. His wife and crew are killed in the incident; Aguirre and the boy Chico are the sole survivors. With vengeance in his heart, Aguirre arrives on the island of Ibiza, a pirate hangout. He is accepted into their ranks, no little thanks to Cuchillo "Knife," the red-haired daughter of the pirate chieftain El Diablo.

Terror enlists the aid of Samurai, "Black Powder" the ace cannonier, the French pistolero Guy, the evenly matched fighters Ramirez and Yogi, and strongman Turco. This motly international group takes up the fight against the tyrant Carlos Fernando on Cuchillo's ship "Flecha" (Arrow), which is rechristened "La Venganza" (Revenge) after some alterations that are to make it maneuverable even in the slightest of breezes.

Capitan Terror stands in the classic tradition of a hero driven into the life of an outlaw by extremity. Nevertheless, he stays true to a standard of morals, a code of conduct that permits him to shape his crew to his ideals and that gives him the necessary strength to fight a dictator who does not care whether his subjects live or die. The stories are fast-paced, well written and drawn, the artwork having been taken over by Sola after Maroto's episode. There is also the additional interest of the growing relationship between Terror and Cuchillo. Although largely escapist literature, *Capitan Terror*, by reflecting on the hero's actions, makes interesting reading. The strip was carried over into *Action Comic* when *primo* was discontinued in December 1974. When Rolf Kauka sold his company, Peter Wiechmann continued writing the feature at Comicon, a company he founded in Barcelona, to be closer to the artists he works with. When Rolf Kauka merged with Springer and took over *Zack* magazine, the feature moved along and was also published in *Zack* albums.

The feature ended in 1981 when production of the *Zack* line of comics ended.

W.F.

CAPITAN TRUENO, EL (Spain) One of the most famous features of the post-World War II Spanish comics, *Capitan Trueno* ("Captain Thunder") was created by Victor Alcazar (pseudonym of Victor Mora) as scriptwriter, and Ambros (pseudonym of Miguel Ambrosio Zaragoza) as illustrator, in June 1956.

"El Capitan Trueno," Victor Mora. © Editorial Bruguera.

A contemporary of Saladin and Richard the Lion-Hearted, Capitan Trueno was a man of action and a defender of the traditional ideals of chivalry, which he upheld against the encroachments of tyrannical authority. His vast cultural knowledge did not prevent him from being a fearless warrior, nor did his wealth inhibit him in his defense of the weak. In spite of his valor, Capitan Trueno was often overwhelmed by his numerous enemies and was subjected to the most terrible tortures, which he bore with courage and fortitude.

In his adventures Trueno had two constant companions, his squire Crispin and Goliath, the big-hearted giant. The trio wandered around the world in search of adventures, which often pitted them against monsters of every description, the succession of which undoubtedly constitutes one of the most important bestiaries in Spanish comics. Humor was alternated with action, romance with fighting, and idyllic interludes with brutal scenes of mayhem and torture.

El Capitan Trueno's long saga ended in March 1968 after no fewer than 618 comic books, 417 issues of its own magazine, and a 232-issue run in the weekly *Pulgarcito*. Not long after its demise, the feature went into three successive reprintings, the last of them in full color. In its first period it was one of the most enjoyable of adventure strips, thanks to Mora's inventive scripts and Ambros' dynamic renderings, but it later fell into mediocrity, without losing, however, the public's favor. The two original authors were succeeded by a swarm of lesser lights, among whom mention can be made of Acedo, Cassarell, and Ortega (as scriptwriters), and of Beaumont, Marco, Martinez Osets, Fuentes Man, Casamitjana, and Comos (as illustrators).

El Capitan Trueno was adapted into novels, anchored several advertising campaigns, and has inspired a number of toys and cut-outs. It made a brief return in 1986, drawn by Jesús Blasco.

L.G.

CAPLIN, ELLIOT (1913-) American writer, younger brother of Al Capp, born in New Haven, Connecticut, on December 25, 1913. The young Caplin moved a lot with his family and attended Ohio State University and Yale, receiving a B.A. from the latter institution in 1935.

He went to work for the old rotogravure *Midweek Pictorial* of the *New York Times*, and, in succession, *Judge* magazine, *Parents'* magazine, and Toby Press, where he edited several magazine titles.

Always interested in comics, a fairly inevitable proclivity, Caplin's first effort was authoring *Hippo and Hookey* for artist John Pierotti; King Features bought the ill-fated strip on the phone.

In short order, however, Caplin-scripted strips were appearing everywhere. *Abbie an' Slats*, conceived by Al Capp, was written for a "trial week" by Caplin—a week that lasted 23 successful years. Another United Features strip, *Long Sam*, was written by Caplin on a basic theme by his brother; Raeburn van Buren and Bob Lubbers were the two very competent artists engaged, respectively, for the two strips.

His first successful strip for King Features was *Dr. Bobbs*, followed by a host of others, notably *The Heart of Juliet Jones*, *Big Ben Bolt*, and *Dr. Kildare*. He has also created and authored a bevy of strips for other syndicates through the years, many running simultaneously.

Caplin has a genius for continuity writing that seems to sustain half the industry. Some titles show the effect of formula production, and his handling of *Little Orphan Annie* (with another brother, Jerry) after Harold Gray's death in 1968 until 1973 was at best neglectful and at worst malevolent.

But the art of the comic strip owes much to Caplin—in terms of sheer volume and quality of production. His versatility is remarkable; one day's comic section could include the folksy humor of *Abbie an' Slats*, the soap-opera doings of *Juliet Jones*, the stilted moralizing of his version of *Orphan Annie*, the Herriman-like craziness of another of his creations, and many more just as diversified—all from the same typewriter.

Some have argued—including King Features comic editor Sylvan Byck—that the decline of the story strip is due as much to decline in quality as other factors of reproduction, competing entertainment media, etc. Caplin must share the praise or blame for the state of the business that he, to a large extent, dominates. But his value to the development of the art is clear and ongoing; Caplin continues to both write and develop new comic features. In his entry to the 1996 *National Cartoonists Society Album* he modestly noted that he had been "employed by King Features since 1937 as a writer."

R.M.

CAPP, AL (1909-1979) Alfred Gerald Caplin, creator of *Li'l Abner*, was born in New Haven, Connecticut, on September 28, 1909, to a father with a silver pencil in his hand. The elder Caplin used the pencil to draw comic strips for the family's amusement (using family members as characters), and entranced the young Alfred. Finding himself talented as well, the son ignored university work and went to a number of art schools, landing a job with Associated Press doing a strip called *Col. Gilfeather* in 1927 at 19. When Caplin left to tackle New York, the strip was turned over to a young Milton Caniff. In New York, Caplin was persuaded to ghost the *Joe Palooka* strip by its creator, Ham Fisher, who made him exaggerated promises of fame and fortune in the immediate future.

Caplin made the *Palooka* prize-fighting strip into a hilariously attractive work by his renovative art and his fanciful rendering of such presumed Fisher characters as Senator Weidebottom, women athletes, Russian boxers, and—above all—the hillbilly menage of Big Leviticus and his Mammy and Pappy, with which the strip reached its all-time heights of art and humor in 1933 and 1934. But Caplin was feeling his ink by now, and he had become thoroughly tired of making millions for Fisher while Fisher paid him in castoff artboard—a situation he later satirized in a July 1950 Sunday sequence of *Li'l Abner*. The 26-year-old cartoonist took his own strip idea to the syndicates, where (after being tempted to change his strip idea wholly to one syndicate's specifications in return for a fat contract) he found United Feature willing to try *Li'l Abner* as Caplin had prepared it.

In mid-1934 the first daily episode was released, and Caplin made use of his now-famous abbreviation (initially "Al G. Cap"). In early 1935, the Sunday *Abner* page was released, together with a third-page feature by Capp called *Washable Jones*. This weekly continued fairy tale (about a hill boy of 12 or so who pulls a ghost out of a fishing hole and gets involved with a Granny Groggins, a Squire Grunch, a monstrous horror named Zork, sneezing Beezars, talking trees, and a li'l girl named Majorie) was charming, unaffected, and wholly entertaining. It lasted only 16 weeks, unfortunately.

Li'l Abner quickly became a hit. By 1935, the daily and Sunday strip were being syndicated in most major American cities. Part of the reason was the topical response: the jobless or short-houred readers of the depression were being given portraits of impoverished hillbilly characters far worse off than they were—yet apparently able to enjoy it. The lift to morale that this daily look at such people gave in the 1930s is hard to estimate now, but it must have been considerable. The prime reason for Capp's immediate success, however, was his own tremendous imagination, humor, and obvious desire to break fresh ground in strip narrative and gag content. For years, the Capp strip looked fresh, new, and different—mainly because it was.

Capp's later life was one of large personal and financial success: his gain of effective control of *Li'l Abner* and its adaptive uses (he headed Capp Enterprises in Boston for this purpose); his defeat of an attempt by a disgruntled Ham Fisher to railroad him into jail on forged evidence of obscenity in *Li'l Abner* in the 1950s; his establishment of a Disneyland-like amusement park in Kentucky called Dogpatch, U.S.A.; his weathering, both with the strip and personally, a legal hassle involving alleged seduction of college women (an accusation possibly evoked more by dislike of Capp's right-wing politics and campus-stumping for them than his actual bedroom manner), etc. Capp adequately demonstrated his abilities as a humorous writer and critic in numerous articles (for the *Atlantic Monthly* and elsewhere), books, and a cantankerous syndicated column of comment. Once the darling of liberally inclined individuals, Capp was (as the result of his liberal-denouncing political reorientation of the 1950s) able to observe how much of the once-ample liberal praise given his art and story in *Abner* was the result of his political stance at the time, rather than of any objective viewing of the worth of the strip itself. Individuals who enjoyed good strip art, regardless of political slant, however, relished *Abner* both before and after Capp's change of viewpoint, although many of them came to regret the disappearance of the once-suspenseful, relatively serious daily story line of the 1930s and early 1940s and its total replacement by the surreal narratives of the 1950s and later, enjoyable as these often were in their own right. Capp brought *Li'l Abner* to an end in 1977; he died two years later, on November 5, 1979, in Cambridge, Massachusetts.

B.B.

CAPRIOLI, FRANCO (1912-1974) Italian cartoonist, born in Rieti into a wealthy family on April 5, 1912. Franco Caprioli started his career as a fresco painter in a Benedictine abbey, before moving to Rome, where he exhibited his paintings and etchings. Caprioli entered the comics field in 1937, working for the illustrated weeklies *Argentovivo* and especially *Il Vittorioso*, in whose pages he created *Gino e Piero* and *Pino il Mozzo* ("Pino the Cabin-Boy") in 1939. In 1940 he worked for *Topolino* (producing several *Mickey Mouse* stories), and in 1943 he illustrated *Le Aquile de Roma* ("The Eagles of Rome") for Edizioni Alpe. Toward the end of the war, his works also appeared in the *Corriere dei Piccoli* and in *Giramondo*.

After the war, Caprioli resumed his prolific career, contributing *Mino e Dario* (1947), *I Pescatori di Perle* ("The Pearl-Divers," 1950), *Dakota Jim* (1954), *Wild Yukon*, as well as a good number of educational panels, to the Catholic weekly *Il Vittorioso*. For the Mondadori weekly *Topolino*, Caprioli produced several adventure stories, the most notable being *I Tigri di Sumatra* ("The Tigers of Sumatra," 1948).

In 1970 Caprioli joined the staff of the newly formed Catholic weekly *Il Giornalino*, for which he illustrated adaptations of novels by such writers as Jules Verne and Mark Twain. Caprioli also illustrated books for children, the most famous being an adaptation of *Moby Dick* for Mondadori.

Franco Caprioli was known as "the artist with the dots" because of his peculiar graphic style, closely derived from the *pointillisme* of such painters as Seurat and Pissaro. A special element is common to all his stories: the sea, which he loved so much and which he represents in every detail with graphic faithfulness; an imaginary sea, romanticized and idealized by a native of the mountains.

Franco Caprioli was awarded the distinction of "Best Italian Cartoonist" at the Genoa Comics Festival in 1973. He died in Rome of heart failure on February 8, 1974.

G.B.

CAP STUBBS AND TIPPIE (U.S.) The beginnings of *Cap Stubbs and Tippie* are clouded in mystery. Edwina Dumm, the strip's author, has always contended that she was asked to undertake the feature at the behest of George Matthew Adams a few months after she got her diploma from the Landon Correspondence Course. As Dumm was born in 1893, that would place the start of *Cap Stubbs* somewhere in the mid-1910s. The earliest recorded date of any *Cap Stubbs* strip, however, is

1918. The latter date seems more likely, as it is probable that Edwina (as she signed her work) might have indulged in some innocent fibbing about her age to later interviewers. A Sunday page simply called *Tippie* was added in 1934.

Adams reportedly asked for a strip about a boy and a dog, and that was what he got. Cap Stubbs is the boy—a nice, well-behaved, clean-cut, if high-spirited, little man. His pranks are quite innocent, although they always seem to upset in some way his equally nice and concerned Grandma Bailey. The dog is, of course, Tippie, a bedraggled mutt who always manages to be in the way.

In retrospect it takes time to understand all the praise heaped upon the strip: the plots are minimal, the gags slight, yet it all comes together in the end. Coulton Wugh justly wrote: "Edwina's work succeeds through a delicate balance of factors; she stops at that point in human interest and warmth before sentiment begins to rot the idea. She draws straight, natural people doing natural things."

Dumm left the daily strip in 1966 and the Sunday page some time later. She has since been sorely missed.

M.H.

CAPTAIN AMERICA (U.S.) *Captain America* was created in March 1941 by Jack Kirby and Joe Simon and made its first appearance in Timely's *Captain America* number one. Garbed in a dazzling red, white, and blue flag-inspired costume, Captain America quickly became one of the foremost manifestations of American patriotism during World War II. A bigger-than-life all-American, Steve (Captain America) Rogers soon epitomized all that the country claimed to be fighting for.

The character's origin, which has been told and retold dozens of times, explained how scrawny Steve Rogers, previously rejected for military service, drank a secret potion that turned him into a superhuman. The government planned to create a whole army of Captain Americas, but the creator was immediately assassinated by Nazis and the secret died with him. Adopting the guise of Captain America, Rogers and his sidekick Bucky spent the war attacking and conquering horde after horde of Axis enemies. But, as the war ended, *Captain America* began to falter. Created to capture the emotions of the wartime American public, the Captain simply could not make the postwar transition from Nazis and Japanese to garden-variety criminals. And despite frantic attempts to keep the strip from folding—Bucky was dropped in favor of Golden Girl, and the magazine was retitled *Captain America's Weird Tales*—the Captain's adventures ceased after May 1949's 74th issue.

When Timely's successor, Atlas Comics, reentered the superhero market in May 1954, *Captain America* was one of the returnees. But it was a short-lived revival, and the strip appeared in only two issues of *Men's Adventures* and three more issues of *Captain America*.

The character was revived again in the *Avengers* number four (March 1964). Although saddled with a hokey explanation of his 15-year absence—he was supposedly trapped in an iceberg—the Captain caught on again and the strip began appearing in *Tales of Suspense* (beginning with October 1964's 58th issue). It was finally awarded a new *Captain America* magazine (beginning with number 100) in April 1968. During the

"Captain America," Jim Steranko, © Marvel Comics Group.

subsequent years, changes came in rapid-fire succession: a new Bucky was added but eventually dropped; The Red Skull, the quintessential opposite of Captain America, was revived; Steve Rogers became a spy, then a cop, then a drifter, and finally a neurotic introvert who considered himself an anachronism; the Falcon, a black, crime-fighting ghetto-dweller, was brought in as the Captain's partner; and, in the strangest quirk, the 1950s Captain America was revealed as a reactionary fraud.

There have been close to 100 artists and writers on the feature, but Jack Kirby is clearly the definitive artist. His version is legendary and is often praised as the best comic book work ever produced. Handling the first three dozen stories in the 1940s and several years' worth of adventures in the 1960s, Kirby used stylized, highly detailed, and action-laden artwork to make the character a legend in its own time. He elevated *Captain America* from comic book strip to Americana. Stan Lee, who authored and edited material on the strip from its conception to 1972, is considered the definitive writer.

Besides dozens of comic book guest appearances, *Captain America* has also been published in paperback, drawn in animated cartoons, depicted in a 1943 Republic movie serial, and shown up in dozens of other items.

Over the years, *Captain America* has always mirrored the American psyche: in the 1940s, he was the superpatriot; in the 1950s, he was the reactionary; in the Vietnam era, he was the unsure giant. He is America.

J.B.

In the last two decades Cap, as he is familiarly called, has known a somewhat checkered career. For two years in the mid-1970s Kirby came back to draw the character again. He was followed by a legion of artists, Jim Steranko, Sal Buscema, Gene Colan, John Byrne, and Frank Miller being the most notable of the bunch, with every succeeding illustrator changing Cap's appearance. The writers working on the series also altered the character to suit their inclinations or prejudices, recasting him up and down the line from rabid jingo to liberal do-gooder. All these changes did not help the hero's image, and neither did two disastrous movie versions (in 1979 and 1992). *Captain America*, however, limps on, with Rob Liefeld cast by Marvel in 1995 in the unlikely role of the title's savior. Liefeld has since left the strip.

M.H.

CAPTAIN AND THE KIDS, THE (U.S.) After the celebrated court decision that gave him the right to use his *Katzenjammer Kids* characters, Rudolph Dirks wasted no time in starting a new strip for the *New York World*. The first Sunday page appeared on June 14, 1914; in the beginning the strip had a different caption every week followed by the words: "by Rudolph Dirks, Originator of the Katzenjammer Kids," and it

"The Captain and the Kids," Rudolph Dirks. © United Feature Syndicate.

was not called *Hans and Fritz* until May 23, 1915. In June 1918, in response to anti-German feelings, the title was dropped, and the strip was rechristened *The Captain and the Kids* on August 25, 1918. (There was a panel explaining that Hans and Fritz were actually Dutch and not German!)

Dutch or German, Hans and Fritz are of course none other than the terrible Katzenjammer Kids (minus the surname). Dirks also retained the cast of characters that had done yeomen's service in his earlier strip: der Captain, as irascible and bumbling as ever; and his foil der Inspector; the long-suffering Mama; not to forget "Chon Silver" and his crew of comic-opera pirates— all the above-mentioned and many more still being the unwilling butts of the Kids' destructive shenanigans. From time to time Dirks tried to introduce new permanent characters into the cast, often relatives, such as der Captain's explorer brother and die Mama's twin sister, but none of them clicked with the public. (At the same time Hearst, who had retained the right to the title, entrusted *The Katzenjammer Kids* to Harold Knerr, and a lively competition resulted between the rival strips.)

In 1930 the *World* went out of business, and *The Captain and the Kids*, along with other *World* features, was taken over by United Feature Syndicate. In 1932 a daily strip was added, but later that same year Dirks left, following a contractual dispute (both the dailies and the Sunday were taken over by Bernard Dibble). Dirks returned in 1937, taking charge of the Sunday page again. (The daily strip remained in Dibble's hands but lasted only a few more months.)

Rudolph Dirks' son John started assisting his father as early as 1946, and he gradually took over the strip when illness kept his father away from the drawing board. After his father's death in 1968, *The Captain and the Kids* was officially signed by John Dirks.

Dirks Jr. preserved the unique flavor and charm of the strip, often taking his juvenile heroes into the fields of science fiction and fantasy. In the 1960s and '70s John Dirks went back to the more basic plot and theme of the strip, often re-creating with loving and nostalgic care the situations and settings of his father's early pages.

The Captain and the Kids has often been reprinted in comic book form; in the 1940s and 1950s it had its own comic book, with John Dirks contributing most of the artwork and continuity of the original stories. *The Captain and the Kids*, unfortunately, did not enjoy the circulation that its reputation and quality warranted, and in the 1970s it could be seen only in a handful of newspapers across the country. It was terminated by the syndicate in May 1979.

M.H.

CAPTAIN EASY *see* Wash Tubbs.

CAPTAIN MARVEL (U.S.) When Fawcett decided to enter comics publishing in 1939, writer Bill Parker was chosen to spearhead the drive. Together with artist C. C. Beck, he created *Captain Thunder* for *Whiz* number one. Written and drawn solely to secure copyrights, the issue never appeared publicly, but the feature was retitled *Captain Marvel* and published in February 1940's *Whiz* number two. Modeled after motion picture actor Fred MacMurray, Captain Marvel was really a homeless orphan named Billy Batson who was taken to see the old wizard Shazam. When Billy spoke his name, he was magically transformed into "The Big Red Cheese"—complete with orange-and-gold superhero suit.

Artist Beck's visualization of the strip was the cleanest and most straightforward yet to appear in comics. Often devoid of backgrounds, stories were easy to read and children doubtlessly identified with the young Billy Batson. *Captain Marvel* became a phenomenal success and was soon outselling all the competition. In short order there was a Mary Marvel, a Captain Marvel Jr., an Uncle Marvel, three Lt. Marvels, and even a feature called *Hoppy, The Marvel Bunny*. The lure of simply yelling "Shazam"—which stood for *Solomon's* wisdom, *Hercules'* strength, *Atlas'* stamina, *Zeus'* power, *Achilles'* courage, and *Mercury's* speed—and becoming the "World's Mightest Mortal" was so enticing to readers, *Captain Marvel Adventures* was soon selling over a million copies every two weeks. A serial, *The Adventures of Captain Marvel*, was released by Republic in 1940, and Captain Marvel soon began appearing in dozens of comic books.

To keep pace with the tremendous demand for stories, many artists were employed under the strict supervision of chief artist C. C. Beck. Even Jack Kirby produced material—he drew the first issue of *Captain Marvel Adventures*. There were also many writers on the feature, but Otto Binder emerged as the strip's major architect in 1941. His gently satirical stories set the style for secondary writers like Ron Reed, Bill Woolfolk, and Bob Kanigher. Editors Bill Parker, Ed Herron, Ron Reed, Will Lieberson, and especially Wendell Crowley, the last editor, kept the strip on an even keel. Everyone worked to make *Captain Marvel* the most consistently entertaining feature produced during the 1940s.

The strip's downfall came primarily from a long, oppressive lawsuit. Soon after *Whiz* appeared, *Superman* publisher National Comics filed a celebrated copyright infringement suit against *Captain Marvel*. The features showed circumstantial similarities, Fawcett readily admitted, but they claimed the heroes were both unique. But after several time-consuming trials and National's dogged determination—they even engaged famed Louis Nizer as Superman's counsel—Fawcett decided not to continue the costly defense. They voluntarily killed not only *Captain Marvel*, but the complete Fawcett comics line.

The *Captain Marvel* feature appeared in 155 issues of *Whiz* and 150 issues of *Captain Marvel Adventures* before the ax fell after January 1954's *Marvel Family* 89. Dozens of toys and novelties had also spun off from the World's Mightiest Mortal in its 13-year history. And many outstanding subsidiary characters were developed, including Mr. Mind, the evil genius of a worm; Mr. Tawny, the talking tiger with urbane pretentions; Dr. Sivana, the mad-scientist-you-loved-to-hate whose family was the arch-enemy of the Marvel Family; and a long series of inventive criminals like Ibac, Black Adam, and Captain Nazi. Ironically, *Captain Marvel* was revived in February 1973's *Shazam* number one. The publisher was National Comics, the people who originally put the feature out of business!

Captain Marvel is part of Americana. "Shazam" became part of the English language as an interjection expressing surprise or astonishment. He was and is the classic example of America's naivete, cheerfulness, and undying optimism. He's a Horatio Alger in superhero tights. The new version lasted only for 35 issues, to

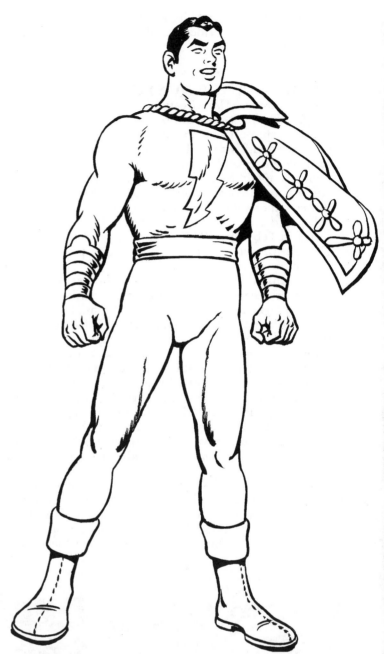

"Captain Marvel," C.C. Beck. © D.C. Comics.

mid-1978, although it was revived in a 1987 miniseries.

A second Captain Marvel character was introduced in *Captain Marvel* number one, published in April 1966 by Country-Wide comics. An obvious attempt to capitalize on the now-legendary name, this Captain Marvel had the ability to parcel his body into five parts by yelling the magic word "Split!" The short-lived feature suffered an obscure death in November 1966 after five issues.

A third *Captain Marvel* feature was introduced in the 12th issue of Marvel Comics' *Marvel Super-Heroes* (December 1967). In an original story written by editor Stan Lee and illustrated by artists Gene Colan and Frank Giacoia, "Captain Mar-vell" was an officer from the Kree Galaxy sent to scout Earth. The feature was given its own book in May 1968 and the origin, motivation, and costume of Captain Marvel changed continually. The title was dropped in August 1970, but was later revived in September 1972. Late in 1973, writer Al Milgrom and artist Jim Starlin brought to

Captain Marvel the stability and respectability it needed to compete side-by-side with the original *Captain Marvel* feature.

J.B.

CAPTAIN MARVEL JR. (U.S.) The phenomenal success of *Captain Marvel* caught the Fawcett company off-guard, and it was almost two years before they added a spin-off feature to their line. It was finally introduced in *Whiz* number 25 for December 1941, created by writer and editor Ed Herron. Drawn by Mac Raboy, Captain Marvel Jr. was a boy-turned-superboy and a natural companion for Captain Marvel, a boy-turned-superadult. The readers appreciated the difference, and the feature immediately began a regular series in February 1942's *Master Comics* number 23. *Captain Marvel Jr.* comics number one premiered in November of the same year.

Captain Marvel Jr. was really crippled newsboy Freddy Freeman. Viciously attacked by a villain named Captain Nazi, an old enemy of Bulletman, Freddy was near death until Billy (Captain Marvel) Batson took him to Old Shazam, the wizard who'd originally endowed Captain Marvel with his abilities. Unfortunately, Shazam said only Captain Marvel could help, so when Freddy spoke the words "Captain Marvel," he was miraculously transformed into the blue, gold, and red-suited Captain Marvel Jr. Ironically, for all the new powers granted to his alter ego, Freddy Freeman was still crippled. And it was never explained why Billy Batson became a super*man* and Freddy Freeman became a super*boy*!

Writer Otto Binder, who scripted the bulk of all the Marvel Family tales, also directed the fortunes of the *Captain Marvel Jr.* series. But for all his excellent, fast-paced stories starring villains like Captain Nippon and The Piped Piper, Binder never developed the strong secondary characters for Junior as he had for the Captain himself. There were never characters as ingenious as Mr. Tawny, the talking tiger, or Mr. Mind, the evil worm, in *Captain Marvel Jr.* The feature limped along with mundane and pedestrian supporters like landlady Mrs. Wagner and banker Mr. Davenport.

The strip did have some outstanding artistic moments, however. Mac Raboy, who handled almost all the stories drawn in 1942 and 1943, was more illustrator than cartoon artist. Unlike the simple, almost comedic style set by C. C. Beck for *Captain Marvel*, Raboy handled *Captain Marvel Jr.* far more realistically. A disciple of *Flash Gordon* artist Alex Raymond, Raboy made his stories brilliantly detailed, with anatomically perfect characters and a lavishness strange for comic books. His covers, drawn almost at the printed size, looked more like rich, expressive poster art than comic book drawings. When he left the strip in 1944, artists like Bud Thompson and Joe Certa worked especially hard to maintain the style he had established.

Captain Marvel Jr. continued until April 1953—just months before Fawcett folded their complete comic book line. The character was revived in 1973 when National Periodicals began republishing all the Marvel Family heroes in *Shazam!* comics. He vanished again, along with *Shazam!* comics, in 1978.

J.B.

CAPTAIN MIDNIGHT (U.S.) The Captain Midnight character was created by radio writers Willfred Moore and Robert Murit and premiered in his own radio show on September 30, 1940. His first comic book appearance was in Dell's *The Funnies* number 57 in July 1941. After eight issues, the *Captain Midnight* feature moved

"Captain Marvel, Jr.," Mac Raboy. © D.C. Comics.

"Captain Midnight." © Fawcett Publications.

to Dell's *Popular Comics* in June 1942, but it was not until Fawcett Comics purchased the character that *Captain Midnight* became a major comic book feature. He made his first Fawcett appearance in September 1942's *Captain Midnight* number one.

As set out in his radio program, Captain Midnight was really aviator Captain Albright, a crack flyer assigned to defeat Nazi mastermind Ivan Shark before midnight. If he failed, the Allied cause would be defeated. Despite the herculean proportions of his task, Albright accomplished the mission at exactly midnight, hence the name Captain Midnight. He later added a group of assistants known as the Secret Squadron.

In his 11 Dell stories, *Captain Midnight* followed the radio adventures closely. He wore a brown leather jacket and aviator's cap, goggles, and the ever-present Captain Midnight emblem—a winged clock with both hands at 12. And, as in the radio program, Captain Midnight was heavily assisted by the Secret Squadron. But when Fawcett assumed the strip's direction, Captain Midnight was decked out in a colorful new costume (primarily bright red and gray), operated almost totally independent of the Secret Squadron, and added a sidekick, Ichabod Mudd (a Secret Squadron member who often called himself "Sgt. Twilight"). The Fawcett series, written primarily by Otto Binder, also equipped the Captain with a wealth of gadgets, including blackout bombs, a "swing spring," and a "doom beam" torch.

The strip lasted until September 1948's *Captain Midnight* number 67. Comic books were never the feature's strong suit, however, and Captain Midnight's radio show was constantly more popular than the comic. He also appeared in a Columbia movie serial starring Dave O'Brien (1942), had a short-lived newspaper strip, was published by Whitman as a "big little book" hero, and had a sought-after series of radio premiums and giveaways.

J.B.

CAPTAIN WINGS (U.S.) Fiction House was one of the companies that switched from pulp magazines to comic books in the late 1930s and early 1940s. One of their comic titles, *Wings*, was simply a compilation of old Fiction House pulp stories with drawings added. But in the 16th issue, the company decided to develop a "lead" strip entitled *Captain Wings*. It premiered in December 1941, though the credits for the strip's creation are unclear: the story, as did all future *Captain Wings* adventures, carried the byline "Major T. E. Bowen," but that was probably a pen name. Likely creators include Gene Fawcette, who drew the Captain Wings cover for *Wings* 16; interior artist Artie Saaf; art studio head S. M. "Jerry" Iger; and pulp-writer-turned-comic-scripter Joe Archibald. Company president Thurman Scott probably suggested the name Captain Wings.

In reality, Captain Wings was really Captain Boggs, an efficient but hard-hearted commander who gave orders but never took the risks his fliers did. Unknown to the fliers who hated him, however, after he had issued the often-suicidal orders, Captain Boggs snuck into his plane and joined them as Captain Wings. None of his fliers knew Boggs and Wings were one and the same—"a man with two faces, two souls, two names," as the scripts said—which reflected little intelligence on their part since neither Wings nor Boggs wore a mask at any time. Captain Wings eventually dropped the

Captain Boggs ruse and led the Captain Wings squadron into action.

The stories themselves centered on the Captain and his P-51 Mustang—painted black and white to look like a huge eagle—and his adventures fighting Nazi and Japanese aces. Scantily clad women were strip staples—as they were in all Fiction House titles—and after the war, Wings fought those Axis pilots who refused to believe that the war had ended. Among later villains of this type were Mr. Atlantis and Mr. Pupin.

Besides artists like Artie Saaf and Ruben Moreira, who handled some early stories in 1942 and 1943, *Captain Wings* had two major artists: Bub Lubbers, who drew the strip from 1942 to 1943, and again from 1946 to 1948; and Lee Elias, who handled the strip from 1944 to 1946 while Lubbers was in the service.

Lubbers' stories were highly action-oriented and featured the obligatory bare-legged and barely clad females. Elias, on the other hand, was an expert at drawing planes, and his stories tended to feature long dogfights between Wings and his adversaries.

The air ace could fight unconvinced enemy pilots for only so long, and the strip finally ended in 1952. *Captain Wings* appeared in all issues of *Wings* between 16 and 113, and then appeared in three later issues before disappearing.

J.B.

CAREY, ED (d. 1920) Ed Carey, virtually forgotten today, was one of the most popular and prolific comic strip artists of his time.

His first major works can be found in the pages of the old *Life* magazine at the turn of the century and the following two decades. His work matured from tight line drawings to exaggerations to comical wash renderings. Carey contributed infrequently—only several panels a year—but the quality of both his art and gags compensated for the "dry spells" in between. His major occupation at this time was drawing color comic strips, and it was in the Sunday supplements that Carey made his mark.

Many of that era's most published comic artists are forgotten today—the Hearst stable had big-city clout, reaching influential readers and surviving to modern syndication. On the other hand, artists with the early preprint houses faded from sight when the major syndicates took over around 1920, unless they were snapped up by Hearst, as were Herriman, Carl Anderson, C. H. Wellington, and others.

Ed Carey is perhaps the foremost example of a big name who never made it to the history books because he didn't draw for a major paper or syndicate. But in 1905 he was the highest-paid comic strip artist of his day, earning $500 for one page of *Simon Simple*.

Carey's first strip was a spoof on the Conan Doyle rage of the day: *Sherlock Holmes*. Other early strips were *Jack Webster's Dictionary* and *Brainy Bowers*, a tramp comic he inherited from R. W. Taylor.

In 1905 we find his *Simon Simple* distributed by T. C. McClure. Simon was one of the great early comic characters. He was a red-haired simpleton—an early Boob McNutt—whose collars and ties were as enormous as his pants and whose swallow-tail jackets were always too small.

Simon was a victim (in the already-familiar comic strip convention) of a society that seemed to conspire against him. He had luckless experiences with girlfriends, cops, strangers. Among the regular characters was a half-pint black boy whose success in each page contrasted with Simon's bad luck. Simon for a while has a pet tiger, and in 1908 the strip, then distributed by Otis F. Wood, was called *Simon Simple and Ben-Gal.*

In 1907-8 Carey illustrated the very popular *Dickenspiel Stories* on comic pages. These were German dialect tales (Dickenspiel was a Teutonic Mr. Dooley) written by George V. Hobart. Originally Frederick Opper had illustrated the first collection of these columns from the *New York Journal.*

Carey's last published work was *Pa's Family and Their Friends* for the new McClure Syndicate in 1915; he succeeded C. H. Wellington, who carried on the characters in *Pa's Son-In-Law* for the *New York Tribune.* Carey also introduced the character of Charlie Chaplin into the strip (it would also be done by Elzie Segar and others in other features). Chaplin was the rage across America in the mid-teens and Carey's strip fared well, although not with the verve of earlier efforts, until 1918. After that his work disappeared from sight, and reports list his death around 1920.

If he had done the same work, but had moved to New York and major syndication with some of his coworkers from the early distribution houses, Carey's name and work would need little introduction today.

R.M.

CARLSON, WALLACE A. (1884-1967) American cartoonist, born March 28, 1884, in St. Louis, Missouri. In 1905 W. A. Carlson moved with his family to Chicago and started his career as a copy boy for the *Chicago Inter-Ocean,* where he soon had several sports and humor cartoons published at the age of 11. When the *Inter-Ocean* folded in 1914, Carlson turned to animation, single-handedly producing in 1915 a five-minute animated cartoon. He later joined the Essanay studio, where he spent two-and-a-half years. In 1919 he founded the Carlson Studios, releasing through Metro-Goldwyn-Mayer. When later that year Paramount decided to animate Sidney Smith's *The Gumps,* they called on Carlson to oversee the animation. The series was a flop, but during the course of production, Carlson met Sol Hess, who was then writing *The Gumps'* continuity. Later, when he was approached to do a new family strip, Hess remembered Carlson, and together they created *The Nebbs* (May 22, 1923).

W. A. Carlson drew *The Nebbs* (along with its top strip *Simp O'Dill*) until 1946, when it was finally discontinued. After *The Nebbs'* demise, Carlson created a gag strip, *Mostly Malarkey,* about the shenanigans of a bumbling office worker. W. A. Carlson died in 1967 on the West Coast and left behind a long record that still has not been fully evaluated.

W. A. Carlson was one of those cartoonist boy prodigies whose talents for some reason never fully blossomed. His drawings for *The Nebbs* have an endearing charm, which gave him at least modest fame in the history of comic art.

M.H.

CARPANTA (Spain) Created in 1947 for the weekly *Pulgarcito, Carpanta* was the brainchild of Josep Escobar, who was also the author of a number of animated cartoons produced at that time. The word "carpanta" means ravenous hunger, but it was not widely used until Escobar made it famous in his comic strip.

Carpanta the tramp is characterized by his insatiable hunger, epitomized by his daydreams of people with inaccessible barbecued chickens (the zenith of his aspirations), from which nothing can distract him. He embodies the widespread hunger suffered by the people in this period, the difficult years following the Spanish Civil War, with its obsession for food and its daily struggle for survival. These were the years when barbecued chicken was the symbol of wealth and well-being.

Carpanta is a gag feature unfolding in one or two pages. Its bum hero is a lovable vagabond, clean despite his poverty, whose attire, with its neat black hat and high collar, parodies that of a banker. He makes his home under a bridge and each morning he sets out, confident that some bright idea will, if not get him out of his poverty, at least provide him with a hot meal. His failures, as inevitable as taxes, serve only to reinforce Carpanta's stoical attitude and his lonely life, only shared by his friend Protasio.

The strip, besides giving rise to a number of Carpanta toys and dolls, also inspired a TV series at a time when this medium was still in its infancy in Spain. It is no longer being published.

L.G.

CARR, EUGENE (1881-1959) American cartoonist, born in New York City on January 17, 1881. Born into a very poor family, Eugene (Gene) Carr had to go to work at an early age. At nine he was an errand boy for the *New York Recorder,* where he liked to hang around the art department and learn the tricks of the trade. At 15 he launched his prolific cartooning career. During the course of his life, he was to work at one time or another for the *Herald,* the *World,* and the *Evening Journal* in New York; the *Times* in Philadelphia; and McClure and King Features Syndicates. The comic strips that he either created or took over are innumerable, although only a few attained any popularity. There was *Lady Bountiful,* a modern fairy tale that he created for the *Herald,* in 1904; *Nobody Works Like Father* (1906, in the *World*), which Coulton Waugh dismisses as "a comic which was too reminiscent of the ancient days of Dickens and Cruikshank to last long in a modern world," but which today has a period charm; *The Bad Dream That Made Billy a Better Boy* (a forerunner of *Little Nemo,* which Carr had taken over from William Steinigans); and a host of others whose titles will suffice: *All the Comforts of Home, Buddy, Uncle Crabapple, Phyllis, The Jones Boys, Father, Romeo, Willie Wise, Reddy and Caruso,* and *Flirting Flora.*

In 1913 Carr took over the famous panel *Metropolitan Movies,* which had been created by Rollin Kirby, and he did a creditable job; *Metropolitan Movies* was to become Carr's most noted feature, and it was popular enough to be reprinted in book form under the title *Kid Kartoons.*

Gene Carr represents the quintessential cartoonist of the start of the century: restless, experimental, and highly prolific. Had he stayed with one feature instead of rolling around like the proverbial stone, he might have become one of the more respected names in comic art. He died of a heart attack at his home in Walpole, New Hampshire, on December 9, 1959.

M.H.

CARREÑO, ALBERT (1905-1964) American comic strip and comic book artist, born in Mexico City in 1905. Albert (Al) Carreño's father was a bank manager who was once abducted by Pancho Villa but managed to escape, and he lived to the ripe age of 96. Carreño Jr. attended the University of Mexico and was expected to follow in his father's footsteps; but his love was art, not banking, and he moved to the United States in the mid-1920s to make his mark as a cartoonist. Working first as a caricaturist on the *Chicago Daily News*, he later went on to New York, where he became the roommate of Miguel Covarrubias and contributed cartoons and illustrations to various national magazines.

In 1935 Carreño, while working for United Theater Advertisers turning out movie ads and posters, was contacted by the George Matthew Adams Service to do a comic strip for an eight-page tabloid comic section they planned to offer to client newspapers. The result was *Ted Strong*, an atmospheric and lovingly rendered Western, one of the better efforts in the genre. Unfortunately the service's comic section (which featured such other obscure strips as Paul H. Jepsen's *Rod Rian of the Sky Police*) picked up only scant circulation and was dropped after a few years.

From there Carreño went on (as do many other disappointed strip artists) to comic book illustration (*Ted Strong* had appeared in reprints as early as 1937), working variously at Fox, Fawcett, Marvel, National, Pines, Prize and Ziff-Davis throughout the 1940s and 1950s. He turned out love, horror, superhero, and Western stories by the bushel. His best efforts were on the *Ibis*, *Red Gaucho*, and *Captain Marvel Jr.* titles for Fawcett, and on *The Blue Beetle* for Fox. In the 1950s he also became active in the National Cartoonists Society and became NCS membership chairman. Al Carreño died in September 1964.

Carreño is one of a number of obscure laborers in the comic vineyards whose work deserves to be re-examined in a new light.

M.H.

CARTER, AUGUSTUS DANIELS (1895-1957) The cartoonist father of Mush Stebbins and Fatso Dolan—*Just Kids*—known by millions of newspaper readers as Ad Carter, was born Augustus Daniels Carter near Baltimore in 1895. He claimed later that two school friends at Baltimore's Donaldson School were the originals for Mush and Fatso (Mush, he said, died on the western front in World War I, while Fatso went on to success in the insurance field). Orphaned at 11 by the death of his mother, Carter missed much of the childhood fun he created for his kid characters, and had to go to work as soon as he could, where he could. Until he could market his talent, Clare Briggs, then established as one of the foremost panel cartoonists in the country, got Carter a job as a reporter on the *Brooklyn Times*. After a stint on the *Brooklyn Eagle* as well, Carter had his strip idea shaped up and submitted it, again with the encouragement and assistance of Briggs, to King Features Syndicate in 1922. The King Features people liked Carter's kids and gave the strip an old King Features title that had been used on and off in its Sunday supplement since the 1890s.

Popular from the outset, Carter's *Just Kids* was always a King Features second-string Sunday strip, never appearing for any prolonged time in *Puck*, but running in many other papers around the country. Daily, however, it ran in most Hearst afternoon papers and was published widely beyond these. Perhaps the best-known accomplishment of the strip was its emphasis on children's safety. Carter introduced the Just Kids Safety Club into the daily and Sunday feature

in 1927, then augmented the idea with a separate series of panels focusing on commonsense ways for kids to avoid injury and danger, which ran in many papers not subscribing to the strip as well as all those that did.

In the late 1920s, Carter added *Nicodemus O'Malley* to his Sunday page; this was another kid strip that ultimately developed a theme of pure fantasy with the addition of a whale in the 1930s. Fathering three children of his own, the rotund Carter lived on a broad estate at Mamaroneck, New York, until his death there from a heart attack on June 26, 1957, at the age of 62. *Just Kids* was interred with its creator.

B.B.

CARTER, REG (1886-1949) Reginald Arthur Lay Carter, also known as Reg, was born on December 6, 1886, in Southwold, East Suffolk, England. His earliest published works were the many colored comic postcards he drew in the early 1900s, following the craze created by Tom Browne and others. Carter's style was distinctive: his urchins wore large berets, his adults wore cloth caps with peaks, beads of sweat flew everywhere, and most of all he pioneered squared-off speech balloons with cutaway corners. Radiating from people's heads were descriptive words such as "Rage!" or "Wrath!" when they were angry, and he also added the word "Throw!" when one of his characters threw something. He continued to use this same style when he began to create children's comics in 1920.

His earliest strip was of the comedian Oliver Hardy, who appeared in a full-page strip in the new comic *Film Fun* (1920), under the popular sobriquet of "Babe Hardy." This was many years before the comedian paired up with Stan Laurel to form their famous duo. In 1921 he drew the adventures or, as they were called, *Astonishing Stunts* of Ernie Mayne, a bulbous Music Hall comedian, for *Merry-and-Bright*, a penny comic. No further real-life characters came from his pen, despite his obvious ability as a caricaturist, but a string of alliterative heroes ensued for the next 20 years. There was *Priceless Percy* in *Sports Fun*; *Wireless Willie and Bertie Broadcast* in *The Monster Comic*; *Horace Horseradish* and *Ferdinand the Fire Fighter* also appeared in *Monster*; while *Nathaniel Nodd* and *Benjamin Beetroot* starred in that comic's companion, *Golden Penny*.

A slew of working-class heroes came next, beginning with *Daniel Dole and Oscar Outofwork* in *Tip Top*; *Oswold the Odd Job Man* in *Up-to-Date*; *Filleter Fish and Jack Sprat* in *Sunny*; and *Gussy the Gas Meter Manipulator* in *Happy*. In 1936 the new comic *Mickey Mouse Weekly* was started, and Carter found a new venue with such series as *Bob the Bugler*, about an army cadet, and the unusual strip *Sea Shanties*, which was set beneath the ocean. In 1938 he found a new home and his best showcase with *The Beano*, a new comic launched by the Scottish publisher D.C. Thomson. He won the full-color front cover of *The Beano* with his carefully drawn adventures of Big Eggo, an ostrich in search of his egg. Eggo ran on the cover for 10 years, a record for that comic. His final features, also for *The Beano*, were *Freddy Flipperfeet* (1947), about a comic seal, and *Peter Penguin* (1948). Carter died on April 24, 1949.

D.G.

CASEY COURT (G.B.) On May 24, 1902, a large single panel depicting the opening of the Casey Court Rowing Season appeared on the back page of the pink

"Casey Court," Charlie Pease. © CHIPS.

comic paper *Illustrated Chips*. On September 12, 1953, a larger single panel depicting the Casey Court Funny Face Contest appeared on page nine of the pink comic paper *Chips*. Little had changed in the interim. The original cartoonist was Julius Stafford Baker, the last cartoonist "Charlie" Pease. In between, M. C. Veitch, Louis Briault, and others have drawn the weekly escapades of this gang of back-street urchins in much the same crowded manner, with the boys bossed about by Billy Baggs, the girls in the charge of Sally Trotters, and the usual background signs of "Boots Mendid" and "Washin Dun Ere." In all there were 2,385 episodes (including a few reprints).

J.S. Baker was clearly inspired by the single-panel happenings featuring the American *Yellow Kid,* and his early urchins all had that monkey-faced look that popularly suggested the Irish. But his ideas were British, for he quickly established a pattern. Whatever was topical, the Casey Court "Nibs" would stage, build, or construct their own version. Be it a fireworks display, tennis at Wimbledon, racing at Ascot, the Lord Mayor's Show, or even the threatened invasion of England, the Casey Court Kids were ready with their home-made answer.

The only British comic characters to take to the vaudeville stage, *Casey Court* toured the music halls from 1905 with Will Murray as Mrs. Casey. The 1906 tour had young Charlie Chaplin as Billy Baggs!

D.G.

CASEY RUGGLES (U.S.) Unquestionably the finest Western adventure strip yet created, Warren Tufts' *Casey Ruggles* first appeared in a number of Sunday papers around the country as a half-page United Features release on May 22, 1949, with the daily starting on September 19, 1949. Subtitled *A Saga of the West,* Tufts' impeccably researched, grippingly cast, brutal, bloody, and fast-moving strip stunned readers of the early 1950s as it single-handedly lifted the possibilities of serious strip drama several daring notches—only to

find that no one followed. Casey himself is an army sergeant serving with Fremont in California who is eager to get in on the California gold rush. He returns to the East to pick up his fiancée, Chris, only to become entangled with Lilli Lafitte, the daughter of pirate Jean Lafitte. Although some of the strip action takes place in the East, the general narrative locale is California, featuring the gold-rushing Americans, native Spanish, and Indians (a later major character is Kit Fox, an Indian boy).

With its narrative themes including graphically portrayed rape and torture, the strip tended to be published only in the Sunday and daily papers of the more sophisticated cities, and it was subject to recurrent waves of protest even there. Tufts' trampling on the genteel traditions of the earlier Western confections in strips and films anticipated the same steps later taken by Sergio Leone in *A Fistful of Dollars* and other films, although the public was not ready for this in the early 1950s. Although no specific data is available, as Tufts does not discuss his strip work, syndicate requests that he "tone down" his material seem to have led him to abandon the *Casey Ruggles* property to United Features (which continued it for a while with an inept ghost) on Sunday, September 5, 1954 (he had dropped the daily on April 3 of the same year), while he prepared *Lance*.

If any recent strip deserves a memorial reprinting in full, daily and Sunday, it is *Casey Ruggles*. Gripping, colorful, exciting, and mature, the strip should be packaged and sold as a graphic novel of several volumes.

B.B.

CASPER (U.S.) *Casper the Friendly Ghost,* which later became the keystone feature of the Harvey Comics line, debuted in animated cartoons in 1946. The debut film, *The Friendly Ghost,* was produced by Famous Studios (formerly Fleischer) based on an unsold children's book conceived by Joe Oriolo and written by him and Sy Reit. Oriolo, a Famous Studios animator, had invented the character two years earlier and collaborated with Reit on the book, which dealt with a meek little ghost who desires only to make friends—a difficult task when his transparent appearance frightens everyone off. In 1946, on an impulse, Oriolo and Reit submitted their story to Famous and the cartoon, intended as a one-shot, blossomed into an entire series. *Casper* and other Famous Studios characters were licensed for comic book use to Jubilee in 1949, which issued *Casper* number one in the fall of that year.

The comic book was not successful, and after a year, Jubilee allowed its contract to lapse, whereupon it was taken over by St. John, which issued a new *Casper* number one in 1950. As was the case with St. John's comics based on Paul Terry's characters, the comic book company worked closely with the New York animation studios, employing many studio employees to write and draw the comic books. A roster of supporting characters developed in the St. John issues, based upon characters who had appeared in the cartoons. When the *Casper* series switched over to Harvey Publishing Company, these characters, who included Wendy the Good Little Witch, Nightmare the Ghost Horse, Spooky, and the evil Ghostly Trio, graduated to star status and their own features.

Harvey's association with *Casper* began with a new number one issue in 1953, the third numbering for the comic. A number of companion comics, featuring Casper and his co-stars, soon followed with titles like *Casper's Ghostland, Casper and Spooky, Casper and Wendy, Casper and the Ghostly Trio, Casper and the Cub Scouts, Casper and Nightmare, Casper and Richie Rich, TV Casper and Company,* plus several magazines starring Wendy and Spooky. Since 1986 Harvey Publications has been issuing a digest-size *Casper* magazine in addition to their regular line of comic books.

The *Casper* series and its spin-offs soon became the cornerstone of the Harvey line, and when Famous Studios ceased production, the parent company, Paramount Pictures, sold Harvey all rights to the characters, including television rights to the cartoons. The films were retitled with a "Harveytoons" logo and subsequently enjoyed great popularity, which in turn bolstered the sales of Harvey comics. Through judicious use of reprints, Harvey managed to keep an ample supply of *Casper* adventures on the newsstand, much to the delight of younger comic book readers.

As with most Harvey features, Casper artists received almost no recognition for their work. Only Dom Sileo—whose works hang in the Brooklyn Museum's Community Gallery—is generally known for his participation.

M.E.

CASSON, MELVIN (Ca. 1920-   ) Mel Casson was born in Boston on a date he refuses to divulge. He grew up in New York City, attended the Art Students League on scholarship, and studied under George Bridgman and Kunyiosha.

Casson always wanted to be a cartoonist and was no doubt inspired by his talented father, a "Sunday artist." While in art school, he sold his first magazine cartoons. At 19, he sold to the *Saturday Evening Post* and became the youngest artist in the magazine's history to sign a first-refusal contract.

He saw bitter action in World War II and was wounded as an infantry captain in the European theater. He returned to the U.S. with a Bronze Star and two Purple Hearts and took another plunge into the

magazine gag field. Casson was the first Secretary of the American Society of Magazine Cartoonists.

His first strip was *Jeff Crockett* for the Herald Tribune Syndicate, about a small-town lawyer. Casson strained for a satirical slant; the editors wanted straight laughs and the feature died after a modest five-year run (1948-1952).

Next came *Sparky*, a little kid panel for Publishers Syndicate, and *Angel*, a baby panel for the same distributor, which fared well and ran from 1953-1966 with merchandising and a series of books. With Alfred Andriola (under the name of Alfred James) he created *It's Me, Dilly!* for the Hall Syndicate; it ran from 1958-1962.

Dilly was a bright, smart, and funny glamour-girl strip that might have been more successful a decade later. After this strip, Casson coedited a cartoon book with Andriola, *Ever Since Adam and Eve*, and worked in advertising, books, and TV writing and production.

In November 1972, Casson and veteran gag cartoonist William F. Brown created *Mixed Singles*, a trendy strip about young adults. Brown, one of the best funnymen in comics, also had credits in Juluis Monk's off-Broadway revues and was responsible for the book of Broadway's *The Wiz*.

Mixed Singles achieved moderate success through United Features. It starred an array of hip, square, sexy, and troubled singles, with sophisticated gags and sharp, poster-effect art (both partners wrote and drew the strip). The slick style was achieved by the use of rapidograph pens. In early 1975, in an effort to revitalize the strip, which had leveled off in sales at around 150 papers, it was renamed *Boomer*, after the lead character, who married shortly thereafter.

Casson's art through the years has mirrored the style in vogue. He is an accomplished draftsman and dedicated worker in cartoonists' causes.

In 1973, he and Brown won the Philips Award from the 24th Festival of International Humor in Italy.

R.M.

The Sunday version of *Boomer* was discontinued on April 29, 1979; and on August 1, 1981, the daily strip also came to an end. From 1990 on, Casson has been drawing the *Redeye* newspaper feature on texts by Bill Yates.

M.H.

CASTELLI, ALFREDO (1947-   ) Italian writer and editor, born June 26, 1947, in Milan. Alfredo Castelli began his career drawing and writing a filler, *Scheletrino*, in the pages of the popular *Diabolik* comic book. In 1966 he started writing the scripts of well-established features: *Diabolik, Pedrito El Drito, Cucciolo, Tiramolla,* and *Topolino* (Mickey Mouse Italian style), for different magazines. In 1969, with a group of friends, he edited *Tilt*, an Italian *Mad* magazine; it published parodies of established comics (both American and Italian), such as *Peanuts, The Wizard of Id, Valentina,* and *Feiffer*, and spoofs of movies, as well as satires on contemporary subjects. This was the first attempt to establish the *Mad* type of humor in Italy, and it failed.

In 1969 Castelli founded and coedited *Horror*, a fine magazine devoted to horror and the supernatural, for which he wrote a number of stories, illustrated by leading Italian artists (Dino Battaglia, Sergio Zaniboni, Marco Rostagno, Sergio Tuis, et al.). For *Horror* he also created the humor strip *Zio Boris* ("Uncle Boris"), the story of a mad scientist and his friends:—a vampire, a werewolf, and a ghoul. *Zio Boris*, drawn in the beginning by Carlo Perini and later by Daniele Fagarazzi, was published in many Italian newspapers and magazines and has been translated in a number of European and Latin American countries. At the same time, Castelli wrote the stories of *Van Helsing*, about a vampire turned detective, and other *Tilt*-type series.

In 1972 Castelli became a member of the editorial staff of the leading Italian weekly *Corriere dei Ragazzi*, for which he continued the *Zio Boris* and *Tilt* series; created a humor strip, *Otto Kruntz*; and created two adventure series, *L'Ombra* ("The Shadow") drawn by Mario Cubbino, and *Gli Aristocratici* ("The Aristocrats") drawn by Fernando Tacconi. (The latter strip relates the exploits of a gang of British gentlemen-thieves. It has been widely reprinted throughout the world.) Alfredo Castelli has also written stories about famous characters of lore and legend (Aladdin, Sinbad, Gulliver, etc.) for the French weekly *Pif*, and his prolific career also includes writing TV commercials and magazine stories. In 1978 he created the highly successful *Martin Mystere* comic strip, and most of his efforts since that time have focused on developing this very lucrative property.

G.B.

CATHY (U.S.) "Cathy" was born on November 22, 1976, and quickly came to represent the prototypical busy modern woman who tries to balance career and relationships with parents, friends, and lovers while she struggles (unsuccessfully) with weight gain and constantly changing fashions. Created by her namesake Cathy Guisewite, the comic strip's heroine takes on the world alternately with anger and resignation, as when she rants against Valentine's Day for having become "capitalism at its worst" or when she lists all the things she should have done but didn't for one reason or another, except "Wanted to eat cake. Ate cake," concluding with a self-indulgent smile, "The only time I ever live in the moment is when it has to do with chocolate."

Other characters include Cathy's parents, Mr. and Mrs. Andrews. Whereas Mr. Andrews is ineffectual but properly sympathetic to his daughter's situation, the mother works on Cathy by indirection, ladling equal portions of advice (what she calls "wisdom") and guilt on subjects as diverse as how to follow a recipe, shopping for food or clothes, Cathy's single status, or life in general. Regardless of Cathy's avowed desire for independence, ultimately she still needs the advice and support of her family—much to her mother's delight. Rounding out the cast of characters in Cathy's world are Mr. Pinkley, her manipulative boss; her coworkers with a mob mentality; lying salespeople working on commissions; a dog who understands her too well; her insensitive boyfriends; and female friends to pal around with but who are also rivals for the insensitive men they complain about.

However, in spite of insecurities fostered not only by her mother but also by countless advice columns, self-help books, and ad campaigns, Cathy knows that deep down she is not a brainless young woman programmed by clearance sales and fashion magazines, with low self-esteem and a craving for male affection. Thanks to her deprecating sense of humor, often directed at herself, she remains an optimist about life, love, family, and friends, even after setbacks: "I've given up my quest for perfection and am shooting for five good minutes in a row."

Drawn in a simple, almost caricature style, *Cathy* is distributed by Universal Press Syndicate and runs daily and on Sundays in over 1,200 newspapers worldwide. The strip, which has been reprinted in numerous paperback collections, received the Reuben Award from the National Cartoonists Society in 1993, and its characters appear on sundry merchandise. In 1987, Guisewite won an Emmy Award for the first of several animated television cartoons based on Cathy's amusing, though frustrating, travails.

P.L.H.

CAT-MAN, THE (U.S.) 1—The first strip entitled *The Cat-Man* appeared in Centaur's *Amazing Man* numbers five (September 1939) and eight (December 1939). The strip was created by writer and artist Tarpe Mills, and was a rather pedestrian feature starring Barton Stone as The Cat-Man.

2—The second strip entitled *The Cat-Man* was created by Charles Quinlan for Holyoke (Helnit) Publications and made its first appearance in number one for May 1941. This Cat-Man was really David Merrywether, the sole survivor of a caravan of Americans attacked by bandits in Burma. Merrywether was reared, educated, and cared for by a tigress—just as

"Cathy," Cathy Guisewite. © Universal Press Syndicate.

Tarzan was cared for by apes—and eventually adopted all the traits of the cat family. He had great strength, was extremely agile, was able to see in the dark, and had tremendous leaping ability. As was the custom in comic books of the 1940s, Merrywether came to America, adopted the Cat-Man identity, and set out to save the world from crime. His costume was an orange tunic with a "C" emblazoned on the chest, red gloves, boots, cape and hood, and bare legs. He also sported a pair of catlike ears.

Most of the material was produced by Quinlan, who was not a stellar artist or writer. (He created another animal-inspired character for Fox, *The Blue Beetle*.) In the fifth issue, a female sidekick was added. Katie Conn, dubbed The Kitten, was orphaned when her parents were killed in a train wreck. She joined The Cat-Man to fight crime because she was a trained acrobat—just as Dick Grayson, alias Robin, was a trained acrobat and joined Batman to fight crime—and had the ingratiating habit of calling Merrywether "Uncle David." She later appeared in another strip, *Little Leaders*, another of the 1940s group of "sidekicks banded together to fight crime without the aid of their mentors."

In all, *The Cat-Man* contains just about every comic book cliché of the 1940s—Holyoke was a house known for producing just such characters. It lasted until *Cat-Man Comics* folded after August 1946's 32nd issue.

J.B.

CAVAZZANO, GIORGIO (1947-   ) Italian cartoonist, born on October 9, 1947, in Venice. As an assistant to Romano Scarpa, the famous Italian illustrator of Disney characters, Giorgio Cavazzano inked a Donald Duck adventure that appeared in the Italian magazine *Topolino* ("Mickey Mouse") in 1962. His first pencil and ink work was published in the same magazine in 1967. Since then his contribution to the Italian Disney production has been vast and important: it totals more than 250 stories involving Donald Duck,

Mickey Mouse, and other Disney characters. He has also drawn several other comic characters: *Oscar e Tango* (1974) for the magazine *Messaggero dei Ragazzi*, and *Walkie & Talkie* for the weekly *Corriere dei Pioccoli*, both written by Giorgio Pezzin. In 1975 he drew *Altai & Jonson*, written by Tiziano Sclavi, for the weekly *Corriere dei Ragazzi* and later for the magazines *Il Mago* and *Orient Express*. Cavazzano's body of work also includes *Smalto & Jonny* (1976), written by Pezzin, for the monthly *Il Mago*; *Captain Rogers* (1981), written by Pezzin and later by François Corteggiani, for the weekly *Il Giornalino*; *Silas Finn* (1985), written by Sclavi, for the magazine *Messaggero dei Ragazzi*; and *Timothy Titan* (1991), written by Corteggiani for *Il Giornalino*. In all of his series, he merges humor with adventure, and his artwork is marked by the realism of the settings and the caricatural drawings of the characters, both of which are drawn with a thick and supple line. Several of these adventures have been reprinted in book form.

Cavazzano has also drawn the French animal strip *Pif*, and he coordinated the art production for *Pif* magazine from 1988 to 1991. *Timothy Titan* has been reprinted in the German magazine *Zack!* under the name *Peter O'Pencil*. Cavazzano's talents have also been displayed on illustrated posters, booklets, and other promotional materials for various advertising campaigns. In 1992 he was awarded a Yellow Kid prize in Lucca, Italy.

G.C.C.

CELARDO, JOHN (1918-   ) American artist, writer, and editor, born in Staten Island, New York, on December 27, 1918. Celardo attended public schools in Staten Island (he has remained there all his life) and later enrolled as a student in the Arts Students League and the New York School of Industrial Arts. His ambitions were to be a painter and illustrator.

Celardo's first professional work was doing sports cartoons and spots for Street and Smith publications in 1937. From there he graduated to comic books and worked for Eisner and Iger. When Quality Comics

Giorgio Cavazzano and Tiziano Sclavi, "Altai & Jonson." © the authors.

gathered its own staff and raided the Iger shop, Celardo was one of the artists; there he worked on *Dollman, Wonder Boy, Uncle Sam, Paul Bunyan, Espionage, Hercules, Old Witch,* and *Zero* comics. He sometimes signed his work John C. Lardo.

In 1940 Celardo also worked for Fiction House (only to be interrupted by the draft in the next year). There he drew *Hawk, Red Comet, Powerman, Captain West,* and *Kaanga;* after the war, from 1946-49, he rejoined Fiction and worked on the *Tiger Man, Suicide Smith,* and other titles.

After a short stint with Ziff-Davis in 1950, Celardo freelanced until landing the position of artist on the *Tarzan* newspaper strip, succeeding Bob Lubbers. His first daily strips appeared in 1953 (Sunday in 1954), scripted by Dick van Buren (son of Raeburn van Buren of *Abbie an' Slats*) and others.

In 1960 Celardo took over the writing chores and had control over Tarzan. His drawing was stiffer and heavier than other Tarzan artists, and Tarzan was taken to meet Red Chinese spies and various new antagonists in and out of the jungle.

In 1967 he left United Features to take over *The Green Berets* at Chicago Tribune-New York News Syndicate from Joe Kubert. This assignment lasted until the strip died in 1969, at which time Celardo found himself back at United finishing the career of *Davy Jones,* which had been created by Sam Leff and Alden McWilliams. *Jones* sank in 1970.

In 1968 and thereafter Celardo freelanced the comic book market again, drawing *Believe It or Not* for Western and miscellaneous work for National. In 1973 he was hired as a comics editor at King Features and soon bowed out of the drawing-board side of the business. He returned, however, to draw the *Buz Sawyer* newspaper strip from 1983 to its end in 1989.

R.M.

CELLULITE (France) *Cellulite* was created by female cartoonist Claire Bretécher in the French magazine *Pilote* of June 19, 1969.

Claire Bretécher conceived Cellulite as the antithesis of the stereotyped fairy-tale princess: she is ugly, with dull hair and a blotched face, sniveling, sex-starved, avaricious, mean, and stupid. In spite of her rank, she has been unable to find a husband, although she spares no effort in this endeavor—from booby-trapping the highway leading to the castle in the hope that some prince will get caught, to blackmailing her father's counsellor. If Cellulite is grotesque, the strip's male characters fare no better, confirming the cynical judgment of the misbegotten princess that, "while women aren't much, men are nothing at all." Her father the king is a feckless, self-absorbed moron, a certified coward and an unabashed lecher; the knights are conniving flunkeys, and the peasants a bunch of uncouth louts well deserving of their lot.

The resemblance to *The Wizard of Id* is inescapable; but, if anything, Bretécher is even more pessimistic than Hart about the worth of the human race. *Cellulite* is often very funny, yet the laughs always leave a bitter aftertaste—perhaps because they hit too close to home. The misadventures of Cellulite have been reprinted in book form by Dargaud. Bretécher definitively abandoned *Cellulite* in 1977, after which time she restricted her cartoon work almost exclusively to the pages of the newsweekly *Le Nouvel Observateur.*

M.H.

"Cellulite," Claire Bretécher. © Editions Dargaud.

CEREBUS (Canada) In the mid-1970s barbarian comics, spurred by the success of *Conan* comic books, were all the rage. A young Canadian cartoonist named David Sim decided to design a Conan parody starring—of all creatures—an aardvark. With his wife Deni Loubert he self-published a black-and-white comic book titled *Cerebus,* whose first issue hit the newsstands in December 1977.

Described as being "five hands high, with a lengthy snout, a long tail, and short grey fur," Cerebus, the unlikely protagonist, mimicked everything Conan was doing at the time in the Marvel comics. Soon, however, he evolved a personality and a history of his own, helped by such supporting characters as the female barbarian Red Sophia, the ineffectual wizard Elrod the Albino, not to mention Lord Julius, who looked, behaved, and presumably talked like Groucho Marx. In the course of his adventures in the pre-industrial human world of Lower Felda, the "mean and lethal aardvark" has battled such worthy opponents as the Moon Roach (a malevolent version of Batman) and the Woman-Thing, was appointed prime minister of the mythical country Iest, and even managed to get crowned pope.

Well drawn and humorously plotted, *Cerebus* has enjoyed growing popularity since its inception. The series has been regularly reprinted in 500-plus-page anthologies, the so-called "telephone books"; it has also received its share of controversy, because of Sim's frank depiction of sex and rape scenes, his long disquisitions on the war between the sexes, and his occasional racial allusions. At the outset Sim vowed to complete the saga in 300 issues; at the rate of 12 issues a year coming out like clockwork, this should put *finis* to the whole enterprise sometime in the year 2002.

M.H.

CÉZARD, JEAN (1925-1977) A French cartoonist born in 1925, Jean Cézard started his prolific cartooning career in 1946 with a humor strip, *Monsieur Toudou,* published in the children's magazine *Francs-Jeux.* This was followed by more comic creations: *Pilul* (1946-1948), a series of humorous adventures; *Les Mirobolantes Aventures du Professeur Pipe* ("The Out-of-

"Cerebus," Dave Sim. © Dave Sim.

Sight Adventures of Professor Pipe," 1949); *Jim Minimum*; and three adventure features, *Brik* (a pirate strip), *Yak* (about a superhero), and *Kiwi*, his most famous creation in the action genre (1952).

Cézard is best noted, however, for the hilariously funny strip that he created for *Vaillant* (now *Pif*) in 1953, *Arthur le Fantôme Justicier* ("Arthur the Justice-Fighting Phantom"). This saga of a mischievous little ghost always in search of wrongs to redress is one of the funniest strips to come out of post-World War II France. Along with *Arthur,* Cézard produced several short-lived strips for *Vaillant-Pif*: *Les Rigoius et les Tristus*, a comic fable in the manner of Rabelais, and *Les Facéties du Père Passe-Passe* ("The Pranks of Pop Legerdemain").

Jean Cézard was awarded the First International Prize in the comic strip category at the Brussels Humor Salon of 1968. He died on April 8, 1977.

M.H.

CHAI RACHAWAT (1941-   ) Thai cartoonist, born in 1941. Chai Rachawat did not start out as a cartoonist; in fact, he was college-educated as a bookkeeper. Cartooning was a hobby he practiced while working as a bank bookkeeper in the early 1970s. By 1973 he landed his first full-time cartooning position with Bangkok's *Daily News*, where his antigovernment vitriol quickly drew the attention of the authorities. Inevitably, Chai landed on the government's blacklist, and in 1976, he sought refuge in the United States, settling in Los Angeles, where he worked in a variety of menial jobs for two years. In 1978 he returned home and joined Thailand's largest and most influential daily newspaper, *Thai Rath*.

Chai has been voted by readers as Thailand's most popular cartoonist. He is easily recognized in Bangkok's popular culture scene and appears frequently on television talk shows. His major strip in *Thai Rath, Poo Yai Ma Kap Tung Ma Muen*, described as Thailand's

Chai Rachawat, a typical Chai strip. © Chai Rachawat.

Doonesbury, has been made into a full-length film and featured in television commercials, many articles, and a graduate-school dissertation. The two major characters, Poo Yai Ma, a village headman, and Ah Joy, his spunky deputy, are symbolic of the government and the common people and are used by Chai to express his strong opinions about political and social issues. Chai has survived various authoritarian regimes despite his hard-hitting style; at times, he has been forced to abandon his career. In the politically turbulent times of May 1992, he stopped drawing altogether for fear of possible retribution and as a tribute to the hundreds of pro-democracy demonstrators killed or injured in anti-government riots. Even then he seemed to have the upper hand, vowing not to resume his drawing until the dictators were removed from office, and in the last published sequence of his strip, he turned the once lively fictional village into a wasteland.

Along with the *Thai Rath* comic strip, Chai draws other cartoons and strips for weeklies and monthlies and for advertising agencies. He also presides over his own television production company, where he script-writes a weekly talk show, handles numerous land investment interests, and teaches the first cartooning course in Thailand at Silpokorn University.

J.A.L.

CHALAND, YVES (1957-1990) Inarguably one of the more brilliant representatives of the much-touted Franco-Belgian school of comics, Yves Chaland was in the process of transcending this artistic concept and attitude that had become somewhat outdated when his career was tragically cut short in its prime. Born in Lyon, France, on April 3, 1957, he started contributing to various comic fanzines while still in high school, and after studying at the School of Fine Arts in Saint-Etienne in central France, he made his professional debut in the magazine *Métal Hurlant* in 1978. There he produced a series of masterly spoofs of the Belgian comics of the 1950s that had charmed him since childhood, while at the same time he denounced the subtle racism, chauvinism, and sense of superiority inherent in most of these stories.

In the pages of *Métal Hurlant* Chaland also created in 1980 the first of his many comic characters: Bob Fish, a Belgian private eye in the mold of Humphrey Bogart, living precariously in a Brussels of the future occupied by the Chinese. Following hard on the heels of Bob Fish, Adolphus Claar made his appearance the next year. A citizen of the 23rd century, Claar reflected ironically on the lunacies of our own times. In 1982 Al Memory, better known as *le jeune Albert* ("Young Albert"), formerly a sidekick of Bob Fish, was promoted to his own series, a succession of cruel vignettes in which the artist expressed his revulsion at the cruelties and hypocrisies of contemporary society. His most famous creation, however, remains *Freddy Lombard*, about a go-getting teenager and his two inseparable companions, a boy and a girl; set in the artist's favorite time and place—Brussels in the 1950s—it satirized not only many of the Belgian cartoonists of the period (Hergé, Jijé, Franquin, et al.) but also slyly subverted the values they stood for.

Yves Chaland, "Bob Fish." © Humanoides Associés.

"Chanoc," Angel Mora. © Publicaciones Herrerias.

Chaland was slowly emerging from the shadow of his elders and developing an exciting style of his own, as his posthumously published sketches and drawings demonstrated, when he was killed in a fiery car crash on a French highway on July 18, 1990.

M.H.

CHANOC (Mexico) Created on October 16, 1959, as a comic book by cartoonist Angel José Mora and script-writer Martin de Lucenay, *Chanoc* soon became the best sea-adventure feature in Mexico, with its clever blend of humor and pathos.

Chanoc, who lives in the village of Ixtac, earns his living as a fisherman, although, through his experience and curiosity, he has become a respected zoologist and an eminent oceanographer. An accomplished athlete who has mastered many skills, and a courageous man, Chanoc devotes his life to the preservation of wildlife and the fight against injustice. As in the case of *Alma Grande, Chanoc* develops over many adventures without chronological consistency. As a humorous counter-point to the hero, the authors have created the character of the ancient and bewhiskered Tsekub, as excitable as his companion and of incredible physical strength in spite of his age. Chanoc's extensive love life is characterized by a healthy and youthful eroticism: well-endowed and liberated females are as abundant in the strip as the sports events in which the two friends can shine.

With the assistance of Javier Robles, Antonio Hernandez, and his brother Ulises, Angel José Mora has continued drawing the adventures of Chanoc to this day, while de Lucenay was later succeeded by the equally excellent Pedro Zapiain. Chanoc, the hero of no fewer than six movies, has been used to introduce a brand of chocolate into the Mexican market.

L.G.

CHARLIE CHAN (U.S.) Alfred Andriola created *Charlie Chan* as both a daily strip and a Sunday page for the McNaught Syndicate. Based on Earl Derr Biggers' famous Chinese detective, the *Charlie Chan* strip appeared from October 1938 to May 1942.

Graphically, Al Andriola modeled his hero after actor Warner Oland (who played the title role in many of the *Charlie Chan* movies). In the course of his investigations Inspector Chan of the Honolulu police fights crooks, international conspirators, spies, and saboteurs in many parts of the world. He is very ably assisted in his endeavors by Kirk Barrow, a handsome, tall adventurer in the tradition of the 1930s, and by Kirk's actress sweetheart, the lovely and enterprising Gina Lane.

"Charlie Chan," Alfred Andriola. © McNaught Syndicate.

Characterized by witty dialogue and brisk plotting, *Charlie Chan* figures among the best comic strips of the "Caniff school" and is highly entertaining as well as excellently drawn.

In comic books, *Charlie Chan* has known a slightly longer, if checkered, career. Prize Publications issued a series of nine *Charlie Chan* comic books in 1948-49 (among its contributing writers and artists were Joe Simon and Jack Kirby). From 1955 to 1959 the character was run by Charlton (under the title *The New Adventures of Charlie Chan*) and then by National. In 1965-66 it was briefly revived by Dell.

M.H.

CHARLIE CHAPLIN'S COMIC CAPERS (U.S.)
Drawn by several artists, *Charlie Chaplin's Comic Capers* was introduced early in 1915 by publisher James Keeley into his newly purchased *Chicago Record-Herald and Inter-Ocean* (later the *Chicago Herald*.) A Sunday and daily strip based on the screen character of Charles Chaplin, it attained nationwide syndication within six months through the publisher's J. Keeley Co. Keeley, whose *Herald* was the first paper to discover the talents of such later famed cartoonists as Frank Willard and Billy De Beck, had noted the popularity of comic strips based on screen personalities in England (where Chaplin, Fatty Arbuckle, and others were featured in comic magazines), and decided to try the same thing stateside in his new paper. The immensely popular figure of Chaplin (released for strip use to Keeley by Essanay Films in 1915) sold the strip; the art and narrative, contributed by a number of now-unknown *Herald* staff cartoonists (some of whom signed themselves only as "Bud" or "Aurie," etc.), varied from poor to terrible. Once subscribing papers realized this, the strip was frequently dropped, and its run in a given paper was unlikely to be longer than a year at most.

Yet to a newcomer to strip cartooning in 1916 like Elzie Crisler Segar (later creator of *Popeye*), the Chaplin epic looked like a royal chance to make a major public bow. R. F. Outcault, realizing this, persuaded Keeley's staff to give the ambitious young man a chance on *Capers*. The job didn't pay much (and what it did pay was cut considerably when Keeley dropped the daily *Capers* in 1917), but Segar was eager, and he published his first Chaplin page on March 12, 1916.

The humor of the strip picked up at once, although Segar's style at the time left much to be desired. The ambitious cartoonist added a comic companion for Chaplin, a shrimp named Luke the Gook (later kidded as a strip figure by Segar himself in his *Thimble Theatre* of the mid-1930s), but generally followed the story content of the Chaplin shorts of the time. Segar made his only sharp departure from the films when he put Chaplin into the European war in mid-1917, with a new buddy named Brutis (Luke the Gook having been dropped earlier).

When Chaplin left Essanay to sign with the Mutual Company in February 1916, Essanay's deal with Keeley was apparently continued by Chaplin's business manager of the time, his brother Sydney. After Chaplin contracted for film release with the First National Circuit in 1917, however, he or his brother seemed to feel a need to call a halt to the strip, for it ended abruptly in the *Herald* of Sunday, September 16, 1917. Segar remained with Keeley another year, but the *Capers* strip was finished—and with it any real prospect of a widespread use of screen stars in the American comic strip (although Charlie McCarthy was featured much later in his own newspaper strip, and W. C. Fields was utilized as a character named The Great Gusto in *Big Chief Wahoo*, for example).

B.B.

CHARLIER, JEAN-MICHEL (1924-1989) One of the most prolific and successful of European comic strip writers, Jean-Michel Charlier was born in Liège, Belgium, on October 30, 1924. After studies at the University of Liège law school, he started working for different newspapers. In 1945 he met cartoonist Victor Hubinon and together, with Charlier writing and Hubinon drawing, they created *Buck Danny* (1947), an aviation strip. The success of *Buck Danny* prompted Charlier to write scenarios for a number of other strips: *Kim Devil, Marc Dacier, Jean Valhardi, Tiger Joe*, etc.

After a stint as a professional pilot for Sabena Airlines, Charlier moved to Paris, where he became coeditor of the newly formed comic weekly *Pilote* in 1959. In addition to his editorial duties, Charlier contributed a number of well-crafted scripts to the paper: he created, among others, *Le Démon des Caraïbes* ("The Demon of the Caribbean"), a pirate story drawn by Victor Hubinon, and *Michel Tanguy*, an aviation strip, first drawn by Albert Uderzo, both in 1959; and in 1963 he created a Western with Jean Giraud, the widely acclaimed *Fort Navajo* (later *Lieutenant Blueberry*.)

Charlier was coeditor of *Pilote* until 1972, and he brought the weekly to unprecedented heights of popularity. While continuing to provide scripts for his comics series, he also wrote a number of adventure novels for the French publisher Hachette. In the 1970s he increasingly turned to television as an outlet for his creative talents: he adapted his own *Michel Tanguy* as a successful television series and produced numerous documentaries for French television on subjects ranging from the St. Valentine's Day massacre to the development of the Concorde airplane. He was working on a script for a projected *Blueberry* theatrical movie when he died in Paris on July 10, 1989.

Charlier was the recipient of many distinctions and awards, including the Order of the Crown of Belgium and the French Medal for Arts and Letters.

M.H.

CHARTIER, ALBERT (1912-   ) Canadian cartoonist, born June 16, 1912, in Quebec. After studies at Mont Saint-Louis, the Montreal School of Fine Arts, and Chicago's Meyer Both, Albert Chartier started his career as a cartoonist in the 1930s with a daily strip, *Bouboule* (written by René Boivin), for the Québec newspaper *La Patrie*. In 1940 he went to New York, where he stayed for two years, drawing a humor panel for Columbia Comics Corporation. During World War II Chartier worked at the Information Office in Ottawa as an editorial cartoonist whose drawings were published in English-speaking countries around the world.

In 1943 Albert Chartier created what is now the oldest Canadian comic strip in existence, *Onésime*, for the obscure *Bulletin des Agriculteurs* ("Farmers' Bulletin"). Recounting the adventures and misadventures of a middle-aged Québecois of that name, *Onésime* is today credited with upholding the tradition of French-Canadian comic art at a time when Canadian newspapers were inundated with American imports. (In 1974 a collection of the best pages of *Onésime* was reprinted with the subtitle: "The adventures of a typical Québe-

Albert Chartier, "Onésime." © Editions de l'Aurore.

cois.'') For the same publication Chartier produced another comic strip from 1950 to 1968, *Séraphin*, with Claude-Henri Grignon as scriptwriter.

In addition to his work as a comic strip artist, Chartier has also drawn many illustrations and covers for the French-Canadian magazines *Le Samedi* and *La Revue Populaire* from 1945 to 1960, a number of panels and cartoons for the *Montreal Star* and *Weekend Magazine* (1950-1965), as well as a good deal of advertising cartoons for the McKim agency, Vickers & Benson, and others. From 1945 to 1960 he also did a number of editorial cartoons and illustrations for *Le Petit Journal*. In 1968 Chartier created a bilingual strip for the Toronto Telegram News Service, *Les Canadiens* ("The Canadians"), which took place at the time when Canada was a French colony, in an effort to promote bilingualism.

Albert Chartier, whose work has long been neglected even in his native province, is now regarded as the dean of French-Canadian cartoonists. His style and humor are typically Québecois and often accurately reflect the views and attitudes of the French-Canadian community. He retired in the mid-1980s.

M.H.

CHATILLO Y FEDERICO (Spain) The first episode of *Chatillo y Federico* was published in issue 73 of the weekly *Chicos* (July 26, 1939), with later episodes issued in book format, on scripts credited to José Maria Huertas Ventosa, and with illustrations by Emilio Freixas. Chatillo is a busboy at a military officers' club, and Federico is the nephew of Colonel Bustamente, a Phalangist soldier, agent of the Information Service. In the first stories, uncle and nephew are wearing the blue shirt of Franco's Phalangists, while Chatillo dresses like any other young boy of the period.

In the course of their first adventure, the two young heroes explore a hidden country in the recesses of a hollow mountain where they are pitted against a Soviet agent. In successive episodes they discovered a medieval kingdom and faced a hostile sect of assassins

in what was then French Indochina. Coinciding with this third episode, their adventures were simultaneously published as a straight narrative in the monthly *Chiquitito* (April 1942). When this publication disappeared in 1943, these illustrated tales were taken back to the pages of *Chicos* where they were born, with scripts by Antonio Torralbo Marin. Fantasy was abandoned in favor of action and espionage.

The main characteristic of this first stage in the history of *Chatillo y Federico* is the absence of speech balloons. These were replaced by a straight narrative that inserted itself between the panels of irregular sizes and shapes. Years later, in 1954, the cartoonist Borne revived the feature in the pages of *Chicos*, this time as a traditional comic strip, blatantly plagiarizing Emilio Freixas' earlier drawings and illustrations. This version did not last long.

L.G.

CHAYKIN, HOWARD (1950-) American comic-book artist and illustrator, born October 7, 1950, in Newark, New Jersey. Of his education, Howard Chaykin admitted that he received "precious little," but learned much from his apprenticeship with such masters as Wally Wood and Gil Kane. After turning out a Wood-inspired erotic Western, *Shattuck*, for an army publication, followed by a passage at Neal Adams' studio, Chaykin started work at Marvel Comics in the mid-1970s; there, in 1977, he attracted critical notice with his artwork on the *Star Wars* comic-book adaptation.

It was for his work for independent publishers, however, that he really made his mark. After his profusely illustrated adaptation of Alfred Bester's *The Stars My Destination*, he returned to comic books with *Cody Starbuck* (1978). A space-opera of uncertain merit, it was mostly notable for Chaykin's restless line and unconventional compositions. But it was with his next project, *American Flagg!*, that he finally came into his own as an artist and writer. Created in October 1983 and published by First Comics, the title became an overnight sensation.

A dystopian science-fiction tale set in the year 2031 in an America that had been ravaged by thermonuclear warfare and was now run by a gigantic conglomerate called Plex-USA, it unfolded in a district of Chicago "nameless, lawless, and devastated by sexually transmitted diseases." In this urban jungle, scene of incessant combat between such gangs as the Genetic Warlords and the Ethical Mutants, Reuben Flagg, former video star Plexus Ranger, tried to restore some semblance of order with the help of Raul the talking cat and a robot named Luther Ironheart, not to mention the liberal use of the euphoria-inducing drug Somnambutol, nicknamed "the tender riot-ender." An amalgam of Aldous Huxley's *Brave New World* and George Orwell's *1984* with comic-book boilerplate and a generous dose of eroticism, it was innovative, fast-paced and highly entertaining.

Chaykin turned out another science-fiction series, involving time travel, *Time²*, for First Comics. When that company started to falter, he worked for DC Comics briefly, doing a Batman tale and working on the miniseries of *The Shadow* (1986) and on the first issues of the revived *Blackhawk* comic book (1988). He then returned to his earlier specialty, erotic fantasy, in a violent story of murder and sex titled *Black Kiss*, later *Thick Black Kiss*. In recent years he has only occasionally contributed to the comic-book field, preferring to concentrate on illustration and on television work; he was the executive script consultant on the *Viper* and *The Flash* television series.

M.H.

CHENDI, CARLO (1933-   ) Italian comic strip writer, born in 1933 in Ferrara. Carlo Chendi had a passion for comics since childhood; at 14 he moved to Rapallo, where he began to work variously as an electrician, cheese salesman, etc. In the meantime he met Luciano Bottaro, then an accounting student, and like himself a comic fan.

In 1952 Bottaro, who had begun to draw two years before, asked Chendi to write some stories for him. A year later Chendi decided to become a professional comic writer. Besides writing Bottaro's strips, such as *Baldo*, *Pepito*, *Pik e Pok*, and *Papi Papero*, Chendi contributed texts for *Cucciolo*, *Tiramolla*, and *Il Sceriffo Fox*. In 1957 he began a long and fruitful collaboration with the Italian branch of Walt Disney Productions, for which he contributed stories featuring Donald Duck, Mickey Mouse, and Uncle Scrooge. These stories, drawn by Luciano Bottaro, G. B. Carpi, Romano Scarpa, and Giorgio Rebuffi, are considered classics and have been reprinted in 25 countries (excluding the United States).

Chendi was one of the founders of Studio Bierreci, along with Bottaro and Rebuffi, and has contributed scripts for *Big Tom*, *Vita di un Commesso Viaggiatore* ("The Life of a Traveling Salesman"), *Whisky e Gogo*, and *Vita col Gatto* ("Life with the Cat") for the magazines *Redipicche* and *Whisky & Gogo*. Some of his stories, drawn by Bottaro and Rebuffi, have been anthologized in two volumes published by Cenisio, *Un Mondo di Fumetti* 1 and 2.

Besides being a scriptwriter, Carlo Chendi is also a student of comic art. In 1956, along with Bottaro, Rebuffi, Nino Palumbi, and Guiseppe Greco, he organized a conference on the comics in Rapallo. He was responsible for public relations at the Comics Festival in Genoa, and was the organizer of the International Comics Conventions held in Rapallo in 1973 and 1975. He is now planning a museum of comic art in Rapallo.

Carlo Chendi also finds time for writing, notably for Bottaro's *Pon Pon* and *Il Paese dell'Alfabeto* ("Alphabet Land"), and for the Disney productions in Italy. "I still write stories," he declared in 1996, "and carry out new comic-magazine projects for the Walt Disney Company Italy with the same enthusiasm as ever."

G.B.

CHEVALIER ARDENT (Belgium) François Craenhals created *Chevalier Ardent* ("Knight Ardent") in 1966 for the comic weekly *Tintin*. Ardent is a young nobleman of the Middle Ages, full of chivalrous ideals, youthful dreams, and righteous ardor (hence his name). Inheriting the estate of Rougecogne, he must fight to reclaim it from a murderous bunch of cutthroats (whose chiefs later become his friends and retainers in feudal fashion). Having thus established his manhood, Ardent becomes a knight at the court of King Arthus (the author's spelling), where he promptly falls in love with Arthus' own daughter Gwendoline. Later, for the greater glory of King Arthus and for the love of Gwendoline, Ardent will fight robber barons and renegades all over Europe, and will even venture as far as the Holy Land in quest of the mysterious Lady of the Sands.

The plot sounds familiar, but Craenhals makes it all seem fresh, mainly through his well-plotted adventures and his flair for the period. The drawing is vigorous and full of dash, and the depictions of tournaments, pageants, and battles are not unworthy of comparison with some of the best *Prince Valiant* scenes. Starting in the 1980s, Craenhals also introduced fantastic and supernatural elements into his story lines.

Chevalier Ardent is one of the few historical strips of note, and it has enjoyed a solid, if not overwhelming, success from its inception. A number of episodes have been reprinted in book form by Casterman in Belgium.

M.H.

CHIBA, TETSUYA (1939-   ) Japanese comic book artist born January 11, 1939, in Chiba. When Chiba was a senior in high school he decided to become a comic book artist and at 17 made his professional debut with the 1956 publication of *Fukushū no Semushiotoko* ("The Hunchbacked Avenger"). In 1958 his strip *Odettojō no Niji* ("The Rainbow of Odetto Castle")

"Chevalier Ardent," François Craenhals. © Editions du Lombard.

began publication in the girls' monthly *Shōjo Kurabu*. More famous strips were to follow: *Mama no Violin* ("Mama's Violin") in 1958; *Rina* (a story about a young girl by that name) in 1960; *Chikai no Makyū* (Chiba's first boy's strip) in 1961; *Shidenkai no Taka*, a highly popular Japanese war strip, in 1963; *Yukino Taiyō* ("Yuki's Sun") in 1963; *Harisu no Kaze* ("The Whirlwind Boy of Harisu School") in 1965; *Ashita no Joe* (a noted boxing strip) in 1968; *Ore wa Teppei* (another boy's strip) in 1973; *Notari Matsutaro* (Chiba's first strip for young adults, also in 1973), and more.

Most of Chiba's strips met with great success. Because he thought highly of the comic art field, he devoted much care to his drawings and stories. Once the top girl's-strip artist, he became bored with the formula and switched to more action-oriented series.

Chiba's graphic style is delicate and charming, his compositions as warm as his stories. Chiba's strip protagonists are ordinary people rather than superheroes, and so his characters are popular because one can easily identify with them. Chiba has influenced a whole school of young artists, including his younger brother Akio Chiba, Tashiya Masaoka, Sachio Umemoto, and Shin Ebara.

Chiba's strips (with the exception of his early efforts) have all been reprinted in book form, and he is currently the highest-paid of all boy's comic strip artists. *Ashita no Joe* ended in 1973, and *Ore wa Teppei* in 1980, and since that time the artist has branched out into even more exotic sports, such as kendo, sumo, and even golf.

H.K.

CHIEF WAHOO *see* Steve Roper.

"Chikaino Makyū," Tetsuya Chiba. © Shōnen.

CHIKAINO MAKYŪ (Japan) *Chikaino Makyū* ("The Miracle Ball of Great Promise") was created by writer Kazuya Fukumoto and artist Tetsuya Chiba. Soon after its first appearance in the weekly *Shōnen* magazine (January 1961), *Chikaino Makyū* became the foremost sports strip of its time.

Hikaru Ninomiya was an ace pitcher at Fuji High School, and he would throw miracle balls (his first miracle ball jumped in front of the batter); he became known as the miracle pitcher. He was soon spotted by a baseball scout named Yagi, who hired him as pitcher for the Yomiuri Giants. Hikaru's friend Tagosaku Kubo later joined him on the team as catcher. His miracle

balls continued to prove effective until the day his ball was hit by Henry Nakagawa, a half-breed player on the Taiyo Whales team.

Hikaru worked out a new miracle pitch (in which the ball would spin so violently that the batter thought he saw several balls) with his coach Aikawa. Only Kubo could catch this ball. With this pitch he won the "most valuable player" award and entered the Nihon Series (the Japanese equivalent of the World Series); but his ball was hit by Ichiro Otawara of the opposing Hanshin Tigers, and again Hikaru felt despondent. He soon recovered, however, and mastered a third pitch: the vanishing miracle ball, which disappeared before the batter's very eyes, which was taught to him by a mysterious old amateur pitcher.

During the deciding match between the American and Japanese top teams, Hikaru bedeviled his opposition with three miracle balls. Because of the strain put on his shoulder by his efforts, however, he was badly hurt and had to leave the Yomiuri Giants as a result. Turning to coaching, Hikaru brought the team of his old high school to victory.

Chikaino Makyū was the pioneer of baseball strips and exercised a strong influence on *Kyoshin no Hoshi*, which was soon to surpass *Chikaino* in popularity. The strip's last appearance was in December 1962.

Chikaino Makyū was Tetsuya Chiba's first boy's strip, and it made him into the most noted artist of the genre. Chiba did not know the first thing about baseball when he started work on the strip; but he studied the game and soon became a baseball nut, to the extent of creating a baseball team called the Whiters.

H.K.

CHIP *see* Bellew, Frank.

CHLOROPHYLLE (Belgium) On December 1, 1953, in the pages of the Belgian weekly *Tintin*, Raymond Macherot revitalized the tradition of the European animal strip with *Chlorophylle et Minimum* (later called simply *Chlorophylle*).

Chlorophylle and Minimum are a couple of field mice, the former brave, resolute and resourceful, the latter troublesome and loud-mouthed, but loyal and ingenious, and their adventures, in the company of

"Chlorophylle," Raymond Macherot. © Editions Dargaud.

other animals or in the land of the humans, are always mixed with a large dose of humor and more than a touch of poetry. The first episode involved our two diminutive heroes in a long struggle against a pack of black rats who tried to take over their territory. Led by the dreaded and cunning Anthracite, the black rats almost won the day, and Chlorophylle had to enlist the help of more allies: Sybilline the mischievous mouse, Verboten the tenacious hedgehog, and Torpille the unstoppable otter. Representing the forces of justice and fair play, Chlorophylle and his friends never give up, even in the face of overwhelming odds; and in the end their perseverance defeats the deviousness of the villains, be they Anthracite (who had usurped the throne of Croquefredouille), or the bloodthirsty Croquillards, a gang that terrorizes the country in their homemade tank.

In 1963 Macherot left Chlorophylle, which was taken over first by Guilmard and Hubuc, and later by Dupa and Greg. Since 1985 the title has been drawn by Willi (André van der Elst) on scripts by Bob de Groot and later by Michel de Bom.

Chlorophylle is not only an entertaining strip of humorous adventure (in the illustrious tradition of *Felix the Cat, Mickey Mouse,* and *Popeye*), but also an excellent parody of human foibles and follies and a satire of modern civilization.

The adventures of Chlorophylle and his gang have been reprinted in book form by Dargaud. They are now published by Editions du Lombard.

M.H.

CHIMEL, PAPCIP *see Chmielewski, Henryk Jerzy.*

CHMIELEWSKI, HENRYK JERZY (1923-   ) Polish cartoonist born in 1923 near Warsaw. After studies at the Warsaw Academy of Fine Arts, from which he received a degree in graphic art, Henryk Chmielewski started working for *Swiat Modlich*, a scouting publication, in whose pages he published such now-classic comic strips as *Tytus, Romek* and *Tomek*, under the penname "Papcio Chimel." These are the oldest comic series still in existence, and they have been reprinted in a number of books since 1966. (The latest volume of his comics, the twenty-second, was published in May 1996.)

A pioneer of postwar Polish comics, Chimel (as he is better known) has seen his efforts in the field finally recognized in the early 1990's. Since 1992 he has been producing and editing comics for the prestigious Prusynski i S-ka publishing house. His graphic style, an harmonious blend of old-time cartooning and straight illustration, has been widely imitated in his native country. His work during the 1940's signaled a revival of comic art activity in Poland.

K.R.

CHRISTMAN, BERT (1915-1942) American cartoonist born May 31, 1915 at Fort Collins, Colorado. Bert Christman displayed artistic qualities at an early age, and he began his career (while in high school) as a department store artist. After graduation from Colorado State College as an engineer, he came to New York in 1936, and became a staff artist for the Associated Press. Christman, whom a fellow worker was later to describe as "a nice quiet kid" got his first break, after only a few months, as Noel Sickles' successor on the *Scorchy Smith* daily strip. Christman did a creditable job on *Scorchy* (after the initial awkward period of "breaking in") and he might have gone on to become one of the top adventure strip artists, but he was restless (and A.P. was notoriously cheap towards their cartoonists) and so, after 18 months of drawing the strip, he left. He then briefly worked for the newly emerging medium of comic books: on the super-hero feature *The Sandman* at National, where he later created *The Three Aces* (1939) described as: "three winged soldiers-of-fortune, sick of war and tragedy, who pledge themselves to a new kind of adventure."

Christman must have heeded the same call for "a new kind of adventure": in 1940 he became an air cadet at the Naval Air School in Pensacola, and later joined Clare Chennault's fabled "Flying Tigers" in Burma. On January 23, 1942, during a heavy Japanese raid over Rangoon, Christman's P-40 plane was shot down; Christman himself bailed out but was machine-gunned to death by a Japanese strafing plane while hanging helplessly in the parachute harness (his death was to inspire one of the most memorable sequences in Howard Hawks' 1943 movie *Air Force*).

Even during his service with the American Volunteer Group (as the Flying Tigers were officially called) Bert Christman never stopped drawing. In a letter to Coulton Waugh, Zachary Taylor, comic editor of the Associated Press, recounting the circumstances of Christman's death, added this postscript: "Not many weeks ago, his effects reached his mother at Fort Collins, Colorado. Among them was his scrapbook of sketches of Burma, flying pals, insignia designs."

M.H.

CHRISTOPHE *see Colomb, Georges.*

CHU, RONALD *see Chu Teh-Yung.*

CHU TEH-YUNG (1960-   ) Taiwanese cartoonist Chu Teh-Yung was interested in drawing from the age of four, and by the time he was a film student at the World Junior College of Journalism in Taipei, his cartoons were appearing in campus publications. However, it was during his two-year, compulsory military duty in the mid-1980s that he created the strip that made him famous—*Shuang Hsiang Pao* ("Double Big Guns," also known as "The Couple"). To evade military harassment and censorship while in the army, Chu drew many of the strips under a blanket while holding a flashlight. He would then cut up the four panels and mail them one by one to his father, who relayed them to the *China Times*. He had no idea how successful the strip had become until he left the military and was offered a full-time position drawing for the *China Times*.

Shuang Hsiang Pao is Taiwan's longest-running newspaper comic strip; it now appears in *China Times Express*. Its immense popularity has led to book compilations that have sold hundreds of thousands of copies in Taiwan, Hong Kong, and South Korea. The plot of *Shuang Hsiang Pao* revolves around the domestic life of a nameless couple in their sixties who constantly berate and put each other down. The wife is bug-eyed, mean-spirited, and domineering; the husband is spindly and hen-pecked, but capable of retaliating in their constant bouts of verbal abuse.

In 1989, Ronald Chu (as he is professionally known) created *Chu Liu Chu* ("Wayward Lovers"), a strip in the *China Times* that lampoons Taiwan's unmarried yup-

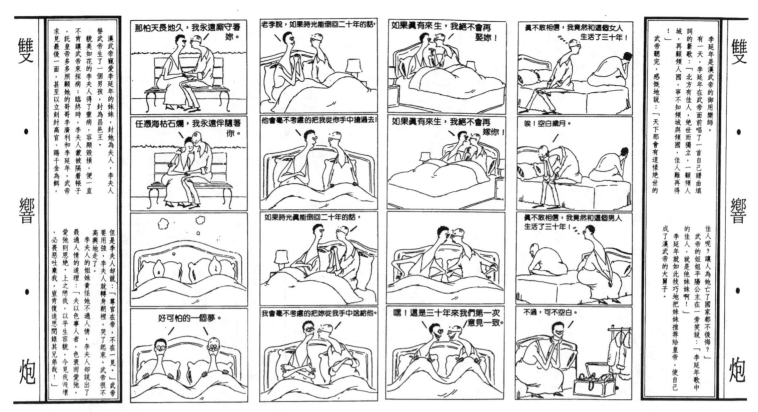

Chu Teh-Yung ("Ronald Chu"), "The Couple." © Ronald Chu.

pies. Less slapstick than *Shuang Hsiang Pao*, the strip is just as sarcastic and derisive as its predecessor. It too has been compiled into best-selling books. Other Chu strips include *Capitalists* for *Commercial Daily* and *Bitter Olive* for *Liberty Times*.

Chu's strips offer up large doses of sardonic wit and are universally appealing. They are fondly reminiscent of the comic art prevalent in the United States before the days of political correctness.

J.A.L.

CHUPAMIRTO (Mexico) During the winter of 1925-1926 the daily newspaper *El Universal* sponsored a contest aimed at discovering fresh Mexican comic strip

"Chupamirto," Jesus Acosta. © Jesus Acosta.

talent. Among the artists thus discovered was Jesus Acosta Cabrera, who that same year created one of the most popular comic strips in Mexican history, *Chupamirto*.

Chupamirto (literally "myrtle sucker," a synonym for hobo) was a disheveled, unshaven little tramp who always wore a snap-brimmed hat and whose tongue perpetually hung out. His wanderings took him to all parts of Mexico, thus giving Acosta the opportunity of satirically depicting many of Mexico's social shortcomings. Chupamirto's persona is said to have inspired the screen characterization of Cantinflas, Mexico's most renowned comedian.

Chupamirto enjoyed tremendous success in Mexico until it was discontinued in 1963, following its creator's death.

M.H.

CICERO'S CAT (U.S.) From its first appearance on the *Mutt and Jeff* Sunday page on December 3, 1933, the weekly *Cicero's Cat* was the work of Al Smith, who had then just begun his ghosting of Bud Fisher's signed work. The cat of the title, Desdemona, was the pet of Mutt's son, Cicero, and the bulk of the action in the color feature concerned the cat (often humanized in hat and coat) in various domestic, backyard, and neighborhood adventures with other cats and dogs (the humans of the *Mutt and Jeff* strip being only infrequently involved). Some of them were extremely humorous—Smith having a competency with comic animals that his work with the older Fisher human characters often lacked. (In an amusing corollary, Desdemona's humanized escapades were rarely as effective as her purely catlike sequences, where Smith's pen was most inspired.)

A single strip of a few panels at the top of the Sunday Fisher page at the start (*Cicero's Cat* took over an untitled space long given to a separate Sunday gag

"Cicero's Cat," Al Smith. © Bell Syndicate.

sequence also featuring Mutt and Jeff above the main narrative layout), the Smith cat opus was abruptly and startlingly switched to a full half-page of three rows with several panels each on August 26, 1934, while the *Mutt and Jeff* portion of the page was correspondingly reduced to a companion half-page, reflecting the general reshaping of Sunday pages going on in the early 1930s. In following episodes, however, the *Mutt and Jeff* half-page appropriated a row of panels from *Cicero's Cat* and turned it into a one-panel logo for the main strip, while *Cicero's Cat* became and remained a two-row, third-page feature below *Mutt and Jeff* for the next 12 years. With the new division of Sunday page space in the late 1940s, however, *Cicero's Cat* and *Mutt and Jeff* both often ran as third-page features, sometimes separated by several pages in the same Sunday section. As a separated second-fiddle feature, Smith's *Cat* strip suffered frequent omissions from papers when advertisements were run, and it steadily lost circulation until it was eased into limbo in the early 1960s, survived by the Smith *Mutt and Jeff* feature. Initially distributed by H. C. Fisher, Inc., *Cicero's Cat* was later a Bell Syndicate property till its demise.

B.B.

CIFRE, GUILLERMO (1922-1962) In the course of his short but extraordinarily fecund career, Spanish cartoonist Guillermo Cifre produced a great many comic strips of quality, most of them for Editorial Bruguera's children's publications. His most popular creation remains the hilarious *El Reporter Tribulete que en Todas Partes se Mete* ("The Reporter Tribulete who Meddles in Everything"). Another successful strip was *Don Furcio Buscabollos* (literally "Don Furcio Troubleseeker"), about an Italian knight in medieval times; the series inspired a number of popular expressions with its peculiar Hispano-Italian jargon and the fabled conversations held between Don Furcio and his mare, Isabelita.

For many years Cifre also drew numerous cover illustrations (mostly of well-endowed females) while ceaselessly turning out weekly comic features, among which mention should be made of *Amapolo Nevera, El Sabio Megaton* ("Megaton the Scientist"), *Golondrino Perez,* and *Don Tele.*

Guillermo Cifre died in 1962 at the age of 39.

L.G.

CIMPELLIN, LEONE (1926-) Italian cartoonist, born June 6, 1926, in Rovigo. Leone Cimpellin moved to Milan while a child; there he started his cartooning career some years later as assistant to Lina Buffolente. His first works were adventure series. The imitation of Alex Raymond's *Rip Kirby* was obvious, but Cimpellin added a touch of the grotesque, which was later to find its full utilization in *Johnny Logan.*

After continuing the Italian version of Warren Tufts' *Casey Ruggles,* written by Giovanni Bonelli, Cimpellin created *Pultos* in 1949, a masked-avenger strip for Edizioni Audace, and *Il Tamburino del Re* ("Drummer of the King") for Edizioni Alpe. In 1953 he joined the art staff of the weekly *Corriere dei Piccoli,* where his talents as a humor cartoonist first flowered. In the *Corriere* he created *Papero Grosso e Fiorello* (1954), about a fat peasant and his little pig; *Codinzolo,* about a little faun; and *Gibernetta,* a hilarious parody of army life (1958). In 1961 Cimpellin created *Charlie Sprint,* the adventures of a racing-car enthusiast, written by Guglielmo Zucconi, and in 1966 he produced *Tribunzio* in collaboration with Carlo Triberti (the latter strip recounted the tragicomic adventures of a Roman legionary). In 1967 there was *Gigi Bizz,* a newspaper satire.

Leone Cimpellin, "Johnny Logan." © Editrice Dardo.

"Cinco por Infinito," Esteban Maroto. © Selecciones Illustradas.

Meanwhile Cimpellin, hesitating between a realistic and a "big-foot" style, again tried his hand at adventure with *Oklahoma* (1952), a Western written by Guido Martina, and diverse series for other publishers. Only in 1972 did Cimpellin find his niche with *Johnny Logan*, his weird depiction of the antihero created by Romano Garofalo for Edizioni Dardo. Since the early 1990s he has illustrated a number of *Martin Mystere* stories.

G.B.

CINCO POR INFINITO (Spain) *Cinco por Infinito* ("Five for Infinity") started in September 1967, vaguely inspired by Jean Hougron's novel *The Sign of the Dog*. The team responsible for this series was initially made up of Esteban Maroto, who wrote the scripts and pencilled the pages; Ramon Torrens, who drew the female characters; Adolfo Usero, who did the male protagonists; and Suso (pen name of Jesus Paña), who did the backgrounds. The first three episodes were done in this way; the fourth was the work of Usero and Maroto, after which Maroto remained in sole control of the 26 remaining episodes.

The protagonists are five earthlings who help Infinito, the survivor of an extinct extraterrestrial race, to keep order in the cosmos. Each of the five possesses special abilities that complement those of the rest of the team. Aline, the woman doctor, is endowed with exceptional mental powers, Sirio enjoys great agility and keen reflexes, Orion has herculean strength, Altar is gifted with vast intelligence, and Hidra, who has been incorporated into the team by accident, is extremely beautiful.

The special quality of the feature is the conception of each page as a whole, in which panel limitations are ignored in favor of a fusion of the images into one single baroque composition. Maroto was then in search of his style, and it is easy to discover in this work the stages of his graphic evolution, the excellence of his draftsmanship, and the influences that were at work on him over the course of the years. Initially intended to be reproduced in black and white, the feature was later printed in color, which gave it an added dimension, but which also eliminated Ben Day and hatchings; negative images and floral motifs, so decorative in black and white, lost their qualities with the imposition of color.

L.G.

CIOCCA, WALTER (1910-   ) An Argentine cartoonist and illustrator born in 1910, Walter Ciocca studied architecture, majoring in urban projects. He became interested in comic art in the 1940s. Drawing his inspiration from Argentine folklore and the legends of gaucho life in the pampas, he produced a series of daily strips for the newspapers of Buenos Aires, all drawn in his energetic and austere style. The first was *Hilario Leiva*, created in 1948, followed by *Santos Vega*, *Hormiga Negra* ("The Black Ant," 1950), and *Fuerte Argentino* ("Argentine Fort"). Since 1954 he has been devoting himself to his most famous comic creation, *Lindor Covas*, subtitled "*El Cimarrón*" ("The Untamed").

Walter Ciocca is famous for his virile and unsentimental depiction of Indian and gaucho life. His graphic style is forceful, direct, and minutely realistic.

L.G.

CIRCUS SOLLY *see* Slim Jim.

CISCO KID, THE (U.S.) The character of the Cisco Kid (from O. Henry's story "The Caballero's Way") was made famous in a series of Fox movies, the first of which was *In Old Arizona* (1929) starring Warner Baxter, who won an Oscar for his interpretation of the Kid. The success of the Cisco Kid in movies (and later in television) prompted King Features Syndicate to make a comic strip version, which was entrusted to the talented Argentinian artist José-Luis Salinas (for the drawing) and to Rod Reed for the writing. *The Cisco Kid* made its debut on January 15, 1951, as a daily strip (there never was a Sunday version).

Like his *compadre* Zorro, the Cisco Kid is a Mexican righter of wrongs, an indefatigable fighter against the crime and corruption afflicting the territory of New Mexico at the turn of the century. Impeccably attired in a richly embroidered black outfit and wearing a huge sombrero, he is one of the legendary figures of the American West. In the company of his comic sidekick, the potbellied and crafty Pancho, his rides often take him—in the best tradition of the Western—far from his usual field of operations. His specialty seems to be damsels-in-distress whom the Kid invariably woos in the most stereotyped Latin fashion, with flowery phrases and large sweeps of the sombrero.

In spite of a creditable story line, some good characterization, and Salinas' lyrical evocation of the limitless vistas and the magnificent scenery of the West, *The Cisco Kid* never fared well with the public, and it was finally discontinued in August 1968.

M.H.

"The Cisco Kid," José-Luis Salinas. © King Features Syndicate.

CLASSICS ILLUSTRATED (U.S.) The comic-book medium has been used mostly for entertainment, as everyone knows, but occasionally it has served educational purposes. Such has been the case with *Classics Illustrated*.

Albert L. Kanter conceived the idea of introducing children to the classics of literature via comic books in 1941. In October of that year the first issue of what was originally called *Classic Comics* was published; it was an adaptation of *The Three Musketeers*. Scores upon scores of new titles would follow, mixing literature high and low in almost equal doses, such as *Macbeth* and *The Prisoner of Zenda*, *The Iliad* and *King of the Khyber Rifles*, or *Crime and Punishment* and *Swiss Family Robinson*. The first three titles in the series were issued under the Elliot Publishing imprint, and the rest of the titles were released by Gilberton Publications; with issue number 35, *The Last Days of Pompeii*, the series acquired its familiar Classics Illustrated logo.

The first 20 or so adaptations were characterized by uneven artwork, ranging from the barely adequate to the impersonally professional. In 1944 Jerry Iger took over production of the series, bringing in a number of excellent artists from his shop, including Alex Blum, Henry Kiefer, and Matt Baker. The demise of the E.C. Comics line in 1954 resulted in many former E.C. artists moving to *Classics Illustrated*, and the series soon boasted artwork by the likes of Joe Orlando, George Evans, and Graham Ingels.

The original *Classics Illustrated* series ended in the spring of 1969 with issue number 169. An offshoot of the original, titled *Classics Illustrated Junior*—a series for the very young (sporting titles like *Jack and the Beanstalk* and *The Ugly Duckling*)—lasted for over 70 issues from 1953 to 1971. The end of the original *Classics Illustrated* was not the end of the story, however, as new titles continued to be published in Europe. In addition, reprints of the original *Classics* were issued throughout the 1970s and 1980s.

Early in 1990, First Publishing, in association with Berkley Books, acquired the rights to the Classics Illustrated name and released a new series of Classics with original art by such outstanding talents as Gahan Wilson, Kyle Baker, and Mike Ploog. A noble experiment, it lasted for only 27 issues, coming to a close in the fall of 1991.

Undaunted by First Publishing's experience, Acclaim Comics started reprinting some of the old *Classics Illustrated* in December 1996, recoloring the original artwork and reformatting the titles to digest size (approximately 5¼ by 7½ inches). Calling the new series "your doorway to the classics," a press release averred that, "Featuring essays on the author, background, theme, characters, and significance of the work . . . these editions make perfect study guides." Time will tell whether this latest effort will prove successful.

M.H.

CLIVE (G.B.) On January 8, 1968, a mop-haired teenager introduced himself to readers of the *Evening Standard*: "I'm Clive. Clive Bravo. Clive Genet Marat-Sade Bravo. Of course, my parents didn't call me Genet Marat-Sade, but that's typical of parents. No thought for others!" He scorns his "Aged Parents" (his father is 41!), and when his sister Augusta demands a bedtime story, he reads her *The Forsyte Saga*. At his parent's

"Clive," Dominic Poelsma. © Evening Standard.

party he discusses "Flagellation, le vice Anglais" with the wife of his father's chairman, Sir Reginald Bull, and recommends *The Naked Lunch* to the vicar's wife. Actually, Augusta isn't much better: her nighty-night question to Mummy is "Do you think Rodney Harrington's on pot?" Clive, in quest of fame and fortune, joins Imperial Imperials and gets his first girlfriend, Enid, secretary to the secretary's secretary of Sir Percival Hubbard Browne's secretary. He winds up as lift boy and gives up commerce for school. More adventures in the same wacky vein have been going on for over two decades now.

A daily gag strip, *Clive* is written by *Standard* columnist Angus McGill and drawn by Dominic Poelsma. Reprints include *Clive* (1968), *Clive in Love* (1970), and *Clive and Augusta* (1971).

D.G.

COCCO BILL (Italy) *Cocco Bill* started on March 28, 1957, in the pages of the *Giorno dei Ragazzi*, the weekly supplement of the Milanese daily *Il Giorno*, and it turned out to be the most hilarious comic strip parody ever concocted by Benito Jacovitti. During his long career, this cartoonist (whose distinctive trademark is a fishbone) had already shown a marked taste for the mock Western epic. This predilection is easy to see in the many strips he produced, from the first, *Il Barbiere della Prateria* ("The Barber of the Prairie," 1941), to the more recent *Pippo Cow Boy* (1946) and *Tex Revolver* (1955). But with *Cocco Bill* Jacovitti summoned all the resources of his sarcastic mind to demolish the myths and legends of the Old West.

The hero, Cocco Bill ("Soft-hearted Bill"), whose name has become a byword of the Italian language, is a heavy drinker of chamomile tea and a teetotaller. Otherwise he has all the requisite qualities of the Western hero: flawless marksmanship, fists of steel, herculean strength, gift of gab (especially with the Indians); all these are used by the author to satirize the godlike figure of the traditional hero.

The text is not contained only in the balloons: Jacovitti's most scathing lines can be found here and there in the middle of the large crowds who so often fill up his panels. These pithy aphorisms can be found on walls, on the bellies of cows, on the backsides of his characters. This characteristic, coupled with the screwball dialogue (often on a topic wholly unrelated to the action), makes *Cocco Bill* one of the most outrageously funny Italian strips. The same approach can be found in the surrealistic and chaotic drawings in which the characters elbow their way among the panels disposed any which way, and directly address the reader.

"Cocco Bill," Benito Jacovitti. © Jacovitti.

Cocco Bill and his faithful horse Trottalemme (Slowpoke) have been the heroes of a great number of stories, first in *Il Giorno dei Ragazzi*, then, after it ceased publication in 1968, in the *Corriere dei Piccoli*, and finally in *Il Corriere dei Ragazzi* (1972). Since 1980 *Cocco Bill* has appeared in the pages of *Il Giornalino*.

Eldorado, a confectionery manufacturer, used Cocco Bill to advertise its ice creams in newspapers and on television. The ad campaign was produced by the Pagot brothers.

G.B.

COCKING, PERCY (1881-1964) Percival James Cocking was perhaps the widest-known, yet unknown, comic artist in the British Empire: in a cartooning career that lasted well over half a century, his signature appeared just once. The rest of the huge volume of his weekly work was anonymous, save for his waning years when he signed his work with the pen name "Jack Daw."

Percy Cocking was born in London on March 10, 1881. He grew up less than a mile from the home of Amalgamated Press, where he would work for most of his life. The exact date when he began to draw for children's comics is unknown, but he was known well enough in the industry to be given an entire tabloid page in *The Jester & Wonder* under the heading "Our Artist's Page" on June 25, 1903. This was the only time his name appeared on one of his cartoons.

His drawing style, like so many cartoonists of the period, imitated that of Tom Browne, the father of British comics. In 1908 Cocking took over Browne's famous tramp characters *Weary Willie and Tired Tim* for *Illustrated Chips*. He continued to draw this 12-panel series until the last issue of *Chips* on September 12, 1953—a record run of 45 years, give or take a week or two when he was ill or on vacation.

From 1903 his work, recognizable mainly through his characteristic lettering and extremely neat and precise style, included *Sunbeam and the Innocent*, a "good little girl" character in *Illustrated Chips*, and two unusual series set on a street of shops and buildings, *Racketty Row* in *Jester* (1906) and *Mulberry Flats* in *Comic Cuts* (1906). In 1910 he created *Tom the Ticket of Leave Man* for *Comic Cuts*, a full front page series starring a well-meaning ex-convict. In a later, clean-up-the-comics campaign, Tom was turned into *Jolly Tom the Menagerie Man* (1917), which in turn became the adventures of *Jackie and Sammy* (1931), twins to whom Jolly Tom was a sort of guardian. These cartoon kids continued to be published with variations for several years.

Cocking worked on many other series, totaling 40 in all, including *Happy Hambone* (*Funny Wonder*), *Constable Cuddlecook* (*Jolly Jester*), *Hip Pip and Hoo Ray* (*Butterfly*), *Oliver Twister* (*Jester*), *Doctor Doodah* (*Joker*), *Tinwhiskers the Pirate* (*Chips*), and the cinema stars Joe E. Brown and Old Mother Riley in *Film Fun* during World War II. In 1949, by now considered too old by the Amalgamated Press, Cocking began working for the independent publisher Gerald G. Swan and began producing series for *Slick Fun*, *Comicolour*, and *Cute Fun*. These series included *Puny Peter Pieface*, *Fuller Gusto*, *Ossie Oddsocks*, and *Konko the Clown*. Cocking died at St. Francis Hospital on January 17, 1964, and his widow died just three weeks later. It is a cruel irony that a cartoonist who spent his lifetime making millions of children laugh should be denied any acknowledgement by Amalgamated Press, the publisher to whom he devoted his talent and most of his life.

D.G.

COLAN, EUGENE (1926-   ) American comic book artist, born September 1, 1926, in New York City. With art training from his years at George Washington High School and the Art Students League, Gene Colan broke into the comic book field in 1944 and has since become one of the industry's most durable contributors. Often using the name "Adam Austin," he has worked for a dozen companies here and abroad and is also an illustrator and commercial artist.

Colan's first work in comic books appeared in 1944 and 1945 on Fiction House strips like *Wing Tips, Clipper Kirk,* and *Suicide Brigade.* All were airplane adventure strips, and Colan used a clean illustrative style that he has continued to improve over the years. Throughout his career, he has also worked for Ziff-Davis (*Ken Brady*), Dell (illustrating two television spin-off titles, *Burke's Law,* which starred Gene Barry, and *Ben Casey,* which starred Vincent Edwards), Quality, St. Johns, Charlton, Ace, EC, and Warren. Colan also worked sporadically for National between 1947 and 1965; there he illustrated all types of stories (romance, science fiction, war, weird, adventure). His flexible style was best utilized on two diverse strips at National, however; he drew the *Hopalong Cassidy* Western strip for several years during the early 1950s, and then contributed some finely rendered material to the *Sea Devils* adventure feature during the early 1960s.

Undoubtedly, Gene Colan's finest material has been done for the Timely/Atlas/Marvel group edited by Stan Lee. Throughout his many years there—he began in 1948—he has contributed to hundreds of features of all kinds. Although he has drawn mostly for Marvel's war, horror, and romance departments, his most recognizable work has been in the superhero field. Colan draws incredibly handsome figures in majestic poses, and this fits perfectly with editor Lee's concept of the "noble-bearing" hero. His most productive years were between 1965 and 1972, when he handled the *Sub-Mariner* and *Daredevil* strips concurrently. On the former, he is perhaps the best-known artist after creator Bill Everett. Like most of the other illustrators who assumed *Sub-Mariner* after Everett, Colan's handling differed radically from the creators; but only Colan's material can stand on its own and compare favorably to the uniqueness of Everett's. He had even more success with *Daredevil.* Preceded by such top-notch artists as Everett, Wally Wood, John Romita, and Joe Orlando, Colan went on to become the feature's definitive artist. His handling of the blind-lawyer-cum-superhero was tastefully direct, and his well-paced stories did much to keep Lee's often confusing plot lines believable. Colan finally abandoned both features, illustrating *Sub-Mariner* between 1965 and 1971 and *Daredevil* between 1966 and 1972.

Also at Marvel, Colan has contributed work to *Captain America, Dracula, Silver Surfer,* and many others. In recent years, however, ill health forced him to give up drawing mainstream comics, and he has been working mainly (and episodically) for independent publishers; his latest efforts can be seen on Dark Horse's *Predator* (1997).

J.B.

COLE, JACK (1918-1958) American comic book artist, writer, and editor born in New Castle, Pennsylvania, on December 14, 1918. Although his only formal art training was the Landon Correspondence Course, Cole was a natural-born "bigfoot" comedy artist and began drawing humor features for the Harry "A" Chesler Shop in 1937. Using the pen name "Ralph Johns," he turned out comedy strips like *Peewee Throttle* and *Officer Clancy* until he became the editor of the New Friday Comics group in 1939. There he wrote and drew adventure strips like *Silver Streak* and *Daredevil* in a tight, realistic style that caught the eye of Quality Comics publisher "Busy" Arnold.

Joining Quality in 1940, Cole quickly began producing outstanding superhero and adventure features like *Quicksilver, Midnight, The Barker,* and the tongue-in-cheek *Death Patrol.* But August 1941 brought *Police Comics* number one and Jack Cole's *Plastic Man*—a superb, highly inventive strip that propelled him to the top of the comic book humor field. Utilizing a judicious and tasteful mix of his realistic and bigfoot art styles, Cole made the unpredictable and zany "Indian Rubber Man" an instant best-seller. His *Plastic Man* material was unique, using breathless storytelling and a refined, semi-slapstick type of humor—all of it showing influences of George McManus and Elzie Segar. Assisted by Woozy Winks, his roly-poly assistant of dubious character, "Plas" laughed, stretched, and gimmicked his way through crime fighting, all the time allowing Cole to gently poke fun at superhero strips that took themselves too seriously. The *Plastic Man* feature soon merited its own book in 1943 and even a short-lived syndicated strip.

Cole continued creating his goggled crime fighter until 1950 and then began a full-time freelance cartooning career. Over the years he had become a highly successful magazine illustrator who frequently contributed cartoons to *Collier's Judge* and *The Saturday Evening Post,* and by 1955, *Playboy* began featuring his *Females by Cole,* a cartoonist's view of the modern feminine mystique. His sophisticated and beautifully rendered full-color cartoons were also well received, and they remain among the finest cartoons ever printed in *Playboy.*

In 1958, the Chicago Sun-Times Syndicate commissioned Cole to create a new feature, *Betsy and Me,* a humorous look at American family life. But, on August 15, 1958, only months after the strip had started, Jack Cole shot himself to death with a .22 caliber pistol. At the height of his career, Cole ended it with his own hand. No one ever learned why.

J.B.

COLOMB, GEORGES (1856-1945) French artist, writer, and teacher, born in 1856 in Lure (Haute-Saône) in northeastern France. After graduating from the prestigious Ecole Normale in Paris, Colomb taught natural history, but his passion for drawing prompted him to become a contributor to various illustrated magazines. Using the pen name "Christophe," a play on words derived from his surname (Christophe Colomb is French for Christopher Colombus), he created in 1889 what some consider the first modern comic strip, *La Famille Fenouillard* ("The Fenouillard Family"), followed in 1890 by *Les Facéties du Sapeur Camember* ("The Antics of Sapper Camember") in the tradition of service comedies, and *L'Idée Fixe du Savant Cosinus* ("The Fixed Idea of Dr. Cosinus"), about an

Gene Colan, "Daredevil." © Marvel Comics.

absent-minded professor who is thwarted by cruel fate in all his efforts to get out of Paris (1893). Two lesser series, *Plick et Plock* (1894), about the doings of two mischievous gnomes, and *Le Haut et Puissant Seigneur Baron de Cramoisy* ("The High and Mighty Lord Baron of Cramoisy"), begun in 1899 but left unfinished, and a natural history textbook in comic strip form complete Christophe's *oeuvre* as a comic strip artist.

In 1903 Colomb, abandoning the comic field, devoted himself entirely to his academic career and later became director of the botany laboratory at the Sorbonne. He died in 1945.

Colomb never used balloons but inserted a text (of excellent literary quality) under his pictures. Far from being an outmoded pioneer, however, he contributed a number of important stylistic innovations, such as action depicted from odd angles, and accelerated narratives, thus foreshadowing techniques that would later become hallmarks of the comic strip. In his delineation of action and in his use of motion to link different pictures together, Colomb was also far ahead of his time, and he accordingly deserves to be ranked among the major contributors to the then-nascent art of the comics.

M.H.

"Colonel Pewter," Arthur Horner. © Associated Newspapers.

COLONEL PEWTER (G.B.) Col. Hugo Pewter (retired), late the Duffs (Bull's Foot) and Pewter's Pike, resides at "The Chukkas," a half-hidden mansion among the bandanna trees and dense placebos that outskirt the village of Much Overdun (turn right at Great Twittering, along the narrow road through Wits End and Dipping Hemline), outside the Market Town of Quirk, beyond the County Town of Whimchester, in the County of Whimshire (which in turn, bounded to the north by Nossex, nestles between John's End and Land o' Groats).

The Colonel lives quietly with his great-nephew Master Martin and housekeeper Mrs. Aspic, when he is not busy in his pottering shed with a tea-cozy on his head ("It's to keep my brain simmering, my boy!"), inventing the Pewter Rotor-Bike Mark One. This foot-powered helicycle bears man and boy through the clouds to the Lost City of Ironicus, complete with Chloe the Cat asleep in the saddlebag. King Leo XXXVII turns out to be a talking lion. A later adventure, "Dog Star," introduces Sirius the Wonder Dog, a thoughtful part-Salmanian Putschound and part-Spacedog, expert at telepathy, telekinesis, and teleportation, much to the distress of Glub, the Colonel's man, who has been quick-frozen in a pothole since Palaeolithic Times.

Created and written by Arthur Horner in 1956 as the *News Chronicle*'s answer to *Flook*, *Colonel Pewter* was the replacement for *Japhet and Happy*. This daily strip for children (but more for their parents) moved to the *Daily Mail* upon the *Chronicle*'s demise (October 18, 1960), then moved again to *The Guardian* on May 24, 1964, an unprecedented double crossing. But, surprisingly, the rarer air of that classier newspaper did not prove conducive, and Horner was obliged to replace it with a more overtly adult strip. This was ingenious from a different angle: *The Thoughts of Citizen Doe* (1970) made readers the heroes by depicting everything from their point of view. It, too, disappeared, overtaken by John Kent's sexy *Varoomshka*.

Reprints of the strip include *Colonel Pewter in Ironicus*, a large paperback with an introduction by Christopher Fry, and *Sirius Dog Star* (1972), a hardback.

D.G.

COLONEL POTTERBY AND THE DUCHESS (U.S.) Chic Young started *Colonel Potterby and the Duchess* in 1934 as a top to *Blondie*, along with *The Family Foursome*, with which it alternated and eventually replaced.

Colonel Potterby is an amiable, bemoustached, jolly old gentleman, always attired in coat-and-tails and opera hat. His only goal and occupation in life seems to be the wooing of "the Duchess," an angular, homely spinster who fights the colonel's amorous advances with all and every means at hand. Never daunted, the colonel displays the utmost (if crackbrained) inventiveness in order to get the Duchess to marry him, but he is thwarted week after week by the Duchess' obsessive chastity.

Colonel Potterby was probably conceived by Young as a relaxation from the domesticity of Blondie: the humor there is looser and more fanciful, and there is no attempt at realism, sentimentality, or even verisimilitude. Because of this, *Colonel Potterby* is a delightful little strip, unpretentious, whimsical, and very funny.

It is doubtful whether Young himself worked on the strip after the 1940s. From that time on *Colonel Potterby* steadily declined in both interest and readership, and it finally folded in November 1963.

M.H.

COLQUHOUN, JOE (1927-1987) Joseph William Colquhoun (pronounced "ca-hoon") "was not just one

"Colonel Potterby and the Duchess," Chic Young. © King Features Syndicate.

of the best comic artists Britain has ever produced—he was the best!" Praise indeed. This quote came from Barrie Tomlinson, Joe's last editor at the Amalgamated Press/Fleetway comics empire. Among the many heroes Joe created there, one still survives; *Roy of the Rovers*, a popular football hero whom Joe first drew for the first issue of *Tiger* weekly in 1954, which was scripted by Frank S. Pepper.

Joe was born in 1927, and as a boy was more interested in the illustrations that accompanied the stories and serials in the "Tuppenny Bloods," the popular boys' story weeklies of the 1930s. His early influences were Steve Chapman, who drew for *Triumph*, and R. Simmons, who drew for *Champion*. Curiously, both artists illustrated stories written by the same Frank Pepper (who scripted *Roy of the Rovers*), who was using the pen name "Hal Wilton" at the time. An American influence was Alex Raymond, who drew *Flash Gordon*, which was being reprinted in *Modern Wonder*.

After attending art school, Colquhoun enlisted in the navy in 1943 and returned to art college in 1947, upon his discharge from the navy. Colquhoun saw a newspaper advertisement for comic-strip artists and sent samples of his work to the new studio, formed by two ex-GIs and financed with their army severance pay. King-Ganteaume was in the business of packaging 28-page comic books for various small publishers, such as L. Miller and Son and the United Anglo-American Book Company, under whose trade name, Streamline, *Masterman Comics* (1952) was published. Colquhoun tried his hand at scripting and wrote a four-part serial entitled *The Naval Stowaways* for *Lion* (1952), his first encounter with the Amalgamated Press. In the same year he joined the freelance artists on *Champion*, one of his favorite prewar papers. Colquhoun drew a long-running series entitled *Legionnaire Terry's Desert Quest*, which ran for 44 weeks, followed by *Biff Benbow* and *Wildfire*, published through 1953.

Roy of the Rovers first appeared on September 11, 1954, and after the fourth strip Colquhoun took over the scripting and continued the strip, somewhat unhappily, until 1959. "Writing never came terribly naturally to me, compared with drawing," he said. In 1959 he moved to *Lion Comic* to draw the adventures of the World War II fighter pilot *Paddy Payne* through 1964. Many other series followed, usually two-page spreads, plus a return of *Roy of the Rovers* in 1965. Titles included *Saber, King of the Jungle* (*Tiger*, 1967), *Football Family Robinson* (*Jag*, 1968), *Adam Eterno*, (*Thunder*, 1970), *Kid Chameleon*, (*Cor*, 1970), *Zarga, Man of Mystery*, (*Buster*, 1972), the television comedians *The Goodies* (*Cor*, 1973), *Zip Nolan* (*Valiant*, 1974), and a 64-page comic book, *Flash Point*, in the monthly series *Air Ace Picture Library* (1961). Colquhoun's most popular and arguably best series was, however, *Charley's War*, a long saga about a soldier serving in World War I. It ran for seven-and-a-half years, which was three-and-a-half years longer than the war itself. Scripted by Pat Mills, it was later reprinted as two books by Titan Publishing. It was also reprinted in the original *Battle Action* series (1979) in both *Battle* and *Eagle*, but the reruns were heavily censored for a younger audience.

Colquhoun retired from full-time comic drawing in 1986, but died shortly thereafter of a heart attack on April 13, 1987.

D.G

"Comanche," Greg and Hermann. © Editions du Lombard.

COMANCHE (Belgium) The team of Hermann and Greg, already responsible for the brilliant *Bernard Prince*, conceived a new adventure strip in 1971, *Comanche*, also for *Tintin*.

Comanche is a conventional but solid Western about a ranch hand named Red Dust, his comic sidekick Ten Gallons, and Comanche, the young and pretty ranch owner they work for. Comanche manages her ranch with a firm hand and a level head, Red Dust is strong and silent as befits a Western hero, Ten Gallons is the fabled crotchety old man with a heart of gold, and Clem is the callow youth who drinks at Dust's feet, not to forget the Western's latest wrinkle, the black cowboy (in this case his name is Toby and he is, of course, courageous, tolerant, and wise).

The stories are well researched and well written but, as in the case of so many European Westerns, they are somewhat disappointing, refusing to strictly conform to the mythology of the West, but never quite succeeding in giving us a genuine sense of the time and the place either (but Greg is *trying*).

Hermann's style is bold and powerful, his compositions visually striking, although he tends to overload his imagery with too much detail. *Comanche* tries hard to emulate *Lieutenant Blueberry* in realism and color, and in sheer skill Hermann is often the equal of Gir, but lacks his narrative skill and sense of pace. Yet *Comanche* must be ranked as one of the more interesting creations of the 1970s adventure-strip genre.

Editions du Lombard have been reprinting the adventures of Comanche and Red Dust in book form since 1972. In 1983 Hermann abandoned the feature, sending it into a prolonged hiatus, which ended in 1989 when Michel Rouge picked up the series on continuities still written by Greg.

M.H.

"Come on, Steve!", Roland Davies. © Sunday Dispatch.

COME ON, STEVE! (G.B.) "A lovable, usually stupid, occasionally artful animal." This was Steve the cart horse, in the words of Charles Eade, editor of the national newspaper *Sunday Dispatch*, in his introduction to a collation of the weekly *Come On, Steve!* strips, entitled *Adventures of Steve* and published in 1947 as a

P. J. Press paperback. Steve galloped into the *Dispatch* in 1939, a few months before the outbreak of the war. He survived Adolf Hitler by some years, despite the paper shortage that reduced his strip to a pocket-sized two panels. In fact, *Steve* lived longer than his 10 years in the *Dispatch*, for he had come there from an earlier existence in a rival newspaper, the *Sunday Express*. Such a radical change of venue was unheard-of in British newspaper strips of the 1930s.

Steve was created by Roland Davies and was the very opposite of all Davies loved: speed and power. A cartoonist and illustrator obsessed with racing cars and aircraft, Davies christened his stolid old cart-horse, almost an anachronism in the 1930s, Steve, after the catchphrase shouted by crowds at the racetrack when Steve Donoghue, champion jockey, came roaring in to win: "Come on, Steve!" Davies tried his strip, a pantomime gag, as a daily for the *London Evening Standard*, but they turned it down, and so he then tried the *Daily Express*. Arthur Christiansen, the bright assistant editor, took it in to John Gordon, editor of the Sunday edition, who snapped it up immediately to commence the very next Sunday. Within a few years Steve was so popular that Davies taught himself animation, set up a studio in his kitchen, and with a stop-frame camera costing 18 shillings spent seven months making an animated cartoon. He showed it to Butcher's Film Distributors and secured a contract for six sound cartoons. With some professional animators and local talent from the Ipswich Art School, the films were made. *Steve Steps Out* (1936) was crude, but *Steve of the River* (1936), a burlesque of Edgar Wallace's *Sanders of the River*, was good. Story books were published using drawings from

Didier Comés, "Silence." © Casterman.

the films. After the *Dispatch* discontinued the strip, Davies retained his copyright and produced an excellent series of full-color picture books lithographed by Perry's Colourprint: *Steve Goes to London* (1946); *Steve and the Little Engine* (1947); *Steve's Christmas Holiday* (1947); *Steve on the Farm* (1948); *Steve's Dream* (1948); *Steve and the Burglar* (1949); *Steve and the Racing Car* (1949). There were also *Come on, Steve!* annuals in 1947 and 1950.

D.G.

COMÉS, DIDIER (1942-   ) Belgian cartoonist and illustrator, born December 11, 1942, in Sourbrodt, in that part of eastern Belgium that was annexed by the Germans during World War II; given the name Dieter at birth, Comés was rechristened Didier after Belgium's liberation in 1944. Following studies at a vocational art school, he became an industrial designer, working in that capacity from 1959 to 1969.

His career as a professional cartoonist started in earnest in the early 1970s, when Comés contributed several short comic stories to Belgian and French publications, such as the daily *Le Soir* and the comic weeklies *Spirou* and *Pilote*. In the pages of the latter he published his first long-breathed creation, *Ergun l'Errant* ("Ergun the Wanderer"), in 1973. It was the saga of a space traveler, in which arresting images and imaginative layouts counterpoint a rather conventional script.

Having refined and simplified his style in *L'Ombre du Corbeau* ("The Shadow of the Raven," 1976-77), a nature story blending the commonplace with the fantastic, Comés unfolded what turned out to be his masterpiece, *Silence*, from 1979 to 1981. A legend-drenched graphic novel full of mystery, magic, and yes, silence, set amidst the forests, the ponds, and the mists of the artist's native region, it brought a welcome breath of fresh air to the claustrophobic Franco-Belgian comics scene. He followed this up with more gripping tales of magic realism, *La Belette* ("The Weasel," 1981-82), *Eva* (1985), and *Iris* (1990). From 1985 to 1986 he also produced *L'Arbre-Coeur* ("The Heart-Tree"), the romantic adventure of a female reporter returning from assign-

ment in Afghanistan. In his narratives as in his compositions, Comés has shown himself to be a highly original talent, the poet of the eerie, the magical, the unspoken.

M.H.

COMMISSARIO SPADA, IL (Italy) Few Italian mystery writers have ever made it big under their own names: the almost single exception is Giorgio Scerbanendo, who acquired fame and honors toward the end of his long career. On the other hand, many other writers had no trouble selling their works by using an Anglo-Saxon pseudonym. The shibboleth that a good mystery story had to be written by an Englishman or an American carried even to the characters, who had to have English-sounding names, and to the locale, which had to closely resemble an American metropolis. This prejudice held true not only in novels and stories, but in comic strips as well.

Il Commissario Spada ("Commissioner Spada") was the first exception to the rule. It was created on April 19, 1970, by Gian Luigi Gonano (writer) and Gianni DeLuca (artist). Spada is the commissioner of the Squadra Mobile (mobile squad), and he is often engaged in everyday cases full of human interest, all of them cleverly told and solved by Gonano. DeLuca, in his turn, cinematically translates the suspenseful action into comic strip terms, focusing not only on the athletic commissioner but also on his subordinates and adversaries, who are all realistically drawn with broad strokes.

The themes of the stories are those of everyday life, and the problems Commissioner Spada has to face are not only professional but also personal (Spada is a widower with a young son named Mario). *Commissario Spada* appeared in the pages of the widely circulated Catholic weekly *Il Giornalino* (whose editor, Gino Tomaselli, physically resembled the hero—and not by coincidence). The series ended in the early 1980s.

G.B.

CONAN (U.S.) For years, the late Robert E. Howard's *Conan* series had seen many editions in paperbacks.

"Il Commissario Spada," Gianni DeLuca. © Ed. Paoline.

...AS THE GLEAMING FANGS OF THE *BEAST* HEAD, WHICH IS SURELY *DEATH* ITSELF, GNASH AND CHAMP!

THE EYELIDS OF THE *OTHER* HEAD... *SLEEP,* IT MUST BE... ARE *CLOSED* IN EERIE TRANQUILITY.

TO AWAKEN THEM, THEN -- TO SEE *THOSE* EYES OPEN, AND THE BEAST'S *CLOSE* -- BUT *HOW*??

"Conan," Gil Kane. © Marvel Comics Group.

Graced with cover artwork by illustrator Frank Frazetta or others of equal note, the barbarian from mythical Cimmeria had occasional revivals and celebrations. But the comic book industry, never receptive to, or willing to experiment with, sword and sorcery material of the Howard/Conan ilk, ignored the character and its attendant popularity like a plague.

But then Marvel Comics purchased the rights to the Howard stories and planned to issue a *Conan the Barbarian* comic book. Roy Thomas was assigned to write the title, and young Barry Smith to illustrate, even though Thomas had publicly indicated a preference for John Buscema, who was unavailable. The first issue of the full-color *Conan the Barbarian* was issued in October 1970, and it immediately became that rare kind of title: a book hailed by the critics that sold well to the general comic-buying public. As issues progressed, Thomas managed to balance Conan's essentially violent nature—Howard had characterized him as a barbarian in the true sense of the word; he was mean, cruel, ruthless, unmannered, and mercenary, with a conscience guided only by personal survival—and the restrictions of the oft-condemned comics code. But perhaps more amazing was that the talented Thomas even managed to save Conan from becoming just another Marvel character. Whereas most of Marvel's minions were standard types—usually noble-bearing, upright, considerate, and more often than not, gifted with superhuman powers but normal intellect—Thomas maintained Conan as a demigod fighting unnatural phenomona with none of the strictures inherent in the Marvel world of superheroes with problems.

Writer Thomas, who also edited the book, relied mostly on adaptations of Howard stories, and later adapted unfinished Howard manuscripts. Still later, when the volume of Howard material was exhausted and the Conan work by writers such as De Camp, Carter, and Nyborg was contractually unavailable, Thomas turned to adapting sword-and-sorcery work by writers like Edgar Rice Burroughs and Gardner F. Fox. Under his constant tutelage, the *Conan the Barbarian* book has won a score of comic art awards from fans and professionals alike.

Artistically, the book has gone through many changes. Young Smith developed quickly, and although his Conan was not nearly as brutal-looking as described by Howard, his characterizations gained a quick following. His material was heavily laden with intricate designs—at times bordering on ornate, art deco-like scenes and backgrounds—and eye-pleasing page composition and layout; his coloring was delicate and compatible. But, by early 1973 differences between Smith and Marvel came to a boil and he left the strip. After several fill-in issues by Gil Kane, John Buscema, Thomas's original choice, assumed the strip in April 1973. His Conan was even less vicious-looking, but Buscema's design and execution were excellent and two quite diverse factions developed, some favoring Smith and others preferring the Buscema version, which was inked by Ernie Chua, among others. Neal Adams and Esteban Maroto also rendered the character.

The Conan character was also highly saleable and has appeared in many of Marvel's newer formats. A second Conan title, a one-dollar black-and-white book entitled *Savage Sword of Conan*, premiered in August 1974.

J.B.

In the late 1970s Thomas's increasingly sloppy writing almost doomed the barbarian in a way his enemies had not been able to do. The title was rescued by the two movies based on the character, the 1981 *Conan the Barbarian* and the 1985 *Conan the Destroyer*, both starring Arnold Schwarzenegger in the title role. Despite this shot in the arm and the contributions of some good artists (Howard Chaykin, Walt Simonson), the title continued to falter, and it was discontinued in December 1993. Several spin-offs (*Conan the King, The Conan Saga*, etc.) that had sprouted in the meantime proved to be short-lived. Since August 1995 the barbarian's adventures have been carried in the black-and-white *Conan the Savage* magazine.

M.H.

CONNIE (U.S.) Frank Godwin's *Connie* is, along with Noel Sickles' *Scorchy Smith* and Burne Hogarth's *Tarzan*, one of the causes célèbres of comic strip scholarship. Distributed by the obscure Ledger Syndicate from 1927 to 1944, it ran in only a few newspapers (including the *Brooklyn Eagle*) and was completely ignored by the early historians of the medium. Even as late as 1974 Jerry Robinson's *The Comics* does not mention it (an unjustifiable omission, since the earlier *History of the Comic Strip* and *75 Years of the Comics* not only discussed the strip but also reprinted illustrations). Yet a close study of *Connie* reveals it as one of the most fascinating strips of the era.

"Connie," Frank Godwin. © Ledger Syndicate.

In the early years of the strip, Connie was a pretty blonde living with her parents and going to picnics and masquerade parties in the company of eligible young men with such names as Percival Llewellyn-Smith and Clarence Dillingworth. Then came the depression and Connie turned out to be a girl with a social conscience; she helped her mother with her charity work and often visited the men on the breadlines (one of the very few instances where the depression was graphically depicted in a comic strip).

In 1934 Connie went to work, first as a reporter, then as the operator of a detective agency (a kind of female Sam Spade). Her assignments led her to all parts of the United States and as far as Mexico and South America. Her most unusual adventure took place in Russia, where she helped foil a plot against the Soviet regime (certainly an oddity in comic strips of the 1930s). Then, to top it all, Connie joined an interplanetary expedition headed by another woman, Dr. Alden, and her son Hugh. Connie's explorations of the solar system—which were to last over two years—is one of the most remarkable sequences in the history of the adventure strip, and in the power of its imagery and suspense, it can be ranked alongside the best episodes of Raymond's *Flash Gordon*, Caniff's *Terry*, and Foster's and Hogarth's *Tarzan*.

The narrative, good as it often is, is overshadowed by the personality of the heroine and her chaste, cool beauty. Connie is a liberated woman: intelligent, self-reliant, at ease in all situations. Holding her own against any man, she would certainly have made a better representative for the women's movement than the masochistic, dull-witted Wonder Woman.

Connie was sparsely reprinted in comic books and was never adapted to radio or the screen. The strip was rescued from total oblivion only through the efforts of dedicated lovers of the medium. *Connie* is a constant visual delight, even when the narrative falters, and it deserves to be exhumed from dusty library archives into the light of print.

M.H.

CONTI, OSCAR (1914-1979) Oscar Conti (better known as "Oski") was born in Buenos Aires in 1914. After studies at the Buenos Aires Academy of Fine Arts, Conti became a poster designer. In 1942 he started his collaboration as a humor cartoonist with Carlos Warnes, who used the pseudonym "César Bruto." A man of great culture, obsessed by the oppression exercised by Latin American dictators, concerned about the life of the Indians, the inventions of mankind, and the re-creation of the old didactic texts from world literature, Conti transferred his deep knowledge of these subjects into his thematic treatment.

Conti edited many collections of his graphic work gathered from magazines from many countries. With his comic strip *Amarrotto*, published in the comic magazine *Rico Tipo*, he influenced many cartoonists who later become his disciples. At the same time he wrote the daily *Versos y Noticias de César Bruto* ("Rhymes and Notes of César Bruto").

Conti's fertile creativity led him to combine many of his hobbies into one: he repaired pocketwatches, put in a new setting, and decorated them in his own masterly style. He died in Buenos Aires on October 30, 1979.

L.G.

CORBEN, RICHARD VANCE (1940-   ) American comic book and underground artist and animator, born October 1, 1940 in Anderson, Missouri. Rich

Richard Corben, "Rowlf." © Richard Corben.

Corben—or "Gore" Corben as he often signed his work—was educated at BFA, Kansas City (Missouri) Art Institute.

Corben is one of the groundbreakers of comic art, but also extremely unique. His first experience with comics was with Calvin productions in Kansas City, where he worked in the animation department from 1963 to 1972. His first published comic work in printed form appeared not in a professional magazine, but in a fanzine—*Voice of Comicdom* number 12 (1968). He moved into the underground market in mid-1970 when his first story, "Lame Lems Love" appeared in *Skull* number two. His first traditional, "above-ground" comic book work appeared in the November 1970 issue of Warren's *Creepy* black-and-white magazine (number 36). Since that time, he has continued to work in all three veins, becoming at one time the best fanzine artist, the most-respected underground horror artist, and the best horror artist in the black-and-white mainstream magazines.

Most of Corben's appeal and popularity—which grew steadily and has recently reached cult proportions—comes from his highly stylized, completely individual approach to a comic story. Much of his style developed from his animation work. Corben's anatomy is always grossly exaggerated: his men are unbelievably muscular and his women abnormally well-endowed. His figures are sometimes amazingly three-dimensional, other times agonizingly two-dimensional. Most of his panels have highly developed foreground action with just the barest detail in the background. He often works in color—both in the underground and with special sections of Warren's black-and-white books—and his work there is exceedingly vibrant, eerie, and always well conceived.

Corben usually develops three distinct types of stories with repetitive trends and ideas. His sword-and-sorcery work was done mostly for a vast number of out-of-print and hard-to-find fanzines. His neo-EC, gory horror tales are usually found in underground comix like *Skull*, *Death Rattle*, and *Weird Fantasies*. Science fiction is Corben's other major theme and these stories are found in undergrounds like *Fever Dreams* and *Slow Death* and fanzines like Mike Barrier's outstanding *Funnyworld*. Corben uses all three types of stories in his above-ground work, but they are considerably more sedate and sexually demure than his underground and fanzine work.

Perhaps his best-known work is *Rowlf*, which originally appeared in fanzines and was republished as an underground in 1971. It is a strange tale about a woman named Maryara, her dog Rowlf, and their eerie devotion to each other.

Corben has racked up several awards in a relatively short professional career in comic books. In addition, one of his animated films—*Neverworld*, a completely Corben animation-and-line action film—has won three awards.

J.B.

The last 20 years have been extremely productive for Richard Corben. *Bloodstar* (1976), *Neverwhere* (1978), and *New Tales of the Arabian Nights* (with Jan Strnad, 1979) strengthened his reputation as a master storyteller. It is in *Den* and *Den II* (both 1984) that all of the artist's narrative strands—heroic fantasy, speculative fiction, horror play—came together, building up to what is perhaps the author's most representative work.

With *Werewolf* and *Edgar Allan Poe* Corben explored further the twin themes of horror and madness that run through his oeuvre as a scarlet thread. While continuing the saga of Den, in the late 1980s and early 1990s he also touched upon more science-fictional and even metaphysical themes; at the same time the more openly erotic aspects of his work have found since 1994 their ideal vehicle in *Penthouse Comix*. Corben has also evidenced great strength as an animator, especially in the "Den" segment of the *Heavy Metal* theatrical feature.

M.H.

"Corentin," Paul Cuvelier. © Editions du Lombard.

CORENTIN (Belgium) Started as *Les Aventures de Corentin Feldoë* in the first issue of the comic weekly *Tintin* (September 26, 1946), the strip was the brainchild of cartoonist Paul Cuvelier and writer Jacques van Melkebeke (who also happened to be *Tintin's* first editor).

Corentin Feldoë was a young Breton orphan of the 17th century who was sent to join his uncle in India. There he was to experience many adventures in the company of the young Indian boy Kim, whom he had befriended, and his two pet animals, Belzebuth the gorilla and Moloch the tiger (as one can see, in the beginning at least, the series was strongly influenced by Rudyard Kipling's tales). Later Corentin traveled to China, North America, Arabia, and anywhere else under the sun. Very often magic and the supernatural played an important role in the series, which was consistently well plotted and always exciting. Corentin grew up over the years into a handsome adolescent; his appearances in *Tintin*, however, became fewer and farther between, due to the author's preoccupations with other series (such as *Line*, a circus strip) and with other pursuits (painting, sculpture). Following van Melkebeke's departure as scriptwriter after two episodes, *Corentin* was written by Greg, Jean van Hamme, and Cuvelier himself. Cuvelier died in 1978, and *Corentin* died with him.

Corentin is probably one of the best adventure series to come out of the immediate postwar years. The situations and plots are very imaginative, the characters interesting and colorful, and the backgrounds lovingly detailed. Cuvelier's graphic style helped in no small measure the success of the strip: clean, uncluttered, and very dynamic, it is the classic style of the adventure strip of the 1930s, but brought up to date, with a dash of European sophistication and flair.

M.H.

Jayme Cortez, "Sergio Amazonas." © Jayme Cortez.

"Corto Maltese," Hugo Pratt. © Pratt.

a retrospective exhibition of his work organized by the Museu de Arte de São Paulo, the most important art museum in Latin America. He died in 1987, a few months before the publication of an anthology of his horror stories titled *A Saga do Terror*.

A.M.

CORTEZ, JAYME (1926-1987) Brazilian cartoonist and comic strip artist of Portuguese origin, born in Lisbon in 1926. Jayme Cortez started his career as a disciple of E.T. Coelho, working for the weekly *O Mosquito*, where he drew such series as *Os Dois Amigos* ("The Two Pals"). In 1947 he moved to Brazil, where he produced a number of comic strips for the São Paulo daily *O Diario da Noite*, notably *Caça aos Tubaroes*, a jungle strip, and *O Guarany*, a saga of Indian life. He married a Brazilian woman in 1948 and became a permanent resident of the country. He worked alongside veteran cartoonist Messias de Melho in *A Gazeta Juvenil* and *A Gazeta Esportiva*, and he drew the covers for the horror comic-book title *O Terror Negro,* published by Editora La Selva. When horror comics were banned in the United States in the mid-1950s, La Selva hired Brazilian cartoonists to keep the market going. From the late 1950s through the 1970s Cortez drew *Dick Peter*, a detective story, as well as *Zodiac* for the Italian market.

In 1951 Cortez, along with Syllas Roberg, Miguel Penteado, Reynaldo de Oliveira, and Alvaro de Moya, organized the first international exhibition of comics; rare originals by George Herriman, Milton Caniff, Alex Raymond, Hal Foster, and other American cartoonists were displayed alongside the work of Brazilian and European artists. Cortez was the inspiration for a whole generation of Brazilian cartoonists, especially Mauricio de Souza. He authored three how-to books on drawing and cartooning. He received the Caran d'Ache Lifetime Achievement Award in Italy and had

CORTO MALTESE (France and Belgium) One of the most popular of French-language strips, *Corto Maltese* is the work of an Italian, Hugo Pratt, who created it as a spin-off from one of his earlier efforts, *Una Ballata del Mare Salato* ("A Ballad of the Salty Sea"). *Corto* first appeared in the French weekly *Pif-Gadget* on April 1, 1970.

Corto Maltese is a sea captain without a ship and, by all appearances, without a country. The action takes place around 1910, when there were still worlds to conquer, treasures to discover, and causes to fight for. There is a heavy atmosphere in these tales full of sound and fury, in which magic and witchcraft play a large part.

In adventures that lead him from South America to Europe (where he takes part in the fighting of World War I) to North Africa, Corto always sides with the rebels and the oppressed. He fights alongside the Indians against the military and the settlers, with the Irish revolutionaries against the British, and with the Arabs against the Turks. A host of secondary characters lend color and relief to the action, like the old pirate captain Rasputin, the dypsomaniacal professor Steiner, Banshee the fiery Irish lass, and the voluptuous adventuress Venexiana Stevenson, among others.

In 1974 Pratt left *Pif* for the Belgian *Tintin*, where the adventures of Corto Maltese appeared in full color (they were published in black and white in *Pif*). New *Corto Maltese* episodes continued to appear like clockwork over the years, up to the time of the author's death in 1995.

In the space of a few years, *Corto Maltese* has risen to the top of the list of adventure strips. All the episodes have been reprinted in book form and translated into a halfdozen languages. *Corto Maltese* has also been adapted (in animated form) to the television screen. Several book-length studies have been devoted to the seafaring adventurer, the most notable being Michel Pierre's *Corto Maltese Memoires* in 1988.

M.H.

CORY, FANNY YOUNG (1877-1972) American cartoonist and illustrator born in Waukegan, Illinois, in 1877, Fanny Young grew up in Montana and started her art studies at age 14 in Helena, then went to New

York. She sold her first drawing in 1896 to *St. Nicholas* magazine. She then became very much in demand, with contributions to *Life, Scribner's* and the *Saturday Evening Post.* In 1901 she went back to Montana, married the next year, and settled on a 1,800-acre ranch near Helena. She became a noted illustrator of children's books (her illustrations for Frank Baum's novels are best known, along with *The Fanny Cory Mother Goose*).

In 1928 Fanny Cory created a one-column panel, *Sonnysayings,* for the Philadelphia Ledger Syndicate. Encouraged by her first foray into the newspaper field, she then decided to become a comic strip artist. After a few false starts, she finally came up with *Babe Bunting,* an orphan strip, in 1934. *Babe* was successful enough for King Features to take notice, and the following year, Cory left *Babe Bunting* to create *Little Miss Muffet,* another little girl adventure strip, for King. The feature enjoyed reasonable success and Cory continued it until 1956.

Fanny Cory's comic strip style was delicate and clean, perhaps a little too elaborate for the simple stories she was given to illustrate. While not outstanding, her contribution (usually ignored in comic strip histories) is worthy of mention. She died on her Montana ranch in 1972.

M.H.

COSSIO, CARLO (1907-1964) Italian cartoonist, born January 1, 1907, in Udine. Along with his younger brother Vittorio (born in 1911), Carlo Cossio moved to Milan during childhood. He started his career as a decorator but in 1928 became interested in animation. Around this time he did a number of advertising cartoons in collaboration with his brother (Carlo Cossio was among the first Italian animators to draw directly on animation "cells") and also drew a number of magazine illustrations and book covers. In 1932 the Cossio brothers produced their first commercially successful animated cartoon, *Zibillo e l'Orso* ("Zibillo and the Bear"), and thereafter went on to create more cartoons.

Carlo Cossio's most famous creation, however, was not an animated cartoon but a comic strip, *Dick Fulmine,* which he created in 1938 for the illustrated weekly *L'Audace.* Centering on the extraordinary adventures of a muscular superhero, *Dick Fulmine* ("Lightning Dick") enjoyed a tremendous success, and Cossio worked on the feature almost uninterruptedly until 1955.

In 1940, after a series of run-ins with Mussolini's Ministry of Popular Culture (the infamous "Minculpop"), Carlo Cossio judged it prudent to leave the comics field for a while, and returned to the animated cartoon with *Pulcinella nel Bosco* ("Punch in the Woods"). His exile did not last long, however, and he made his comeback later that same year with *X-1 il Pugile Misterioso* ("X-1 the Mysterious Prizefighter"), about a boxer-turned-crimefighter, which he left to his brother Vittorio after a few episodes. (Under the title of *Furio Almirante,* it was to have a great career and almost eclipsed *Dick Fulmine* at one time.)

During and after the war, Cossio created a number of other comic strips: *Franca* (about a youthful and spirited heroine), *Tank* (a superhero after the fashion of American comic books), *La Freccia d'Argente* ("The Silver Arrow," 1941, depicting the exploits of another justice-fighter), and *Bufalo Bill* (1950; an entertaining, if

spurious biography of the legendary American scout, which he drew for the weekly *L'Intrepido*).

All the while Carlo Cossio had been working on *Dick Fulmine* (with the assistance of his brother Vittorio on some episodes). It is therefore not surprising that he suffered a complete breakdown, which forced him to leave the field in 1955. He tried to make a comeback unsuccessfully in 1963, and he died (of cancer) in Milan on August 10, 1964.

Carlo Cossio was made famous by *Dick Fulmine* and was perhaps the victim of his own success. Working hastily and at times mindlessly (he once boasted of having drawn an entire 16-page episode in one night), he was never able to display his undeniable graphic talents to their best advantage. He left behind a legacy of dubious achievements, with a few diamonds sparkling brightly amidst heaps of rubbish.

M.H.

"Count Screwloose," Milt Gross. © Milt Gross.

COUNT SCREWLOOSE OF TOOLOOSE (U.S.) One of the most fondly remembered, quoted, and described of all departed U.S. comic strips, Milt Gross' weekly *Count Screwloose of Tooloose,* which began on Sunday, February 17, 1929, with the *New York World*'s syndicate, was partly prefigured by a wild scene in a madhouse involving the characters of Gross' immediately preceding strip, *Nize Baby,* early in 1927. For the springboard of the early *Screwloose* adventures was a madhouse—an institution called Nuttycrest, to which the chronic escapee, Count Screwloose, was always glad to return after a weekly experience in the outside world that convinced him that the asylum was a far saner place. The Count (whose nobility, with his appropriately misspelled notion of an aristocratic place of origin, the French city of Toulouse, was his only delusion) was a shrimpish, balding, daffily cross-eyed brunette dressed neatly in fedora and vest. His closest asylum companion and later co-escapee, a black-collared, cross-eyed, humanized mutt in a Napoleonic hat, named Iggy (not seen in the strip until the third episode, of March 10, 1929), and who appears as first a white, then yellow, and finally an orange dog over the run of the strip, was the Count's steadfast welcomer back to Nuttycrest in the early years of the feature, and Screwloose's admonitory, last-panel refrain of this period, "Iggy, keep an eye on me," became a widely used term for professed dismay at someone else's foolishness.

After two years with the *World*, Gross took *Count Screwloose* to Hearst's King Features in early 1931, which began national distribution of its new acquisition on March 1, 1931. Now sharing the Sunday page with a new page-top Gross feature, *Babbling Brooks* (about a fat fellow who talks himself into weekly disasters), *Screwloose* continued as before—but with the "of Tooloose" dropped from the title—until June 1931, when the strip was moved into the page-top space (*Babbling Brooks* being discarded) and was replaced below by a new feature, *Dave's Delicatessen*. In its new, smaller Sunday spot, *Screwloose* dropped the weekly escape-and-return routine, and focused on the Count and Iggy as edgy but continuing denizens of the outside world, fearful of being found out and returned to the asylum, but managing by nervy inventiveness to make out.

In early 1933, a single-panel feature called *That's My Pop* cut down the size of *Screwloose* even more, until its space was turned over entirely on June 24, 1934, to a new strip featuring two penguins, while the Count himself, who had entered the *Dave's Delicatessen* strip below in December of the previous year, continued there as a close companion of that strip's hero, Honest Dave. The new comic team joined the Foreign Legion in November 1934, for a prolonged stint of comic adventure in the course of which the *Dave's Delicatessen* strip was retitled *Count Screwloose* (January 20, 1935). In June 1938, a third of the *Count Screwloose* half-page space was given over to a new Gross gag panel called *Grossly Xaggerated,* which ran there through October 1938. *Count Screwloose* continued to run (by now almost exclusively in the *Mirror*) until Gross was forced in 1945 by a heart attack to refrain from further comic strip work.

A great strip in its early years, but of declining quality after 1934, *Count Screwloose* remains one of the most continually funny, inventive, and sophisticated comics of all time.

B.B.

COYOTE, EL (Spain) El Coyote's adventures were first published as a series of novels in the collection "Oeste," starting in December 1943. The aim of the publishers was to establish a hero similar to the protagonists of the American pulps; the success of the hero created by the novelist José Mallorqui was so widespread that his novels were translated into several foreign languages and inspired adaptations in all mass media.

In 1946 *El Coyote* started its long career as a weekly comic book with illustrations by Francisco Batet, who had previously drawn the hundreds of Coyote novels. El Coyote, whose first adventure took place during the Mexican-American War, is in actuality the young César de Echague, who conceals his identity under a mask and a curious disguise, in order to fight with impunity the "yanquis" and brigands who devastate his lands. His life is far removed from that of the traditional American West, closer to the traditional ways of the Spaniards of California: he is a caballero who has known struggles, loves, and marriages; he has created

"El Coyote," Francisco Batet. © Ediciones Cliper.

a dynasty, represented in the persons of his children, in the course of the hundreds of comic books depicting his adventures. Batet's version was unfortunately afflicted by lengthy and meandering dialogues and a verbose narrative that considerably choked up the action. Batet's style was very individual, fine and light, without any research or innovation, but effective in its preservation of the Coyote myth, then at the height of its popularity. When Batet left for France and a new career in the early 1950s, he was succeeded by the less inspired José Ramon Larraz. The character managed to survive in his and other artists's hands into the 1980s.

El Coyote was made into three motion pictures, was adapted to the stage, and inspired a musical comedy as well as several records. A fan club further helped to maintain its popularity, and there were also many Coyote toys and costumes.

L.G.

CRAENHALS, FRANÇOIS (1926-   ) Belgian cartoonist, born November 15, 1926, at Ixelles, near Brussels. After studies at the Brussels Royal Academy, Craenhals started his cartooning career with a series of caricatures (which he signed "F. Hals") for the Belgian magazine *Vrai*.

In 1948 Craenhals entered the field of comic art with *Druka*, a medieval adventure strip strongly influenced by *Prince Valiant*, for the weekly *Le Soir Illustré*, where it ran from July to October. Craenhals originated a new feature, *Karan*, also short-lived, for *Heroic-Albums* in 1950, the same year that he started his long collaboration with the comic weekly *Tintin*, first as an illustrator, and later as a comic strip artist. For *Tintin* Craenhals was to create a number of features over the years: *Rémy et Ghislaine* (1951); *Pom et Teddy*, a kid adventure strip that started in 1953; *Luc Tremplin*, an adventure tale (1962); and more importantly *Chevalier Ardent* ("Knight Ardent"), a story of adventure in King Arthur's time (1966). Craenhals has also drawn a daily gag strip, *Primus et Musette*, for the newspaper *La Libre Belgique* (1958-1961), and is, since 1965, the illustrator of *Les 4 As* ("The 4 Aces"), yet another kid adventure strip written by François Georges (George Chaulet). While continuing his work on *Chevalier Ardent*, he also

MAMA'S BOYZ®

BY JERRY CRAFT

Jerry Craft, "Mama's Boyz." © King Features Syndicate.

drew *Fantomette*, a teenage mystery strip, for Editions Hachette from 1982 to 1983; and in the 1990s he turned out a number of short stories for foreign (mainly German) publishers.

A cartoonist with a versatile and free style, François Craenhals is somewhat underrated in Europe, where his traditional outlook and introverted personality do not attract as much attention as the flashier idiosyncrasies of some of his colleagues. Yet he is an artist of solid and noteworthy accomplishment.

M.H.

CRAFT, JERRY (1963-) Cartoonist Jerry Craft was born in New York City on January 22, 1963. He graduated from the School of Visual Arts in 1984. Currently a staff artist at King Features, his strip *Mama's Boyz* is part of a weekly package distributed by King Features to over 1,500 newspapers in the United States.

The main characters in *Mama's Boyz* are Pauline Porter, a widow, and her teenage sons Tyrell and Yusuf. The Porters own a bookstore featuring a large selection of African-American books, and they live in an apartment above the store. The strip's setting, extended family, and friends are all true-to-life and believable, which adds to the appeal of the strip set in a large city. Jerry Craft has designed *Mama's Boyz* to specifically bring African-American family experiences and humor to the general public. Craft has volunteered the characters for use by the American Diabetes Association to educate readers about diabetes and its impact on those who have the disease. In the strip, diabetes was the cause of the father's death.

Prior to having his work syndicated, Craft worked on *New Kids on the Block* for Harvey Comics and *Sweet 16* for Marvel Comics. His work has been published in the *Village Voice, Ebony* magazine, *Street News*, and *Jewish Weekly*. A Sunday-page comic, *Mama's Boyz* is a regular feature in the *City Sun*, a New York City African-American-owned newspaper. It is one of the leaders in the next generation of African-American comic strips, which include such big names as *Curtis, Herb & Jamal*, Jump Start, and *Where I'm Coming From*.

Craft's clean, distinctive style, family humor, and ability to keep up with the latest trends among teenagers, as well as the fact that he presents a pair of African-American young men coping with the teenage years, make his strip a good alternative for newspapers

looking for an African-American strip besides the current big four.

B.C.

CRAIG, CHASE (1910-) American comic book and strip writer, artist, and editor, born August 28, 1910, in Ennis, Texas. Following study at the Chicago Academy of Fine Arts, Craig moved to California in 1935 and joined Walter Lantz's animation studio. In 1936, he switched over to Warner Brothers to work as an animator and story man in Fred (Tex) Avery's unit, followed two years later by a stint drawing a short-lived comic strip, *Hollywood Hams*, for the *Los Angeles Daily News*. While the strip never achieved national syndication, Craig did. V. V. McNitt of the McNaught syndicate saw the strip and liked it, and so Craig and his collaborator, Carl Buettner, were hired to take over the Charlie McCarthy newspaper strip based on Edgar Bergen's popular character. Originally, Craig was to function as Buettner's art assistant, but he soon assumed most of the scripting duties. Buettner, a former contributor to *Capt. Billy's Whiz Bang* and a Disney veteran, subsequently joined Western Publishing Company, where he worked on various comic books in addition to supervising, writing, and illustrating many "Little Golden Books."

After *Charlie McCarthy* folded in 1940, Craig worked with writer Fred Fox on another daily strip, *Odd Bodkins* (Esquire Syndicate), which was probably the first parody of *Superman*. He also began freelancing for Western, writing and drawing the first *Porky Pig* stories for the *Looney Tunes* comic book and many of the early *Bugs Bunny* one-shots. Also for *Looney Tunes*, Craig took a cartoon mouse (Sniffles) from the Warner Brothers films, added a heroine named after Mrs. Craig, and thus launched the very popular strip *Mary Jane and Sniffles*. Craig also wrote and drew the first few *Bugs Bunny* Sunday newspaper pages. The strip was sold to NEA Syndicate in 1942, about the time *Odd Bodkins* ended and Craig went into the navy.

In 1945, after leaving the service, he returned to freelance writing for Western. He did thousands of scripts for various Western comics, including *Looney Tunes, Bugs Bunny, Porky Pig*, and the various Walt Disney comics. In 1950, he joined the firm as an editor, subsequently becoming managing editor and then executive editor. He supervised the stories and artwork of many different comics, ranging from *Tarzan* to various television-based titles to the Disney books, such as

Mickey Mouse and *Donald Duck*. He also created many originals for the line, such as *The Little Monsters, Baby Snoots, The Jungle Twins,* and *Magnus, Robot Fighter*. In each of these comics, he worked closely with his staff of writers and artists to maintain the highest possible standard of quality.

M.E.

CRAIG, JOHN (1926-   ) American comic book artist, writer, and editor, born April 25, 1926, in Pleasantville, New York. After training at the Art Students League, Johnny Craig broke into the comic book industry in 1938 as an assistant to National Comics artist Harry Lampert, who was then illustrating *The King*. He later lettered for Sheldon Mayer's *Scribbly* strip. When World War II erupted, Craig joined the Merchant Marine and then the U.S. Army and fought in Germany.

After the war, Craig spent 1947 and 1948 drawing for the old Fox, ME, and Lev Gleason lines. He then joined the EC group, which was producing nondescript love, crime, and adventure titles. However, when editor and publisher Bill Gaines ushered in the "New Trend" EC line in 1950, Craig immediately became a mainstay and drew outstanding covers and stories for virtually all the horror, crime, and suspense titles. He later became the chief writer and editor of *Vault of Horror* and *Extra!* from 1953-1955.

While Craig was a notoriously slow worker and Gaines once commented that he drew the "cleanest" horror stories he had ever seen, the artist's work drew an inordinate amount of public scrutiny for its alleged violent excesses. His cover for *Crime SuspenStories* 20—showing a close-up view of a hanging victim—was reproduced in *Seduction of the Innocent,* Dr. Frederic Wertham's highly controversial 1953 study of comics and violence. And his cover drawing for *Crime Suspen-Stories* 22—depicting a man holding a bloodied ax and a severed head—sparked a celebrated encounter between Gaines and Tennessee Democratic Senator Estes Kefauver, chairman of the Senate Judiciary Committee's 1954 hearings on comic books. On the other hand, comic art critics consider Craig's 1953 adaptation of Ray Bradbury's *Touch and Go* a comic book classic.

When E.C. folded, Craig left the field and became a commercial artist. He was later an art director and then vice president of a Pennsylvania advertising agency. He made several brief reentries into the comic book field in the 1960s. After drawing stories for the now-defunct

ACG group and Warren's black-and-white magazines, Craig illustrated for National in 1967 (*Batman* and *Hawkman*) and Marvel (*Ironman* and others, from 1968 through 1970). He now maintains a commercial art studio in Pennsylvania.

J.B.

CRANDALL, REED (1917-1982) American comic book artist, born in Winslow, Indiana, on February 22, 1917. After studies at the Cleveland School of Art (1935-1939), Crandall began his career in 1940 as an editorial cartoonist for the NEA Syndicate, later moving to the Eisner-Iger shop, where he produced top-notch material for Fiction House and Quality comic books.

"Reed was a real problem for Iger," fellow shop artist Gerry Altman once said. "His stuff was so great, everytime he came into the shop we all stopped to look at his stuff. Iger eventually had to tell him not to come to the office with his pages." When Quality publisher "Busy" Arnold saw Crandall's fine-line draftsmanship, he hired him exclusively in 1941, and over the next 12 years, Crandall turned out several dozen features, including *Uncle Sam, The Ray, Capt. Triumph,* and *Dollman*. But he did his greatest work on Quality's top-selling feature, *Blackhawk*.

Created by artist Chuck Cuidera in *Military* (later *Modern*) *Comics, Blackhawk* was a difficult strip to draw. It required an intricate knowledge of guns, tanks, and planes, as well as an exceptional ability to draw exciting "group" shots. Crandall, whose fine art training led him to be influenced by the likes of N. C. Wyeth, Howard Pyle, and James Montgomery Flagg, was one of the few who could draw the feature. His stories were amazingly realistic, leaning more toward classic illustration than cartooning; and aided by Crandall's acute attention to details and his great anatomical skill, *Blackhawk* quickly became one of the most popular strips ever created. Crandall was the feature's main artist from 1942 through 1944, and after a short stint in the Army Air Force, he returned to *Blackhawk* in 1946 and continued to draw it until 1953.

After leaving Quality in the 1950s, Crandall applied his fine-line technique to several highly acclaimed EC "New Trend" and "New Direction" stories, features for the educational *Treasure Chest,* and material for Charles Biro's ill-fated *Tops*—a forerunner of today's black-and-white magazines.

In the 1960s, Crandall collaborated with George Evans to produce several outstanding *Classics Illustrated*

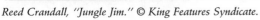
Reed Crandall, "Jungle Jim." © King Features Syndicate.

comics, and he later drew for Gold Key's *Twilight Zone* (1961-1965), for Tower's *Thunder Agents* (1965), and for the comic book version of *Flash Gordon* (1965, 1969). His best later comic book work was for the black-and-white magazines of the Warren Publishing Company. Unfettered by the poor coloring and smaller page size of standard comic books, Crandall's work for Warren during the middle and late 1960's was outstanding in its detail. Always superbly drawn and flawlessly shaded, his horror and "weird" stories were among the best supernatural tales ever produced.

Crandall also drew a lavish, highly acclaimed series of illustrated Edgar Rice Burroughs books for Canaveral Press in the 1960s. Using pen and ink, dry brush, and wash techniques, Crandall's renditions of the Burroughs characters have become classics in a field dominated by artistic giants like Frank Frazetta, J. Allen St. John, Hal Foster, and Burne Hogarth. In later years ill health forced him to give up drawing; he died in 1982.

J.B.

CRANE, ROYSTON CAMPBELL (1901-1977) Roy Crane, whose *Wash Tubbs* daily strip did much to revolutionize graphic and narrative content in the American comic strip, and whose *Captain Easy* Sunday page was one of the half dozen finest color-strips, was born Royston Campbell Crane in Abilene, Texas, on November 22, 1901. Digging oilfield pipelines and jerking sodas while he went to school, the young Roy drew continuously as he grew up in nearby Sweetwater. Stints at the University of Texas and Hardin-Simmons bored him, and Crane struck out for adventure in the Southwest, rail-riding, panhandling, and even working now and again; then he went to sea. Finally he settled in New York, after taking a correspondence course in cartooning, and landed a job as assistant to H. T. Webster on the old *New York World* in the early 1920s. Trying a gag panel series called *Music to the Ear* with United Features, he sold it to two small papers at a dollar each—and went over to the local NEA office to take another flyer. Here the visiting syndicate head turned out to be the same man who managed the correspondence course Crane had taken—and was not averse to hiring a former pupil. He liked a strip notion Crane had built around a curly-headed little fellow named George Washington Tubbs II, and told Crane to shape the character up a bit and put him to work in a grocery store, perhaps, so the working public would like the strip. Crane was too delighted to do more than murmur that the young hero of NEA's *Salesman Sam* strip was also working in a grocery store, but his new boss failed to see why a good idea shouldn't be used twice, and that was that: the *Wash Tubbs* strip was born, and the first episode, a splash layout about Wash, appeared in many NEA papers on April 21, 1924.

By 1929, the popularity of *Wash Tubbs* (and Harold Gray's *Little Orphan Annie*, also a pioneer in bloodcurdling suspense) had sparked numerous imitators, from *Tailspin Tommy* to *Bobby Thatcher*, and Crane had to hustle to keep up his lead. Then Crane launched his stunning display of technical and imaginative virtuosity, the *Captain Easy* Sunday page, on July 30, 1933. The Sunday *Easy* capped Crane's work, and it has never been surpassed for sheer graphic verve and narrative movement, although Alex Raymond's early *Flash Gordon* equalled it for a while. Easy, based on the face and easy movement of Crane's brother-in-law, was

Roy Crane, self-caricature.

never as nationally famed as he should have been, because of the syndication policies of NEA, which preferred to move its strips in packages to small-town dailies, often lacking Sunday editions. So, when Crane moved to Orlando, Florida, in the summer of 1938, he was already considering the line of action that resulted in his outright ownership of his own strip and its appearance in the largest-circulation Sunday papers in the country.

This strip was *Buz Sawyer*, a swift-paced, wartime story of a navy aviator, which Crane launched (owning all rights) via King Features on Monday, November 2, 1943. The Sunday half-page started on November 23, focusing on Sawyer's gunner, Roscoe Sweeney. (NEA kept *Tubbs* and *Easy* going with Crane's understudy, Leslie Turner.) Within a few weeks, it was obvious that Crane had another hit—one that would keep going in hundreds of newspapers for more than four decades. In the 1960s an ulcer condition forced Crane to give up most of the *Buz* work, so that the strip of this period lacked much of the pictorial and narrative zest that characterized it through its first 20 years. But the story line remained entertaining, and the art retained the fundamental characteristics of Crane's work, and it continued to be one of the nation's outstanding adventure strips.

Full of accomplishments, honors, and awards (winner of both a Reuben and a silver plaque from the National Cartoonists' Society; the U.S. Navy Gold Medal for Distinguished Service; U.S. Navy War Correspondent Citation; the Silver Lady award for Outstanding Cartoonist of the Year, 1961, etc.), Crane lived in the lake area of Orlando on an estate of several acres, working with Ed Granberry, creative writing instructor at Rollins College, on the *Buz* story line, and the talented Harry Schlensker on the strip's art. He died on July 8, 1977, in Orlando, Florida.

B.B.

Guido Crepax, "Anita." © Crepax.

CRAVERI, SEBASTIANO (1899-1973) Italian cartoonist, born March 30, 1899, in Turin. His middle-class family sent him to study the classics, but when Italy entered World War I, Sebastiano Craveri was drafted into the army. After the war he worked at a publishing house but quit after a short time to devote himself fully to painting and newspaper reporting; from 1930 to 1934 he contributed humorous sketches to the weekly magazine *Radiocorriere*. In 1931 the first of his humanized animals appeared in the color pages of the *Giornale dei Fanciulli*; in 1932 he also drew a comic feature for the publication *Doposcuola, Porcellino* (whose hero was a little pig that had previously appeared in the *Giornale*). When this publication folded, Craveri, under the pen name "Pin-Tin," edited, wrote, and drew *Quidi*, a magazine for young children published by SEI (1935).

In 1937 Sebastiano Craveri started his long collaboration with the Catholic weekly *Il Vittorioso*, for which he created a great number of animal strips: *Zoo Film, Zoolandia*, the comic adventures of *Pinco Pallino, Giraffone, Tony*, not to mention uncounted stories without permanent characters, fables, and topical illustrations. In 1939 he created a weekly feature for *L'Aspirante* titled *Avventure di Spinarello, Moccolino e Zaratustra*.

In addition to his work for *Il Vittorioso* (which lasted until 1962) Craveri also wrote and drew for the weekly *Corrierino*, in which he created more animal strips: *Buffo, Orsetto* ("Little Bear"), and *Pentonino* (1946-49); for *La Bussola* of Turin (1946); *Famiglia Cristiana* (1953), *Il Giornalino* (1955-66), and others.

During his long career Craveri also illustrated books, worked in advertising, and designed stage plays. His works were all directed at children, for whom he wrote very simple stories illustrated with strongly delineated drawings.

In 1969 a grave illness consigned Craveri to absolute immobility, and he died in Rome on October 25, 1973. His drawings, collected by the "craverian" Mario Giubbolini, are now being reprinted in totality by Camillo Conti.

G.B.

CREPAX, GUIDO (1933-   ) Italian artist and illustrator, born in 1933 in Milan. After high school, Guido Crepax attended the School of Architecture of the University of Milan, from which he graduated in 1958, while supporting himself in the meantime as an illus-trator of book covers and record jackets. Crepax started his cartooning career in 1959 with drawings for the medical magazine *Tempo Medico*. In 1965 he was one of the first contributors to the newly created comic monthly *Linus*, with a fantastic strip called *Neutron*, about an artist with superhuman faculties. From the strip there evolved Crepax's most celebrated creation, *Valentina* (Valentina was at first a girl-reporter playing a secondary role in *Neutron*).

Valentina brought Crepax fame and recognition, and he embarked on new strip creations: *L'Astronave Pirata* ("The Pirate Spaceship," 1968), a strip midway between science fiction and satire, which was published in book form by Rizzoli; *La Casa Matta* ("The Mad House," 1969), a sadomasochistic fantasy published in the magazine *New Kent*, about a young girl in a nightmarish universe; *La Calata di Mac Similiano* ("The Fall of Mac Similiano," also in 1969), a war story and an allegory on American intervention in Viet Nam; the epic *Alexandre Newski*, and two other series about victimized young girls (a theme evidently dear to Crepax's heart): *Belinda* and *Bianca* (the latter an elaborate reworking of the themes of *La Casa Matta*).

At the same time Crepax has been able to pursue his career as an illustrator for books and magazines, and in 1970 he successfully branched out into animation with a series of animated cartoons for Italian television.

Called by some "the Raphael of the comics," Guido Crepax is one of the most controversial, as well as one of the most fascinating, comic strip artists. His universe is unmistakably and uniquely his own, a universe of violence and sex, where innocence is constantly outraged and vice often rewarded. Crepax's line is a model of elegant decadence, and his inspiration places him in the ranks of the "écrivains maudits," alongside the Marquis de Sade and Baudelaire.

While sporadically continuing to draw the adventures of Valentina, Crepax in the last 20 years has devoted much of his time to illustrating the classics of erotic literature, from the Marquis de Sade's *Justine* and *Juliette* to Pauline Réage's *Story of O* by way of Sacher-Masoch's *Venus in Furs*. He has also given a decidedly erotic treatment to such works as *Dr. Jekyll and Mr. Hyde* and *The Turn of the Screw*. The artist has become quite popular in the United States in recent years, and many of his works have been translated into English as well as other languages.

Widely imitated, although never equalled, Guido Crepax has proved himself, within the space of a few years, as not only one of the great masters of the comic idiom, but also as an innovator whose experiments have already revolutionized the comic form, both in structure and in content.

M.H.

CRIMEBUSTER (U.S.) One of the strangest ironies of American comic books of the 1940s was that although the overwhelming majority of readers were children, the overwhelming majority of characters they read about were adult heroes. The few "kid" heroes that did appear were stereotyped: the "Kid Group" of diverse racial background and social status (i.e., the Boy Commandos and Daredevil's Little Wise Guys); the "kid" spin-off of the adult hero (i.e., Captain Marvel Jr.); or the ingratiatory sidekick who was forgettable (i.e., Robin or Bucky). Two features broke away from the mold, however. Street and Smith had great success with *Supersnipe*—which told the story of Koppy McFadden, the boy with the most comic books in the world (all Street and Smith titles, of course)—and Lev Gleason was phenomenally successful with *Crimebuster*.

Created by artists/writers/editors Charles Biro and Bob Wood for the April 1942 issue of *Boy Comics* (number three), *Crimebuster* told the story of Chuck Chandler, an orphan whose parents had been killed by Iron Jaw, the head of all Nazi agents in America. Vowing revenge—it was the thing to do in the 1940s—Chuck adopted the Crimebuster identity, complete with red and white costume and a delightful monkey sidekick named Squeeks. (Only the *Star Spangled Kid*, a National strip, sported a kid hero and an adult sidekick.)

Almost all the stories in the series were written by the innovative and unpredictable Charles Biro. His stories were sometimes overwritten, but they always exuded a tremendous amount of reality and social concern. *Crimebuster* was not a strip about a midget masquerading as a child hero; Chuck Chandler was a child hero and the readers apparently accepted and liked the concept. Artistically, the strip was graced with many fine illustrators. Besides the flexible Biro (who handled art chores sporadically between 1942 and 1956), Joe Kubert (1955), George Tuska (1954-1955), Dan Barry (1947-1948), Frank Bolle (1953), Bob Fujitani (1950), and Norman Maurer (1943-1953) also contributed to the feature.

Crimebuster outlasted many of his older costumed compatriots, appearing in *Boy Comics* until March 1956's 119th issue. The last nine issues carried the name *Chuck Chandler, Crimebuster* because the character had abandoned his costume. The Crimebuster character also appeared in text stories in the *Daredevil* book from 1942 until 1952.

J.B.

CRIME SMASHER *see Spy Smasher.*

CROSBY, PERCY LEO (1891-1964) When Percy Leo Crosby was the age and size of the 10-year-old hero of his famed *Skippy* comic strip, he used to sit on the curb of a street in the Brooklyn neighborhood where he was born on December 8, 1891, and draw comic pictures in the summer dust with a crooked branch. He forgot little of his boisterous, lower-middle-class Irish boy-

hood, and much of it surfaced for decades in the ragamuffin kid strips he drew from the first moment a newspaper editor let him sketch out an idea of his own. This happened on the old *New York World*, where he received his first job as a strip cartoonist after he had finished high school and gotten work on two other papers briefly as a news artist at 19. Gifted with a great natural talent for easy handling of line and mass, and an amusing if often quirky sense of humor, the young Crosby quickly discovered on the *World* that the kid antics that amused him also delighted his editor and the paper's readers, and he moved from one child-oriented strip to another, fielding such titles as *Baby-ettes*, *Toddles*, and *Beany and the Gang* in the early 1910s. In 1915, the McClure Syndicate hired him to do a new strip, *The Clancy Kids*, one of whose title characters, Timmie Clancy, was the prototype of Skippy. Crosby turned out this strip with increasing success until World War I intervened, and he went overseas with the American Expeditionary Force.

Returning to active cartoon work in 1919, Crosby freelanced for many markets, notably the old *Life* humor magazine, where he sold a comic strip called *Skippy* by one-page installments. This first-rate showcase for Crosby's talents got him many newspaper offers, and he began his own syndication of *Skippy* in the mid-1920s. The strip's popularity led Hearst to make him several offers, and finally Crosby accepted King Features distribution of his daily and Sunday feature in 1928.

Skippy, like *Peanuts*, was much more than a kid strip, however, and it often reflected its creator's ardent right-wing political biases in amusing ways. More eccentric and strident statements appeared over Crosby's signature in full-page newspaper advertisements in New York and elsewhere, however, as well as in a series of bizarre books he published himself, such as *A Cartoonist's Philosophy* (1931) and *Three Cheers For the Red, Red, and Red* (1936). Needless to say, the sales of these curious works were minor compared to those of Crosby's illustrated *Skippy* novels and strip collections (such as *Skippy, Always Belittlin'*, etc.) in the 1930s. An adaptation of the strip for film starring Jackie Cooper (*Skippy*, 1931) made Cooper a star and *Skippy* an even

Percy Crosby.

more widely known character than Crosby's strip had made him.

Crosby developed his artistry in many mediums, from watercolor to oil painting to sculpture, and he had many acclaimed exhibits of his wide talents in the 1930s and 1940s. In 1942, however, Crosby's health began to fail, and he had increased trouble in maintaining control of his lines (a difficulty strikingly apparent in a number of his last published episodes). Refusing to hire a ghost for the strip, he withdrew it from King Features and formally retired from commercial work in 1943. Married three times, he lived in continuing ill health with his third wife of 1940, Carolyn, until she died in 1960. Finally death came to Crosby too, in New York City on his 73rd birthday, 1964. (According to Jerry Robinson's biography *Skippy and Percy Crosby*, he had spent the last 15 years of his life in a mental institution.)

B.B.

CROSS, STANLEY GEORGE (1888-1977) Australian cartoonist, born in 1888 in Los Angeles, California. His English parents, who had married in Australia, returned there in 1892 and settled in Perth. A brilliant schoolboy scholar, Stan Cross left school at the age of 16 and joined the Railways Department as a cadet clerk and, a few years later, enrolled for an art course at Perth Technical School. In 1912, he resigned from his job to spend a year in London studying art at St. Martins School and other studios—during which time his cartoons were accepted and published by *Punch*. He returned to Perth, where he contributed freelance drawings to the *Western Mail* and the *Sunday Times*.

In 1919, Robert Clyde Packer, the managing director of *Smith's Weekly*, induced Cross to join the staff of the new newspaper being founded in Sydney. For *Smith's*, he originated Australia's first and longest-running newspaper strip, *The Potts* (originally called *You and Me*), which he handled from 1919 until late 1939, when the strip was taken over by Jim Russell. For the same paper he created *Smith's Vaudevillians* in 1928, which also passed to Russell. He also drew a huge volume of single-panel cartoons—one of which ("For godsake stop laughing—this is serious!") has been hailed as the most famous in the history of Australian comic art. During his 20 years with *Smith's*, Stan Cross earned the reputation of the finest draftsman ever to work on that paper and produced a great deal of the work that made him the leading black-and-white cartoonist in Australia.

In 1940, Stan Cross received an offer from Sir Keith Murdock of the *Melbourne Herald* to leave *Smith's* and create a new daily strip. He accepted, but the new domestic strip, *The Winks*, was not successful. Cross then transferred two of the characters from this strip and featured them in a new daily, *Wally and the Major*, which proved to be an outstanding success. He continued to draw this strip until his retirement in 1970, when the strip was inherited by Carl Lyon, who had been his assistant for a number of years. It was during his stay with the *Melbourne Herald* that Stan Cross became the highest-paid journalist in Australia. He died in June 1977.

Stan Cross was the pioneer of the Australian comic strip. His work reflected his superb comic sense, while his expressions and characterizations were always perfect for the never-ending variety of types that inhabited his drawings. His bold and distinctive pen style showed great skill in building up his forms and tones.

His work was influenced by the artists of both *The Bulletin* and *Smith's Weekly* eras—including Cecil Hartt, whose traditional humor he admired, and Norman Lindsay, whose excellence in comic art he came close to equalling during the 1930s. Over the years, he made himself an authority on such subjects as economics, social credit, soil conservation, and grammar—the latter interest being responsible for an almost total absence of slang in his *Wally and the Major*.

J.R.

CROWLEY, WENDELL (1921-1970) American comic book writer and editor, born September 1921. After attending the University of Oklahoma, Crowley began his comic book career in 1941, when he took a summer job as a "gofer" in Jack Binder's art studio. He quickly moved up to writing, however, and began turning out scripts for books the Binder studio packaged for comic publishers. Among Crowley's stories was material for *Captain Battle* (Lev Gleason), *Black Owl* (Prize), *Flying Dutchman* (Hillman), and the whole range of Fawcett features like *Captain Marvel* and *Bulletman*. Crowley eventually became the shop's editor, a position that entailed considerable business work and art directorial decisions. In 1943, however, he moved over to become the editor of the Beck-Constanza studios, which was then primarily responsible for the Captain Marvel family of books.

In 1944, Crowley elected to go with Fawcett as their general editor and assumed control of not only Captain Marvel and family, but of the whole Fawcett line of comics. But his best work was done on the Marvel family, and he is regarded as the best of the Captain's many editors. "He was totally committed to the comic medium," artist/historian Jim Steranko wrote in 1972. "His enthusiasm showed in his work."

Indeed, much of the finest material in the Marvel lore appeared under Crowley's hand. He was instrumental in the creation of the "Society of Evil" serial that eventually brought about the creation of the delightful but deadly Mr. Mind, the world's evilest villain, who just happened to be an intelligent worm from another planet. And Crowley was editor when Mr. Tawny, the talking tiger, was introduced. Crowley was also financially good for Fawcett, as *Captain Marvel Adventures* garnered its best sales reports with him as editor. Crowley finally left as Fawcett's editor during 1950, and Captain Marvel and company faded away several years later.

Crowley made only one brief return to comics. In 1967, he teamed up with longtime *Captain Marvel* writer Otto Binder and artist C. C. Beck to create *Fatman, The Human Flying Saucer*. It was an unabashed and nostalgic imitation of *Captain Marvel*, and Crowley functioned as the editor, but the title lasted only three issues.

Crowley died in February 1970.

J.B.

CRUIKSHANK, GEORGE (1792-1878) English cartoonist, illustrator, and engraver, born in London on September 27, 1792, into a highly artistic family. George's father, Isaac Cruikshank (1756-1810), was a renowned caricaturist, and his older brother Isaac Robert (1790-1856) was at one time more famous as an illustrator than the younger George. A sister, Eliza, and a nephew, Percy, also added artistic distinction to this extraordinarily gifted family.

George Cruikshank.

George Cruikshank was the last cartoonist of note to follow in the footsteps of Rowlandson and Gillray, and provided the link between the 18th-century school of violently contrasted etchings and the realistic style of *Punch* wood engravings. He started his career as a cartoonist for the satiric monthly *The Scourge* and also illustrated several newspaper serials. In 1823 he became equally famous as a book illustrator, but his style remained rooted in caricature. He was called the perfect illustrator for Dickens (and the appeal of his illustrations contributed in no small measure to the novelist's popular success), but he also illustrated *Don Quixote*, *Robinson Crusoe*, *John Gilpin's Ride*, and the brothers Grimm's fairy tales. Cruikshank added painting to his already numerous activities in 1853, and he remained creative until his death on February 1, 1878.

George Cruikshank continued and consolidated the work of the early English cartoonists, contributing further innovations to the medium, such as the dynamic use of balloons (he is particularly noted for his invention of the interlocking balloons to mark a rapid-fire exchange of repartees and *bons mots*—a convention still widely used in satiric strips, vide *Mad* magazine). This alone should give Cruikshank a place in the pantheon of the patron saints of the comic medium, somewhere between Rowlandson and Töpffer.

M.H.

CRUMB, ROBERT (1943-   ) In any compendium of this nature, there is always someone who does not fit the strictures of the established pattern. Robert Crumb is such a writer and artist. One hesitates before writing anything about him or his characters, mainly because so much of his work consists of raw, uncensored, unfettered fantasies drawn and written on paper. None of Crumb's work was done for "art's sake," and most of it was done simply for fun, and not to make money. Additionally, Crumb the human being is as elusive as his work. As Mark Estren writes in his underground comix history, "no two people come away from him with the same impression—he seems to change his opinion of himself almost every hour."

Born in Philadelphia on August 30, 1943, Crumb never had any formal art training, and as a teenager, he and his brother began drawing a series of single-copy comic books, usually relying heavily on funny animal material. It was here he developed Fritz the Cat, one of his most important characters, a con-man cat who more resembled humans than the humans Crumb would later depict. In 1962, Crumb moved to Cleveland and began drawing for the American Greeting Card company. In 1964, he married and began traveling and contributing to other outlets. He did several pieces for *Help!*, an offbeat humor book published by James Warren and edited by Harvey Kurtzman. He also began contributing heavily to the blossoming underground newspaper market, which was headed by *Yarrowstalks* (Philadelphia) and the *East Village Other*. He settled down in San Francisco in 1966, about the time the city's Haight-Ashbury section was becoming the home of the "hippie" movement. But, while Crumb might have wanted to be a hippie, he was not. He was an introvert, different not only from the flower children who were his neighbors, but also from the flock of other underground cartoonists who were making the Bay area a hotbed of underground publishing.

Although the underground comix business had "officially" started when Jack Jaxon published *God Nose* in Texas in 1963, it was Crumb's *Zap #0 and Zap #1* (1967) and his two issues of *Snatch* (1968) that began the modern movement as it was now known. Crumb never published his own books, however; Don Donahue and Charlie Plymell were instrumental in the distribution and publishing of the *Zaps* and *Snatchs*, and after that, Crumb went from underground publisher to underground publisher. His main concern was never money; it seemed he was more interested in working out his fantasies ("The pleasure is ours, folks!" Crumb told his audience in *Snatch* number two, "we really like drawing dirty cartoons!"), having fun, and giving his readers enjoyment. Over the years, Crumb's work has been in dozens of underground publications, including *Uneeda*; *Big Ass*; and *Motor City Comics*, among many others.

The body of Crumb's work can be divided into two distinct groups. The first is his overtly sexual work. Often indulging every possible fantasy, Crumb's work was shockingly explicit for the late 1960s. Each and every story centered around lovemaking, or kinky variations of it. Crumb pictured himself as an unabashed sex craver who would do anything for any woman. This sexual material was roundly criticized by some (mainly by feminists who complained that almost all his women were stereotypic sex objects; they were right, and even Lenore Goldberg, Crumb's feminist character, eventually was shown to be a closet "Jewish mother"). Crumb was censored by others (Viking Press' *R. Crumb's Head Comix* was unusually explicit for the book market, but they drew the line at Crumb's singing vagina and censored that panel). And occasionally his work led to criminal prosecution (Crumb's celebrated incest story in *Zap* number four caused it to be prosecuted in New York before Judge Joel Tyler in the famed "Zap Obscenity Trial").

Many famous characters came out of Crumb's sexual lore, however: Whiteman, a typical sexually repressed man of modern-day America; Angelfood McSpade, an African amazon, who was a totally sexual and unthinking child of nature; and the "yetti," another Amazonian, hair-covered "woman" who

Snarf #6 cover, Robert Crumb. © Robert Crumb.

eventually captured Whiteman and took him for her lover.

Crumb's other school of work was more philosophical, although not without a healthy dose of sexual fantasy. Out of those works came characters like Mr. Natural, the con-man guru who became a symbol of the younger generation; Flakey Foont, Natural's repressed, hung-up disciple who will probably grow up into Whiteman; Schuman the Human, and many more.

Crumb's art style has traces of many of the old masters, including Segar, Wolverton, Barks, and Herriman. It is sometimes sloppy, rarely cinematic, but always

natural and powerful. It totally changed the traditional standards of "good comic art," and eventually became an art style as recognizable as Peter Max's or Art Déco.

In short, Crumb, a living anachronism in personal life, an introvert outdone only by Howard Hughes, completely changed American mores in the 1960s and early 1970s. He has since sharply curtailed his art production and moved to a secluded farm in California.

J.B.

In the 1980s Crumb edited his own magazine, *Weirdo*, to which he contributed a number of original stories. He also wrote and drew numerous autobio-

Howard Cruse, "Death." © Howard Cruse.

graphical anecdotes of diminishing wit and interest for different publications. The already shaky underground press almost collapsed at the end of the decade, and in 1990 the artist moved to France with his wife Aline Kominsky. The couple was the subject of a 1995 award-winning documentary tersely called *Crumb*. His last work of note has been the 1996 *Kafka*: in it writer David Mairowitz adapted a number of the Czech author's most famous stories (including *The Trial* and *Metamorphosis*), some of which Crumb simply illustrated and others he told in comic-strip fashion.

M.H.

CRUSE, HOWARD (1944-   ) An American cartoonist and illustrator, born on May 2, 1944, in Birmingham, Alabama, Howard Cruse, the son of a Baptist minister, was fascinated by the comics from earliest childhood. "When he was 6 years old," Clarke Stallworth wrote in the *Birmingham News*, "the preacher's son drew his first comic book. It was an adaptation of *Alice in Wonderland,* and little Howard Cruse showed the crude drawings to his parents Clyde and Irma Cruse." With the encouragement of his parents

Cruse continued to draw comics in his spare time, while pursuing a more conventional career as a staff artist and illustrator.

In the 1970s Cruse's comic-strip work started appearing regularly in the pages of underground comic publications such as *Yellow Dog, Snarf,* and *Dope Comix;* he gained national recognition with *Barefootz*, a strip about a naive (and, of course, barefoot) Southern boy, which appeared from 1973 to 1979 in a number of underground and college newspapers. Moving to New York City in 1977, he enjoyed a brief stint as art director of the science-fiction magazine *Starlog*. He came into his own as a comics creator in *Gay Comix* (of which he was the founding editor) with such stories as "Billy Goes Out" which, he said in 1985, "got more response . . . than anything else I've done." From there he went on to develop more features in the same vein, including *Wendel*, which appeared in the pages of the gay magazine *The Advocate* from 1983 to 1989.

Cruse has also contributed a number of comic strips, cartoons, and illustrations to magazines as diverse as *Playboy, Heavy Metal,* and the *Village Voice*. It was with the publication in 1995 of *Stuck Rubber Baby*, a poi-

"Cucciolo," Rino Anzi. © Edizione Alpe.

gnant coming of age (and coming out of the closet) graphic novel set in the South against the backdrop of the civil rights struggle, that Cruse garnered his greatest critical acclaim, along with many commendations and awards.

M.H.

CUBITUS (Belgium) *Cubitus* was created in 1968 for the weekly magazine *Tintin* by the Belgian cartoonist Dupa (Luc Dupanloup).

Looking somewhat like a huge ball of down, Cubitus is a dog who lives in a dilapidated house—in the company of a moth-eaten retired sailor named Semaphore. Cubitus' life would be idyllic were it not for a number of nuisances like the neighbors' cat Senechal; a bothersome (and sports-crazy) phantom who had decided to take up residence in Semaphore's beaten-up motorcycle; and the mysterious Isidore, whose elusive presence sometimes disturbs the canine's generally placid digestion.

"Cubitus," Dupa (Luc Dupanloup). © Editions du Lombard.

When left to himself, Cubitus turns out to be a day-dreamer (not unlike Schulz's Snoopy), but his dreams display a peculiar, put-down quality. Whether impersonating Humphrey Bogart or James Bond, Cubitus always manages to remain true to his old self. The most hilarious gags, however, have Cubitus reinterpreting old fairy tales such as "Red Riding Hood" or "Puss in Boots" in a devastating parody usually ending in mayhem.

Dupa's humor, which is unpredictable, fast, and loony, coupled with his easygoing but accurate drawing line, made *Cubitus* into one of the best European gag strips of recent years. It has been reprinted in paperback and hardbound form, and there has also been a *Cubitus* animated cartoon. In 1989 the roly-poly dog even got his own magazine; and in 1990 a series of animated *Cubitus* shorts made in Japan aired on French television.

M.H.

CUCCIOLO (Italy) Around 1940 publisher Giuseppe Caregaro and cartoonist Rino Anzi got together and conceived two new characters: Cucciolo and Beppe. In the beginning these were two little dogs in the Walt Disney tradition. At the end of World War II Cucciolo and Beppe were completely altered and became fully human. This operation proved successful; after a trial balloon the publisher decided to issue a pocket-size comic book featuring the lead character. On December 22, 1951, the first issue of *Cucciolo* (dated January 1, 1952) hit the newsstands.

Some stylistic changes had also taken place in the meantime: in the late 1940s Giorgio Rebuffi had taken over the feature and given it its current graphic line. Some other talented cartoonists assisted Rebuffi over the years: Umberto Manfrin, Tiberio Colantuoni, Motta, etc. Starting in 1959 Pugacioff the steppe wolf (wolfski!) was one character that became very popular with the reader, and in the 1960s he eclipsed Cucciolo as the star of the show.

The *Cucciolo* comic book has also revealed a number of other outstanding cartoonists. For instance, Luciano Bottaro's *Pepito* first appeared in *Cucciolo*, as did Egidio Gherlizza's *Serafino*; Rebuffi also created *Il Sceriffo Fox* (continued afterwards by Colantuoni and Maria Luisa Uggetti), and Antonio Terenghi produced two series, *Gionni e Geppina* and *Caribu*, in the pages of the comic book. Among the writers working for the publication were Roberto Renzi, Attilio Mazzanti, Carlo Chendi, Franco Frescura, Roberto Catalano, and Giorgio Rebuffi.

Cucciolo continues, strong as ever. At first monthly, it was changed to a fortnightly, but it is once more issued on a monthly basis. A good many of the *Cucciolo* features have been published in other European countries, especially France.

C.B.

CULLIFORD, PIERRE (1928-1992) Belgian cartoonist, born in Brussels on June 25, 1928, of a Belgian mother and an English father. After a brief stay at the Brussels Academy of Fine Arts, Pierre Culliford started working at the age of 17 in an animated cartoon studio, alongside such future luminaries of the comic strip as Franquin, Jije, and Morris. In 1947 Culliford created *Johan* (under the nom-de-plume Peyo), his first comic strip, about a young page in medieval times, for the Belgian daily *La Derniere Heure*; it was followed the next year by *Pied Tendre* ("Tender Foot"), the story of a little Indian, which he did for the Boy Scouts' publication *Mowgli*.

In 1954 Peyo (to give him his chosen name) started his long collaboration with the comic weekly *Spirou*, to which he brought his first creation, retitled *Johan et Pirlouit* (Pirlouit was Johan's bumbling companion). From this strip evolved *Les Schtroumpfs* (1957), Peyo's most durable and endearing creation. In 1960 *Benoit Brisefer* made its appearance, written by Peyo and drawn by Will—about a little boy endowed with superhuman strength—followed a few years later by *Poussy* (a kitten), which Peyo created for the women's magazine *Bonnes Soirees* (eventually *Poussy* also ended up in the pages of *Spirou*).

In the 1960's Peyo assisted on the series of animated cartoons adapted from *Les Schtroumpfs*, and he has also done illustration and advertising work. Peyo is the recipient of several cartooning awards, mostly for his work on *Les Schtroumpfs*.

One of the most original of European cartoonists, Pierre Culliford is also a storyteller full of imagination and fancy. His work sets him apart from his contemporaries, and while his style has been widely imitated in Europe, he is one of the few European creators who has been able to construct an entirely original comic strip vision of the world.

In the 1980s the Schtroumpfs enjoyed phenomenal worldwide success, especially in the United States, where they became known as the Smurfs. Animated cartoons, comic books, dolls, toys, and other merchandise soon followed, and in later years Peyo devoted most of his time to overseeing his growing corporate empire. After his death in Brussels in 1992, his son Thierry Culliford took over the family interests.

M.H.

CUORE GARIBALDINO (Italy) Like every other Italian publication, the comic weekly *L'Intrepido* had to close down all its American features (which included *Connie* and *Gordon, Soldier of Fortune*) on orders from the Fascist government in 1938. The publishers, the brothers Del Duca, then decided to concentrate their reinforced national production on one theme: the melodramatic story, of which they became the acknowledged masters.

One such novel was *Cuore Garibaldino* ("Garibaldian Heart"), a title full of patriotic and nationalistic connotations, Garibaldi being Italy's foremost independence hero. Begun in 1939, the story, subtly propagandistic, was written by Ferdinando Vichi and illustrated by Carlo Cossio.

The narrative opens in 19th-century South America where Leardo Stigli, a Garibaldi supporter and foreign agent, falls in love with the beautiful Italian immigrant girl, Stella Natoli. Their love is thwarted by the cruel and unfaithful Carmensita and by the despotic governor of the colony in which they live. The Austrian Captain Stern aids and abets them in their vicious deeds.

These patriotic adventures unfold at length, generation after generation until the present day, with every melodramatic device milked in the process. After the Italian capitulation, the grandchildren of Leardo and Stella make a quick about-face and, as the dialogue indicates, they now stand ready to fight "the Teutonic invaders and their Fascist henchmen."

The saga ends with the inevitable triumph of true love. While a terrible strip, *Cuore Garibaldino* is a fascinating document for anyone interested in understanding Italy's troubled modern history.

G.B.

CURLEY HARPER (U.S.) Started as *Curley Harper at Lakespur* on March 31, 1935 (and later shortened to *Curley Harper*), this strip replaced *The Kid Sister* as the top piece to *Tim Tyler's Luck*. It was distributed by King Features Syndicate and signed by Lyman Young (who had several "ghosts" working on it).

Curley Harper was first an athlete at Lakespur College who constantly won championships and other distinctions for his alma mater, often thwarting the schemes of shady game-fixers and corrupt managers in the process. This clean-cut and clean-living all-American later became an investigative reporter, fearlessly exposing graft in high places and fighting rackets and corruption.

During the war Curley found even better use for his talents as the nemesis of German spies, fifth columnists, and Axis saboteurs. After the war he tried to reconvert himself into an insurance investigator, but the kind of hero he personified had gone out of fashion, and his adventures ended in the mid-1940s.

In spite of its limitations, *Curley Harper* is quite an entertaining strip, always competently drawn and well plotted. In its lack of sophistication it is most revealing of some of the American dreams, prejudices, and fears of the 1930s and 1940s.

M.H.

CURLEY KAYOE *see* Joe Jinks.

CURTIS (U.S.) A carefully crafted daily and Sunday comic strip about an inner-city African-American family, *Curtis*, by Ray Billingsley, began syndication by King Features on October 3, 1988. This strip followed on the heels of another humor strip by an African-American artist also syndicated by King Features. From mid-1970 until 1988, *Quincy*, a strip about an 11-year-old boy living with his grandmother, was drawn by Ted Shearer. Two years after the death of Shearer and the end of *Quincy*, *Curtis* appeared.

As a 12-year-old living in New York City's Harlem area, Ray Billingsley came to the attention of an editor

"Curtis," Ray Billingsley. © King Features Syndicate.

at *Kids* magazine and worked as a cartoonist from then on. Born in 1957, Billingsley graduated from New York City's High School of Music and Art and was awarded a full scholarship to the School of Visual Arts in New York. He also completed a Walt Disney animation internship. At age 21 his first feature, *Lookin' Fine*, was syndicated for a time by United Features Syndicate. Between *Lookin' Fine* and the first appearance of *Curtis*, Billingsley did extensive freelance work.

As an African-American who grew up in an urban environment, Billingsley draws on his own childhood experiences for inspiration for the characters in *Curtis*. His own parents are models for Greg and Diane Wilkins. Rounding out the family are Curtis and his nosy eight-year-old brother Barry. Like most 11-year-olds, Curtis's life revolves around home, family, school, and a series of inner-city perils not found in family comic strips situated in the suburbs.

Billingsley has stated that his goals in *Curtis* are to make his readers laugh, to present a realistic day-to-day view of urban African-American family life, and to encourage inner-city children. He has succeeded in all three goals. Living in a rented apartment in the city, the Wilkins family is hardworking and religious. Two neighborhood fixtures, the church with Reverend Woodward and the local barbershop with proprietor Gunther, are prominently featured.

At home Curtis and his father constantly bicker over Curtis's love of loud rap music and his father's love of cigarettes. Barry, the devilish brother, does his best to get Curtis in trouble, but it is evident that deep down the brothers love one another. Curtis's mother is the glue that holds the family together.

At school, Curtis has yet to appreciate his teacher's message of the importance of education. He is wrapped up in a puppy love triangle. He longs for the spoiled, aloof Michelle, who knows that she is way too cool for Curtis, while fending off the advances of tomboy Chutney. His best friend is Gunk, a white boy in a student exchange program from Flyspeck Island, part of the northeastern tip of the Bermuda Triangle. Derrick, the school bully, represents the underbelly of inner-city life.

In his standard four-panel dailies, Billingsley uses as much situational humor as gags. Situations involving drug abuse, crime, and the problems of the inner city are handled in a realistic fashion. *Curtis* is a funny strip, but it mixes in hard social commentary with great success.

B.C.

CUTO (Spain) The most famous character in the history of Spanish comics saw the light of print in 1935, in the pages of the comic magazine *Boliche*, under the title of *Cuto, Gurripato y Camarilla*; it was a series of gag strips, without continuity, and its success was scant (it was discontinued after a short run). Its creator, Jesus Blasco, in this first comic strip effort, decided to revive the character, this time without his battery of friends, for the comic weekly *Chicos* (November 27, 1940). With its small boy-hero and a style that was to improve with each passing year, *Cuto* soon became the main staple of the magazine, reaching unheard-of heights of popularity. A newspaper-boy in his first adventure, he converted soon afterwards into a roving adventurer, who lived adventures in the Orient, the American West, the Pacific Islands, and the Egypt of the pharaohs. He was equally at ease among the New York skyscrapers or the snowfields of Alaska.

Cuto's appearance also changed with the years, and he went from young boy to young man, remaining always an adolescent afterwards. With increasing frequency he could be found in the company of his girl-friend Mary, with whom he shared soft drinks and

"Cuto," Jesus Blasco. © Chicos.

adventures. He was always characterized by his wit, thanks to which he got himself out of the most perilous situations that could be concocted by Jesus Blasco. The author had recourse to all the conventions of the comics to enhance the suspense of his strip. *Cuto* is a highly personal work in which the author never stopped experimenting from the start of the feature, playing with color schemes, innovating in the layouts, and sometimes succeeding in making Cuto a genuine masterpiece.

Cuto was made into a radio program and adapted into novel form and a series of short stories. Beginning in the 1970s, the character appeared in the Portuguese magazine *Jornal do Cuto* and in the Spanish comic weekly *Chito*. It is now no longer published, but the character lives on in countless reprints of the earlier adventures.

L.G.

CYBORG 009 (Japan) *Cyborg 009*, created by Shotarō Ishimori, made its first appearance in the Japanese weekly *Shōnen King* in July 1964. Featuring the exploits of Cyborg 009 and his colleagues (Cyborgs 001 through 008), it soon became the most popular science-fiction strip in Japan.

Initially a half-caste juvenile delinquent who had escaped from prison, Joe Shimamura was captured by the evil Black Ghost, the leader of the world's Merchants of Death, who subjected him to experiments aimed at making him into the perfect soldier of future wars. Reborn as a cyborg, 009 could run at speeds higher than Mach 3, had the strength of a hundred men, and could jump over 100 feet. Cyborg 009 and his colleagues, also endowed with special powers, rebelled against the Black Ghost and blew up his secret base with a nuclear device. The battle between the cyborgs and the Black Ghost then started in earnest.

After having vanquished the Black Ghost, Cyborg 009 and his colleagues found many more enemies to combat: Cyborg 0012 (who was as big as a brick mansion), Cyborg 0013 (who controlled a huge robot by means of brain waves), not to mention the Robot Monster, the One-Eyed Robots, the human Bombs, the Skull, the Giant Monsters created by a mad scientist, and the Giant Warriors. Cyborg 009 and his companions also fought against a human race of the future, and even against the gods themselves.

"Cyborg 009," Shotarō Ishimori. © Shonen King.

Ishimori's most popular and longest-lasting work, *Cyborg 009* was published in *Shōnen King*, of the weekly *Shōnen* magazine, and in the monthly *Bōkenō*, before going on to the monthly *Com*, where it appeared for the last time in November 1970.

Cyborg 009 has inspired a series of TV animated cartoons, as well as a full-length animated feature.

H.K.

DAFFY DUCK (U.S.) *Daffy Duck* was created by Fred ("Tex") Avery for a 1936 *Porky Pig* cartoon, "Porky's Duck Hunt," produced by Leon Schlesinger and released by Warner Brothers. The character was originally called "that darnfool duck" but was named Daffy for his second appearance a year later in "Daffy and Egghead." He quickly became a regular in the Warner Brothers stable of characters, often appearing with Bugs Bunny or Porky Pig in cartoons directed by Frank Tashlin, Robert McKimson, Chuck Jones, Fritz Freleng, and others. In 1951, he joined the other W.B. characters in the *Looney Tunes* and *Merrie Melodies* comic book produced by Western Publishing Company under the Dell logo.

Previously, a duck resembling Daffy had guest-starred in some stories in that comic and a duck named Daffy (but not resembling him in appearance or actions) had appeared in some one-page gags. In 1951, however, the Daffy Duck of the cartoons joined the magazine, guest-starring first in the *Henery Hawk* strip and later as permanent guest star of the *Elmer Fudd* strip, beginning with the November issue of that year. In December 1954, Daffy took over the *Elmer Fudd* strip and began a popular series in *Looney Tunes* until it was discontinued in 1962. Daffy was featured as a zany, crazy duck who delighted in mooching free meals off Elmer Fudd and, later, Porky Pig and Yosemite Sam.

In 1953, Dell also issued a one-shot test issue of *Daffy* in the Dell Color Comics series, number 457. It proved so popular that two more followed before the first issue of *Daffy*, released in April 1955. In 1959, the title was expanded to *Daffy Duck*, and in 1963 the magazine made the transition when Western Publishing Company shifted its books from the Dell logo to Gold Key. The character appeared in all other magazines based on Warner Brothers characters, including a number of *Bugs Bunny* giant specials, *Elmer Fudd*, *The Tasmanian Devil and his Tasty Friends*, *Golden Comics Digest*, *March of Comics*, and the revived *Looney Tunes* book (1975).The *Daffy Duck* comic book ended its run in 1983.

Scripts for *Daffy Duck* were supplied by, among others, Lloyd Turner, Don Christensen, Bob Ogle, Jerry Belson, and Mark Evanier. Most of the artwork was done by Phil DeLara until his death in 1973. Other artists include Jack Manning, Joe Messerli, and John Carey.

M.E.

DAIHEIGENJI (Japan) *Daiheigenji* ("A Boy of the Western Plains") was created by Shigeru Komatsuzaki and made its first appearance in the June 1950 issue of the monthly *Omoshiro Book*.

The strip featured the exploits of Daiheigenji Jim, a 15-year-old western scout whose parents had been killed by the King Hell Gang. Brought up by his father's friend Petousu, Jim became an expert marksman and horse rider. Mounted on his white stallion Bright Moon, Daiheigenji fought against the Apaches, the King Hell Gang, the Wolf Girl, and Red Bear (both of them King Hell's accomplices), with the assistance of Tomahawk Morgan, the mysterious chief of the Chitsupetsu tribe whose weapon was a golden tomahawk, and of the beautiful Cherio. There was also a heroine named Jane who had a mole in the form of a butterfly on her left arm and was a missing person with a prize on her head.

The main theme of *Daiheigenji* was the American pioneer spirit of the frontier. In addition to the excellent stories, *Daiheigenji*'s greatest charm resided in Komatsuzaki's graphic style. His drawings were realistic and minutely documented; his compositions powerful and dramatic. Komatsuzaki made especially good use of the double-page center spread. *Daiheigenji* was the first Western strip born in the postwar era, and its popularity was due in great part to Komatsuzaki's art.

Daiheigenji last appeared in October 1952.

H.K.

DALLIS, NICHOLAS (1911-1991) American psychiatrist and author, born in New York City on December 15, 1911. Dallis' family moved to Glen Cove, Long Island, when he was a young boy, and he was educated in public schools there and at Washington and Jefferson College in Washington, Pennsylvania. He graduated from Temple School of Medicine in 1938 and became a general practitioner near Reading, Pennsylvania. Dallis decided to become a psychiatrist and completed four years of residency at Henry Ford Hospital in Detroit before setting up private practice in Toledo, Ohio.

Dallis always loved comics and drew cartoons for his college newspaper. He developed the idea for a "doctor strip" in 1948, and with the help of Allen Saunders, a Toledo acquaintance, took the concept to Publishers Syndicate. Two artists were engaged: Marvin Bradley and Frank Edgington, and the product, *Rex Morgan, M.D.*, debuted on May 10, 1948.

With its success, Dallis and publishers developed another story-strip, this time based on the legal profession—*Judge Parker*. Dan Heilman was the first artist, succeeded upon his death by his assistant, Harold LeDoux. Further success led to a third collaboration, *Apartment 3-G*, with the art supplied by Alex Kotzky.

Dallis abandoned his psychiatric practice in 1959 as the pressure of writing necessitated the abandonment of medicine. Before his work in comics, Dallis had edited his college newspaper and written periodically for pulp magazines.

The trio of Dallis and his friends Allen Saunders and Elliot Caplin account for the major portion of contemporary story strip production. Dallis exemplifies the conversion of the straight strip from adventure to domestic, soap-opera continuity. His story lines were solid and respectable, although rarely exacting. Dallis' characterizations could be interesting (especially in 3-G) but were seldom as mature and never as versatile as Elliot Caplin's. He died on July 6, 1991, in Scottsdale, Arizona, where he had retired.

It should be noted that Dallis' three strips are relatively healthy survivors in the days of the twilight of the story strip, when many of their straight neighbors are dying.

R.M.

DAMONTE TABORDA, RAUL (1939-1987) An Argentine cartoonist born in Buenos Aires in 1939, Raul Damonte Taborda (better known as "Copi") started his cartooning career in the 1950s in the humor magazine *Tía Vicenta*. He then went to the satirical publication *Cuatro Patas*, before moving to Paris in 1961. There he worked with great success, contributing to such publications as *Bizarre* and *Le Nouvel Observateur*; soon his cartoon pages made him famous throughout Europe.

Copi's distinctive graphic style, his wiggly line, and the situations in which he put his characters became a trademark. His famous chicken, his woman sitting on a chair, and his questioning little girl became known in France, the United States, Italy, and Spain and helped him win the Prize of Black Humor.

In addition to his magazine work, Copi made several animated cartoons and wrote several plays (in which he also acted): *El Día de una Soñadora* ("The Day of a Girl Dreamer"), *Té Inglés* ("English Tea"), *Navidad en Ia Isla de los Pacíficos* ("Christmas on a Pacific Island"), *El Caimán, La Cola del Pescado* ("Fish Tail"), and the comedy in drag, *Eva Perón*. He died of AIDS in Paris on December 14, 1987; his last play, *La Visite Inopportune*, was staged after his death.

L.G.

DAN DARE (G.B.) Daniel MacGregor Dare, Colonel O.U.N. Interplanet Space Fleet, was awarded the Order of the United Nations for leadership in the Venus Expedition of 1996. Born on February 5, 1967, in Manchester, England, and educated at Rossall, he finished Cambridge and Harvard Universities and became a Class 3 Space Pilot by the time he was 20. Two years after a Planetary Exploration Course on the moon, he became Chief Pilot of the I.S.F. at the age of 30. His hobbies are cricket, fencing, riding, painting, and model-making.

The official biography differs slightly from the real one. *Dan Dare*, created by Frank Hampson and the Rev. Marcus Morris, was born on the first and second pages of *Eagle* number one, April 14, 1950. His subtitle, *Pilot of the Future*, narrowly missed being *Chaplain of the Future*; it was first intended as a Christian comic of limited sales. However, publisher Edward Hulton took up the idea and helped Morris and Hampson launch the weekly comic that changed the face of British children's publications.

Dare, with his lightning-jagged eyebrows, was pure invention, but Sir Hubert Gascoine Guest, Marshal of Space, K.C.B., O.M., O.U.N., D.S.O., D.F.C. (born 1943) was modeled on Hampson's father. Dare's faithful companion and batman was Spaceman Class 1 Albert Fitzwilliam Digby ("Dig" for short), born Wigan. Others in the regular crew were Professor Jocelyn Mabel Peabody ("Prof"), expert on nutrition, agriculture, and botany, and honorary Pilot/Captain;

"Hank," Pilot/Captain Henry Brennan Hogan of Houston, Texas, red-tape hater; and "Pierre," Pilot/Major Pierre August Lafayette from Dijon, an analytical mathematician whose hobby was gastronomy. There was also Dig's Aunt Anastasia, after whom a two-seater spaceship was named in recognition of the old lady's part in the overthrow of the Mekon of Venus, oppressor of the green Treens, in 1996. (The Mekon was Dare's archenemy.)

Writers of *Dan Dare* after Hampson included Alan Stranks, David Motton, and Eric Eden. Artists who worked on Hampson's pencilings or, later, in his style were Harold Johns, Donald Harley, Bruce Cornwell, Desmond Walduck, Frank Bellamy, and Keith Watson. Harley drew the weekly newspaper strip that ran in *The People* on Sundays (1964).

At the height of Dare's fame, a daily radio serial sponsored by Horlick's was broadcast over Radio Luxembourg. Dan was played by the former *Dick Barton* (actor Noel Johnson). There was considerable merchandising, apart from special appearances in *Eagle Annual* and *Dan Dare's Spacebook*: Dan Dare ray guns, wrist compasses, card games, filmstrips and viewers, inflatable rings, telescopes, periscopes, bagatelle, uniforms (playsuits), Lifebuoy soap stamps, etc. A Dare fanzine, *Astral*, official journal of the International Dan Dare Club, was published through Volume 3, Number 12.

Eagle was taken over from Hultons by Longacre Press/Odhams on March 19, 1960, but the rot began to set in. Clifford Makins took over the editorship, printing changed from color gravure to litho, and Frank Hampson left, disillusioned. *Dan* was reduced to monochrome reproduction in 1962, but restored to the front page in 1964. In 1966 it was down to a single page. Reprinting began in 1967 under the title *Dan Dare's Memoirs*. I.P.C. took over the comic in 1969 and killed it on April 26 (issue 991). For a while the title continued as part of another comic, *Lion and Eagle*, with Dan relettered and redrawn from the originals. By 1971 even that subtitle had gone. However, a happy revival occurred in September 1973, when *Dan Dare Annual* was published, reprinting *Red Moon Mystery* and *Safari in Space* in full color and in their entirety. A "modernized" Dan Dare series started in the all sci-fi comic *2000 AD* (1977) drawn by Dave Gibbons; and later still the original *Eagle* was revived as a part-photo, part-comic magazine in 1982. Once again Dan was reborn with further "modernization," all of which upset the original Dan fans. Finally a book publisher brought out the entire original run of *Eagle* strips in a series of facsimile volumes. Of the many plans to make television and cinema films of Dan's adventures, the only one to reach the screen has been a commercial.

D.G.

DAN DUNN (U.S.) Norman Marsh's imaginative, well-paced, but stiffly drawn and ill-plotted detective strip, *Dan Dunn, Secret Operative 48*, began daily on October 16, 1933, and Sunday the following week, with the daily and Sunday narrative continuous for many years. Created for Publishers' Syndicate as an inexpensive alternative to *Dick Tracy*, *Dan Dunn* featured a detective hero who was in the U.S. Secret Service, as the subtitle indicated. Dunn had a pet "wolf dog" (apparently a German shepherd) named Wolf, who frequently attacked a hood or two. Later, Dunn befriended an adopted orphan girl named Babs. Babs

"Dan Dunn," Norman Marsh. © Publishers Syndicate.

and Wolf pal around together during much of the continuity, thus making the strip a competitor with *Little Orphan Annie*. Dunn also acquired a fat, comic assistant named Irwin Higgs, who appeared in a number of routine Sunday-page gag sequences in the late 1930s, as well as bumbling about in the daily narrative. With many of its plot devices borrowed straight from the pulp magazines of the day, *Dan Dunn* provided a wilder and stranger story mix than *Dick Tracy* much of the time. It featured such master villains as a Fu Manchu parallel named Wu Fang and a death-ray wielder (who operated a dirigible from a mysterious island) named Eviloff.

Popular until Marsh began to dilute the fearsome story lines with more routine criminal material (and featured in several 1930s Big Little Book reprints), *Dan Dunn* declined sharply in readership after 1940, chiefly because subscribing papers decided to go the higher price and buy *Dick Tracy*. Marsh himself enlisted in the Marine Corps in 1942 after wangling a commission, and the strip was continued by a Paul Pinson, then by Alfred Andriola. The latter's slicker art did not help, and *Dan Dunn* finally folded obscurely in the pages of a handful of small newspapers before the close of the war (1943).

Marsh went to King Features on his return and immediately undertook a direct imitation of his own *Dan Dunn*, complete with Irwin, called *Hunter Keene*, which lasted a year, from April 15, 1946, to April 12, 1947. This was followed by a second strip named *Danny Hale*, a pioneer epic, which was similarly short-lived. Perhaps the "pulpiest" of the 1930s crime strips—in fact, the strip itself was the basis for a briefly extant dime novel pulp called *Dan Dunn*, which ran for two issues in the fall of 1936—*Dan Dunn* deserves at least partial reprinting as an often amusing record of the taste in strips during its time.

B.B.

DANNY DINGLE (U.S.) Certainly the most obscure of the really memorable strips of the 1920s and 1930s, Bernard Dibble's *Danny Dingle* is difficult to pinpoint as to its beginning and ending dates. Launched in early 1927 by King Features as a bottom-string strip, *Danny*

Dingle began as a daffy romantic comedy with rapid-fire continuity, unlike anything else in print. Wildly slapstick and hilariously drawn—Dibble's art here, as elsewhere, is infectiously funny—the new strip was too unusual and insufficiently exploited by an obviously dubious King Features to catch on. When Dibble was hired by United Features to ghost *The Captain and the Kids* for Rudolph Dirks (and actually byline the strip for a short period in the early 1930s), he renewed *Danny Dingle* with the new syndicate, this time with larger success. Accompanied by an anecdotal Sunday page (where the companion half-page, a weird extravaganza involving slobbish and hirsute men with little, mockingly angelic wings on their backs, was called *Dub-Dabs*), *Danny Dingle* ran from the early 1930s until the latter part of the decade, being reprinted regularly in *Tip-Top Comics*, and even appearing in a comic book collection of its own in 1939.

Notable in the *Dingle* cast were Danny himself, a "lemon-haired" youth; Pa Dingle, Danny's father and most frequent companion; Ma Dingle; Nellie Maloney, Danny's girl; and Otto Maloney, her father. Intermixed were a variety of crackpot inventors, men from outer space, political revolutionaries, gangsters, corrupt politicians, etc., all done with a fresh and ingenious touch. After 1940, when Dingle disappeared as a strip and when Dibble was ghosting much of *Fritzi Ritz*, as well as drawing *Iron Vic* in *Tip-Top Comics*, the cartoonist took over *Looy Dot Dope* from Johnny Devlin (who had originally carried the strip on after its creator, Milt Gross, left it), and continued it in much the same manner as *Danny Dingle*, actually carrying over Pa Dingle (renamed Dilbury) as Looy's buddy. Dibble's *Looy* ran for several years in the 1940s, largely as a reprint feature in *Tip Top Comics*, then vanished as abruptly and unascertainably as *Danny Dingle*. One of the great comic narrators and artists of the strip form, Bernard Dibble reached his creative peak in *Danny Dingle* and its *Looy Dot Dope* appendage—yet went largely unseen and unappreciated because of his offbeat content and his syndicate's inadequate understanding of the worth of his work. Needless to say, this area of Dibble's work should be reprinted in full, as soon as an adequate and reproducible run has been assembled.

B.B.

DAREDEVIL (U.S.) 1—Even though Siegel and Shuster's *Superman* didn't start the costumed hero boom until 1938, by 1940 the comic book industry was already overrun with "superheroes." But Don Rico and Jack Binder combined to create one of comic book's most unique strips, *Daredevil*, in the September 1940 issue of *Silver Streak* (number six); it was published by Comic House (later Lev Gleason). Even the character of Bart (Daredevil) Hill was innovative: not only didn't he have any powers, but he also used a boomerang, perhaps the only hero of his time to do so; instead of the standard cloth belt, Daredevil used a spiked steel one; and rather than some pedestrian superhero jumpsuit, Daredevil sported a suit that was blue on the left and red on the right.

The earliest *Daredevil* stories were fast-paced, but relatively standard: Daredevil and his constant companion/fiancée Tonia Saunders locked horns and eventually defeated some tremendous menace to the country. The paramount menace was the evil Claw, a particularly malevolent villain who flitted from Lev Gleason title to Lev Gleason title to battle the book's paramount superhero. In July 1941, this mix of action and intrigue merited Daredevil his own book, which was first entitled *Daredevil Battles Hitler*, and then simply *Daredevil*.

The year 1941 brought a new editor, Charles Biro, who proved to be one of the most innovative artist/writer/editors in the field. In *Daredevil* number 13 (October 1942), Biro introduced the Little Wise Guys and then very quickly moved into the spotlight, eventually easing Daredevil out of his own feature. And it was here Biro shone, as his Little Wise Guys became the most popular kid group in comics. As it happened, the group was formed when one of them, Meatball, ran away from his orphanage and met up with Scarecrow, another runaway. Meanwhile, Jocko (later called Jock) saves Pee Wee (who adopted the name Slugger) from a beating, and the four meet in a barn and declare their friendship for one another. Shortly after, the group is saved by the millionaire playboy Daredevil, and he and the Wise Guys begin a long series of adventures together.

Writer Biro was a gutsy, innovative scripter, and tradition was broken when Biro killed off Meatball and replaced him with Curly, an unsavory-looking convert from a street gang called the Steamrollers. Even more gutsy was Biro's totally shocking decision to write Daredevil out of his own strip and let the Wise Guys carry the ball. He last appeared in *Daredevil* number 69 (December 1950), but the boys carried on for five years without him.

Over the years, *Daredevil* showcased many fine artists, too, including Biro himself (1941-1943 and covers until 1950), coeditor Bob Wood (1941), Dan Barry (1947-1948), Norman Maurer (1943-1948), cocreators Rico and Binder (1940-1941), and later Tony DiPreta. In all, *Daredevil* appeared in *Silver Streak* until December 1941's 17th issue, in 134 issues of *Daredevil* (the last issue dated 1955), and in text stories in Boy comics sporadically during the 1940s.

2—The second *Daredevil* strip was created by writer/editor Stan Lee in June 1964 and premiered in the first issue of Marvel's *Daredevil*. In reality a lawyer named Matt Murdock, Daredevil was blind but compensated for that fact by increased hearing, strength, and radar senses. The strip was more action-oriented than most Marvel features, but also had strong supporting characters like Matt's partner Foggy Nelson; his first love interest, Karen Page; and even a bogus brother Matt, invented to allay suspicions that he was Daredevil. Later in the series, after Karen Page was written out, The Black Widow, a Communist spy-turned-American-superheroine, became Daredevil's love interest and partner.

Over the years, *Daredevil* has had a group of good artists, including Bill Everett, Joe Orlando, Wallace Wood, Jack Kirby, John Romita, and definitive illustrator Gene Colan. Among the writers were Lee, Colan himself, Gerry Conway, Tony Isabella, and definitive writer Roy Thomas.

J.B.

The character received a makeover at the hands of Frank Miller, who arrived on the scene in 1979; starting as a penciller on the series, he also took over the writing chores in 1981. During his tenure Daredevil engaged in a grim battle against the almost invincible Kingpin and the female assassin (and the hero's former lover) Elektra. After Miller's departure in 1983, the strip, despite some occasional flashes of brilliance, turned mostly into just another humdrum superhero comic book.

M.H.

DATELINE: DANGER! (U.S.) Writer Allen Saunders's son John and artist Alden McWilliams teamed up to

"Daredevil." © Marvel Comics Group.

"Dateline: Danger!" John Saunders and Al McWilliams. © Field Newspaper Syndicate.

produce *Dateline: Danger!* in November 1968 for Publishers Hall Syndicate.

The strip introduces Danny Raven, a black man and former football hero, currently a reporter for the Global News Co., and his white colleague Troy (short for Theodore Randolph Oscar Young). Danny and Troy are also U.S. undercover men on the side, and their adventures take them from Africa to Europe to South America, where they cover (and uncover) riots, coups d'etat, and other assorted upheavals and conspiracies (the overall idea was obviously inspired by the then-popular TV show *I Spy*).

Closer to home, Danny, along with his sister Wendy and his younger brother Lee Roy, often has to foil the plots hatched by black extremist Robin Jackson, publisher of the underground newspaper *The Revolt*.

Dateline: Danger! is not, as some have claimed, the first "integrated" strip (there has been Mandrake and Lothar; the Spirit and Ebony White) but it is the first one to represent black and white heroes on an equal footing.

Although not on a par with the adventure classics of the 1930s and 1940s, *Dateline: Danger!* is among the very few worthwhile action strips to come out of the adventure-starved 1960s. It was discontinued in 1974.

M.H.

DAUNTLESS DURHAM   *see* Desperate Desmond.

DAVE (U.S.)   David Miller's comic strip *Dave*, about the life of a twentysomething single guy, was first syndicated by Tribune Media Services in 1992. The strip focuses on relationships, using them to provide both humor and insight. As a member of Generation X straddling the space between his college years and a more responsible adult life, Dave claims that he detests everything Yuppies stand for, "everything . . . except the part about owning all that neat stuff!!!"

Miller first drew a precursor to *Dave* as an undergraduate at the Rhode Island School of Design. Following his graduation and a turn as an automobile designer, Miller settled on cartooning as his career choice. His timing was good, and *Dave* became Tribune Media's offering to appeal to not only twentysomethings, but also to men and women of a variety of ages.

Of great importance in Dave's life is his relationship with his childhood sweetheart, Darla. The relationship does not always go smoothly, and Dave and Darla have broken up on occasion. At work, where he is a mid-level office worker, Dave's relationship with his boss has more of the personal Dagwood Bumstead overtones rather than the alienated relationship *Dilbert* has with his boss. Miller combines the realism of a

"Dave," David Miller. © Tribune Media Services.

bachelor's life with politically incorrect moments with humorous results.

For example, in a strip that showed Dave double-dating at a restaurant, Miller has the women at the table thinking, "I'd like something fattening, but I'll probably have a salad." Simultaneously both men look at the waitress and think, "That waitress was hot. She probably wants me!"

David Miller is a mountain-bike enthusiast and has successfully worked his interest in the sport into the strip. He uses brisk, clean lines with little crosshatching or benday in drawing the strip. As often happens as a strip evolves, Dave's appearance has changed to a chubbier fellow with a more filled-out face in the years the strip has been in syndication. Darla, who initially was a full-figured young woman with a head of wild hair, has been toned down with a more slender figure and a simple ponytail hairstyle.

A contemporary strip for the 1990s, Dave has many story lines to continue to develop. Will he drift from Generation X to Generation Next as a commitment-challenged bachelor? Will he marry Darla or another woman and become a family man? As always in David Miller's Dave, relationships will be key to the future and the humor of the strip.

B.C.

DAVE'S DELICATESSEN (U.S.) Milt Gross's least-remembered major strip, *Dave's Delicatessen*, a wildly fanciful work, was begun for King Features in June 1931 as both a daily and Sunday strip. Usually called "Dave," "Davey," "Honest Dave," or (by his employees) "Mr. Dave," but otherwise unnamed, Dave operates a zany, down-at-the-heel delicatessen in a middle-sized town, with the bumbling assistance of a nephew named Chester. The imaginative range of the strip is extensive, however, quickly involving Dave and Chester with spies, racketeers, labor thugs, and locals over a good part of the globe. Both Sunday and daily strips involved ongoing continuity interspersed with one-episode gags, with the Sunday strip more inclined toward the latter, but the tone of both was lunacy and absurdity.

In December 1933, Count Screwloose joined Dave in his concern with the movie career of Dave's dalmatian, J. R. (known as *The Spotted Wonder*, he was featured briefly in a daily strip of the same name in late 1933), and became engaged in Hollywood-scene escapades on and off the movie lots, reflecting Gross's own script-writing background of the time.

During a later adventure of Dave and the Count in the French Foreign Legion, the title of the Gross King Features strip was changed (on January 20, 1935) from *Dave's Delicatessen* to *Count Screwloose*. The daily *Dave's Delicatessen* had already been dropped in 1934. Thus the strip of that name was effectively ended, although Dave himself continued as a central character in the newly named strip for a short while.

B.B.

DAVIES, ROLAND (1910-198?) British cartoonist, animator, illustrator, and painter, Roland Oxford Davies was born at Stourport, Worcestershire, on July 22, 1910. Educated at Hanley schools, he studied art at Ipswich Art School from 1926-28. For seven years he was a lithographic artist and designer of cinema posters at a printer in West Drayton. He first freelanced cartoons to *Motor Cycle* magazine, and gags in the form of a strip. Always obsessed by cars, planes, and speed, he freelanced illustrations to *Autocar* and *Modern Boy* weeklies. Curiously, the antithesis of these drawings was the inspiration for his first newspaper strip: *Come On, Steve!*, which described in a weekly pantomime gag the adventures of a horse and cart! The strip moved from the *Sunday Express* to the rival *Sunday Dispatch*, where it continued for another 10 years. While on the *Express* group, he drew his first comic page, *Larry Leopard*, for the colored cover of the weekly comic supplement, *Daily Express Children's Own* (1933-34). Also for the *Sunday Express*, he did a weekly sports cartoon and the strip *Percy the Policeman*. Signing himself "Pip" he drew a daily pocket cartoon for the *Evening News*, and *Bessie*, a weekly strip featuring a charlady, in the green-paper Saturday Magazine of the *News Chronicle*.

Davies taught himself animation in 1936 and produced his own series of cartoon films starring *Come On, Steve!*, opening a studio in Ipswich. Six cartoons were made in all, but the venture failed through lack of financial support. He drew strips for D. C. Thomson's new weekly comic *Beano* (July 1938), *Whoopee Hank*, and *Contrary Mary*; the latter strip, featuring Mary the Moke (a close relation to Steve), was reprinted years later in *Weekly News* as *Neddy the Cuddy*. He then drew *Charlie Chasem*, a speed cop, in *Knockout* (1939), and joined the staff of the *Sunday Dispatch* as topical/political cartoonist throughout the war.

He returned to comics in 1949 by taking over the long-running serial *Sexton Blake* in *Knockout*, beginning with *The Red Rapier* series on December 10, 1949. He also did the comic series *Old Phibber* and *Sparks & Flash* in 1950, adapted the film *Ambush* in *Knockout*, and then changed publishers for the *T.V. Comic* series: *Norman and Henry Bones* (1953), *Jack & His Baby Jet*, and a superhero, *Red Ray, Space Raynger* (1954), who grew popular enough to have his own club and badge. Also in 1954, he did *Roddy the Road Scout* and *Topple Twins* in *Swift*. *Snowfire* (1959) in *T.V. Comic*; *Pete Madden* (1961) in *Knockout*; *What's Cooking* (1962) in *Girl*. He took over *Sally* in *School Friend*, and *The Trolls* in *Princess*, and he drew the British version of *Beetle Bailey* in *T.V. Comic* (1965). He did children's series (panels) in *Woman's Realm: Pedro* and *Sheepy*; and also drew in full color many episodes of Walt Disney's *Jungle Book, Peter Pan, Winnie the Pooh in Disneyland* (1971), and war strips: *Victor* (1974).

Books: *Steve Steps Out* (1937); *Steve of the River* (1937); *Great Deeds of the War* (1941); *Knights of the Air* (1943); *Steve Goes to London* (1946); *Adventures of Steve* (1947); *Come On, Steve! Annual* (1947); *Steve's Xmas Holiday* (1947); *Steve on the Farm* (1948); *Steve's Dream* (1948); *Steve and the Little Engine* (1947); *All About Engines* (1948); *Daily Mail Speedway Book* (1949); *Steve & the Burglar* (1949); *Steve & the Racing Car* (1949); *Daily Mail Motorcycling Book* (1949); *Come On, Steve! Annual* (1950); *Ace Book of Speed* (1952); *Famous Trains* (1953). Retiring from the weekly grind of strip cartooning, Davies took up painting in his late years. With former comic-book publisher Alan Class as his agent, he staged several successful exhibitions before his death in the late 1980s.

D.G.

DAVIS, JACK (1926-   ) American comic book and comic strip writer and artist, born in 1926 in Atlanta, Georgia. After studies at the University of Georgia, Davis went north in 1951 and entered the comic book field as a writer and artist for the fledgling "New

..."SHOTS FROM THE HILL! DOUSE THAT LIGHT!"

Jack Davis, comic book illustration. © E.C. Comics.

Trend" line of William Gaines' EC comics. His unique, personalized art style made him an instant favorite and his work stands as some of the finest to come from the EC era of 1950-56.

In the serious vein, although Davis did some work on the EC crime and science-fiction titles, his best work came under the direction of Al Feldstein's horror titles and Harvey Kurtzman's war and Western line. His horror work was always extremely effective because of its contrast; while Feldstein was writing heavy tales of gore and retribution, Davis was illustrating in an almost comic style. His characters were always common-looking, but almost always depraved and disheveled. Many consider his finest horror tale "'Taint the Meat, It's the Humanity," a grotesque story of a crooked butcher during the rationing days of World War II. After killing his own child with poisoned meat, he is hacked to death by his wife, who displays the dismembered butcher's body in his display cases. In another story, "Foul Play," Davis rendered several controversial panels in which a ball player is ripped apart and used as baseball equipment.

Under the direction of Harvey Kurtzman, Davis produced some absolutely breathtaking war, Western, and adventure stories, but the best was probably "Betsy," a Western tale written and sparklingly illustrated by Davis. But Kurtzman and Davis' collaboration reached fruition in Kurtzman's *Mad*, perhaps the finest American satire and parody book ever produced. Collaborating with other fine humor talents—Wallace Wood and Will Elder among others—Davis helped contribute to the cluttered *Mad* style. Besides his zany figures, always in motion and exaggerated to humorous extremes, Davis crammed his panels with dozens of sight gags, funny people, and crazy illustrations.

When Kurtzman left *Mad*, Davis followed him to *Trump, Help!* and even *Playboy*'s lush *Little Annie Fanny*, but also eventually returned to *Mad* and remains one of its most talented and prolific contributors.

When the bulk of the EC line folded in 1956, Davis made a brief attempt to continue work in serious comics at Atlas, but his stylized and innovative humor work led him into the illustrating field. Within several years, he became the most sought-after advertising artist in the country and has worked in almost every

advertising medium. Davis developed into a top-notch cartoonist as well as a cover artist (*Time, TV Guide,* and many others), and he may well have been the best-known and most often seen artist of the 1970s.

Davis has also worked on several syndicated strips, including *The Saint* and *Beauregard*, in addition to the *Superfan* strip for *Quarterback* magazine. In 1973, Nick Meglin wrote an excellent chapter on Davis' humor work in his Watson-Guptill book, *The Art of Humorous Illustration*. In the last 20 years Davis has become famous for his album covers, illustrations, humorous ads, and work for such high-circulation magazines as *TV Guide, Esquire,* and *Time* (for which by his own count he has drawn over 30 covers to date). He was the subject of a book-length study, *The Art of Jack Davis*, published in 1987.

J.B.

DAVIS, JIM (1945-   ) Creator of the most famous cat in newspaper comics, cartoonist Jim Davis was born on July 28, 1945, in Marion, Indiana. Surrounded by nearly 25 cats while growing up on a farm near Fairmont, Indiana, he became aware of their mystical appeal and instinctive behavior. While he was kept indoors often due to his asthma, his mother provided him with pencil and paper, prompting Davis to focus his boyhood imagination on drawing funny animals. In 1963 Davis entered Ball State University as an art and business major, followed by two years as a pasteup artist with an advertising agency. For nine years beginning in 1969, Davis was assistant to Tom K. Ryan on the Western humor strip *Tumbleweeds*, providing backgrounds, borders, and speech balloons. In addition to rendering freelance commercial art and copywriting at this time, he also developed his first strip, *Gnorm Gnat*, which was rejected by syndicate editors because of its insect characters. Davis noticed that there were virtually no felines in contemporary comics and developed *Garfield*, about a curmudgeon of a cat with a sardonic sense of humor but a heart of gold. United Feature Syndicate accepted the idea and launched the feature in 41 newspapers in 1978. Perfectly suited in concept and appearance to both cat lovers and those who appreciated *Garfield*'s wit, the strip quickly flourished.

In the beginning, Valette Greene assisted Jim Davis on the strip, while now dozens are employed at his company—Paws, Incorporated—which develops and manages the media and merchandising industry the strip has spawned. In 1986 the cartoonist saluted his rural roots with the publication of his short-lived strip *U.S. Acres*, a comic that featured the zany escapades of farm animals, aimed exclusively at younger readers.

Recognized by the National Cartoonists Society with its Best Humor Strip, Reuben, and Elzie Segar Awards for unique and outstanding contributions to the comics field, Jim Davis has helped redefine the modern humor strip by adhering to his philosophy that "the only legitimate reason for a comic strip to be is to entertain." He lives with his family in Albany, Indiana.

B.J.

DAVIS, PHIL (1906-1964) American cartoonist and illustrator, born March 4, 1906, in St. Louis, Missouri. Phil Davis studied at the Washington University Art School while working as a commercial artist for the local telephone company. In 1928 he started work on the *St. Louis Post-Dispatch* as an advertising artist while at the same time contributing illustrations and covers for various magazines. In 1933 he met writer Lee Falk and together they created *Mandrake the Magician* for King Features Syndicate. *Mandrake* appeared as a daily on June 11, 1934, and as a Sunday feature in February of 1935.

During the war Davis was drafted as art director of the Curtiss-Wright aircraft company; as such he edited and partially illustrated the instruction manual for the A-25 bomber. At about the same time his wife Martha (a talented fashion designer in her own right) joined him to work on the drawing of *Mandrake*. Phil Davis died of a heart attack on December 16, 1964.

Davis' ability to create subtle moods and tones with a few simple lines, the right placement of objects and characters, and a touch of shading, has earned him the admiration of many artists and filmmakers, such as Alain Resnais and Federico Fellini.

M.H.

DE BECK, BILLY (1890-1942) Billy De Beck, the comic strip poet of America's big-city and sporting life of the Jazz Age and depression, was appropriately born in Chicago, on April 15, 1890. He grew up in middle-class surroundings and attended the city's prestigious Academy of Fine Arts, graduating in 1910. After some early success on a local paper, he returned to the academy in 1918 to head a cartoon school for a short time.

De Beck landed his first job as a cartoonist on the Youngstown (Ohio) Telegram in 1910. In 1912, he left the *Telegram* to do political cartoons for the *Pittsburgh Gazette-Times* until 1914, when he obtained his first Chicago opportunity on the old *Herald* and launched his first two comic strips: *Movies Featuring Haphazard Helen* (an anonymously drawn Sunday-page takeoff on film melodrama), and *Married Life* (a daily and Sunday gag strip featuring a number of argumentative married couples, one of which would later serve as prototypes for the early Barney Google and wife). De Beck also did a panel on the daily sports page for the *Herald*, which ran under various topical titles. When the *Herald* was done in by the *Chicago Tribune's* infamous newsprint-cornering tactics in 1917, De Beck and his *Herald* strip peer, E. C. Segar, found jobs on the two Hearst Chicago papers: De Beck taking the sports cartoonist's seat on the old *Examiner*.

After a few months there, De Beck introduced *Barney Google* as a quasi-daily strip, reviving the last of the *Married Life* squabble teams as the stars. The story line

focused on husband Barney's attempts to sneak out to the racetrack without his wife finding out. *Examiner* readers loved it and howled for more; Hearst took note, and abruptly De Beck found himself in New York, on the great *American* comic strip staff, doing *Barney* as a nationally syndicated sports page feature. Barney's 1922 acquisition of the horse Spark Plug cost him his home, of course, but gained him nationwide fame. A Sunday page was slow in coming, but by 1923, *Barney* was running in full color weekly almost everywhere. In 1925, De Beck added a subtle takeoff on *Little Orphan Annie* to the Sunday *Barney* page, entitled *Parlor, Bedroom, and Sink, Starring Bunky*, whose most famed character, aside from the diminutive, nightcapped Bunky, was the despicable Fagin. In 1934, after racing an ostrich as well as Spark Plug and other horses, and managing a prizefighter named Sully, who was as preternaturally strong as Popeye, De Beck's Barney took to the Kentucky hills and met the hillbilly duo of Snuffy and Lowizie Smith (or Smif), who became so enormously popular that they took over the strip by the early 1940s.

When De Beck died in 1942, after a full and active life of travel, golf, and exhaustive socializing (his assistant from 1933, Fred Lasswell, often remarked on how much of the world he got to see with De Beck: Havana, Lake Placid, New York, etc.), his strip was continued by Lasswell, with the emphasis increasingly on Snuffy Smith, as it is today. This De Beck classic, easily one of the 10 greatest American comic strips of all time, was marked by its stunning graphic imagery from the outset, its often hilarious visual and verbal comedy (De Beck coined such once-famed comic terms as "Sweet Mama," "the heebie-jeebies," "horse feathers," "OKMNX," "Osky-Wow-Wow," and "So I took the $50,000"), and a rare mastery of narrative suspense and intrigue—the latter evidenced in the daily strip of the 1920s and in the Sunday *Bunky*, and often overlooked by students of the genre.

B.B.

DELAČ, VLADIMIR (1927-1969) A Yugoslav cartoonist born in Slavonski Brod, on October 13, 1927, Vladimir Delač graduated from grammar school in Zagreb and in 1946 sold his first cartoon for 200 dinars to the humorous paper *Kerempuh*. The subject of his cartoon was the United Nations. Very soon he became a member of the *Kerempuh's* editorial staff and eventu-

Vladimir Delać, "Marina." © *Vladimir Delać.*

"Delta 99," Carlos Gimenez. © IMDE.

ally published over 1,500 cartoons in that paper. In 1950, together with Walter Neugebauer and Borivoj Dovniković, he produced the first Yugoslav cartoon film, *Veliki miting* ("The Big Meeting"). In 1952 Delač finished his own cartoon film, *Revija na dvoristu* ("The Review on the Yard").

Comic strips were Delač's great love, and in 1950 *Ornladinski borac* published his first comic strip, *Vuna Kićo orasi Mićo*. In the following years he published many comic strips in *Vjesnikov zabavni tjednik, Petko,* and *Miki strip*. His most popular character, *Svernirko,* was born in 1957 and started appearing in the *Globus* magazine, but in 1959 Delač moved his little hero from outer space to the pages of *Plavi vjesnik*, where his gags were published for almost 10 years. Delač's other characters—*Ivica Bucko, Viki and Niki, Marina, Davor, Tramvajko, Toma Vank*, and others—were also very popular in Yugoslavia, thanks to his fine style and original humor.

During the last months of his life, Delač was very ill, but Svemirko and Davor did not leave the pages of *Plavi Vjesnik* and *Arena* until their creator died in 1969. Delač's very last gags were done standing near the drawing board on long winter nights, because he was unable to sit down or to sleep.

E.R.

DEL CASTILLO, ARTURO (1925-1992) Chilean cartoonist and illustrator Arturo Del Castillo was born in Concepción in 1925. Del Castillo started his professional career as a commercial artist. Following in the footsteps of his brother, Jorge, also an illustrator, he moved to Buenos Aires in 1948. There he got a job as a letterer on the comic weekly *Aventuras*. A year later he started his collaboration with *Intervalo* magazine with a series of comic strips, and he quickly became famous among comic strip scholars for his incredibly skillful and detailed penwork, an artistic mode in which he is an acknowledged world master.

In the late 1950s Del Castillo worked for Fleetway Publications, contributing a number of comic strip

adaptations of Alexandre Dumas's novels, such as *The Three Musketeers* and *The Man in the Iron Mask*. His most famous creation, however, remains *Randall*, a Western he brought to life in 1957 on a script by Hector Oesterheld; in *Randall* Del Castillo refined his graphic style even further, drawing his backgrounds with a fine network of pen lines that imitated benday and gave his work a highly personalized look. Other important works by Del Castillo followed: *Garret* (1962), published in the magazine *Misterix*, with scripts by Ray Collins (pseudonym, E. Zappietto); *Larrigan* and *Ringo* (both 1964); two more Westerns, *Dan Dakota* and *Los Tres Mosqueteros en el Oeste* ("The Three Musketeers in the West"); and *El Cobra* (also written by Ray Collins), which is currently being published in the Buenos Aires review *Skorpio*. In his later career he worked mainly for an Italian publisher and for the Argentinian Ediciones Record until his retirement in 1989. He died in Buenos Aires in January 1992.

L.G.

DELTA 99 (Spain) *Delta 99* was created by cartoonist Carlos Giménez in 1968, on a script by Flores Thies, and it lasted for 30 complete episodes, each published separately.

The locale of *Delta 99* is a faraway galaxy from which the titular hero is sent to Earth on a peace mission by the confederation of planets to which he belongs. Intelligent, but without any super power or herculean strength, Delta 99 is a curious character, at once sensuous and cold. He lives with a wealthy woman pirate named Lu, who maintains, spoils and adores him at the end of each adventure.

In a second stage, after Giménez had left and the illustration work had passed into the hands of Usero, Mascaro, Nebot, and especially Manuel Ferrer, and with new scripts by Roger (the pseudonym of series producer José Toutain) and Victor Mora, Delta 99 was changed from a sex-hunting extraterrestrial being into a secret agent with a lively sense of humor. In his new adventures (in which could now be found a number of

Gianni De Luca (and William Shakespeare), "Ofelia." © De Luca.

private jokes) he eschewed the woman-robots of his first exploits to tangle with female adventurers and ballerinas.

Created in black and white, *Delta 99* was later reprinted in its entirety in color, with new texts by novelist José Maria Mendiola.

L.G.

DE LUCA, GIANNI (1927-1991) Italian artist and cartoonist, born January 25, 1927, in Gagliano (Catanzaro); died June 6, 1991, in Milan. While studying architecture, Gianni De Luca started drawing comics for the Catholic weekly *Il Vittorioso*. After his comic book *Anac il distruttore* ("Anac the Destroyer," 1946) was published, he drew *Il Mago da Vinci* ("The Wizard from Vinci," 1947-48), which highlighted some aspects of the artist Leonardo da Vinci's life. Then came a succession of remarkable adventures set against historical backgrounds: *Prora vichinga* ("The Viking Prow," 1949),

L'impero del sole ("The Empire of the Sun," 1949), *La Sfinge nera* ("The Black Sphynx," 1950), *Il tempio delle genti* ("The Peoples' Temple," 1950).

In 1951 he published *Gli ultimi della Terra* ("The Last Survivors on the Earth"), the story of the tragedy of those who have survived an atomic disaster. De Luca's elegant and impressive style is enriched by the use of unusual shading to counterpoint the emotions of the characters and by the different psychological expressions he gives his characters.

In 1957 De Luca left *Il Vittorioso* and started collaborating with the other Italian weekly, *Il Giornalino*, for which he produced several illustrated series on the Bible and the history of the Catholic Church. In 1969 the weekly's content was revised and its graphics were updated. Beginning in 1970, De Luca illustrated a new series of comics written by Gian Luigi Gonano, *Il Commissario Spada* ("Commissioner of Police Spada"), a character who deals more with the social implications of criminal cases than with solving the crime. Here De Luca experimented with his technique. In the years 1975-76 he reached the peak of his creative graphic invention with the so-called Shakespearean trilogy: *La Tempesta* ("The Tempest"), *Amleto* ("Hamlet"), and *Romeo e Giulietta* ("Romeo and Juliet").

In these comic adaptations of the plays, De Luca begins to employ, instead of the single panel, the entire page as a basic graphic unit. The page, which has a single setting, is divided into panels to advance the narration through the images of the characters in action. Instead of dividing the page into geometrical and artificial panels, he utilizes the natural (e.g., a tree) or architectural (e.g., a column) elements of the single setting to divide the successive stages of the narration. Later on he eliminated all divisions within the single setting, instead depicting the characters in different successive positions in order to describe the action, with a final strobe effect.

In the following years De Luca drew several covers for the Comic Art reprints of American vintage comics, which were done in album form. He continued to draw the *Il Commissario Spada* series and other stories for *Il Giornalino*, including *Il giornalino di Gian Burrasca* (1983), an adaptation of Vamba's humorous novel for children, *Paulus* (1987), *Avventura sull'Orinoco* ("Adventure on the Orinoco River," 1988), and *La freccia nera* (1988), an adaptation from R. L. Stevenson's *The Black Arrow*. With the graphic novel *Paulus*, De Luca carried on his research in graphic style. Here he tells on parallel planes, on the same page, two stories: one set in the distant past, dealing with Saint Paul's conversion and the spread of Christianity; the other of the science-fiction genre, set in the distant future.

De Luca worked up to the end of his life: the story *I giorni dell' impero* ("The Days of the Empire") was published posthumously in 1990-91 in *Il giornalino*. In 1977 he was awarded a Yellow Kid prize in Lucca.

G.C.C.

DÉMON DES CARAÏBES, LE (France) An enjoyable sea-adventure story created by Jean-Michel Charlier (script) and Victor Hubinon (art), *Le Démon des Caraïbes* ("The Devil of the Caribbean") ran in *Pilote* magazine from the first issue (October 29, 1959) until September 1967.

The titular hero (or antihero) is the one-eyed, red-bearded pirate, Barbe-Rouge, who sails the Spanish Main aboard his ship, the *Black Hawk*, spreading slaughter and terror in his wake. He is assisted by his adopted son, Eric, who follows his father out of a sense of loyalty, and by his two henchmen, the gigantic black Baba and the lame and devious Triple Patte ("Triple Paw").

A healthy dose of humor, good draftsmanship (Hubinon's improvement is quite impressive when compared to his shaky start on *Buck Danny*), and hearty adventure made *Le Démon des Caraïbes* into a quite entertaining strip. After Hubinon's death in 1979 the series was sporadically continued by Joseph Gillain and his son Laurent (who signed "Lorg"); Patrice Pellerin and Christian Gaty have carried on from 1982 to this day.

M.H.

DENNIS THE MENACE (G.B.) Not to be confused with the American *Dennis the Menace*, the British character who bears the same name has little in common with his Yankee cousin other than a love for mischief. Actually his is more a mania for mischief, and so the British Dennis is closer to those practical jokesters, the Katzenjammer Kids, than to Hank Ketcham's lovable moppet.

The late David Law created Dennis for D. C. Thomson's weekly *Beano*, drawing him in a style that got looser and wilder through the years. Dennis's first appearance was on March 17, 1951, in a half-page strip headlined "Look! Here's a new pal you'll enjoy—He's the world's wildest boy!" When Dennis persists in walking on the park grass, his dad puts him on the leash instead of the dog! On September 8 Dennis moved to the red and blue of page two, mowing down fences with a homemade steamroller made from a garden roller and a soapbox.

On March 7, 1953, the strip increased to a full page of 15 panels, and on February 13, 1954, it moved to the full-color back page. Dennis celebrated by taking over a railway engine! In 1969 he was joined in his escapades by an incredible mess of black hair and teeth, a dog called Gnasher. So popular was this beast that the title was changed to *Dennis the Menace and Gnasher* in 1971. The ultimate triumph came on September 14, 1974, when Dennis and Gnasher took over the front page of *Beano*, moving the previous occupant, *Biffo the Bear*, to the inside!

"Dennis the Menace," David Law. © Beano.

Law created a female counterpart to Dennis, *Beryl the Peril*, and other descendants of his original include *Minnie the Minx*, by Leo Baxendale, and *Roger the Dodger*, by Ken Reid. An annual reprint, *Dennis the Menace Book*, began publication in 1959.

So well established is this British Dennis that Ketcham's American character had to be rechristened *The Pickle* for his British reprint. In the 1990s Dennis became the first British children's comic character to be animated, and a series of half-hour cartoons was released to television and for home-screen viewing as *The Beano Video* (1994). In support were other *Beano* comic heroes, the Bash Street Kids, the Three Bears, and Ivy the Terrible. They were produced by Flicks Films and directed by Terry Ward. The credits included 58 names, but nowhere were the original cartoonist-creators mentioned.

D.G.

DENNIS THE MENACE (U.S.) Hank Ketcham's *Dennis the Menace* appeared for the first time, as a single-panel daily, on March 12, 1951, and soon became so popular that the Hall Syndicate, which distributed the feature, added a Sunday page a year later.

With *Dennis the Menace* Hank Ketcham proved that the kid strip was not yet dead (as many syndicate editors then believed). His tiny hero is a tousle-haired, enterprising tot whose counterfeit innocence, unflattering candor, and joyous vandalism are in delightful contrast to the docile conformity of the adult world. Dennis (who was inspired by the cartoonist's own four-year-old son) is the terror of his suburban neighborhood, whose quiet he disrupts with his devilry and high jinks: his targets are often his harassed parents, Henry and Alice Mitchell, who usually stare in helpless wonder at their son's irrepressible shenanigans.

"*NOT THAT ONE, MARGARET! YOU WANT ONE THAT'LL MAKE YA LOOK WORSE!*"

"Dennis the Menace," Hank Ketcham. © Field Newspaper Syndicate.

The Mitchells' next-door neighbor, the grouchy and miserly Mr. Wilson, also figures high on the list of Dennis's hapless victims. Margaret, a precocious prig often at odds with Dennis, Joey (Dennis's inseparable friend and accessory in mischief), and Ruff (his idiot dog possessed of an irrational fear of cats), complete the merry cast of characters.

Ketcham's scripts for his Sunday page are always funny and refreshingly acerbic, while his daily one-line gags often display a barbed point. His graphic style is unobtrusive in its appearance, yet highly effective in its purpose. Since the late 1980s Ketcham has left most of the artwork to his assistants, Ron Ferdinand and Marcus Hamilton.

Dennis the Menace has been consistently popular for close to 50 years: its very title has become a household word. It has been reprinted in hardcover by Holt and in paperback by Fawcett (over 20 titles published to date), and has its own Dell comic book. In the 1960s a long-running television series starring Jay North as Dennis was broadcast by CBS. A live-action *Dennis the Menace* movie, with Mason Gamble in the title role and Walter Matthau as Mr. Wilson, came out in 1993.

M.H.

DERICKSON DENE (G.B.) *Derickson Dene Super Inventor* can lay claim to being the first British superhero strip. Although its heroes possess no physical superpowers, their fantastic adventures qualify the strip for the distinction. It was certainly the first British strip to follow the American comic book format. The captionless strip, with dialogue carried purely through speech balloons, was considered so revolutionary by the traditional Amalgamated Press that they billed the strip as "A Thrilling Story You Don't have to Read!" The comic book technique was also imitated in that Dene's strip formed a four-page detachable center section to a weekly story paper, *Triumph*, although in later issues the space was somewhat reduced.

Dene, working on a detector device to protect London's banks, was kidnapped by flying batmen and taken to the hideout of the Vampire, who sought his collaboration on a Planet-Rocket. They arrive on an unknown planet where they are attacked by Giant Rhamdhorns, Medusa Snakes, and Apemen. Dene's metal-melter saves the day.

The first serial ran from July 8 to July 29, 1939, when *Dene* was replaced by the first British reprint of *Superman*. But popular demand brought him back, and on September 23 *Derickson Dene in the Valley of Frozen*

PULL YOURSELF TOGETHER AND TELL ME HOW TO WORK THIS THING

"Derickson Dene," Nat Brand. © Triumph.

Monsters began. Still marooned in space, Dene took an ice-car to the realm of the Snow-Mammoths and tunneled his way to a tropical jungle where Dryptosaurs threatened and Basilisks flew. In November came a new saga, *Sabotage and War*, which took Dene under the sea to Marshland. This scenario concluded with his rocket return to Earth on February 17, 1940. However, that proved to be Dene's farewell appearance, although a new serial was trailered: *The Nazi Spy Ring*.

Dene was written and drawn by Nat Brand, who modeled his hero, and his drawing style, on Alex Raymond's *Flash Gordon*. His artwork improved considerably during the series, but the "Yankee" style was frowned upon by A.P. and Brand found no more work. He turned to the minor publisher A. Soloway and created some excellent serial heroes for their comic books: *Crash Carew* (Daredevil of the Stratosphere) in *Comic Adventures*; *Argo Under the Ocean* in *All Star*, which also featured *Dandy McQueen* (of the Royal Mounted); *Halcon* (Lord of the Crater Land) in *Comic Capers*; and *Bentley Price* (Scientific Detective). These ran approximately quarterly throughout 1940-49. Brand later created *Steve Samson* (Strongman of Sport) for the Mans' World Comics series, but seems to have drawn remarkably little for so promising and exciting a talent.

D.G.

DE SOUZA, MAURICIO (1936-   ) Brazilian cartoonist, born October 7, 1936, in Santa Isabel, a city near São Paulo, but raised in Mogi das Cruzes. At age 17, Mauricio De Souza moved to São Paulo and worked for the daily newspaper *Folha de S. Paulo* as a crime reporter. He often submitted daily comic strips to the newspaper, until the editors accepted one entitled *Bidu and Franjinha* about a boy and his dog. In 1959, he quit his reporting job and dedicated his career to the comics. He married and had a daughter, Monica, who was the inspiration for one of his strips: *Monica and her gang*. De Souza started creating strips with male characters inspired by boys he knew from childhood: *Cascão*, a boy who hated baths, and *Cebolinha*, a boy with only three strands of hair. He developed a gallery of children characters: *Penadinho*, about a small phantom; *Chico Bento*, a hillbilly; *Astronauta, Nico Demo*, a demon boy; *Anjinho* ("Li'l Angel"); and *Horacio*, a dinosaur orphan. His strips were distributed in the small newspapers in Brazil. A food company bought the rights to one of his characters, a green elephant, to use in a television campaign, and the character was a hit. In 1970, Editora Abril launched a full-color monthly magazine,

Monica, and eventually other De Souza characters were given their own titles. The sales of these monthly magazines were good, and once he moved to the Editora Globo, which was owned by the TV Globo group, sales of his magazines reached the millions each month, surpassing Disney publications. Today De Souza makes feature films for theatrical release, animates cartoons for television and home video, shows, theme parks, theater, CDs, CD-ROM, phone answering services, and the Internet. He has become the most successful cartoonist in the Brazilian comics industry. He was awarded Italy's Yellow Kid.

A.M.

"Desperate Dan," Dudley Watkins. © Dandy.

DESPERATE DAN (G.B.) "Desperate Dan was born in the town of Tombstone, and all the natives of that town are tough, but Desperate Dan was the toughest of them all." So begins the official biography of this famous comic hero as published in *The Wizard Midget Comic*, a one-shot giveaway dated September 11, 1954. It continues: "His Paw was a quarry-man at the granite quarries. When Dan was six months old his Paw used to bring home useless hunks of granite too hard for making tombstones, for his baby to chew. That helped his teeth to come through the gums." The extraordinary mixture of British and American lore that gives this strip so much of its charm comes in the following paragraph, which describes how 12-year-old Dan loved playing cricket and hit every ball a mile out of town! Cactusville, where Dan settled, is noted for its quaint British lampposts and, from time to time, its trams and gasworks!

Dan's real birthday was December 4, 1937, and his birthplace was number one of *Dandy*, the first weekly

Mauricio De Souza, "Monica." © Mauricio De Souza.

comic published by the Scots firm of D. C. Thomson. His three rows of pictures on page two expanded to a full page of five rows in 1940, and he fills a similar page to this day.

Created by Dudley D. Watkins, Dan has been drawn in his style ever since. Originally something of a bad hat, Dan mellows to use his super-strength on the side of law and order. He lives with his Aunt Aggie, who bakes him cow-pie (with the horns in) for supper, and the bane of his life is Desperate Danny, his tough little nephew, who came on a visit on June 4, 1949, and is still around—so is niece Katey, who arrived in 1957. A hardback reprint, *The Dandy's Desperate Dan*, was published in 1963.

D.G.

DESPERATE DESMOND (U.S.) The young Harry Hershfield's first comic strip for the Hearst papers was a direct imitation of C. W. Kahles' popular *Philadelphia Press* Sunday half-page, *Hairbreadth Harry*. Unlike *Harry*, Hershfield's new *Desperate Desmond* strip was daily, although it ran only six times in the first month of its appearance in the *N.Y. Journal*, where it began on March 11, 1910. Its popularity grew rapidly, and it ran regularly in Hearst dailies and other papers around the country for the next few years.

Hershfield's *Desmond* copied Kahles' early *Harry* format in featuring a stalwart hero and his betrothed lady-love faced with a fiendish villain in a top hat and tails, and by running a largely redundant narrative text beneath each panel. Hershfield's strip, however, was named for its villain rather than its hero and showed greater ingenuity and wit from the outset than did the more labored Kahles work.

The burlesque melodrama content of Desmond lent itself to suspenseful continuity from episode to episode. It was the first daily strip after *Mutt and Jeff* to utilize this device. The first episode, for example, opens with Desmond trying to throw lovely Rosamund from a high tower of the Brooklyn Bridge, from whence she is rescued by Claude Eclair, the hero, who has

"Desperate Desmond," Harry Hershfield. © International Feature Service.

tightrope-walked a cable to save her in the nick of time, and closes with Claude trussed loosely by Desmond to the minute hand of a huge tower clock, from which he will fall 900 feet at 5:27.

On July 12, 1912, Hershfield gave Desmond, Claude, and Rosamund an announced "vacation," effectively ending their adventures after 28 months, in order to do a political burlesque with the strip—to Hearst specifications, of course. The new version featured Rosamund Election, Desmond Prohibition, and three heroes: Claude Taft, Claude Roosevelt, and Claude Wilson. This hastily conceived epic was switched to the editorial page, where it ran intermittently over the election months, while Hershfield introduced *Homeless Hector*, his old pre-Hearst strip, to the *Journal* comic page.

By 1913, the political nonsense was over, and Hershfield replaced Hector on January 22 with a new daily strip called *Dauntless Durham of the U.S.A.* This strip, minus the subpictorial text of *Desmond*, followed the same basic pattern (adding a touch of English caricature), with a hero, Durham, a heroine, Katrina, and a dark-eyed villain, Lord Havaglass, who was a moustached Englishman accompanied by a valet, Watkins. By March 12, 1913, Lord Havaglass had become the president of Mexico and Desperate Desmond was reintroduced as the primary heavy. Desmond and Durham went at each other for the remainder of the year, and then on January 31, 1914, Durham wed Katrina, Desmond retired to home life (he had a wife and three kids all the time), and the Desmond odyssey ended for good. It is all entertaining to read even today, and deserves reprinting.

B.B.

DETEKTIV SCHMIDTCHEN (Germany) *Detektiv Schmidtchen* ("Detective Smitty") may have been the only daily newspaper adventure strip to come out of postwar Germany. The series was created and initially written by Frank Lynder, who hoped to raise a German comics emporium of Disney dimensions, but the project never came off, allegedly because of a lack of German comic artists. *Detektiv Schmidtchen* was drawn by Friedrich-Wilhelm Richter-Johnsen, who had moved to Hamburg in 1954 to work for the Springer newspaper chain. It was in the largest of the Springer newspapers, *Bild-Zeitung* (Picture-News), that *Detektiv Schmidtchen* started on May 6, 1954. When Lynder's idea of a large-scale comics production did not work out, he went on to other journalistic pursuits, even abandoning his comic strip creation. The strip had to continue, however, so Richter-Johnsen, while continuing to draw the strip, also started to write it. The strip continued in *Bild* until March 26, 1962. It was killed off not because of lack of reader interest but because it was so decreed by the new editor-in-chief, who disliked comic strips. Since then *Bild*, which at times could boast national sales of almost five million copies per day because of its blood-and-guts sensationalism, has used strips like *Bugs Bunny* and *Sesame Street* as a kind of TV tie-in, but they are usually discontinued after very short runs.

Detektiv Schmidtchen is a very unusual type of detective; he is a tiny white mouse. Schmidtchen is the pet of the elderly, kind, and energetic Kommissar Schmidt ("Police Commissioner Smith"). Schmidt carries his pet along wherever he goes and this is only natural since the pet, whose beady eyes uncover even the tiniest of clues, provides his master with a perfect record of solved crimes. Schmidtchen's incentive may be the special ration of milk and crackers the commissioner offers to him whenever a crime is solved. It goes without saying that Schmidtchen has scared his share of females during Schmidt's investigations.

While never boring, the strip had an aura of calmness, largely due to its artwork of a somewhat academic realism. This was a welcome change in a newspaper of *Bild's* kind of sensationalism. It is regrettable that in Germany editors put their dislike of the strip medium above reader interest.

W.F.

"Diabolik," Angela and Giulana Giussani. © Astorina.

DIABOLIK (Italy) *Diabolik* was created by two sisters from Milan, Angela and Luciana Guissani, in the winter of 1962.

Diabolik is a supercriminal, an athletic antihero. He is cast in the usual hero mold of being both brave and clever. He is also a master of disguise who not only changes his facial features (by the use of plastic masks of his own invention) but also has gadgets that can transform his physical appearance. He is a modern-day version of the fabled rogue Arsene Lupin or the infamous Fantomas, in that he doesn't fight on the side of the law, as do traditional heroes, but against it, for his own amoral purposes. Theft and murder are his *modus vivendi*—but he pursues both with the skill and the intelligence of a master chess player.

While the reading public acclaimed *Diabolik*, the strip was immediately accused by puritans of "exalting crime and violence." Because of this the feature has been nicknamed "fumetto nero" (black comic strip); but Diabolik does not symbolize evil in every respect—one should not grant him total immorality. He is a superman (in the Nietzschean sense), and for him the morality of the average man is irrelevant. Stealing and killing does not ease his conscience, however—for he has a conscience and has demonstrated it many times. His own morality keeps him from breaking his monogamous relationship with Eva Kant, his beautiful and inseparable companion, and an essential figure in the story. Diabolik's code also compels him to come to the help of those loyal to him. On the other hand, Diabolik would destroy those who betray or deceive him, and likewise would eliminate those who might cross his path, not because of blood lust, but for the same reason one might crush an irritating insect.

Diabolik respects only those who are not afraid of him, or those who oppose him with a conviction equal to his. His main opponent is Ginko, a policeman who is Diabolik's double—perhaps an alter ego who has chosen good over evil. The stories in *Diabolik* present the encounter between two equally pure consciences who have deliberately chosen different and opposing paths.

The feature, though now written and drawn by a variety of ghosts, is still under the firm control of the Guissani sisters, who personally supervise the art assignments. The present staff consists of Flavio Bozzoli, Alarico Gattia, Sergio Zaniboni, Franco Paludetti (pencils); Glauco Cretti and Enzio Facciolo (pencils and inks); Paolo Ongaro, Lino Jeva, and Saverio Micheloni (inks).

Diabolik has given rise to a phenomenon of great importance in the Italian comics—the "fumetto nero" or "per adulti" (for adults only). Despite public outcry, political and media denunciation, and even condemnation from the Church, the amoral antihero has been pursuing his nefarious career for over 35 years now.

G.B.

DIAMOND, H. LOUIS (1904-1966) Henry Louis Diamond, British cartoonist, editor, and publisher, was born in 1904 in Bath, Somerset, where he died on October 13, 1966, at age 62. He worked on the *Daily Herald* and began freelancing strips to children's comics published by Fleetway Press. *Sweet Hortense* (1924) in *The Monster Comic* led to his drawing the full front page of *The Golden Penny* from their Hundredth Celebration Number: *High Jinks at High School* (1924). He replaced this with the extraordinary strip *Pot T. Pot and his Pet Patient, Piecan* (1927). Early strips for Amalgamated Press include *Ginjar the Turk* (1926) in *Butterfly*. After A.P. bought out the Fleetway comics, he drew for *Frolix* and *Rover*, the D. C. Thomson boys' paper, but was quick to join a local Bath firm, Provincial Comics, when they tried comic publishing in 1931.

He drew *Micky the Merry Midget* on the front of *The Merry Midget* and *Alfie, Auntie & Annabel* for *The Sparkler*, soon taking over editorial control of these weeklies. The venture failed within six months but, enjoying

H. L. Diamond, "Chuckle Our Own Clown." © Ovaltiney.

the experience, Diamond enlisted another Bath printer and set up Target Publications. After a trial run with two weekly story libraries, *Target* and *C.I.D.*, he brought out his first pair of comic weeklies, *Rattler* and *Dazzler* (August 19, 1933). The first issues were bumper 16-page affairs for one penny, but he soon settled down to 12 pages. Thus, although the artwork was generally lower than A.P. standards (Diamond paid half-a-crown [12-1/2 p; 25 cents] per panel), to indiscriminating children they were a bargain buy, having four more pages for the price than their A.P. counterpart.

Diamond followed with *Chuckler* (1934), *Target* (1935), *Rocket* (1935), *Sunshine* (1938), and *Bouncer* (1939), plus the giveaway *Ovaltiney's Own Comic* (1935), all with artwork by the same team: E. H. Banger, Bert Hill, S. K. Perkins, G. Larkman, and Diamond.

Target publications sold out to A.P. in 1939, and all the titles were immediately discontinued. Diamond was not given the editorial post he had been promised, but returned to freelance drawing for A.P.'s *Jester* and *Crackers*. There was an immediate improvement in his work (*Buster Button*, etc.), which had grown very hasty at Target. During the war he worked for the Admiralty at Lansdown, Bath, freelancing his first adventure strips, *Caleb King's Mine*, etc., to *Comic Capers* (1943) and other Soloway Publications.

He became freelance editor of Martin & Reid's comics in 1947 (*Jolly Western,* etc.) while working as an income tax officer. His last drawings appeared in *Fizz* (1949). Although his style was considered below standard by the major publishers, it was simple and clean and amused undiscerning children.

D.G.

DICK BOS (Netherlands) *Dick Bos* ("*Dick Bush*" is one of the possible translations) is one of the earlier adventure strips to come out of the Netherlands. The strip's creator, Alfred Mazure (born September 8, 1913, in Nijmegen, Netherlands) had already done another private detective comic strip, *De Chef* ("The Boss"), in 1932. The adventures of private eye Dick Bos started on July 20, 1940, with a story entitled "De geval Kleyn" ("The Kleyn Case"). With World War II in progress, it did not take German occupation forces long to discover Dutch comic strips and try to convert them into a propaganda tool. Allegedly it was the Berlin publishing house Ullstein Verlag that offered print runs of one million copies of *Dick Bos* comic books for distribution among the Wehrmacht, if Mazure went along with their plans to change Dick Bos into a Nazi spy. Mazure, an active member of resistance groups at the time, refused to cooperate, and *Dick Bos* was barred from publication. Thus the first run of *Dick Bos* comic book reprints (of nearly square format) ended in 1945. *Dick Bos* shared this fate with a number of Dutch strips.

Dick Bos was back in the private eye business in his "beeldroman" ("picture novel") world after World War II ended. The picture novel became the pattern for a number of books, like *Tarzan*, *Bob Crack*, and *Lex Brand*. The books not only had a tendency toward the same kind of style, more often than not they also sported similar plots. The new series of *Dick Bos* comic books started with reprints of earlier books in a somewhat edited form, then continued with new material until 1964.

Dick Bos started out as a tough guy with whom crooks had to reckon. He not only cleared up crimes but meted out justice as well, much in the tradition of classic private eyes of the day. While his first case hinted at his having killed a criminal, the character was toned down in later years, when he used guns only to shoot other guns out of criminals' hands. *Dick Bos* was done in a style consisting of firm lines with a well-balanced use of black, gray, and white spaces.

W.F.

DICKENSON, FRED (1909-1989) American newspaperman and writer, born in Chicago on January 18, 1909. After studies at the University of Illinois, Fred Dickenson began his career with the Chicago City News Bureau and, as one of his first assignments, covered the St. Valentine's Day Massacre on February 14, 1929.

In subsequent years Dickenson worked as a reporter, rewrite man, and editor for a number of newspapers throughout the country, and for the Associated Press. He covered many of the most important crime stories of the era, including the Winnie Ruth Judd murders, the search for John Dillinger, the murder of Arthur Flegenheimer (alias "Dutch Schultz"), and the capture of Bruno Hauptman, kidnapper of the Lindbergh baby.

Fred Dickenson joined King Features Syndicate as an associate editor in 1943, while continuing to write stories for newspapers and magazines, and a mystery novel (*Kill'em With Kindness*, 1950). In 1952 he began writing the continuity for *Rip Kirby*, the detective strip created by Alex Raymond in 1946.

Fred Dickenson's knowledge of crime, the criminal world, and police procedures was a contributing factor in *Rip Kirby*'s enduring success. Following Alex Raymond's sudden death in 1956, Dickenson worked harmoniously with Raymond's successor, John Prentice. He continued to write the strip, despite ill health, almost until the time of his death in 1989.

M.H.

DICK FULMINE (Italy) In 1938 Mussolini banned all American comic strips from Italian newspapers (with the exception of *Mickey Mouse*), and the unhappy Italian publishers frantically scrambled to replace them with homemade products. *Dick Fulmine*, drawn by Carlo Cossio and written by Vincenzo Baggioli, was

"Dick Fulmine," Carlo Cossio. © Vulcania.

one of these newly minted strips, making its appearance that same year in the illustrated weekly *L'Audace*.

Dick Fulmine (whose name means "lightning") was initially an Italian-American adventurer, vaguely affiliated with an imaginary international law enforcement agency, whose exploits carried him to all corners of the world. Unabashedly modeled after the "giant of Sequals" Primo Carnera, whose popularity was then at its peak in Italy, Dick was a broad-shouldered, square-jawed, thick-boned athlete who used his fists as his most powerful weapons in preference to his guns (or his brains, unfortunately). He could be seen, at least four or five times per episode, ritualistically rolling up his sleeves, while taunting his enemies to a fight with such verbal incitements as: "Don't be afraid, my little turtledoves, I'll take good care of you!" before flattening them with a few well-directed blows from his powerful arms.

Among Fulmine's many enemies were the herculean black Cuban Zambo, the only man able to stand up to Dick for more than a few seconds; the underhanded White Mask, a master criminal who used a gas-filled gun to overcome his opponents; the South American adventurer Barerra; and the mighty hypnotist Flattavion. Try as they might, however, in the end they could never quite measure up to Dick's simple justice.

During World War II our hero became simply Fulmine, and his adventures took a decidedly bellicose turn: he fought on the African and Russian fronts, and even helped the Japanese in the Pacific; after the war he resumed his free-booting ways. When Carlo Cossio retired (for reasons of health) in 1955, his creation disappeared with him.

Dick Fulmine was undeniably Cossio's strip. Others might have at times written some of the scripts (Baggioli, A. Martini, Carlo's brother Vittorio) or even drawn a few of Fulmine's adventures (Vittorio Cossio again, Giorgio Scudellari, Sinchetto), but the strip remains permeated with Carlo Cossio's unique style, a mixture of slapdash (but effective) draftsmanship and breathless showmanship. Cossio had a flair for the colorful pose, the bravura stance, the fast pacing of action, and these qualities made *Dick Fulmine* into one of Italy's most popular strips, and a favorite with many foreign readers as well.

In 1967 Editoriale Corno started reprinting the complete and unexpurgated collection of Fulmine's adventures, and this caused an outcry in Italy, with many critics leveling charges of fascism and racism against the strip. The furor died down, however, and *Dick Fulmine* has now taken its place among the classic Italian comic strips.

M.H.

DICKIE DARE (U.S.) *Dickie Dare* was created by Milton Caniff for Associated Press Newsfeatures in July 1933.

Dickie was a bright young lad with a yen for adventure and a vivid imagination, who would daydream his way into any book that fired his enthusiasm. The first episode involved Dickie and his dog Wags on the side of Robin Hood and his Merry Men; he later fought alongside Jim Hawkins against Long John Silver and even rescued Robinson Crusoe!

The readers, however, did not take overwhelmingly to Dick's imagination, and early in 1934, Caniff remodeled *Dickie Dare* into a slam-bang adventure strip, adding Dan Flynn, a swashbuckling soldier of fortune, as

"Dickie Dare," Milton Caniff. © AP Newsfeatures.

Dick's companion and mentor. The new *Dickie Dare* strip attracted the notice of Colonel Patterson, of the Chicago Tribune-New York News Syndicate, who asked Caniff to create a new action feature for his syndicate (it turned out to be *Terry and the Pirates*, in which Caniff used the same combination of manly hero and boy companion).

Upon Caniff's departure in October 1934, *Dickie Dare* was taken over by Coulton Waugh, who, in the course of his 10-year stewardship over the strip, retained much of Caniff's flavor and added a few personal touches of his own. Unlike Caniff's *Terry*, Waugh's *Dickie Dare* was to remain a strip of pure adventure. Dickie and Dan sailed the seven seas aboard Dan's yacht, getting involved with brigands, gun-runners, international spies, and power-mad potentates along the way (one 1939 episode had Dan and Dickie foiling the evil designs of an Arabian sheik in one of Waugh's most entertaining and exciting stories).

In the spring of 1944, Coulton Waugh was succeeded by his former assistant (and future bride) Mabel Odin Burvik (she signed her name simply "Odin"), who managed to keep the strip on its course for a while; but times had changed, and after a slow decline, *Dickie Dare* was finally dropped in the late 1950s.

Dickie Dare is remembered today chiefly for Caniff's contribution. Yet one should not forget Coulton Waugh, who managed, in his easygoing, winning style, to establish *Dickie Dare* as the most entertaining and agreeable kid-adventure strip of the period.

M.H.

DICK'S ADVENTURES IN DREAMLAND (U.S.) King Features Syndicate's *Dick's Adventures in Dreamland* was created at the express direction of William Randolph Hearst himself. In December of 1945 Hearst sent the following message to J. P. Gortatowsky, then president of KFS: "I have had numerous suggestions for incorporating American history of a vivid kind in the adventure strips of the comic section. It seems to me that something (sic) which told the youthful life of our American heroes and how they developed into great men and their great moments might be interesting." The editors took the hint and on January 12, 1947, *Dick's Adventures* finally saw the light as a Sunday feature written by Max Trell and drawn by Neil O'Keefe.

A FEW MOMENTS LATER THEY ARE AT WHARFSIDE! HERE A BUSTLING CROWD OF STEVEDORES IS ALREADY LOADING A THIRD SHIP! "LOOK," CRIES DICK, "WE'RE ALMOST READY TO SAIL!"

"Dick's Adventures in Dreamland," Neil O'Keefe. © King Features Syndicate.

"Dick Tracy," Chester Gould. © Chicago Tribune.

Utilizing the dream device (in a manner more reminiscent of *Dickie Dare* than of *Little Nemo*), Dick traveled back in time in the company of some of the most illustrious names in American history. He fought alongside George Washington at Valley Forge, sailed the oceans with John Paul Jones, and even witnessed the invention of the cotton gin by Eli Whitney. The successive episodes did not flow naturally into one another but were arbitrarily tied together by Dick's waking up from one dream to relapse into another, a kind of oneiric fade-out fade-in. Dick was slowly dreaming his way toward World War I when, the gimmick having worn thin (and Hearst having died in the meantime), the series was discontinued in October 1956.

Didactic strips have never been popularly accepted, and *Dick's Adventures* was no exception. The strip was not without merit, however. O'Keefe's style is airy and atmospheric, with none of the clutter that many draftsmen feel obligated to bring to the "historical" feature, and one can occasionally learn something from the earnest but pedestrian text.

M.H.

DICK TRACY (U.S.) In 1931 Chester Gould, after several unsuccessful attempts, submitted a strip to Joseph Patterson, editor of the Chicago Tribune-New York News Syndicate, about a Chicago detective tentatively named "Plainclothes Tracy." Patterson accepted the proposed feature but changed the name, and so *Dick Tracy* was born on Sunday, October 4, 1931. The daily strip soon followed, on Monday, October 12, of the same year.

In the first daily episode, Dick Tracy was the powerless witness to a holdup in the course of which his sweetheart, Tess Trueheart, was kidnapped and her father murdered. In revulsion Tracy joined the police force and unrelentingly tracked down the criminals responsible for the act.

Tracy's first adversaries, Ribs Mocco, Larceny Lu, Stooge Viller, Boris Arson, Shirtsleeve Kelton, and Whip Chute, were the conventional villains of pulp and movie fiction—racketeers, killers, kidnappers, bank robbers, counterfeiters, mob lawyers, etc. Gradually these were replaced by a rogues' gallery of grotesque criminals with appropriate faces or mannerisms for their names. One of the first was Frank Redrum, alias "the Blank," who hid his face behind a featureless mask. The Blank was soon followed by Jerome Trohs, a midget with a giant ego and a criminal brain; "the Brow," a master spy whose forehead was a mess of creases and wrinkles; the aptly named Pruneface; Shaky, who must kill in order to steady his shattered nerves; Mr. Bribery, collector of roses and shrunken heads; and many more in this grisly circus of horrors. Most of them met ends as horrible as their deeds. They were shot through the head, impaled on flag poles, buried alive, scalded, hanged, frozen to death.

Tracy's career has also had its vicissitudes; he has been shot countless times, blinded by acid, tortured, stabbed, maimed, and crippled. Not that his personal life has been any quieter. His adopted son, Junior, was kidnapped and beaten on several occasions, his fiancée Tess, a moody and unpredictable lady, jilted him at regular intervals before they finally got married in 1949, and their daughter Bonny Braids was also kidnapped. Tracy's only support has come from his superior, Chief Brandon, and from his associates, Pat Patton, Sam Catchem, and Lizz the policewoman. But the eagle-nosed, square-chinned Tracy has always pursued his relentless crusade against crime.

Dick Tracy was the first realistic police strip. Violent, brutal, often cruel, it has played an important role in the history of American comics by breaking many taboos. Its influence, due both to its massive, dark appearance, and the tightness of its scripts, has been noticeable not only on other detective strips, but also on the whole field of action comics, which have borrowed heavily from its plotting and its techniques.

Dick Tracy was the subject of over a half-dozen movies from 1937 to 1947 (Ralph Byrd played the detective in most of them), a radio program in the forties, a television series in the fifties (starring Ralph Byrd again), and a number of animated cartoons in the sixties. He also inspired Al Capp's parody, *Fearless Fosdick*. In 1970 Chelsea House published a hardbound anthology of his adventures, *The Celebrated Cases of Dick Tracy*, with an introduction by Ellery Queen. A new Dick Tracy movie was released in 1990, with Warren Beatty directing himself in the title role.

Gould retired from the strip at the end of 1977, while still retaining a byline on the feature. Rick Fletcher, who had been Gould's assistant, took over the artwork, and mystery writer Max Allan Collins wrote the scripts. Collins imparted a less grim, more modern tone to the square-jawed detective's adventures, which prompted protests from the creator, who withdrew his name from the strip in 1981. Fletcher's death in 1983 further complicated matters: as his replacement, the syndicate picked editorial cartoonist Dick Locher. In 1992 Collins was abruptly replaced by Michael Kilian, in the latest chapter of the real-life *Dick Tracy* saga.

M.H.

DIEGO VALOR (Spain) In October 1953 the Spanish radio network SER started a daily program devoted to the adventures of Keith Watson's hero Dan Dare under the title of *Diego Valor*. A little later the producers decided to drop the original British scripts in favor of a purely Spanish treatment, which no longer had anything to do with its initial inspiration. The program reached the record number of 1,200 broadcasts before being discontinued in June 1958.

One year after its birth on the air, *Diego Valor* was adapted into comic book form (June 20, 1954). With issue number 10, the comic book version was entrusted to its original creator, the writer Jarber (pseudonym of Enrique Jarnés Bergua), who gave it its definitive characteristics, with the help of his illustrators, Buylla and Bayo (Braulio Rodriguez). With issue 168 (March 1958), the comic book ceased publication, while *Diego Valor* was revived for one short year as a color page in the children's supplement of the magazine *La Revista Española* (1963).

Diego Valor was a Spanish commandant born in the year 2000 and regarded by his fellow men as the great-

"Diego Valor," Buylla. © Editorial Cid.

est hero in the history of the world, no less! At the head of his team, he visited the planet Venus and a satellite of Jupiter named Kelos, where he fought a race of extraordinarily old beings who wanted to conquer the world. Valor's main collaborator and friend was Beatriz Fantana, a shining example of future womanhood, the equal of any man. The scenarios of *Diego Valor* were bellicose and triumphalistic, the drawings simple and without great quality, but the rapid-fire action made up for any artistic deficiency. With the double advantage of a daily radio program and a weekly comic book, *Diego Valor* was, in its time, a phenomenal success. There were several stage adaptations, a television serial, and countless collections of records, color cards, and toys.

L.G.

DILBERT (U.S.) More than 30 years after William H. Whyte Jr. published *The Organization Man,* an engineer with an MBA from Berkeley named Scott Adams created *Dilbert* for United Feature Syndicate, which began its distribution on April 16, 1989.

Dilbert, an engineer and corporate denizen, is the bespectacled, white-shirt-and-tie-wearing, unheroic protagonist working at a company on the proverbial cutting edge of technology. He spends his eight-hour-plus workdays combating the incompetence of his dismissal-proof manager, who, with two spikes of hair on either side of his head reminiscent of the Devil's horns, is too interested in the latest management fads to learn the basics of his job. Dilbert is inundated with meaningless and contradictory memos while forever

DILBERT

"Dilbert," Scott Adams. © United Feature Syndicate.

Ding Cong, a typical pose from a 1985 strip. © Ding Cong.

attending meetings and pre-meetings and reading mission statements from upper management, "visioning" documents from consultants, and team-building morale reports from facilitators.

Fans of the comic strip see a faithful reflection of their own professional world, with its maze-like layout of cubicles, corporate jargonistic gobbledygook, and double-talk (for example, "We have to be more competitive" means "Say goodbye to salary increases," or "We're market driven" means "We blame customers for our lack of innovation"), not to mention outright lies such as "Your input is important to us" and "We reward risk takers."

Dilbert's colleagues share his experiences. Although the frizzy-haired Alice may work 80-hour weeks and donate bone marrow to the company's biggest customer, she receives a 2% raise because her performance for the year "meets expectations." Tina, the public relations person, must put a positive spin on a product that "causes hallucinations and sterility"—not without tiny pangs of conscience, however. For his part, Wally gets a white T-shirt for his 10 years of service to the company, but since he does so little around the office, he gratefully acknowledges his employer's generosity.

Catbert, the evil Human Resources director, aptly portrayed as a cat, enjoys his unlimited pink-slip power as he plays cat-and-mouse games with the employees. Constantly inventing new ways of demeaning them, he shrinks cubicle sizes (the "Densification Project") or orders that employees wear smaller shoes (the "Foot-sizing Program") to reduce wear and tear on the carpeting: "We must do this to be competitive," he gleefully concludes one of his E-mail nastygrams.

Only Dogbert, Dilbert's potato-shaped sidekick and canine master-of-all-trades, views the world clearly: Stupidity, ignorance, morning breath, selfishness, lust, fear, money, and luck—in that order—are the ruling forces of the universe. To him, people (including Dilbert) are morons and prove his theory again and again. He believes people are in desperate need of "a leader whose vision can penetrate the thick fog of human incompetence"—in other words, himself!

What the strip lacks in artistic development, it more than compensates for by its satirical bite and true-to-life workplace situations and characters. This explains the strip's tremendous success—more than 1,000 newspapers carry the strip, while Dilbert and Dogbert have graced the covers of *Newsweek* and *TV Guide*—and the exploding market for *Dilbert* merchandise. In addition, Scott Adams wrote two illustrated, wonderfully funny books, which appeared in 1996 and which were both immediate best-sellers: one, based on Dilbert's life in "cubicle hell," *The Dilbert Principle*, and the other, a highly useful compilation of management wisdom by Dogbert, *Dogbert's Top Secret Management Handbook*.

P.L.H.

DING CONG (1916-   ) Ding Cong's father, Ding Song, was a well-known cartoonist in China in the 1920s who did not want his son to be an artist like himself. Desiring an easier life for Ding Cong, the cartoonist refused to teach him to draw. The only professional training the self-taught Ding Cong had was one semester at the Shanghai Fine Arts Institute. Once he started publishing cartoons at the age of 17, he never stopped creating, with the exceptions of the period from 1957 to 1960 when he was not allowed to publish cartoons after being wrongly accused as a "rightist"; and later during the Cultural Revolution when all cartooning in China ceased for 10 years from 1966 to 1976. His cartoons have brought him fame as one of the best cartoonists in China. He is known not only for his speed in creating his works, but also for the fine drawing and outstanding humor and satire in his comics.

In addition to Ding's single cartoons, his best-known cartoon series includes a comic titled *Reflection of the Society*, which was created in early 1945 during the Sino-Japanese War. Another one of Ding's collections is *Wit and Humour from Ancient China: 100 Cartoons by Ding Cong*, published in 1988 in both English and

Chinese. In this collection, Ding's jokes are inspired by Chinese history, biographies, novels, and anecdotes dating from the third century B.C. to the 17th century A.D. With wit and humor, Ding ridicules stupid government officials and pokes fun at the follies and pretensions of people.

During his more than 60-year career in cartooning, Ding Cong has drawn cartoons, illustrated stories, and designed for many different publications. Although he is an older man, he always signs his work with the name "Xiao Ding" (Little Ding), which indicates his childlike heart with an optimistic, energetic, and diligent spirit.

H.Y.L.L.

DINGBAT FAMILY, THE (U.S.) An oblong, upright strip of six panels, with a separate, illustrated logo, *The Dingbat Family* started in the *New York Journal* on June 20, 1910. Its cast of five was lined up and labeled in the opening logo as "Ma" Dingbat; the family kids named Imogene, Cicero, and Baby; and their father, E. Pluribus Dingbat. Beside the Dingbats, two unnamed family pets, a cat and a dog, were shown, although neither took part in the first episode. (They were to become, after some permutations, two of the stars of the ultimate strip: Krazy Kat and Offisa Pupp.)

The Dingbat Family from the outset was a raffish, knockabout farce about an underpaid, middle-aged office clerk, his lumpish wife, and their difficult prog-

"The Dingbat Family," George Herriman. © King Features Syndicate.

eny. It does not seem to have been too successful, and by July 9, 1910, Herriman had apparently been urged to dump the family conflict and focus on Dingbat, for a series of strips simply titled *Mr. Dingbat* began on that date. On July 26, 1910, however, Herriman had one of those bursts of inspiration that are the prerogatives of genius, and produced an episode titled "Mr. Dingbat Demands His Rights from the Family Upstairs." The action took place in Dingbat's apartment and involved the irritating behavior of an unseen family living in the apartment directly above. This family, which continued in subsequent episodes to keep out of the Dingbats' sight without ceasing to harass them, had become Herriman's focal point. The Dingbats became obsessed with the desire to find out who the upper tenants were, and to get them out of the building—always without success. Readers were fascinated and absorbed, and the Herriman strip (which underwent its second title change in six weeks, this time to *The Family Upstairs* on August 1, 1910) became a *Journal* institution and a feature in Hearst afternoon papers across the country.

On November 15, 1911, Herriman surprised everyone by ending the *Family Upstairs* mystery with the total destruction of the Dingbat apartment building, after which, on November 22, 1911, the Dingbats returned in a strip once again called *The Dingbat Family*. Herriman continued with the feature, drawing it in tandem with *Krazy Kat* (which was given its own berth on October 28, 1913) until the older strip wearied its creator, and he replaced it with a new daily feature, *Baron Bean*, on January 5, 1916.

B.B.

DINGLE, ADRIAN (1912-1974) Born in Wales of Cornish parents in 1912 and brought to Canada at the age of three, Adrian Dingle launched his adult working career as an insurance company employee in Oakville, Ontario, near Toronto, but soon began serious work as a painter, gaining critical attention in the early 1930s. During this period he turned to commercial art to finance his artistic endeavors. In 1941 Dingle created a comic strip called *Nelvana of the Northern Lights* for Triumph-Adventure Comics, an independent "Canadian white" established that June by the Hillborough Studio in Toronto. In 1942 Triumph Adventure, its name pared down to Triumph, was absorbed by Bell Features and Publishing Company, Toronto. Beginning in September 1941 with one publication—Wow Comics—in the wake of a Canadian government embargo on U.S. comic books, it grew to include Dime, Active, Joke, Commando, and Dizzy Don as well as Triumph.

Dingle joined Bell and carried on with Nelvana, a semi-mythological heroine who received fantastic powers from the Aurora Borealis. In addition, he created *The Penguin*, about a crime fighter in birdlike mask, white tie, and tails; *The Sign of Freedom*, the tale of an RCAF pilot turned Underground hero; and *Nils Grant, Private Investigator*.

During his years with Bell, doubling as its art director, Dingle also succeeded other artists on such strips as *Active Jim*, *Rex Baxter*, *Clift Steele*, and *Guy Powers Secret Agent*, the last two done under the pen name Darian. Eventually, Dingle also took on the task of drawing the majority of Bell's color covers, either under his own name or the Darian pseudonym, after the principal cover artist, Edmond Good, left to take over the *Scorchy Smith* comic strip in the United States.

With the reappearance of U.S. comic books on Canadian newsstands near the end of World War II, Canadian publishers geared up for full-color printing. When the changeover came, Dingle continued *Nelvana* and *The Penguin* (which was renamed *The Blue Raven*). Competition from the U.S. was too stiff, however, and Canadian comics faded from the scene by the late 1940s, although publishers kept their presses busy by printing Canadian editions of U.S. titles. By the early 1950s, even this industry had disappeared.

Dingle had kept at his painting through the war years and, with the demise of the Canadian comic book industry, decided to pursue it as a full-time career. Over 25 years he developed into one of Canada's foremost landscape and semi-abstract artists, traveling and painting in France, Italy, Spain, England, Portugal, Ireland, New England, and Canada's Atlantic Provinces, before his death in 1974.

P.H.

"Dinglehoofer und His Dog Adolph," Harold Knerr. © King Features Syndicate.

DINGLEHOOFER UND HIS DOG ADOLPH (U.S.)
Harold Knerr created *Dinglehoofer und His Dog Adolph* in 1926 as a top to his celebrated *Katzenjammer Kids*. Obscured by the fame of its dazzling companion strip, *Dinglehoofer* has remained almost totally unresearched in spite of its undeniable qualities.

Dinglehoofer ("Mr. Dingy") was a small, dumpy middle-class German-American (he spoke in a Teutonized version of English, not too far removed from the Katzenjammers' jargon) who lived with a young boy named Tad and a feisty little bulldog named Adolph. Tad was a good fellow, high-spirited but helpful, mischievous but nice, a far cry from Hans and Fritz. In this strip it was the dog who got the others involved in a variety of escapades. As another (and far more threatening) Adolph arose in the 1930s, Dinglehoofer traded his dog Adolph for a basset named Schnappsy, and the strip retained all of its quality.

Dinglehoofer's humor always remained quiet and serene, a counterpoint to the thunder and lightning of the hectic *Katzenjammers*. The adventures of the Dinglehoofers were in the same low-key mode (Adolph—or Schnappsy—digging up the bones of a prehistoric animal, or befriending a pair of burglars, etc.) and often were continued from week to week. While not on a par with *The Katzenjammers, Dinglehoofer* was nonetheless a minor gem of gentle and engaging fun. *Dinglehoofer* survived its creator's death in 1949 by a few

years. It was continued by Doc Winner until it was finally dropped in 1952.

M.H.

DIRKS, JOHN (1917-   ) American cartoonist, son of Rudolph Dirks, born November 2, 1917, in New York City. He graduated from Yale University in 1939 with degrees in English and fine arts. He started selling cartoons to *Collier's* and the *Saturday Evening Post* while he was still an undergraduate. Drafted during World War II, he was sent to the European theater and was demobilized as a captain in 1945.

Soon after the end of the war, John Dirks returned to illustration and cartooning. He started assisting his father on *The Captain and the Kids* in the mid-1940s and took over the strip in 1958 without altering its original character and spirit.

Since 1960 John Dirks has acquired growing recognition as a metal sculptor as well as a cartoonist. He is particularly noted for the water fountains that he designs and sells all over the world. After *The Captain and the Kids* was discontinued in 1979, he did some drawings of the Kids for promotion and advertising purposes.

M.H.

DIRKS, RUDOLPH (1877-1968) American cartoonist, born in 1877 in Heinde, Germany. The son of a wood-carver, Rudolph Dirks came to Chicago with his immigrant parents at the age of seven. By 1894 he was already selling cartoons to *Judge* and *Life*. In 1897, at the height of the newspaper war between Hearst and Pulitzer, he joined Hearst's *New York Journal*. Rudolph Block, the *Journal's* editor, was then looking for a feature that could compete with the highly successful *Yellow Kid*, the rival *World's* star attraction. He asked the young Dirks to create an original Sunday strip and sug-

Rudolph Dirks.

gested Wilhelm Busch's *Max und Moritz* as a model. On December 12, 1897, *The Katzenjammer Kids* first appeared.

In 1912 Dirks wanted to leave for Europe to devote himself to painting, with the result that Hearst took *The Katzenjammer Kids* away from him. A celebrated court battle ensued, and Dirks won back the right to draw his characters (but not the right to use the title, which went to Hearst), which he did, in 1914, for the *World* under the title of *Hans and Fritz* (later changed to *The Captain and the Kids*).

In addition to his work as a cartoonist, Rudolph Dirks did paintings and engravings. He was associated with different art movements, including the "Ash Can School," and he cofounded the artists colony at Ogunquit, Maine. In 1958 he retired and relinquished *The Captain and the Kids* to his son John. Dirks died in New York City on April 20, 1968.

One of the "founding fathers" of the American comics, Rudolph Dirks has left a permanent imprint on all facets of the medium, which he helped to develop. His themes and style were widely imitated and shamelessly plagiarized in the United States and in Europe; his creative use of balloons and dialogue revolutionized the technique and format of the picture-story; while his legal battle with Hearst created the precedent on which most of the jurisprudence relating to the comic strip is based.

M.H.

DISNEY, WALT (1901-1966) American artist and businessman, born in Chicago on December 5, 1901. Walter Elias Disney, born into a very poor family, studied first in Kansas City, then at the Chicago Art Institute. After a short stint as an ambulance driver on the European front during World War I, Walt Disney started working for an advertising agency in Kansas City. In 1923, in partnership with his brother Roy, he opened a small motion-picture animation studio in Hollywood. After having created two ephemeral series, *Alice in Cartoonland* in 1925 and *Oswald the Rabbit* in 1927, Walt Disney, with the assistance of Ub Iwerks, produced in 1928 the first cartoon of Mickey Mouse, perhaps the most beloved cartoon character ever conceived. Dozens upon dozens of inspired creations followed: the *Silly Symphonies*, *The Three Little Pigs*, *Donald Duck*, *Snow White*, *Pinocchio*, *Dumbo*, and many others. Most of these creations were later adapted into comic strips and comic books with great success (notably *Mickey Mouse* and *Donald Duck*).

Though not a comic strip artist himself, Walt Disney had great impact on the field, either directly through his creations or indirectly through the many cartoonists who served their apprenticeships in his studios—among them Carl Barks, Floyd Gottfredson, and Walt Kelly.

Walt Disney died in Hollywood on December 15, 1966.

M.H.

DI 13 (Philippines) The June 14, 1947, premier issue of *Pilipino Komiks* featured the strip *DI 13* ("DI Trese"). The series was written by Damy Velasquez, the brother of Tony Velasquez, and illustrated by Jesse Santos.

DI 13 was one of the longest-running dramatic features ever to appear in the history of Philippine comic

"DI-13," Tony Velasquez. © Pilipino Komiks.

books. It was also the most popular detective strip in the country.

DI is the abbreviation for the Detective Bureau of Investigation. Trese, the main character, is a James Bond-type of individual—sure of himself, dashing, suave, brave, debonaire, daring, intelligent, and tough. Though he has a regular girlfriend named Sally, he is not averse to tangling with members of the opposite sex.

The tempo of the series varies, depending on the type of story being told. At times the setting is quiet, but there is always a feeling of suspense in the air. In the case of very puzzling crimes, Trese's approach is methodical in order to cope with the perplexity and intricacy of the mystery. Intellect rather than force is used. Then there are other moments when everything is moving at high velocity—cycles dashing about, roaring through the countryside, and cars careening in the city streets, knocking down everything in sight and then exploding into a million fragments. There are also situations in which the hero has to rely on his quick wits and fast reflexes to subdue a swift and tricky assailant, to parry the cobralike lunges of a villainous knife-wielder, or to escape the clutches of a strong and murderous fiend. And when the only thing that separates Trese from certain death is the instinct to survive, though battered and bleeding, he pulls through by sheer tenacity and courage—which almost leaves the reader gasping from the exertion.

The locale is often changed to add variety to the script. Humor is interjected at the right moments to add relief from the suspense and to break the seriousness of a situation. The series combined well-written stories with excellent artwork and lasted into the 1960s.

O.J.

DITKO, STEVE (1927-   ) American comic book artist, born November 2, 1927, in Johnstown, Pennsylvania. He was educated at the Cartoonist and Illustrators School, where he was heavily influenced by renowned comic artist Jerry Robinson. Even Ditko himself is not sure where his first strip appeared—"It was so small," he once said, "I can't even remember the name"—but his material was appearing as early as

WAS IT A *THIEF?* ANYTHING TAKEN?

DOUBT IT...ONLY ROOM DISTURBED IN THE WHOLE PLACE WAS THE LIBRARY... WHO'D WANNA STEAL A *BOOK?*

Steve Ditko, "Collector's Edition." © Warren Publications.

1953 in horror comics published by Farrell, Prize, Charlton, and St. John. In 1956, Ditko began drawing horror and supernatural stories for Atlas (later Marvel).

After a short stint on Charlton's ill-fated *Captain Atom* and *Gorgo* books, Ditko got his first major superhero assignment in 1962—drawing the *Spider-Man* strip in Marvel's *Amazing Fantasy* number 15. It quickly became a phenomenal success, due mainly to a strong story line and Ditko's unique, almost grotesque renderings of Spider-Man and alter ego Peter Parker. Slightly paranoid and always guilt-ridden, *Spider-Man* was a perfect vehicle for Ditko's exciting but simple style. Ditko also began writing and drawing the *Dr. Strange* feature in 1963, which, unlike the realistic *Spider-Man*, afforded him the opportunity to introduce intricate, eerie worlds of mysticism and intrigue. And although he left both strips in 1966—precipitated by a disagreement with editor Stan Lee—his versions remain the definitive ones.

Immediately following his abrupt departure from Marvel, Ditko produced outstanding material for Warren, Tower, Dell, National, and other groups. But his best work during 1966 through 1968 was done for Charlton, where he received two old superheroes, *Blue Beetle* and *Captain Atom*, and created *The Question* strip.

Originally designed as a backup feature in *Blue Beetle*, *The Question* quickly became the most provocative feature on the market. Based on *Mr. A*, a character he created, wrote, and drew for Wally Wood's *Witzend* magazine, *The Question* dealt with the tremendous philosophical battles between the diverse elements of American society. The character's world was a narrow one: there were "black" or evil forces; there were "white" or good forces; but there were no "gray" forces of compromise. *The Question* saw any compromise as an acceptance of evil that could not be tolerated. The quintessential display of the character's philosophy was exhibited in *Mysterious Suspense* number one (Summer, 1968). It consisted of a 25-page battle between the thinly veiled forces of "good" and "evil," and many critics consider the strip one of the best commercial comic books ever published.

After Charlton dropped their superhero titles in 1968, Ditko created two short-lived features for National that same year. Entitled *The Hawk and The Dove* and *The Creeper*, both were less successful ver-

sions of *The Question*. An illness forced Ditko off both strips shortly after their inception, and both were discontinued within a year. When he returned to drawing in late 1969, it was for Charlton's horror and supernatural titles.

Ditko was intent on pursuing the philosophical comics he pioneered, however, and he revived *Mr. A* for many limited-edition magazine appearances. Two collections of his philosophy comics have appeared, *Mr. A* (1973) and *Avenging World* (1974).

J.B.

In 1979 Ditko returned to Marvel, working notably on such titles as *Rom*, *Captain Universe*, and *Indiana Jones*. He left the comic-book field in the mid-1980s but made a much-publicized comeback in February 1997 with the cumbersomely named *Steve Ditko's Strange Avenging Tales*.

M.H.

TRAÉ, NENITO, YO TE INFLO EL GLOBO

Guillermo Divito, "Fulmine". © Rico Tipo.

DIVITO, GUILLERMO (1914-1969) An Argentinian cartoonist and illustrator born in Buenos Aires in 1914, Guillermo Divito owes his early fame to the grace and style with which he depicted the female figure, his famous "Divito girls," tall and luscious beauties with incredibly narrow waists and exaggerated and generous bosoms.

Divito started his career in 1931 in *Paginas de Columba*, and some time later he began his collaboration with Dante Quinterno, producing such comic strips as *El Enemigo del Hombre* ("Man's Enemy") and *Oscar Dientes de Leche* ("Milk Teeth Oscar"), both published in the comic magazine *Patoruzu*. Starting in 1944 he devoted himself to the launching and success of the humor magazine *Rico Tipo*, which he founded. He also inspired a whole school of cartoonists, not only in Argentina but also in Spain. His creations, typically

"Dixie Dugan," John Striebel and J. P. McEvoy. © McNaught Syndicate.

Argentinian, include *Bombolo, Pochita Morfoni, El Doctor Merengue* (his first big success in 1942), *Fulmine* (about a black-hearted villain), and his most popular work, *Fallutelli* (1944).

Guillermo Divito was killed in a car crash in 1969.

L.G.

DIXIE DUGAN (U.S.) The history of *Dixie Dugan's* conception is complicated and in a sense exemplary, as it explains the many factors (artistic, financial, commercial) that go into the making of a syndicated strip.

Artist John Striebel and writer J. P. McEvoy had been friends since boyhood, and when McEvoy sold *Liberty* the serialization rights to his novel *Show Girl*, he insisted that Striebel be the illustrator. Later the novel was adapted to the stage and made into a movie. This prompted the McNaught Syndicate to ask McEvoy and Striebel for a comic strip version, and it made its appearance in October 1929. The strip did not sell, and the editors decided to change the title from *Show Girl* to *Dixie Dugan*, to get the heroine out of show business. A new salesman, aspiring cartoonist Ham Fisher, took the strip on the road and promptly sold it to 30 newspapers. (His success, incidentally, led Fisher to sell his own strip, *Joe Palooka*, the same way a few months later.)

The object of all this maneuvering seems in retrospect not worth the effort. *Dixie Dugan* was never a very distinguished strip, even when judged by the low standards of its genre. The drawing is just adequate and the situations trite. Dixie's countless run-ins with her bosses and relatives and her flirtations with an endless string of suitors are as tiresome as her eternal optimism. *Dixie Dugan's* success represents a greater tribute to Ham Fisher's salesmanship than to the authors' talent or originality.

Dixie Dugan, which died a slow death in the 1960s, was brought to the screen in 1943 by 20th Century Fox (Lois Andrews was Dixie).

M.H.

DIXON, JOHN DANGAR (1929-) Australian cartoonist, born at Newcastle, New South Wales, in 1929, the son of a school principal. After completing his education at Cooks Hill Intermediate School, he joined a soft-goods company as a trainee window dresser. On finishing his course he became interested in art and obtained a position as an advertising artist with the same company. Pursuing his artistic career, he went to Sydney in 1945 and took a series of jobs with department stores and advertising agencies. An agency acquaintance suggested that he try the comic book field, and so he commenced a long association with the H. John Edwards publishing company—one of the newer postwar publishers. In 1946 he created *Tim Valour Comics*, which was to run through three series and over 150 issues. The same year he created *The Crimson Comet Comics*, which also had a long run—but Dixon handled less than 50 issues as he was busy producing other comic features for the company. *Tim Valour*, in particular, allowed him to indulge his passion for airplanes and served as an excellent training ground for his future newspaper strip.

Dixon created a "new" *Catman Comics* for Frew Publications in 1958 and *Captain Strato Comics* for *Young's Merchandising* the same year. His last major comic book work was done in 1959 when he created *The Phantom Commando Comics* for Horwitz Publications. For many months he had been developing a newspaper strip and on June 14, 1959, the Sunday version of *Air Hawk and the Flying Doctors* appeared in the *Sydney Sun-Herald*.

Despite the absence of any formal art training and the obvious crudeness of his early work, Dixon's basic technique had always been reasonably sound. The formative years of *Air Hawk* exhibited many of the slick techniques and treatments used in comic books, but it was obvious that the left-handed Dixon was constantly striving to lift the standard of his work. The introduction of the daily *Air Hawk* strip, in May 1963, seemed to give him added impetus, and by the late 1960s he had polished and refined his technique to the point where it was comparable with that of any comic strip artist in the world.

His careful spotting of black gives his panels great depth and assists in presenting his panel-to-panel continuity dramatically—particularly when he chooses to eliminate all words from the panel and allow the illustration to tell its own story. While impressed by the work of Raymond, Foster, and Caniff, only the latter influenced his art to any noticeable degree, in the early years. With maturity, this influence vanished and the distinctive John Dixon style took over. In the 1970s *Air Hawk* literally took flight, being published in Europe, the United States, and throughout the world; since that time Dixon has largely devoted his time and energies to the production and distribution of his strip.

J.R.

DJON DOMINO (Indonesia) *Djon Domino*, in its many manifestations, has blanketed Indonesian print media since 1970. Created by Johnny Hidajat, Djon was sculpted from a long-nosed, shadow play character known and loved by all Indonesians. The popularity of the strip has been enhanced from the beginning by the numbers Hidajat includes in each sequence; they are used by readers as tips for the national lottery. In describing *Djon Domino*, Hidajat said he has "no special message; he can be a judge, a lawyer, a criminal, a doctor, a bad guy. He changes regularly, day to day." In fact, Djon is a schizophrenic character, appearing under varying names in different media—*Djon Domino* in *Pos Kota* (a daily); *Djon Tik* in *Waspada* (a daily); *Djon Kaget* in *Pos Film*; *Si Djon* in *Terbit*; and *Djon Teremol Ngook* in *Humor Magazine*. Each variation is designed for a specific audience; for example, *Djon Teremol*

"Djon Domino," Johnny Hidajat. © Johnny Hidajat.

Ngook, which is the Indonesian word for conglomerate spelled backward, deals with big business. Hidajat has little trouble cranking out multiple versions of his character; he is both prolific and flexible. From 1970 to 1975, he worked at a breakneck pace, drawing 60 to 75 three- or four-panel strips every day. He said he drew everywhere all the time—in restaurants, the car, at home, or in the office. The leeway he affords himself with Djon's name, personality, and opinion enables him to fit the character to the editorial stances of the periodicals to which he contributes.

J.A.L.

DOBRIĆ, MILORAD (1924-1991) Yugoslav cartoonist, editor, and writer Milorad Dobrić was born in Belgrade on August 18, 1924. Dobrić studied architecture, but his beloved hobby was cartooning. In 1945 it became his profession. His first comic strip was influenced by Louis Forton's *Les Pieds-Nickelés*. Even the characters were drawn in the same way as Forton's, but the strip involved Yugoslavs whose adventures were influenced by events of World War II.

In 1950 Dobrić got a job as political cartoonist on the humor weekly *Jež* in Belgrade. His cartoon comments were inspired by everyday life. It was the time of his professional growing up, and very soon he became one of the top cartoonists in his field in Yugoslavia.

In August 1951 Dobrić wrote and illustrated his first published comic book, *Veliki turnir* ("The Big Rivalry").

The same year he used chessmen as characters in a comic strip written by Yugoslav poet Andra Franićević. In 1952 *Pera Pešak* ("Pera the Pedestrian") became a very popular comic strip. Pera was used as a symbol on three-way traffic lights to signal pedestrians as to when to cross the street. A pantomime gag strip, *Ljuba Truba*, was created in 1954 for *Jež*. The amazing drunkard of the strip still appears there.

Dobrić is also the author of a few comics with animal characters. From 1954 to 1968 Belgrade's newspaper *Borba* published Dobrić's daily comic strip, *Kurir Fića*, which later became a regular daily cartoon panel and is well known today in that format. From 1961 to 1967 Dobrić was editor-in-chief of the comic magazine *Mali Jež*, where he had two very successful comic strips: *Slavuj Gliša* and *Inspektor Žuća*. He returned to *Jež* in 1968 and became that magazine's cartoon editor.

This very prolific and outstanding Yugoslav cartoonist, who won several international and national prizes for his work, was syndicated by Strip Art Features. He died in Belgrade on June 10, 1991.

E.R.

DOC SAVAGE (U.S.) 1—Street and Smith was one of the preeminent pulp magazine publishers of the 1930s, having both *The Shadow* and *Doc Savage* in their stable. The company decided to enter comic books with their features, and the *Doc Savage* strip made its first appearance in March 1940's *The Shadow* number one; it graduated to its own book in May 1940. Unfortu-

"Doc Savage." © Street and Smith.

Milorad Dobrić, "Ljuba Truba." © Strip Art Features.

nately, the series was an artistic disaster. A superman of sorts, who had five assistants, the Doc Savage character never established a firm comic book foothold. He was a weak imitation of his former pulp self. The comic book writers could not inject the excitement that Lester Dent and others had brought to the 181 pulp stories, and comic artists like Jack Binder, Joe Certa, Henry Kiefer, and Bob Powell simply could not match pulp illustrator Edd Cartier.

In all, *Doc Savage* lasted 20 issues until October 1943, and the strip appeared sporadically in *The Shadow* until 1949.

2—Doc Savage made a one-shot appearance in a Gold Key book in 1966 with art by Jack Sparling.

3—Bantam Books began reprinting the *Doc Savage* pulp novels in the 1960s, and more than 20 million copies of over 75 paperback titles have been circulated. Warner Bros. and George Pal began producing a *Doc Savage* movie, and Marvel revived the *Doc Savage* comic in 1972. It was also uninspired, and the feature has been fighting off comic book obscurity although both a black-and-white and color version have apparently been failures.

J.B.

4—Over the years many attempts were made to bring the Man of Bronze back to comic books. First came Marvel (1972-74; 1975-77), then DC Comics (1987-90), Millenium Publications (1991-92), and lastly Dark Horse (which paired Doc with the Shadow in 1995). All these efforts were half-hearted and ultimately unsuccessful.

M.H.

DR. FATE (U.S.) *Dr. Fate* was created by writer Gardner Fox and first illustrated by Howard Sherman for National's *More Fun* number 55 for May 1940. The strip was as colorful as it was inconsistent. Unlike many of his more subdued magical predecessors, the doctor sported a shimmering blue and gold superhero suit, complete with gold amulet and epaulets. In early adventures, he also sported a gold cape and full-face helmet. But, by the strip's end, Dr. Fate had no epaulets, no cape, and only half his original helmet.

The character's origin was just as changeable. One story had the magician placed on earth by elder gods long before the dawn of civilization. Another claimed he was archeologist Kent Nelson, who happened to find the temple of Nabu the Wise. According to this story, Nabu, who came from the planet Cilia, taught Nelson the magic and gave him the costume. Dr. Fate's powers were just as confusing. Often he was portrayed as omnipotent, but at times he couldn't fly, couldn't break out of bonds, or wasn't invulnerable. In fact, the only thing in *Dr. Fate* that remained stable was his secret lair—an ominous, doorless, and windowless brick tower in Salem.

Artistically, Sherman (1940-43) handled the strip competently, though not innovatively. Joe Kubert (1944) and Stan Asch (1941-42) were other contributors. *Dr. Fate* appeared in *More Fun* through January 1944—the 98th issue. The character also appeared as a member of the Justice Society in *All-Star* from issue number three (Winter 1941) through issue number 21 (Summer 1944). The character made two brief appearances in *Showcase* during 1965 as *Hourman*'s partner. *Doctor Fate* is also a member of the revived Justice Society.

"Dr. Kildare," Ken Bald. © King Features Syndicate.

After years of lurking in the shadow of the superheroes' comic books, the mystic hero finally got his own title in 1988. The series, however, lasted only until 1992, after which it was back to the salt mines for the ill-fated Dr. Fate.

J.B.

DR. KILDARE (U.S.) The character of Doctor Kildare was created in 1938 by the prolific writer Max Brand in his script for the MGM film *Interns Can't Take Money*, but it was firmly established by the movie *Young Doctor Kildare*, with Lew Ayres and Lionel Barrymore. Its success was so great that no fewer than nine sequels followed in the period from 1939 to 1947 (as well as a spin-off series based on Kildare's mentor Dr. Gillespie). In 1960, *Dr. Kildare* started its long TV career, and this seemingly inexhaustible success prompted King Features to release a comic strip version of *Dr. Kildare*. Drawn by Ken Bald, it made its daily debut on October 15, 1962, and was followed by a Sunday version on April 19, 1964.

The plot is well known by now: young, idealistic intern Dr. Kildare (modeled after the TV Kildare, Richard Chamberlain) is entirely devoted to his calling, sometimes with a too-youthful élan but moderated by crusty, wise Dr. Gillespie. Kildare's medical and romantic adventures take place in the mythical Blair General Hospital, and there is never a scarcity of attractive young women around, be they nurses or patients. Dr. Kildare, however, shuns any permanent entanglement, always preferring medicine to love.

The comic strip version of *Dr. Kildare* was as good (and sometimes better) than anything that the movies or television was in the same genre. And Ken Bald's enjoyable artwork was always a relief from the well-worn clichés that too often afflicted the script. The feature outlasted the TV series by many years, ending in 1984.

M.H.

DOCTOR MERENGUE, EL (Argentina) First appearing as *El Otro Yo del Doctor Merengue* ("Doctor Merengue's Other Self") in 1942, the feature was created by cartoonist Guillermo Divito as a series of gag strips

"El Doctor Merengue," Guillermo Divito. © Rico Tipo.

"Dr. Merling," Knud Larsen. © Bulls Pressedienst.

without continuity. It was successively published in the magazines *Rico Tipo*, *El Hogar*, and *Dr. Merengue* (a monthly comic magazine whose star attraction it was), and as a daily newspaper strip.

At the beginning of the strip, Dr. Merengue was a middle-aged gentleman, bald-headed and mustachioed. But he had the rare ability of pulling his stomach in, a neat trick he would use with increasing frequency in the course of his life, with the result that his silhouette was to look more stylized with each passing year. A lustful quinquagenarian always attired in a black suit and a hat to match, he had delusions of being a lady-killer, and would parade down the street with his nose held up high. The only bright note in the doctor's attire was a white handkerchief that stuck out ostentatiously from his breast pocket.

Married to a dumpy and benighted woman, Dr. Merengue earns his living as a general practitioner, though he could be seen at times dressed as an explorer or settled in an executive role. He leads a comfortable life, employs a majordomo named Abel, but likes to give himself airs and spends his life faking, because he is a repressed, libidinous, lying, cheating, and hypocritical philanderer. He has a double identity, and this "other self" is the one that always appears in the last panel of each strip, where it tells the truth with an overabundance of gestures and poses. But Dr. Merengue goes on his merry way, seemingly unfazed by the revelations spoken in pure Buenos Aires dialect by his other image. Having survived the death of its creator in 1969, the feature lives on without its former luster.

L.G.

DR. MERLING (Denmark) *Dr. Merling* (also known as Dr. Merlind) was created, written, and drawn by Knud V. Larsen, a Danish artist now living in an old school-house deep in the forests of Småland, Sweden. Albert Merling, the hero of this comic strip that was published in newspapers as renowned as the *Berlingske Tidende* of Copenhagen, Denmark, is the alter ego of the artist, who is also an amateur illusionist performing magic tricks. Although created as far back as 1963, *Dr. Merling* did not see print before 1970.

Just like Larsen, Dr. Merling is an illusionist, a magician. Dr. Merling tours Europe, together with his fam-

ily, in the 1870s, an epoch of scientific advancement that was still surrounded by mysticism and an atmosphere of expectation; in short, the epoch of Jules Verne. True and false ghosts and monsters, magic, mesmerism, hypnotism, and the occult pitted against and/or controlled by Dr. Merling meet the new mysticism of the 20th century halfway and are in line with the flowering of occultism in literature and comics. Depending on the case at hand, *Dr. Merling* shows humorous undertones or is played out for the sheer dramatic effect.

Although largely escapist fantasy, *Dr. Merling* nevertheless was based on Larsen's actual experience combined with the necessary amount of fantasy, according to the artist. This and research into the 1870s made for a genuine atmosphere correctly flavored for the delighted perusal of the modern reader.

The hero of the strip was not a superman but rather a reasoning, more or less normal protagonist who, through insight and learning, was able to master even the craziest situations he encountered. In comics, his type is relatively rare. His adventures, unfortunately, are no longer being published.

Knud V. Larsen, who had a thorough professional education as an artist, employed a bold, very personal style in *Dr. Merling*. Using a special technique, he incorporated details from engravings and illustrations of the 1870s into his artwork in order to add to the aura of authenticity that helped him pull off the fantastic and outlandish occurrences met by his hero.

W.F.

DR. MID-NITE (U.S.) *Dr. Mid-Nite* was created by writer Charles Reizenstein and artist Stanley Aschmeier (Stan Asch) and first appeared in National's *All-American* number 25 in April 1941. One of the most unique characters to appear as a National backup feature, Dr. Mid-Nite was actually blind surgeon Dr. Charles McNider. During the day he saw with the aid of infrared glasses, but at night, his eyesight increased tremendously. His only weapon was a blackout bomb, a pellet that spread a blanket of blackness over the doctor's quarry. Dr. Mid-Nite also sported one of the most original costumes of the 1940s superheroes—black tights, a red blouse, a cape and cowl, goggles, and yellow quarter-moon crescents on the cowl and blouse.

Despite Reizenstein's conceptual overkill (with his goggles and a blackout bomb, Mid-Nite was sharper than most sighted persons), his scripts were always crisp and fast-moving. And while the doctor was usually confined to the standard street crime gambit, his blackout bombs were constant fun. Artistically, Asch stayed with *Dr. Mid-Nite* until 1947. His work was never outstanding, but it was competent and the feature worked well. He was succeeded by Bernard Sachs, Alex Toth, and several others.

Overall, *Dr. Mid-Nite* appeared in *All-American* until October 1948's 102nd issue. As a member of the Justice Society of America, however, he survived in *All-Star Comics* from issue eight (December 1941) through issue 57 (February 1951). He was revived in the mid-1960s and has made several cameo appearances in *Flash* comics.

J.B.

DOCTOR NIEBLA (Spain) Adapted from a series of popular novels written by Rafael Gonzalez, *Doctor Niebla* ("Doctor Fog") appeared for the first time as a mystery strip in issue number 17 of the magazine *El Campeón* (November 1948). After this first publication, the feature was to appear in other publications put out by Editorial Brughera, such as *Superpulgarcito, Almanaques de Pulgarcito,* and *Supplemento de Historietas del DDT,* usually in the form of isolated two-page episodes, before disappearing definitively in 1959.

Rafael Gonzalez was soon succeeded as scriptwriter, first by Silver Kane (pseudonym of F. Gonzalez Ledesma) and Victor Mora. *Doctor Niebla's* only illustrator was Francisco Hidalgo, who succeeded in re-creating, in his use of black and white, the mood of American gangster films of the 1930s and the atmosphere of London and New York, the two cities where most of the action took place.

Dr. Niebla was a man in his thirties who did not deny his admiration for Sam Spade, Dashiell Hammett's private eye hero, and who wore a trench coat, sunglasses, and an ample scarf. A skilled violinist like Sherlock Holmes, a man of refined tastes, and somewhat of a stickler for niceties, he would leave a note of explanation for the police after each case he would solve, along with a small bouquet of heliotropes. In the course of each investigation, Dr. Niebla would take time out to telephone his girlfriend, the newswoman Alice Stark, whom he would scrupulously keep informed of his discoveries and without whose collaboration and patient devotion his life would probably hold no inducement. More than his fight against mas-

ter criminals, Alice's admiration was what kept the hero going through his paces.

Some *Doctor Niebla* stories were printed in two colors, but Hidalgo, like Caniff and Robbins, was at his best in black and white.

L.G.

DOCTOR STRANGE (U.S.) Less than two years after Marvel's *Fantastic Four* premiered in 1961, editor Stan Lee had built a stable of strips that included *Spider-Man, Thor,* and *The Hulk.* He added a fifth strip, *Doctor Strange,* in July 1963. Created by artist Steve Ditko and Lee, this master of the occult made his debut in *Strange Tales* number 110.

Doctor Strange was really prominent surgeon Stephen Strange, a selfish, rather callous man who had abandoned the spirit of the Hippocratic oath. As fate would have it, he was injured in an auto accident and could never operate again. He searched in vain for a cure, finally coming upon "The Ancient One," keeper of the forces of white magic. After some initial reluctance, Strange became his willing pupil and was taught the old one's powers. He also inherited a horde of evil-doers bent on using magic to destroy Strange and the forces of good. Among them were Baron Mordo, the Ancient One's original pupil and Strange's most persistent enemy, the "dread" Dormammu, Nightmare, Umar, and many others of mystic persuasion.

The doctor lived in Greenwich Village, wore an oriental-like costume and cape, possessed the mystic amulet, the power to separate his spirit from his body, and a rich vocabulary that included phrases like "By the hoary hosts of Hoggoth" and "The all seeing eye of Agamotto." *Doctor Strange* was one of the first strips Lee drifted away from, however, and over the years,

"Doctor Niebla," Francisco Hidalgo. © Editorial Bruguera.

"Doctor Strange," Frank Brunner. © Marvel Comics Group.

Don Rico, Roy Thomas, Denny O'Neil, Jim Lawrence, Ray Holloway, Steve Englehart, and even artist Ditko wrote the feature. Unfortunately, no one could capture Lee's flair and the strip never regained its early mystique. For a while, Doctor Strange was even made into a superhero, complete with long johns.

Artistically, Steve Ditko remained on the strip until 1966, creating heretofore unseen fantasy worlds. Most noted for his realistic, "everyman" artwork on *Spider-Man*, Ditko's *Doctor Strange* work was a fantastic trip into the occult. After his departure, Bill Everett, Marie Severin, Dan Adkins, Gene Colan, and others handled the feature with varying degrees of success, but only Frank Brunner's short-lived 1974 rendition ever matched Ditko's inspired originality.

The feature continued in *Strange Tales* until the book was dubbed *Doctor Strange* beginning with June 1968's 169th issue; it folded after November 1969's 183rd issue. After many subsequent guest appearances and a regular spot in *The Defenders* feature, *Doctor Strange* began a new book in June 1974.

J.B.

In the hands of capable artists (Rudy Niebres, Frank Miller, Frank Brunner, etc.) and of writers who involved the hero with such mythical figures as Dracula and Lilith, the revived series fared reasonably well, lasting to 1987. The character was brought back in 1988, given a nifty moniker ("Sorcerer Supreme"), and under this new guise *Doctor Strange* managed to hang on until 1996, when it was finally discontinued (but perhaps not for good).

M.H.

DODD, EDWARD BENTON (1902-1991) American cartoonist and author, born November 7, 1902, in La Fayette, Georgia. Ed Dodd attended the Georgia Institute of Technology and later the Art Students League in New York, where he studied under the noted animal painter and sculptor Daniel Beard. In 1926 his love of the great open spaces took him to Wyoming, where he managed a cattle ranch; he later went on to become a guide and mule packer in Yellowstone National Park. All during this time he kept drawing and sketching people, animals, and scenes around him.

In 1930 Dodd started a nature panel for United Feature Syndicate, *Back Home Again*, which he drew until 1945. In 1946 he created *Mark Trail* for the Hall Syndicate, a strip into which he poured all of his love and knowledge of nature, his feelings for the open spaces and the free life. Dodd won a multiplicity of distinctions in different fields, from the Sigma Delta Chi award for cartooning to an award from the National Forestry Association for his contribution to conservation. He was also the author and illustrator of a nature book, *Mark Trail's Book of North American Mammals*, as well as other books also concerned with the great outdoors and wildlife.

Dodd retired from *Mark Trail* in 1978, although his name continued to appear on the strip for some years thereafter. Along with his wife Rosemary he established the Mark Trail-Ed Dodd Conservation Foundation and was active in environmental issues. He died in Gainesville, Georgia, in May 1991.

M.H.

DOLL MAN (U.S.) *Doll Man* was created by Will Eisner and made its first appearance in Quality's *Feature*

"Doll Man," Reed Crandall. © Comic Magazines, Inc.

Comics number 27 in December 1939. Using more traditional methods of transformation, Darrel Dane simply willed himself into Doll Man, a change that made him shrink from his normal height to Doll Man's five-inch stature.

Wearing a simple blue uniform and red cape, Doll Man spent over 12 years fighting a wide assortment of villains, all of whom were much bigger than he. But because he retained his normal strength at his minuscule height, Doll Man rarely had trouble with foes, though many of the feature's best moments came when Doll Man went searching for a means of transportation. Over the years, he traveled in pockets, on a roller skate, or in briefcases. As the years progressed, he also enlisted the aid of a dog and later a miniplane. Doll Man hid behind inkwells, in books, and in drawers. As the strip began to falter in the 1950s, Doll Girl was added. She was Darrel Dane's fiancée, Martha Roberts, and she made her first appearance in December 1951's *Doll Man* number 37.

Many of Quality's best artists worked on the strip, including Eisner (1939-41) and Reed Crandall (1942-43). But Al Bryant, who drew the feature between 1943 and 1946, became the definitive artist. Although he was not as creative as other Quality artists, his material was always clean and straightforward.

Doll Man continued to appear in *Feature Comics* until the 139th issue in October 1949. The character was also given his own book, starting in autumn 1941 and lasting until October 1953 through 47 issues.

J.B.

DONALD DUCK (U.S.) Donald Duck, a major Walt Disney Studios animated cartoon star, appeared in two major comic strips, one drawn by Al Taliaferro from August 30, 1936, and the other by Carl Barks from April 1943. The bad actor who was to become the biggest hit in the history of animated films initially appeared dancing a hearty hornpipe on the deck of his

"Donald Duck," Floyd Gottfredson. © Walt Disney Productions.

rural scow in a Disney short called *The Wise Little Hen* in 1934. The Disney animators liked working with the new character, and since public response to the first short had been good, Donald was given a supporting part in a Mickey Mouse cartoon, *The Band Concert*. The raucous, popcorn-peddling duck completely stole the show, and his stardom was assured.

Donald's popularity was delayed a bit in the comic strip arena. Although Donald made his initial strip appearance in the first Sunday episode of a strip version of *The Wise Little Hen*, published in the *Silly Symphony* third-page portion of the *Mickey Mouse* page on September 16, 1934, which ran until December 16, 1934, his impact was not comparable to his screen smash. Given minor roles in *Mickey Mouse* daily and Sunday strip continuity of the time by Floyd Gottfredson (first daily *Mickey* appearance was as a newsboy on March 15, 1935; first Sunday, a little earlier, was as a tough neighborhood kid in the *Mickey* for February 10, 1935), Donald did not receive a major role in the comics until Sunday, August 23, 1936. Then, in the last panel of a *Silly Symphony* page otherwise devoted to the closing episode of a Three Little Pigs story, an aggressive-looking Donald, tilting his hat drakishly, glared out at the audience while black and red letters behind him announced: *Next Week*: DONALD DUCK!

Sure enough, next week a full half of the Sunday *Mickey Mouse* page was shared by a new strip titled *Silly Symphony Featuring Donald Duck*. Signed by Walt Disney but drawn by Al Taliaferro, the gag sequence displayed Donald demolishing a wall in his house to blast a mosquito with a shotgun. The new screen legend had come in full bloom to the comic page. The daily *Donald* strip, which started a bit later, was also drawn by Taliaferro and, like the Sunday, featured individual gags with little inter-episode continuity. Goofy, Horace Horsecollar, Pluto, and other *Mickey Mouse* regulars appeared in the new *Donald* strip from the outset. Daisy Duck, Donald's girlfriend, appeared a bit later. The real bombshell of characterization hit the strip on October 17, 1937, when Donald's tormenting nephews, Huey, Louie, and Dewey, appeared, on a visit from Donald's cousin, Della Duck. They stayed, to the delight of millions of readers, for Donald and his

nephews were the magic mixture that made the strip a solid hit.

Donald, Daisy, and the nephews next appeared in comic book form in *Walt Disney's Comics and Stories* for April 1943, as drawn by cartoonist Carl Barks. For a long time, the Disney magazine had been reprinting the Taliaferro *Donald*, but the immediate supply was running low, and the magazine editors wanted more Donald up front right away. The answer was to keep reprinting Taliaferro, but to add new material in the form of monthly 10-page Barks stories. For the first time in comic form, Donald burst the bounds of daily and Sunday gag strip limitations and became involved in longer, more elaborate narratives written by Barks. The readers loved it and wrote in increasing numbers for more. Barks branched into book-length *Donald Duck* narratives published as 64-page comic magazines by the Disney people under titles such as *The Pixilated Parrot*, *Voodoo Hoodoo*, and *The Sheriff of Bullet Valley*. The effort, which earned Barks the magazine Duck assignment, was a 64-page magazine adaptation of a projected Donald Duck feature film in 1942.

Donald as an adventurer intrigued readers as much as Donald the daily gagster, and the magazine feature became as strong a hit as the newspaper strip. Barks introduced some original characters into his work, such as Gladstone Gander and Uncle Scrooge McDuck (who later starred in his own comic books by Barks), while Taliaferro stuck to new studio characters such as Gus Goose and Grandma Duck. Both versions of *Donald* are still appearing: the Barks magazine stories are reprinted each month, and the newspaper strip by a new, less capable Disney hand, although Donald has virtually disappeared from the screen except on occasional TV reruns of his old cartoons. The major *Donald Duck* strip work appears to be in the past, although it will live on in reprint and memory, thanks to the fine work of Al Taliaferro and Carl Barks.

B.B.

Since Taliaferro's death in 1969 Donald has known a bewildering succession of artists, including Frank Grundeen, Frank Smith, and Peter Alvarado; while the writing, done by Bob Karp from the feature's inception to 1974, has been continued by, among others, Bob Foster and Larry Meyer. The strip still appears daily and Sundays (as *Walt Disney's Donald Duck*) to this day. The comic book title meanwhile continued with diminished fortune until 1984, when it was discontinued by Whitman. In 1986 Gladstone Publishing revived the title, carrying on to the present (with a brief interlude in 1990-93 when it was published by the ill-starred Disney Comics).

M.H.

DON BERRINCHE (Spain) Created in 1948 in the magazine *El Campeón*, *Don Berrinche* moved the following year to *Pulgarcito*, another Bruguera publication, while, as was customary with most features distributed by this publishing house, it also appeared in the comic weeklies *DDT* and *Ven y Ven*. The author of this gag strip was Peñarroya, a prolific and talented cartoonist.

Don Berrinche was in the beginning a bitter little man, an irascible curmudgeon, incapable of controlling his temper, who would roam the streets wielding an enormous club surmounted by a nail. The most frequent target of Berrinche's temper was the hapless Gordito Relleno, a slow-witted and good-natured milquetoast, who suffered with resignation all of Berrinche's indignities. The latter would scream, get mad, and end each episode wildly flaying his arms while letting out terrible curses.

With the passing of time, Don Berrinche's character softened considerably, underwent a radical mental transformation, and became a quiet middle-class citizen. He went to work as a company manager, enjoyed a higher standard of living, and got fat; his face did not look as angry, and his eyes were more peaceful. He traded his club for a cane, and for screams and curses he substituted unctuous platitudes. While earlier he was impulsive, he became calculating, hypocritical, and coldly cruel: the very epitome of the petty bourgeois. Don Berrinche continued for some time after José Penarroya's death in 1975, ending when Bruguera closed its doors in the mid-1980s.

L.G.

DONDI (U.S.) Launched on September 25, 1955, *Dondi* was the joint effort of Gus Edson and Irwin Hasen for the Chicago Tribune-New York News Syndicate. Coming at the end of a large number of GI adoptions of war orphans, Dondi was an Italian boy (with a dead American GI father) whose first great battle was attempting to enter the United States over immigration restrictions.

This first continuity was a master stroke on the part of Gus Edson, the author, as it created a national sensation and a great deal of real anxiety about the comic character's fate.

Dondi became enmeshed in a long-running tug-of-war over his guardianship in the States—between rich, matronly Mrs. McGowan, mother of one of Dondi's GI buddies in Europe, and Ted Wills, one of the GIs. The other major characters were Katje, Ted's wife (they would become his parents in Midville, a typical small town); Pop Fligh, Dondi's new "grandfather"; friends Baldy and Web in their Explorer's Club; and Dondi's dog Queenie.

In 1966 Gus Edson died and Hasen assumed the continuity. When Dondi's family affairs were straightened out, much of the pathos left the strip, and it then revolved around incidents with his club members and weird characters who came and went. The strip outlasted such competitors as *On Stage* in the syndicate's flagship papers.

"Dondi," Irwin Hasen. © Chicago Tribune-New York News Syndicate.

Dondi, with its basic appeal formulated for all age groups, was made into a feature movie, with David Janssen, Patti Page, and David Cory in the title role, in 1962. Other spin-offs have included comic books, clothing accessories, and a TV pilot. *Dondi* was awarded the NCS Best Story Strip Award in 1961 and 1962. It ended in June 1986.

R.M.

DON DIXON AND THE HIDDEN EMPIRE (U.S.) *Don Dixon and the Hidden Empire* resulted from the collaboration of writer Bob Moore and artist Carl Pfeufer. The feature (with *Tad of the Tanbark* as a top) ran in the *Brooklyn Eagle* from October 6, 1935, to July 6, 1941.

Don Dixon, his companion Matt Haynes (soon to disappear from the strip), and Dr. Lugoff enter the unknown country of Pharia in the course of their explorations. There Don fights against giants and pygmies, witches and sorcerers; leads the revolt against Karth, who has usurped Pharia's throne; and frequently rescues Princess Wanda from a fate worse than death. After a brief trip back to civilization, Don, Lugoff, and Wanda return to Pharia, where the princess is finally restored to her throne.

"Don Dixon," Carl Pfeufer. © Brooklyn Eagle.

Don Dixon was probably the best of all the *Flash Gordon* imitations. Don looks very much like Flash and Dr. Lugoff is an obvious reference to Dr. Zarkov. Pfeufer's style was at first reminiscent of the early Raymond but it later acquired authority and dash and is not without merit. Bob Moore's stories were imaginative, with a good plot. This evocation of "the hidden empire" is quite enjoyable, even today, and it deserves an honorable mention among science-fiction strips.

M.H.

DON FULGENCIO (Argentina) The humor strip *Don Fulgencio o el Hombre que no Tuvo Infancia* ("Mr. Fulgen-

"Don Fulgencio," Lino Palacio. © La Razón.

cio, or the Man Who Had No Childhood") was created in 1935 by cartoonist Lino Palacio. It was first published in the Buenos Aires daily *La Opinión*, moved in 1939 to *La Prensa* and later to *La Razón*.

In the 60 years of his existence, Don Fulgencio has changed little in his physical appearance. He is still the same middle-aged, black-attired man with a cucumber-shaped head surmounted by a minuscule derby. Bald and short-sighted, he has gotten a little more jowl in the face with the years, but his character has not changed one iota. Well-mannered, indecisive, good-natured, and shy, he goes through life in an optimistic daze.

Like so many men who had to work hard to succeed, it is presumed that Don Fulgencio had to earn a living at a tender age, which is why he never had toys, or a genuine childhood, or had ever been mischievous. Now that he enjoys a good station in life, having money in the bank and servants, all he wants is to drop out of life, chuck everything, and play. If he finds his house empty, he dresses like Tarzan and swings from the dining room chandelier; if his neighbors invite him for a snack, he asks to be given a second helping of cherry pie; if he misses the streetcar, he goes home on a skateboard. Such is Don Fulgencio, more temperamental, impudent, mischievous and childish at 50 than he ever was at 5. The unique adult's toy that he cherishes is his record player on which he plays the songs of his lost love: Shirley Temple!

Don Fulgencio lives in the world of dreams. In recent years he has been saddled with a cheeky nephew whose attitude is opposite to that of his uncle: he wants to be an adult, and he'd rather wear a suit much too large for him than allow Fulgencio to buy him more suitable attire in the children's department. In the *Don Fulgencio* daily strip, as well as in the accompanying *Ramona* strip (about Fulgencio's maid), Palacio has created a whole score of secondary characters such as Tripudio, Pochito, Pototó, Liberato, and Radragaz, who have gotten strips of their own in the magazine *Avivato*.

Don Fulgencio, the most popular Argentine strip in and out of its country of origin, has been adapted to the screen and radio. Among Palacio's assistants on the strip have been cartoonists who later became famous, such as Toño Gallo, Guerrero, Atilio, Montes, Pereda, Haroldo, and Flores.

L.G.

DON PANCHO TALERO (Argentina) *Don Pancho Talero* was created by the pioneering Argentinian cartoonist Arturo Lanteri, for the magazine *El Hogar*, where it ran without interruption from 1922 to 1944.

It is a family strip, deeply rooted in Argentine middle-class life, although Don Pancho Talero himself bears more than a passing resemblance to Jiggs (but only in appearance). A sailor by profession, Talero, when at home, is dominated by his energetic wife, a stout and sturdy woman, who is fond of awaiting her philandering husband, concealed behind a curtain with a bottle in her hands. The household includes Pancho's mother-in-law, his children, his daughter's fiancé, his loafer brother-in-law, and a maid of formidable aspect, an immigrant from Vigo whose peculiar accent contrasts sharply with the typically "porteño" (from Buenos Aires) dialect and mannerisms of the Talero family.

Lanteri started his comic strip career in 1916 with *El Negro Raul*, but *Don Pancho Talero* met with greater popularity, thanks to its familiar roots and to the male readers' easy identification with the main character, whose only preoccupation is to escape this home where everybody screams, and seek refuge in the company of his friends inside a friendly café.

The first talking picture ever produced in Argentina was released in 1931: directed by Lanteri himself, it dealt with Talero's adventures in Hollywood.

L.G.

DON WINSLOW OF THE NAVY (U.S.) The idea for *Don Winslow* came to Lt. Commander Frank V. Martinek when Admiral Watson T. Cluverius, then commandant of the Ninth Naval District and of the Great Lakes Naval Training Station near Chicago, complained of the difficulties of navy recruiting in the Midwest. Martinek started a series of novels with a young naval officer, Don Winslow, as the hero. Colonel Frank Knox, Secretary of the Navy, became interested and helped in selling the concept to the Bell Syndicate. Written by Martinek himself, drawn by Lieutenant Leon A. Beroth, USN, assisted by Carl Hammond, and approved by the Navy Department, *Don Winslow of the Navy* premiered on March 5, 1934.

Commander Don Winslow of navy intelligence, helped by his partner Lieutenant Red Pennington, pursued a long and successful struggle against various espionage and subversive groups that threatened the welfare and security of the United States. His chief opponent in the thirties was the crafty and ruthless "Scorpio," head of the worldwide spy network known as "Scorpia." During World War II Don and Red turned their attention to the Japanese and Germans, and their domestic allies and supporters. From time to time Don Winslow was allowed a rest in the arms of his eternal fiancée, Mercedes Colby, daughter of Don's commanding officer, Admiral Colby.

From 1940 to 1942, Ken Ernst assisted on the strip. In 1942 Hammond was drafted and replaced by Ed Moore, then Al Levin. In the fifties *Don Winslow's* appeal steadily waned, and the strip was discontinued July 30, 1955.

Don Winslow was more a mystery strip than a sea-adventure story. Competently written and carefully

"Don Winslow," Frank Martinek and Leon Beroth. © Bell Syndicate.

"Doonesbury," Garry Trudeau. © G. B. Trudeau.

drawn, it held its own in the crowded adventure field and was popular for over a decade. Commander Winslow's adventures were published in book form, broadcast on the radio, and carried in a series of comic books issued by Fawcett. Two movie serials were also released, *Don Winslow of the Navy* (1941), directed by Ford Beebe and starring Don Terry, and *Don Winslow of the Coast Guard* (1943), also with Don Terry.

M.H.

DOONESBURY (U.S.) Garry Trudeau, then a Yale undergraduate, created a strip called *Bull Tales* in 1968 for the *Yale Record*; from there it went to the *Yale Daily News* in 1969, where it attracted national press coverage. In the following year the strip, retitled *Doonesbury*, started syndication. It was distributed by Universal Press Syndicate; the first issue date was October 26, 1970.

Doonesbury is a C-minus college student—and a minus in most other enterprises as well. He never quite succeeds in asserting himself, or winning an argument with fellow students, or scoring with campus coeds. His friends are almost as hapless as he is—B.D. (inspired by Yale quarterback Brian Dowling) fancies himself a football hero and big man on campus; Mark Slackmeyer (alias Megaphone Mark) is a self-styled campus revolutionary who tries to upset the establishment with the help of his trusted megaphone through which he utters the well-worn clichés of the radical left. Not surprisingly, Mark has lately become a disc jockey on station WBBY.

Obviously inspired by the sophisticated strips of the 1950s and 1960s (Feiffer) Doonesbury often rises to the level of genuine satire. Trudeau is unsparing in his parodies: the coeds are depicted as a bunch of neurotic girls, as pathetic as their male counterparts; the police, as a mob of sadistic bullies whose greatest enjoyment

in life is cracking students' skulls. Political figures are not spared either, and Trudeau did a running commentary on the Watergate situation. A comic strip sensation almost from the first, *Doonesbury* has been reprinted in book form by Holt, Rinehart.

Trudeau received the Pulitzer Prize for cartooning in 1975 for *Doonesbury*. Following marriage (to TV personality Jane Pauley) and fatherhood, he became the first cartoonist in modern times to take a sabbatical from his strip. The feature went on hiatus in January 1983 (subscribing newspapers were supplied with reruns). When it came back in September 1984, it was a changed strip, hovering uncertainly between satire and soap opera. Consequently, it started losing papers, and in order to maintain his income, Trudeau branched out to merchandising *Doonesbury*, a practice he had previously declared he would never resort to.

M.H.

DORGAN, THOMAS ALOYSIUS (1877-1929) "Tad" Dorgan was born Thomas Aloysius Dorgan to laborer parents in San Francisco on April 29, 1877. Erratically schooled and a part-time factory worker before his teens, Dorgan lost the last three fingers on his right hand in a factory machine accident at age 13. Recuperating, he was urged to develop a latent cartooning talent as manual therapy. He became enthusiastically involved and landed his first job at 14 as staff artist on the *San Francisco Bulletin*, where he illustrated news events, did classified-ad-page filler art, and drew visiting celebrities. By 1895 his weekly illustration for the *Bulletin*'s continued children's stories revealed his capacity for arresting humorous art, and within a few years he had been hired by the city's most prestigious paper, the *Chronicle*, as general artist, where he was assigned his first comic strip work, a weekly color-page

"Dot and Carrie," J. F. Horrabin. © Associated Newspapers Ltd.

called *Johnny Wise*, which ran for several months in 1902. Able as ever to spot talent in the pages of rival papers, W. R. Hearst hired Dorgan away from the *Chronicle* in late 1902 and put him to work as a sports-page cartoonist on his *New York Journal*, where he flourished both as a personality able to almost instantly become close friends with virtually every sports celebrity of the period, and as an extremely able sports cartoonist, drawing action poses of boxers and other sports figures so accurately that they are still reprinted as textbook records.

In the lax periods between the major sports seasons, Dorgan began to develop characters out of his own fancy and put them through anecdotal and narrative paces. Most of these were canine figures with human attributes and problems, from Silk Hat Harry, a dog about town with a revengeful wife; through Curlock Holmes, a bulldog detective; to Judge Rummy, Tad's central character. Despite Tad's inconsistent narrative and often flat jokes, the public adored his non-sports work, and particularly relished his relaying of contemporary big city street argot and sports slang into both his strips and his handwritten prose column of wit called *Daffydills*, which accompanied them on the *Journal* sports page. So wide was the popular response to

T. A. Dorgan (Tad), "Indoor Sports." © International Feature Service.

his innovative terms, such as "drug-store cowboy," "the storm-and-strife" (for wife), "Dumb Dora," "Yes, we have no bananas," etc., that many have entered the American idiom permanently.

Dorgan's comic dog continuity eventually acquired a continuing name, *Silk Hat Harry's Divorce Suit*, a name that became one of the half-dozen most popular daily strips of the 1910s. A panel gag series called *Indoor Sports* (poker, dice, pool, etc.) ran concurrently and continued after Dorgan dropped Judge Rummy and the others in the early 1920s. Suffering from recurrent ill health, particularly after his last out-of-town sports assignment—the Dempsey-Miske bout in 1920—Dorgan went into enforced retirement at his Great Neck, Long Island, estate, where he continued his sports-page art until his premature death from a relatively minor case of pneumonia at his home on May 2, 1929.

Hearst papers across the country turned over what amounted to entire editions to commemorate his passing and immediately undertook a reprinting of his *Indoor Sports* panel and boxing history features, which continued for years. Lean and angular, and a familiar figure to his readers through his frequent self-caricatures, Dorgan was remembered as much as a personal friend by his followers as he was a cartoonist. A significant personage of his time, Dorgan deserves the comprehensive memorial biography and collection of his work he never received.

B.B.

DOT AND CARRIE (G.B.) Dorothy and Caroline, dubbed "Dot and Carrie" after the shorthand typist's catchphrase, "Dot and carry on," brought the working girl into British newspaper strips. They were created by J. F. Horrabin, already writing and drawing *Japhet and Happy*, at the request of Wilson Pope, editor of the London evening newspaper *The Star*. He wanted a daily strip in the American mold of *Somebody's Stenog*, and Horrabin obliged. The early credit was "By the Horrabin Brothers," as J. F. drew the scripts written by his brother-in-law, H. O. Batho. The strip, which began on November 18, 1922, was American in style, but soon settled into a more native and individual form. The cast was Dot, the pretty blonde who felt sure she was born for movie stardom; Carrie the plain and bespectacled spinster; their boss, bald and fiery Henry Spilliken (Motto: "Work like Helen B. Gloomy"); the handsome Junior Partner; Adolphus the cheeky office boy; Carrie's rotund boyfriend, Aubrey V. DuPois; and Mrs. Mopps, the cheery cockney charlady. Once a year they would abandon their daily gags for continuity in the form of the Office Pantomime. The strip did not end until Horrabin died, having survived an absorption of *The Star* by the *Evening News*, in which paper it ran from October 18, 1960, to March 2, 1962. The final strip bore the serial number 11,735.

Only three books of *Dot and Carrie* strips were published: *Dot and Carrie* (1923); *Dot and Carrie (and Adolphus)* (1924); *Dot and Carrie (not forgetting Adolphus)* (1925).

D.G.

DOTTOR FAUST, IL (Italy) Wolfgang Goethe's *Faust*, that masterpiece of German literature, seemed in 1939 to be a fit subject for adaptation into comic strip form. Its cultural credentials and high moral tone would put it past the censors without a hitch; and the propaganda value it would give to Italy's ally, Germany, was a further consideration in view of Mondadori's strained relations in the past with the Fascist authorities.

Of course, for a work of such distinction an exceptional talent had to be found, and the publishers picked Gustavo Rosso, who was not a cartoonist but a painter and illustrator of children's books. Rosso (using the pen name "Gustavino") set to work, and on July 20, 1939, the first page of *Il Dottor Faust* appeared in the comic weekly *L'Audace*, following the strip adaptation of Federico Pedrocchi. Unfortunately Rosso fell ill after having completed only four pages, and the publication was suspended.

Mondadori had not given up on his pet project, however, and in 1941, *Il Dottor Faust* was revived by Rino Albertarelli for another one of Mondadori's comic weeklies, *Topolino*. If Rosso's pages had been technically flawless, Albertarelli's artwork proved just as remarkable. His architecture was grandiose or sinister, according to the plot; the backgrounds were exquisitely detailed; the pace was unrelenting; and the color work was matchless. But the artists who continued Albertarelli's work after 1943, the painters Chiletto and Maraja, were markedly inferior.

In the end, the original figure of Doctor Faust, a religious man tormented by his sins, was changed into

"Il Dottor Faust," Gustavino (Gustavo Rosso). © Mondadori.

that of a mindless fop, a portrayal that did not fit either the place or the character. His antagonist Mephistopheles soon became the principal character, owing to the author's sympathetic treatment and, more significantly, to his popularity with the readers; so much so that the second episode of *Il Dottor Faust* was actually devoted to the doctor's fiendish enemy.

G.B.

Borivoj Dovniković, "U Zemlji Lijepog Nogometa." © Dovniković.

DOVNIKOVIĆ, BORIVOJ (1930-) Born in 1930, Borivoj Dovniković today is known as one of the best Yugoslav cartoon filmmakers. He lives in Zagreb and works for "Zagreb film." His childhood was filled with comics—Walt Disney and Harold Foster were his idols.

Dovniković's first comic strip, *Udarnik Ratko*, was published in *Glas Slavonije*; it was the first realistic strip published in Yugoslavia after World War II. After that Dovniković worked at the first Yugoslav cartoon film studio, "Duga film," but when the firm was liquidated in 1952, he and Walter Neugebauer came back to their mutual love—comic strips. From there Dovniković started his collaboration with the new comic magazine *Horizontov Zabavnik*, where he created his most popular strip, *Velika utakmica* ("The Big Match"), which he drew on the verses of Neugebauer's brother, Norbert.

For the Zagreb magazine *Plavi Vjesnik* he drew three episodes of a realistic soccer strip, the scripts for which were written by famous Yugoslav sports journalist Ljubomir Vukadinović. For the same magazine he did a longer comic strip series, *Mendo Mendović*, based on a very popular children's TV series. The strip was discontinued along with the TV series, and it was the last one done by Dovniković. He is now occupied producing cartoon films and sometimes does cartoon illustrations for the TV magazine *Studio* in Zagreb. His hobbies are going to the movies and photography.

E.R.

DOWLING, STEVE (1904-1986) Stephen P. Dowling was born in 1904 in Liverpool. Educated at Liverpool Collegiate, he studied art at the Liverpool School of Art, continuing at the Westminster School of Art in

London. Upon graduating in 1924, he did freelance drawing and advertising work for the Charles W. Hobson Agency. After two years in various art studios, he set up his own in 1927, and in 1928 was made assistant art director of the Dorland Advertising Agency. He drew his first strip, *Tich* (November 21, 1931), for the *Daily Mirror*, a pantomime gag written by his brother, Frank Dowling, who was also an advertising man.

His first successful daily strip was *Ruggles*, at first a daily gag, again by Frank Dowling, but soon becoming a continuity strip. *Ruggles* ran from March 11, 1935, to August 3, 1957. He also took over *Belinda Blue Eyes* for the same paper, and drew both strips daily from 1936 to July 24, 1943, when he started *Garth*. Meanwhile, he did freelance advertising work, notably the Roses Lime Juice series featuring Hawkins the Butler, and served as a captain in the British Home Guard.

After the war he joined the *Daily Mirror* staff, assisting Bill Herbert, the strip editor, continuing *Garth*, visualizing *Jane*, and creating the new daily, *Keeping Up With the Joneses* (March 9, 1960) in conjunction with the paper's city editor. Required to retire at the age of 65 in 1969, Dowling became a full-time farmer, market gardener, and riding-school proprietor in Pett, near Hastings, Sussex. The most prolific British newspaper strip artist, Dowling's style and characters were both popular and influential. He died on March 19, 1986, at the age of 82.

D.G.

DOWN HOGAN'S ALLEY see Yellow Kid, The.

"Drago," Burne Hogarth. © Burne Hogarth.

DRAGO (U.S.) Soon after he left *Tarzan* for the first time in 1945, Burne Hogarth created a Sunday page for the *New York Post*. Called *Drago*, it ran for a year, from November 4, 1945, to November 10, 1946.

Physically and psychologically Drago looks pretty much like Tarzan's kid brother, in his dark and athletic good looks. The locale is Argentina instead of Africa, but the universe of violent landscapes and sinister shadows favored by the author are quickly rediscov-

ered. In the two episodes that make up the entire strip Drago and his comic sidekick Tabasco fight Baron Zodiac, a sinister Nazi with a plan to destroy the world, and foil a plot aimed at discrediting Drago and his father.

Despite its brief existence, *Drago* remains one of the adventure strips most deserving of study, as well as the one most revealing of its author. Hogarth's baroque imagination enjoys free play in the opulence of the women's costumes and in the phantasmagoric atmosphere of the plot. Never before did Hogarth's talent rise to such expressionistic fury as it did in the violent depiction of the action. A song, aptly titled *The Song of Drago the Gaucho*, was composed, to which Hogarth contributed the lyrics, but without much success.

M.H.

DRAKE, STANLEY (1921-1997) American artist, born in Brooklyn on November 9, 1921. Stan Drake moved with his family to New Jersey and grew up in River Edge and Hackensack. In 1939 he attended the Art Students League and studied under the great anatomist George Bridgman. Before and during his training there he was a pulp illustrator, starting with *Popular Detective* and *Popular Sports* at age 17.

Also as a youngster, he drew for early comic books beside Bob Lubbers and Bob Bugg—writing, drawing, and lettering at seven dollars a page. He also worked for Stan Lee before entering the service in August 1941. Discharged in February 1946 after wartime action in the Pacific theater, he immediately went to Madison Avenue and drew for many advertising accounts of the Perlowin Studios. Soon Drake transferred to the training ground for a generation of strip artists—Johnstone and Cushing. Drake successfully opened his own studio, with Bob Lubbers and John Celardo, and had a staff of 12 before exhaustion overtook him.

At the suggestion of Lubbers, Drake decided to draw a newspaper strip, and Gill Fox introduced him to Eliot Caplin. Together they filled King Features' need for a romantic soap opera. *The Heart of Juliet Jones* has been a leader in the story-strip field ever since they created it in 1953.

Drake's strongest influences came at the start of this strip. He moved to Connecticut and became friendly with the inhabitants of the artists' colony around Westport, including Al Parker, Al Dorne, and Robert Fawcett. Drake sought a definite illustrative flavor and a liberation from the comic-book conventions for *Juliet*.

His two goals have been well met. He preserved his integrity in the strip format changes, and his strip lasted in the days of the dying story strip.

Drake's art is strong and his bold men and winsome women vibrate with character and emotion. The attraction of his art lies in the use of benday as a wash, and the pioneering of a confident pen (as opposed to brush work). For the last 13 years of his life he contributed the artwork to *Blondie*. He died at his home in Westport, Connecticut, on March 10, 1997.

R.M.

DRAYTON, GRACE (1877-1936) American cartoonist and illustrator, born in Philadelphia on October 14, 1877. The daughter of Philadelphia's first art publisher, Grace Gebbie married Theodore E. Wiedersheim Jr. in her twenties and, under the name G. Wiedersheim, created the series *Bobbie Blake* and *Dolly Drake* for the *Philadelphia Press*. She also illustrated nursery rhymes

Grace Drayton, "Dimples." © Grace G. Drayton.

"The Dream of the Rarebit Fiend," Silas (Winsor McCay).

written by her sister Margaret G. Hayes, with whom she created, in 1909, *The Terrible Tales of Captain Kiddo*. In 1911 she divorced her first husband and married W. Heyward Drayton III (whom she was subsequently to divorce in 1923). Using the name Grace (Gigi) Drayton she illustrated a number of children's books and created several comic features: *Toodles* (around 1911), *Dolly Dimples* (1915), *The Campbell Kids*. In 1935 she started the series she is best remembered for, *The Pussycat Princess*. She died on January 31, 1936.

Grace Drayton was probably the first and certainly the most successful of American female cartoonists, and her position in the history of the comic strip is unique. As an artist, however, her work is overly cute and mannered, and her creations designed only for younger children.

M.H.

DREAMS OF THE RAREBIT FIEND (U.S.) Winsor McCay's first acknowledged masterwork and first exposition of the oneiric theme was *Dream(s) of the Rarebit Fiend*. It made its appearance in the *New York Evening Telegram* in 1904, signed with McCay's pseudonym "Silas."

In 1907 McCay gave this explanation of the genesis of the unusual strip: "The Dream of the Rarebit Fiend is an evolution of a drawing I made for the New York Telegram two years ago (sic) . . . You know how a cigaret fiend is when he gets up in the morning and can't find a dope stick? Well, I drew a picture once showing a fiend at the north pole without a cigaret and about ready to die. I introduced some other characters who happened to have paper and tobacco and a match, but the only match went out before they got a light. Then I had to frame up a finish and I made it a dream. My employer suggested that I make him a series of pictures and make them as rarebit dreams and you know the result."

The Rarebit Fiend is especially remarkable as a dry run for the later *Little Nemo* and as an earnest effort at exploring the depths of the unconscious—and doing it one year before the publication of Sigmund Freud's *The Interpretation of Dreams*. During the "fiend's" nightmares, caused by his inordinate, manic craving for Welsh rarebits, he encounters situations and themes that examine the nature of a man's fears. Topics include nudity and the taboo that is attached to it, masks, transvestism, the fear of castration, the fear of going insane, and the obsession of impotence. More than in *Little Nemo*, where it is rationalized and sublimated, the dream quest appears here in its naked, spontaneous immediacy.

The Rarebit Fiend appeared with weekly regularity from 1904 to 1907, until McCay became more absorbed elsewhere and the strip appeared intermittently. When McCay joined the Hearst organization in 1911, the Herald Co. (publisher of the *Telegram*) started syndicating reprints of *The Rarebit Fiend* that were hand colored by McCay. Hearst's International News Service tried to compete with a new version variously titled "A January Day Dream," "Midsummer Day Dream," etc. Both versions disappeared in 1914.

Dreams of the Rarebit Fiend enjoyed notable success, presumably due more to the strip's imaginativeness and artistry than to its theme. In 1905 a total of 61 of the fiend's dreams were reprinted in book form by Frederick A. Stokes; they were reprinted by Dover in 1973. In 1906 the American movie pioneer Edwin S. Porter produced a film adaptation called *The Dream of a Rarebit Fiend*, which is widely acknowledged as a masterpiece of the early cinema. In 1916 Winsor McCay himself made an animated version of the strip under the title *The Adventures of a Rarebit Eater*.

M.H.

DROPOUTS, THE (U.S.) Howard Post launched *The Dropouts* in 1968 as a daily strip for United Feature Syndicate, and a Sunday version followed a year later. At first the feature was little more than a one-joke strip. Two young men, the stringy, conceited Alf and the diminutive, naive Sandy, were literally "dropouts," having been washed ashore on a desert island after a shipwreck. Their inept, harebrained attempts at adapting to their new situation provided most of the gags, but they became tiresome after a while.

Post quickly realized he was painting himself into a corner, and in 1969, he transferred his dropouts to another island, inhabited this time by a host of nutty characters. Not only did Alf and Sandy rediscover mankind, mankind came back at them with a vengeance. There were, in addition to the natives, Harbinger, the professional hippie and prophet of doom; the drunkard Chugalug; and an assortment of weird female characters from selfish debutantes to affectionate old maids to shrews. The animal and vegetable kingdoms also played a part in the strip, with such (rare) specimens as Irving the playful gorilla, Elliott the dancing frog, and a horrible carniverous plant.

The Dropouts is in the tradition of the modern sophisticated humor strip (it is close to Johnny Hart's *B.C.* both in intent and treatment). A number of *Dropouts* strips have been reprinted in paperback form. But Post's downbeat humor proved unfortunately at odds with the go-go spirit of the Reagan years, and the Dropouts dropped out of the comic pages for good in 1984.

M.H.

DRUILLET, PHILIPPE (1944-   ) French artist and illustrator, born in Toulouse on June 28, 1944. Philippe Druillet spent his childhood in Spain, returning to France in 1952. After his high school studies, Druillet worked as a photographer. In 1965 he met French publisher Eric Losfeld, for whom he created *Lone Sloane*, a science-fiction strip published in book form in 1967. Druillet also illustrated a number of science-fiction stories and novels, and his work earned him some recog-

Philippe Druillet, "Lone Sloane." © Druillet.

nition. In 1970 he joined the art staff of *Pilote*, for which he revived the adventures of Lone Sloane. In 1973, also for *Pilote*, he created a new feature, *Yarzael ou la Fin des Temps* ("Yarzael or the End of Time") from a scenario written by science-fiction author Michel Demuth. Since the late 1970s he has virtually eschewed comics in favor of painting, sculpture, and set designing.

Philippe Druillet is probably the most overrated of all European cartoonists. He has received an impressive number of prizes at various gatherings of comic art fans, and his publishers keep promoting him with persistent, if misguided, zeal. The trouble with Druillet is that he has been judged more on his professed intentions than on his actual performance. His strips have been few in number and, while high in graphic excellence, they are lacking in narrative construction and in conceptual clarity and do not constitute a truly impressive body of work.

Some have hailed Druillet as a genius, while other observers remain unconvinced. Certainly Druillet's inability to draw the human face does not exhibit a high degree of psychological insight, just as his sterile delineation of character does not show any great enthusiasm for moral examination.

M.H.

DU JIANGUO (1941-   ) Born in Guangdong but raised in Shanghai, Chinese cartoonist Du Jianguo worked as a high school art teacher for about 10 years before he became an art editor at the Children Journals Publishing House in Shanghai. Beginning in 1958 he published cartoons in newspapers and journals and also illustrated and made decorative designs for books. His artwork received more than 20 awards in national and regional competitions. A member of the Chinese Artist Association, the Chinese Animation Society, and the Chinese Cartoon Art Commission, Du has been named one of the best comic artists in China.

Since 1960, Du has concentrated on comics for children. His well-known strips are *Xiaotu Feifei* ("The Little Rabbit Feifei"), *Xiang Gege* ("The Brother Elephant"), *Xiao Moli* ("The Little Jasmin"), *Quan Buzhi* ("The Not-Know-It-All"), and *Xiaoxiong he Xiaoxiaoxiong* ("The Little Bear and the Littler Bear"). His strips are usually not continuous but independent stories in each issue of the children's journals. Among them, "The Little Rabbit Feifei" and "The Brother Elephant" have been adapted to animated television series.

H.Y.L.L.

DUAN JIFU (1935-   ) Before he was sent to study art at Tianjin Art Academy, Duan Jifu worked in a bank as an accountant for three years and then as a public relations person for four years. His first cartoon was published in Tianjin in 1956, and he has continued to create cartoons since then. In 1958 he became an art editor for *Tianjin's Daily*, and since 1981 he has worked at the Xin Lei Publishing House in charge of children's reading material.

He has created numerous cartoons, comics, and illustrations—some of which have received national and international awards. He has been a board member of the Chinese Artist Association Tianjin Branch and vice president of the Tianjin Cartoonist Association.

Duan's comic strip entitled *Lao Ma Zheng Zhuan* ("Old Ma's Adventures") appeared for the first time on

Duan Jifu, "Lao Ma's Adventures." © *Duan Jifu.*

December 18, 1984, in *Jinwan Bao* (Tonight News). It has been published weekly without interruption since it began. Readers find similarities between their own lives and the adventures of Lao Ma, which is the main reason for the strip's popularity and its status as the longest-running comic strip still in existence since the founding of the People's Republic of China. To date, 600 stories of *Lao Ma's Adventures* have been created, some of which were published in three collections.

"Lao Ma" has a double meaning: it is a common family name in China and older men are often called "Lao Ma." At the same time, "Lao Ma" also means "old horse." The double meanings in the stories of Lao Ma reflect the double meanings in the lives of its readers. The strip is done in a four-panel format, and some strips include simple dialogue.

Duan has also published several dozen comic books on other topics. In 1995, his Lao Ma Adventures was chosen to be adapted into a series of animated films by Tewei Humorous Animation Center of Shanghai Xiejin-Hengtong Film and TV Company Limited.

H.Y.L.L.

DUMAS, GERALD (1930-   ) Born in Detroit in 1930, Jerry Dumas went through schooling, including an English degree from Arizona State University in 1955, with very little art training, even though his love of cartoons and comics was an obsession. He cartooned for school, service, and neighborhood publications until he broke the New York gag market in 1955.

In that year, desiring to move closer to the magazines than Arizona, he contacted an acquaintance, Frank Roberge, who had been assisting Dale Messick on *Brenda Starr, Reporter*.

The postcard reached Roberge as he was leaving Mort Walker to draw *Mrs. Fitz's Flats*. Roberge had told Walker of this "kid from Arizona" with a sense of

humor and "bigfoot" drawing style. The rest is history and Dumas continues to assist on all of Walker's creations in lettering, penciling, inking, and gag writing.

His most important contribution was *Sam's Strip*, a joint venture with Walker, in which Dumas did the art. The cast was the roster of all classic comic strip characters, which Dumas drew in styles closely resembling the originals. The ill-fated classic died too soon, running only from 1961 to 1963. Since then Dumas has remained active in Walker's factory, and published children's books, an autobiographical *Afternoon in Waterloo Park* for Houghton Mifflin, and a collection of children's verse, and has done occasional cartoons for the *New Yorker*, among others.

R.M.

In 1977 Dumas and Mort Walker revived *Sam's Strip* (as *Sam and Silo*). In addition to his work for Walker, Dumas has also written several short-lived comic strips, including *Rabbits Rafferty* (with Mel Crawford, 1977-81), *Benchley* (with Mort Drucker, 1984-86), and *McCall of the Wild* (again with Crawford, 1988-90).

M.H.

DUMAS, JACQUES (1904-1994) French cartoonist, writer, editor, and publisher, born in Clermont Ferrand in 1904. After a variety of odd jobs (errand boy, window cleaner, handyman, commercial artist), Jacques Dumas started his cartooning career (under the soon-to-become famous pseudonym "Marijac") with the Catholic weekly *Coeurs Vaillants* in 1934. His first comic strip was *Jim Boum*, a Western so terribly clumsy that it is endearing. The strip enjoyed a fair success due to the excellence of its scripts. At the same time Dumas did a series of comic books with a variety of characters, some humorous, some realistic.

Drafted during World War II, Dumas was taken prisoner by the Germans, escaped, and later joined the

Resistance movement in Auvergne. There he created an underground newspaper, *Le Corbeau Déchaîné* ("The Unleashed Crow"), which gave birth to the first French comic magazine of the postwar era, *Coq Hardi* (1944). Dumas remained the editor of *Coq Hardi* until its demise in 1957. In it he created many comic features, both as a cartoonist and scriptwriter (the best remembered is probably *Les Trois Mousquetaires du Maquis*, "The Three Musketeers of the Maquis"). After 1957 Dumas went on to create more boys' and girls' magazines, such as *Mireille, Frimousse,* and *Nano Nanette.* After suffering a heart attack in 1970, he went into retirement. He died in 1994.

Dumas is best known as Marijac, the inexhaustible purveyor of comic fun. When asked during a 1973 interview to name some of his comic creations, he ticked off in rapid-fire succession: *Jules Barigoule, Jim Boum, Joe Bing, Rouletabosse, Flic et Piaf, Les Trois Mousquetaires du Maquis, Onésime Pellicule, Rozet Cochon de Lait, Capitaine Brisquet, Capitaine Barbedure, Patos Enfant de la Brousse, Costo Chien Policier, Césarin, Sidonie en Vacances, Jim et Joe, Baptistou le Lièvre, Marinette Cheftaine, Line et Zoum, Jim Clopin Clopan, Bill de Clown,* and *François Veyrac l'Emigrant.* He added that he had also been the scriptwriter for over 300 different strips illustrated by such luminaries of French comic art as Poïvet, Forest, Liquois, and Le Rallic.

M.H.

DUMB DORA (U.S.) Feeling a need for another flapper strip in 1925, despite its ownership of *Tillie the Toiler, Hotsy-Totsy,* etc., King Features assigned Chic Young to begin a feature built around a college-age brunette named Dora Bell. Starting first as a Sunday page, fielded by the King affiliate, Premier Syndicate, and then as a daily as well, *Dumb Dora* dealt with boy and girl dating and related college activities. Dora was nicknamed "Dumb Dora," although the nickname is not notably used in the strip dialogue, and always had a thick-witted boyfriend, whom she continually passed up (a la Tillie, et al.) for handsomer, brighter, but less permanent boys. Dora's earliest boyfriend, simply named Ernie, didn't last past 1926. A bespectacled, old-looking oaf, he was quickly replaced by the rotund,

straw-hatted Rodney Ruckett, who stayed on as Dora's steady for a number of years. The strip's famed payoff line, used to the point of inanity in the Sunday page, but much less often in the daily strip, was "She ain't so dumb!", and was usually muttered, shouted, or sobbed by the misused Rodney in the last panel.

Young gave the daily strip an engaging narrative, with a certain amount of wit and character skill, which foreshadowed his later, more mature work on *Blondie.* When Young left the strip in April 1930 to work on *Blondie,* it was turned over to the talented King Features stringer Paul Fung, who did an excellent job in continuing the strip in Young's style and content. Fung kept Rod as Dora's boyfriend until 1932, when he turned the strip over to Bil Dwyer, who gave Dora a new love interest named Bing Brown. Dwyer did away with the old payoff line and drew a fresh, witty, well-scripted strip, but the day of the flapper had gone with the 1920s, and the strip died in the middle 1930s, distributed obscurely by King Features to a few outlets until it ended.

B.B.

DUMM, FRANCES EDWINA (1893-1990) Edwina Dumm was born in Upper Sandusky, Ohio, in 1893, the daughter of newspaperman Frank Edwin Dumm, whose father also ran a newspaper. Printer's ink turned to India ink in the veins of the daughter, though, and she pursued an interest in cartooning. Upon "graduation" from the Landon Correspondence School, she secured a position drawing editorial cartoons for the *Columbus* (Ohio) *Daily Monitor.* In 1916 Edwina Dumm was the only member of her sex to hold such a job in the United States (although female cartoonists were common enough, including Rose O'Neill, Grace Wiedersheim (Drayton), Fay King, Albertine Randall, Bertha Corbett, Kate Carew, and Barksdale Rogers).

She drew a strip for the *Monitor* called *The Meanderings of Minnie,* about a little girl and her dog. The feature caught the eye of syndicate wizard George Matthew Adams in New York, and Edwina was offered a contract to do a dog strip, for Adams was not convinced a little girl was the proper companion. When the offer coincided with the folding of the Ohio newspaper, Edwina moved to New York.

In 1921 the result of her work with Adams debuted: *Cap Stubbs and Tippie* was about a little boy and his dog. The combination was perfect, and although the strip never achieved great heights in terms of syndication, it had widespread appeal and popularity spanning two generations.

Her early work on the strip was engaging, although it sharpened noticeably the first years; two major influences were courses in anatomy under George Bridgman at the Art Students League (for human study), and the drawings of Robert L. Dickey, premier dog cartoonist, in *Life.*

In later years, for a healthy run into the 1960s, Dumm drew *Alec the Great,* little dog drawings (Alec looked just like Tippie) with four-line verses written by Edwina's brother, Robert Dennis.

Edwina's other work in cartooning was also dog-oriented. She illustrated the songsheets for songs written by Helen Thomas in honor of the Edwina dogs: "Tippie and the Circus" (1944); "Tippie's Christmas Carol" (1946); and "Tippie's Hallowe'en Serenade" (1950), recorded by Buffalo Bob Smith. Book illustrations included *Two Gentlemen and a Lady* by Alexander

"Dumb Dora," Milton Caniff (ghosting for Bill Dwyer). © King Features Syndicate.

Edwina Dumm, "Tippie." © Adams Service, Inc.

Woolcott, Burges Johnson's *Sonnets from the Pekinese*, and others.

The drawings for Woolcott's book caught the attention of the editors of the old *Life* magazine, and by the mid-1920s Edwina's full-page dog strips in wash were among the most popular things in the magazine. The puppy star was named in a reader contest: "Sinbad/ Was in bad/ From Trinidad to Rome/ And Edwina's Dog/ 'S in bad/ Wherever he may roam." Ultimately two hardcover collections of *Sinbad* strips were published. And Gluyas Williams noted to Edwina that the London *Tatler* was reprinting the cartoons without her knowledge or *Life*'s; soon, by arrangement, her drawings were a regular fixture in that sophisticated English journal.

Edwina's dog and kid cartoons are among the warmest and friendliest in all of cartooning. She had an uncanny ability to portray the world of a little boy, the relationships of kids, and, especially, the unique bonds between a boy and his dog. Few of her strips are knee-slappers in terms of humor, but that type of laugh would be out of place in the gentle, homey world observed, examined, and so definitively captured by Edwina. The Sunday pages of *Tippie* (distributed by King Features because Adams lacked color distribution and production facilities) allowed greater exposition of the dog's character. But the dailies were charming glimpses into the antics and observations of Tippie, the boyhood pranks of Cap Stubbs, and the fussy exterior but lovable essence of Grandma.

Edwina is a genius; the utter simplicity and sketchiness of her pen lines are as deceptive as the homey themes she mastered. There is a cult of Edwina fans, especially among cartoonists. A smattering of her work was published in 1975 by Ideals, and will hopefully be followed by more collections. She died in April 1990 in New York City.

R.M.

DWIG *see* Dwiggins, Clare Victor.

DWIGGINS, CLARE VICTOR (1874-1959) By far the greatest of the American comic strip's lost and forgotten talents was the late Clare Victor "Dwig" Dwiggins, of *School Days, Tom Sawyer and Huck Finn, Nipper,*

Ophelia, and many other strips. Dwiggins was born in Ohio on June 16, 1874, and was educated in country schools. He apprenticed as a draftsman with an architectural firm, then went into cartooning in 1897, producing gag drawings and panels for newspapers. Dwig's subject was simple and basic—the vanished past of boyhood in rural America between 1870 and 1920. The artist also did some earlier daily and Sunday strips, of which only one is worthy of extended comment.

J. Filliken Wilberfloss, Leap Year Lizzie, Them Was the Happy Days were typical titles among Dwig's pre-1920 work. The exceptional strip was the Sunday feature *School Days*, of the 1910s, a markedly different work from the later panel series of the same name. These Sunday half-pages were usually one large panel, filled with schoolkids involved in mischief inside the one room of a rural schoolhouse or the schoolyard outside, while their lovely, unconcerned schoolmarm was courted by various local gentry in the background. Central to the majority of these panels were elaborate devices cooked up by the kids to carry out various pranks, such as mechanisms of pulleys, wires, and wholly absurd connective parts such as dogs who have to lap up the contents of water buckets so that the emptied buckets will permit a weightier part of the device to lower, and so forth. In short, they were Rube Goldberg inventions before Rube Goldberg drew any inventions.

Interesting as these were, however, Dwig's finest sustained work lies in the daily panel series also called *School Days* (1917-32) with its continuing cast of kid characters and its lovely, sharply etched visual comments on the past these kids knew. Against the wooded hills and riversides that once surrounded or bisected so many American small towns, along the dirt streets and picket fences and haystack-sided barns, in the forest swimming holes and spotless Victorian parlors of their parents, Dwig's children spoke and adventured with stunning authenticity.

Dwig's Sunday pages, such as *Nipper* and *Tom Sawyer*, retained much of the atmosphere of the daily panels, but syndicate requirements for broad gag situations on Sunday too often took Dwig into slapstick and blunted the haunting, ethereal quality of his best work.

Dwig later tried an adventure strip, *The Adventures of Bobby Crusoe*, without success. In 1945 he went back to book illustration, which he had also done in his early career, and worked on that until his death in 1959.

B.B.

DYLAN DOG (Italy)   About 35 years old, handsome, tall, a vegetarian, agnostic, claustrophobic, with a phobia of heights (he never flies), former policeman, rehabilitated alcoholic, clarinet player, miniature galleon builder, and womanizer. These are the main physical and moral characteristics of *Dylan Dog*, the character created in 1986 by Tiziano Sclavi and drawn by Angelo Stano, intentionally copying the features of the British movie actor Rupert Everett.

Sclavi, born in 1953, has contributed to many Italian magazines and dailies as a journalist, novelist, and comic scriptwriter and has created several comic characters: *Altai & Jonson* (1975) and *Silas Finn* (1978), both drawn by Cavazzano; *Agente Allen* and *Vita da cani* ("A Dog's Life"), drawn by Gino Gavioli; *Roy Mann* (1987), drawn by Micheluzzi; and many more.

In 1981 Sclavi started to write scripts for some of the many series of the publisher Sergio Bonelli, and in 1986 *Dylan Dog* inaugurated a new monthly black-and-white comics series in book form. *Dylan Dog*, officially baptized "Nightmare Investigator" because he tries to solve dreadful and supernatural phenomena, began as a sort of horror and splatter comic strip echoing the horror movies of Argento, Romero, Carpenter, and Craven. Soon the plots went beyond the traditional figures of the horror domain—vampires, werewolves, and zombies—and started to present monsters of contemporary society such as serial killers and others who inflict pain and oppression on people. With the passing of time, the *Dylan Dog* saga has dealt with more romantic, fantastic, and psychological problems, which are troubling nonetheless in daily life.

In *Dylan Dog* the borderline between good and evil, the normal and the abnormal, is quite uncertain. There is always a benevolent attitude toward the "monsters" of society and an attempt to understand why these people have become what they are. *Dylan Dog* has been an unexpected success and became a cult hero among male and female Italian teenagers of the 1980s. At the beginning of the 1990s the series sold half a million copies a month, plus another half million of two monthly reprints. The series has also been reprinted in hardbound books and has been extensively merchandised. The success of the strip is due in part to its appeal to the younger generations, to their curiosity of the mysteries of life, and to the questions that trouble our society, which *Dylan Dog* explores in detail. Young readers frequently write to their hero for advice on a variety of problems, from the trivial to the personal. The character has been used in several advertising campaigns for social and humanitarian issues.

In his fight against evil *Dylan Dog* is supported by his assistant Groucho, who, like his namesake Groucho Marx, is garrulous and humorous to compensate for the dark thoughts and silences of his master. They live in a house in London where the doorbell howls instead of ringing. Other characters in the strip include Inspector Bloch of Scotland Yard, a father figure, and *Dylan Dog*'s parents, Dr. Xabaras and Morgana.

Since its inception, many hands have helped Sclavi make *Dylan Dog* a success: scriptwriters Claudio Chiaverotti and Luigi Mignacco; artists Giampiero Casertano, Corrado Roi, Carlo Ambrosini, Luigi Piccatto, Gianni Freghieri, Bruno Brindisi, Montanari & Grassani, and Piero Dell'Agnol. *Dylan Dog* has been published in many European countries and in Brazil, where it failed to find a large readership. Sclavi was awarded a Yellow Kid in Lucca in 1990 for the series.

G.C.C.

DZJENGIS KHAN (Netherlands)   *Dzjengis Khan* ("Genghis Khan") or "De strijd om het bestaan" ("The Fight for Survival") is one of the most interesting new comic series to come out of Holland since the Dutch comic weekly *Pep* (1962) decided to cut back on comic imports in 1968 and build its own stable of Dutch comic artists. This new policy was initiated by the editor-in-chief, Hetty Hagebeuk. It was also her idea to ask Jos Looman, who had already done some short features for *Pep*, to do a strip about the life of Genghis Khan from a script by Anton Kuyten. Thus, in the early 1970s a historic figure was given new life on the comic page.

Looman had to get acquainted with the character and the period before starting work on *Dzjengis Khan*. He did so admirably, the result being an ideally complemented epic sweep of Anton Kuyten's scenario that could have been a motion picture script. The comic strip epic of *Dzjengis Khan* in all probability has a greater semblance to reality than any wide-screen motion picture super-production could ever hope to achieve without spending millions of dollars.

The epic contains everything necessary to hold reader attention: sweeping landscapes, drama, and a strong cast of characters. Whatever Genghis Khan may have meant to history, he also had a personal history. Thus, the reader gets to follow the growing up and coming into power of Temoedzjin Khan (Temujin Khan). The reader is presented with the picture of an epoch, the lives and loves of another time, and their decisions and decision making.

Although bigger than life, Dzjengis Khan is not blown up to superhero proportions in this Dutch comic strip. The strip avoids the pitfall of becoming overly "talky," while making good use of page layouts and composition. Marianne Veldhuizen's colors top off the work on *Dzjengis Khan*. It is comics like this that make up for some of the shortcomings of certain aspects of the history of comics.

W.F.

ED, CARL FRANK LUDWIG (1890-1959)

ED, CARL FRANK LUDWIG (1890-1959)   The man who first celebrated the juvenile teens in a comic strip, *Harold Teen*, Carl Ed (rhymes with "swede"), was born Carl Frank Ludwig Ed in Moline, Illinois, on July 16, 1890. Ed's father, a working man, died when the boy was 13, causing him to leave high school in his freshman year and go to work. Ed continued his studies when and where he could, and later attended Augustana College in Illinois, getting a job as a sports writer on the Rock Island (Illinois) *Argus* at 20. From there, his cartooning ability got him a job as sports cartoonist on the Chicago *American* in 1912. The World Color Syndicate of St. Louis enabled him to try a strip when it circulated his daily feature for a number of years in the 1910s.

His talent was noted by Joseph Patterson, then co-publisher of the *Chicago Tribune*, who hired him to undertake the nation's first strip about a boy in his teens in 1918. Booth Tarkington's minor classic, *Seventeen*, had appeared in 1916. Called *The Love Life of Harold Teen* at the outset, Ed's new daily and Sunday strip was a hit in both the *Tribune* and Patterson's new New York tabloid, the *Daily News*. Aimed at newspaper readers between the ages of 12 and 20, *Harold Teen* was read widely by teenagers of the 1920s because of the wide-eyed Harold's reflection of their lifestyle, from the jalopies to the soda fountain socializing. Among the terms Ed popularized nationally with the kids of the 1920s were "lamb's lettuce" (for a girl) and "fan mah brow" (for surprise). "Panty-waist," a term for a juvenile "sissy," has lasted until the present.

In the grim 1930s, some of the appeal of *Harold Teen* ebbed, and by 1941, Harold was not only in uniform, but also a government spy, and the strip had been given a sharp twist toward melodrama. This was not all that well done, however, and public interest slipped further, not returning even when Ed renewed his teenage content in the post-war years. The strip's peak was reached when a silent film was made of it in 1928 and remade as a talkie in 1933. A few *Harold Teen* strip collections were published in the late 1920s and early 1930s.

Living in Skokie, a Chicago suburb, in his later years, Ed continued drawing his strip until 1959, when an acute illness took him to the Evanston, Illinois, Hospital, where he died a short time later on October 10, 1959, at the age of 69. The strip was laid to rest with its creator.

B.B.

EDSON, GUS (1901-1966)

EDSON, GUS (1901-1966)   Gus Edson, creator of *Dondi* and continuer of *The Gumps* from 1935, was born in Cincinnati, Ohio, on September 20, 1901. Leaving high school at 17 to join the Army just as World War I ended, he served in the U.S. After his discharge, Edson studied art at the Pratt Institute in New York. He landed a job as a sports cartoonist on the sleazy *New York Graphic* in 1925. When that paper col-

lapsed, Edson went in fast succession from the Paul Block newspaper chain to the *New York Evening Post*, and from there to King Features Syndicate as a standby ghost, and finally landed on the *New York Daily News* in the early 1930s, again on the sports page.

After Sidney Smith's tragic death in 1935, a desperate News-Tribune Syndicate contacted, without success, all major cartoonists from Rube Goldberg to Stanley Link to ask them to continue Smith's *The Gumps*. Gus Edson, still with the *Daily News*, was finally tapped to continue the popular Smith strip. With no previous strip experience and no evident talent either as an artist or an author, it is little wonder that he ran the brilliant *Gumps* strip into the ground in less than a decade, making millions wonder what they had ever seen in the once-popular feature.

After the propped-up corpse of *The Gumps* finally embarrassed even the executives of the *News* and the *Chicago Tribune* (which were about the only papers still carrying it), a decision was made to allow Edson to undertake a new strip with the artistic aid of Irwin Hasen in 1955. The new strip, called *Dondi*, appalled even the most astute supporters of the comic strip as an art form with its doe-eyed hero and its wholly insipid sentiment and callow melodrama, while the public loved it. *Dondi* ran in many papers until Edson's death in Stamford, Connecticut, on September 27, 1966, wealthy but little famed (for even the public that adored *Dondi* hardly noticed the name of its author). His only other major attempt at creativity was a script for a film version of *Dondi*, which was a box office

Gus Edson.

bomb. *Dondi* was drawn by Irwin Hasen until 1986, when the strip was discontinued.

B.B.

EDWINA *see* Dumm, Frances Edwina.

"Eek and Meek," Howard Schneider. © NEA Service.

EEK AND MEEK (U.S.) Howie Schneider created *Eek and Meek* in 1965 for NEA service. It was another one of the fables in which creatures in animal form were supposed to reveal the wisdom of the ages to us. In this case the action, or rather what there was of it, took place among mice. Meek, as his name implies, is a rather bland individual, eternally put upon by Eek, the unshaven and discreditable cynic, and eternally put down by Monique, the object of his unrequited love. There are also a couple of teenage mice, a female named Freaky, and a male named Luvable (a misnomer) who indulge in all the activities (protests, marches, sit-ins) once deemed fashionable by their human counterparts.

With the limited *dramatis personae* at his disposal, Howie Schneider bravely tried to make some meaningful statements, although he never managed to sound convincingly original. The trouble with *Eek and Meek* was that it plowed much the same ground previously, and more successfully, worked by *Peanuts*, *Pogo*, *B.C.*, and others. To come up with that kind of strip in 1965, complete with stick figures, settings without background, and contemporary situations showed a marked lack of originality. Yet one has to give Schneider the benefit of his intentions, and granted that, he succeeded reasonably well. Several collections of *Eek and Meek* were reprinted in pocket-book form by Paperback Library.

In 1977 Schneider decided to turn his rodent characters into human beings (or their approximation); the metamorphosis took place gradually and was only completed in 1982. Eek and Meek in human guise behave no differently than their former animal personas, but the strip has benefitted from the change and has substantially increased in readership in recent years.

M.H.

8-MAN (Japan) *8-Man* was created by artist Jirō Kuwata and scriptwriter Kazumasa Hirai (now one of the most famous authors of Japanese science fiction).

The strip made its debut in the weekly *Shōnen* magazine in April 1963.

8-Man was the reincarnation of Detective Rachiro Azuma, who had been killed by the Mukade gang. Dr. Tani remade him into a super-robot, giving him Azuma's memory and cool brains as well as his human appearance. Under his identity of Private Detective Azuma, 8-Man worked out of his office with his two assistants, Ichiro and Sachiko, who did not know his secret. Only Chief Tanaka of the Japanese Metropolitan Police Board knew Azuma's real identity.

8-Man could change his facial appearance at will, due to the special properties of his artificial skin (one of his favorite ploys was to assume the identity of his enemy's girl); he could run a thousand times faster than any human being; he had a small atomic reactor in his body, and concealed strength tablets (in the form of cigarettes) in his belt buckle.

8-Man fought against criminals, and came to the help of people in distress. His enemies have included: Dr. Demon; the Satan brothers, chiefs of a gang of kidnappers; Machine-gun Geren; 007, a powerful but dullwitted robot; Kitō, the boss of an international ring of criminals; Chōnenten, a master of magic and Kung Fu; the knife-wielding Apache; a huge electric brain called Superhuman Saiba; the super-robot 005; Dr. Yūrei, chief of an international spy organization known as "the Black Butterfly"; a witch with extrasensory perception; and superhuman beings trying to conquer the earth.

In spite of the fact that he was a machine, 8-Man had human feelings, and even problems, after the fash-

"8-Man," Jirō Kuwata and Kazumasa Hirai. © Shōnen.

ion of the Marvel superheroes. 8-Man soon became the idol of the comic-book-reading public, and must be ranked as one of the most famous superheroes in the history of Japanese comics.

The strip gave birth to a series of animated cartoons and was the inspiration for a whole line of metamorphic superheroes, such as Ultra Man, Ultra 7, Ultra Man Leo, and Kamen Rider. 8-Man made his last appearance in February 1966.

H.K.

EISELE UND BEISELE (Germany) It is doubtful whether *Eisele und Beisele*, originally titled *Des Herrn Baron Beisele und seines Hofmeisters Dr. Eisele Kreuz- und Querzüge durch Deutschland* ("Baron Beisele and His Private Tutor Dr. Eisele's Trips Through Germany"), should be termed comic strip characters. However, they *are* comic characters. Created by Caspar Braun, one of the founders of the *Fliegenden Blatter* and the *Münchner Bilderbogen*, Eisele and Beisele are two innocents journeying through Germany, later on through various countries. The two characters, who first appeared in the late 1840s, enjoy the distinction of being among the first recurring characters in cartoon history.

While Caspar Braun sometimes had Eisele and Beisele appear in sequential pictures and a sort of narrative figuration, they started out in cartoon illustrations loosely connected by narration that usually commented on some problem. The *Fliegenden Blatter* appeared weekly as a humor magazine with many illustrations by the same artists who also drew the *Münchner Bilderbogen*, most notably, of course, Wilhelm Busch.

What makes *Eisele und Beisele* of interest for the comic historian, however, is the fact that, in addition to being early—if not the first—continued cartoon characters, they have the distinction of being the first cartoon characters involved in litigation over "merchandising" products. At the height of their popularity, the characters were put on cakes and other sweets. This irked Caspar Braun, particularly because the Munich bakeries who used the characters had never asked for his permission.

W.F.

EISNER, WILL (1917-   ) American cartoonist, writer, and businessman. Born March 1917 in New York City, William Erwin Eisner wanted at first to become a stage designer, but upon graduation from high school he studied under George Bridgeman at the New York Art Students' League; this led to a staff job

"Eisele & Beisele," Caspar Braun, 1850's.

on the *New York American*. In 1936 he produced his first comic book work for the short-lived *Wow, What a Magazine*. In 1937, in collaboration with Jerry Iger, he founded his own studio where, along with a number of other beginning cartoonists, he turned out comic strips, games, and cartoon material. Under his own name or pseudonyms such as "Willis Rensie" and "Will Erwin," Eisner created such features as *Muss'em Up Donovan* (a detective strip), *The Three Brothers* (a foreign legion tale), *K-51* (a secret agent strip) and, most noteworthy of all, *Hawk of the Seas*, a beautifully delineated and hauntingly atmospheric tale of pirates and buccaneers.

On June 2, 1940, Eisner created and produced a comic book insert to be carried by Sunday newspapers along with their regular comic section. The 16-page insert, sized as a regular comic book, contained three features: Nick Cardy's *Lady Luck*, Bob Powell's *Mr. Mystic*, and Will Eisner's own *The Spirit*.

In 1942 Eisner was doing *The Spirit* both as a Sunday comic section and as a daily strip (as of 1941) when he was called to service. He was stationed in Washington, D.C., where he contributed, among other things, the character of Joe Dope for the instruction magazine *Army Motors*.

Demobilized in 1946, Eisner went back to *The Spirit*, which he was to draw until 1950. In the meantime, he had founded the American Visual Corporation, which published a host of official manuals and magazines (often in comic book form). Will Eisner's influence on the art and development of the comic book has been tremendous and lasting. He has received a number of awards and citations (including the title of "best comic book artist") both in the United States and in Europe.

Eisner's pedagogical propensities have been very much in evidence in the two books he has devoted to the comics medium, *Comics and Sequential Art* (1985) and *Graphic Storytelling* (1996). In the past 20 years he has also published a number of graphic novels and stories, many of them of an autobiographical nature, such as *A Contract with God*, *The Dreamer*, and *To the Heart of the Storm*. His most ambitious project to date has been the 176-page *Dropsie Avenue*, in which the author chronicled in comic-book form the history of a New York City neighborhood from the time of the Dutch colonization to the present.

M.H.

ELDER, WILLIAM W. (1922-   ) American comic strip and comic book artist born September 22, 1922, in the Bronx, New York. After studies at the High School of Music and Art and the Academy of Design in New York City, "Will" Elder began his comic book career in 1946, writing and drawing the *Rufus DeBree* humor feature for Orbit's *Toy Town* book. In 1947, Elder, Harvey Kurtzman, and Charles Stern formed an art studio, and after doing work for the Prize and Pines groups between 1948 and 1951, Elder joined the E.C. group in 1951.

The E.C. group was launching their vaunted "New Trend" books, and Elder worked on crime, horror, and science fiction stories. Unfortunately, his work on those was stiff. He did better material for the war books—*Frontline Combat* and *Two-Fisted Tales*—but there he was overshadowed by John Severin, whose work he frequently inked. It was not until his friend Harvey Kurtzman began E.C.'s *Mad* in November, 1952, that Elder's style developed and flowered. Under Kurtzman's aegis, Elder cut loose and began filling his panel backgrounds with designs, humorous characters, and outrageous gags. He is credited with developing the early *Mad* style—a panel cluttered with gags and sharp one-liners. When friend and mentor Kurtzman left *Mad* in 1956, Elder went with him to draw for a string of Kurtzman-edited black and white humor books. He continued developing his zany style through the regrettably short lives of *Trump* (1957-1958), *Humbug* (1958-1959), and *Help!* (1960-1962).

When Kurtzman created *Little Annie Fanny* for *Playboy* in 1962, Elder was the logical choice to illustrate the feature. But because the strip was printed in full-process color—the first American strip to be printed so lavishly—Elder was forced to simplify the cluttered style so as not to muddy and darken the rich colors. Instead, he concentrated on understated cleverness and slickness, and with the aid of Kurtzman and humor specialists Allan Jaffee and Jack Davis, Elder's *Annie Fanny* became the most complex and impressive comic material produced in America. Every panel was a painting, and a four-page strip often took several months to complete.

In addition to his comic book and strip work, Elder has also done considerable amounts of commercial art and book illustrating. His *Little Annie Fanny* work was exhibited in a 1974 Brooklyn Museum show, and his paintings have merited several one-man shows. After a brief return to *Mad* in 1985-87, he definitively retired from professional activities in 1988.

J.B.

ELEUTERI SERPIERI, PAOLO (1944-   ) Italian painter, scriptwriter, and cartoonist, born February 29, 1944, in Venice. In 1975 he started drawing comics for the Italian weekly *Lancio Story*, and several years later he distinguished himself as an excellent illustrator of Western adventures written mainly by Raffaele Ambrosio. Many of these Western stories, which were drawn during the 1970s for *Lancio Story* and the first half of the 1980s for the monthlies *L'Eternauta* and *Orient Express*, were reprinted in book form by the publishing house L'Isola Trovata from 1982 to 1987. In this period Serpieri illustrated some episodes of the French *Histoire du Far West en B.D.*, written by Jean Ollivier.

Serpieri's artwork of the Old West is noteworthy because it is rich in references to the works of photographers and painters of the Frontier and it reflects the spirit of the plots, both fictional and biographical. The powerful composition of the figures and the harsh hatching give a sense of crude realism to the strips. In Serpieri's West there is no room for myth.

After contributing artwork to the French collective work *Decouvrir la Bible* (Larousse, 1983-1985), Serpieri devoted himself to a new character of his own and at the end of 1985 his story *Druuna*, and later *Morbus Gravis* ("Serious Disease") appeared in the Italian monthly *L'Eternauta* and in the French *Charlie*.

In a far distant future, after an atomic catastrophe has destroyed the Earth, the last human beings are living aboard a spaceship where life is controlled by the supercomputer Delta. Druuna, the main character, is plunged into a world of depravity and horror, and Serpieri's powerful artwork helps to remind the reader of the possibilities of a technological, dull future, of the fear of losing our lives through atomic catastrophe, and the presence of hidden powers at work.

So far Serpieri has published five long versions of the series in Italy and France: *Morbus Gravis*, *Morbus Gravis 2-Druuna*, *Creatura*, *Carnivora*, and *Mandragola*. In 1982

Paolo Eleuteri-Serpieri "L'indiana bianca." © Editoriale l'Isola Trovata.

Serpieri was awarded a Yellow Kid in Lucca, and he has received many other prizes at home and abroad.

G.C.C.

ELFQUEST (U.S.) Wendy Fletcher always had a fascination for drawing and for fairy tales; eventually she joined the ranks of organized comics fandom, one of the female fans in an otherwise male-dominated field. (Indeed she met her husband, Richard Pini, through their common love of the comics.) All the elements of fairy tale fantasy and comic book imagery coalesced into *Elfquest*, a project the Pinis tried unsuccessfully to sell to every major and minor comic book company. After encountering only rejection and disappointment from all quarters, they decided to form their own publishing company, which they defiantly called WaRP—a name with a definitive science-fiction tinge that also stands for *W*endy *a*nd *R*ichard *P*ini. The first *Elfquest*

"Elfquest," Wendy Pini. © WaRP Graphics.

story (drawn and plotted by Wendy with writing assistance from Richard) appeared in WaRP's *Fantasy Quarterly* in the spring of 1978; it was given its own title in August of that year.

Outwardly *Elfquest* is the story of a clan of elves, the Wolfriders, in their suspenseful search for a new home after their ancestral grounds have been invaded by human barbarians; but it also serves as a metaphor for the eventual triumph of the spirit over brute force. It is also an allegorical projection of the Pinis' inner life and personal turmoil. "*Elfquest* is almost a symbolic autobiography of mine," Wendy told an interviewer. "Many of the incidents that happen in *Elfquest* are symbolic representations of things that have happened to me or to me and Richard. Quite literally some of the dialogue has been spoken by either Richard or me at certain times. We draw from our life experience and translate it into this beautiful fantasy."

When the last of the 21-episode saga was printed in February 1985, it was the culmination of a success story that had resulted in numerous reprintings, several paperback anthologies, and a host of merchandising. Between August 1985 and March 1988 Marvel, under its Epic imprint, reissued in color the stories that had originally appeared in black and white. Since 1987 the Pinis have also published a number of parallel series and miniseries, each under its own subtitle ("New Blood," "Siege at Blue Mountain," "Kings of the Broken Wheel," etc.)

M.H.

ELIAS, LEOPOLD (1920-   ) American comic book and comic strip artist born in Manchester, England, on May 21, 1920. After studies at the High School of Music and Art (with Israel Epstein) and Cooper Union, both in New York City, "Lee" Elias began his comic book career with the Fiction House group in 1943. Perhaps his most remembered work at this "pulp group turned comic house" was as Bob Lubbers's successor on the *Captain Wings* feature.

Appearing in *Wings Comics*, one of the foremost comic-aviation titles of the 1940s, Elias immediately upgraded the strip's treatment of airplanes. While Lubbers was an excellent anatomy artist, his technical work was poor and Elias's lovingly rendered airplanes were among the finest of the time. On the other hand, Elias, whose black-oriented work and economy of line often makes his work resemble that of Alex Toth and Frank Robbins, was not an outstanding figure artist. His characters lacked maturity and the rugged masculinity of the better artists of the time. His women were not particularly beautiful or voluptuous. Nevertheless, Elias also handled features like *Suicide Smith*, *Firehair*, and *Space Rangers* for Fiction House in the 1943-1946 period.

From there, Elias began a long career of journeyman work and illustrated for Western (*Terry and the Pirates*, 1948), Harvey (*Black Cat*, *Green Hornet*, 1946-1958), National (*Black Canary*, *Green Lantern*, 1947-1948), Hillman, and Marvel.

During the 1950s, however, Elias spent most of his time doing comic strips. After a two-year stint as an assistant on Al Capp's legendary *Li'l Abner*, he went on to cocreate with author Jack Williamson the *Beyond Mars* strip. One of a slew of aerospace strips spurred by the country's technological advances, the feature was well written and drawn, but it was as ill-fated as the genre and had a short run.

Elias returned to National and comic books in 1959 and drew for a large number of books. He is probably best remembered for his dark illustrating on the *Green Arrow* series, but he also did some fine work for both the *Cave Carson* adventure feature and the *Eclipso* strip. During 1959-1968 Elias also drew sporadically for the *Adam Strange*, *Ultra*, and *Automan* features, as well as doing a group of science fiction and horror work. In 1972, he once again rejoined National, concentrating almost entirely on the horror work. His last comic book work was on *The Rook* (1980).

Throughout his career, Elias has had great success as a commercial illustrator and has had several painting exhibitions, including one at the New York Metropolitan Museum of Art. In the 1980s he taught at the School of Visual Arts in Manhattan and at the Joe Kubert School of Cartoon and Graphic Art in New Jersey.

J.B.

ELLA CINDERS (U.S.) Originally one of the most popular strips of all time, and the only one to have been printed despite being damaged by fire, from coast to coast, Bill Conselman and Charlie Plumb's *Ella Cinders* began as a daily strip on June 1, 1925, and as a Sunday page on January 1, 1927. The Sunday pages followed the daily continuity. Created by a writer and artist team in Los Angeles, California (Conselman was editor of the *Los Angeles Sunday Times*; Plumb a cartoonist from nearby San Gabriel), *Ella Cinders* was the first strip to focus on the Hollywood scene as its principal locale and theme and involved a Cinderella heroine (toiling, of course, for her selfish mother and sisters) who won a filmland studio contract. Distributed by the Metropolitan Newspaper Service at the outset, *Ella Cinders* was a hit within its first year, and was made into a major studio film starring Colleen Moore by mid-1926.

Drawn with great comic style by Plumb, *Ella Cinders* was witty and fast-paced from the beginning, with imaginative publicity spinoffs from time to time which maintained public involvement beyond the story line level (for example, there was a 1929 request for readers to write in and advise Ella whether to marry or follow a career; there was also a $500 contest for the best letter telling Ella how to spend a million dollars in 1932).

In 1930 Conselman wrote a book-length novel for the Stratford Company of Boston called *Ella Cinders in Hollywood*, based on the early episodes of the strip; in September of the same year, a mail plane carrying a week's originals of *Ella* (October 6-11) from Los Angeles to New York crashed in flames at Warren, Ohio, charring the outside edges of the episodes to a depth of an inch and a half or more. Rushed to the syndicate by the post office, proofs made from the burned originals were sent out to the subscribing papers barely in time for publication and they appeared exactly as rescued from the ruins of the plane: flame-eaten dialogue balloons, panel details, and all. Luckily, enough remained of the episodes to make continuity sense; the publicity engendered for the strip was incalculable.

Built around such memorable characters as Ella herself; her close friend and brother Blackie Cinders; her devoted adventurer-father Samuel Cinders; her domineering mother Mytie Cinders; her two step-sisters, Prissie and Lotta Pill; her dumb but faithful admirer, the powerful Waite Lifter; her Hollywood director, Phil M.

"Ella Cinders," Charles Plumb and Bill Conselman. © United Feature Syndicate.

Waister; her co-star, Fluffy Frizelle; and her arch-enemy, producer O. Watters Neek, *Ella Cinders* reached its imaginative and popular peak in 1929-1931. At this point, however, her creators decided to glamorize Ella, drop the Hollywood setting, and pursue an outright romantic story line on the order of that in *Winnie Winkle* and *Boots and Her Buddies*. The now-comely heroine surrounded by handsome boyfriends in the daily strip, while being actually married to a mystery-man named Patches and plagued by jokebook gags in the Sunday episodes, *Ella* steadily lost its original appeal and its following in the 1930s, moving to a new syndicate, United Features, on January 1, 1933. (A Sunday companion strip, *Chris Crusty*, was added on July 5, 1931. Featuring a spectacularly nervy lead, the strip was often funnier than the main page by the mid-1930s.)

Despite an attempt to return to more imaginative story lines in the late 1930s and 1940s, *Ella Cinders* remained a second-string strip, without any noticeable improvement when the story line was taken over by Fred Fox in the 1950s after the death of Bill Conselman. The strip plummeted in circulation when Plumb's art was lost a few years later and replaced by that of Roger Armstrong. Nevertheless, for its first half-dozen years, *Ella Cinders* was a glittering, absorbing body of comic strip work, graphically outstanding and both amusing and gripping as a narrative.

B.B.

ELMER (U.S.) *Elmer*, the boyhood strip creation of A.C. Fera in 1916, is one of the few strips which achieved its early fame under a different name than the one most contemporary readers know it by. In fact, as long as Fera drew the strip (until 1925), it was titled *Just Boy*, and it was Fera's successor as artist and narrator on the strip, Charles H. (Doc) Winner, who changed the name to *Elmer*.

Just Boy was first released under Hearst syndication on a trial basis as a full weekly Saturday page in the *San Francisco Call* on May 6, 1916; it was not released in other Hearst papers until some time later. Fera's Elmer Tuttle was a tall, lean boy of about 13, growing up in a semirural community. His parents, Clem and Ella Tuttle, were solid, middle-class types; Clem Tuttle apparently held down an office job in the city. The family had a black maid, and a close acquaintance with the local beat cop, Officer Nolan (largely because of Elmer's shenanigans).

Fera had a deep, rich awareness of the lore of American boyhood in the 1910s and 1920s, and his *Just Boy* is as excellent a treatment of that subject as Booth Tarkington's *Penrod* of a slightly earlier period. His

"Elmer," A. G. Fera. © King Features Syndicate.

death in 1925 was a distinct loss to the art of the comic strip. The *Just Boy* feature, by then widely circulated, was continued by Hearst interests under a new title, *Elmer*, and drawn by Hearst cartoonist Doc Winner. The first Winner *Elmer* was released on October 4, 1925, and made a sound attempt to maintain the Fera quality of narrative and art. (By now, Elmer had become the short, rotund kid readers knew in the 1920s and later.)

Winner's *Elmer* speedily became the standard boy and dog gag strip found in a dozen features of the time, however, and its earlier wide appeal faded. By the mid-1930s, it had become a distinct second-string King Features strip, usually running as a Sunday half-page, accompanied by an even more obscure Winner upper half-page, *Alexander Smart, Esq.*, about a henpecked householder in his 50s. Always a Saturday or Sunday page feature from its inception, *Elmer* was folded with Winner's death, the last episode appearing on December 30, 1956. All or most of the Fera *Just Boy* portion of the strip calls for reprinting.

B.B.

ELWORTH, LENNART (1927-   ) Lennart Elworth is a Swedish writer, cartoonist, illustrator, and graphic artist, born February 5, 1927, in Surahammar, Sweden. After finishing public school, Elworth started working in an industrial office. From there he moved on to a technical bureau where he was to draw nuts and bolts, but he soon realized he was not cut out to be an engineer. Then, while serving in the army, he decided to study art. When he returned to civilian life, he started studying commercial art at the Bergh's school of advertising, earning his way through as a jazz musician. Having completed his studies, he started working as an illustrator on work ranging from editorial cartooning to illustrating children's books. In recognition of his work, he received a cultural scholarship from the city of Stockholm in 1968.

One year earlier, in 1967, Elworth had started the comic strip *47:an Löken* (which freely translates into "Soldier 47, Chowderhead") in *Lektyr. 47:an Löken* is in the Swedish tradition of humorous army series, started in 1932 with Rudolf Petersson's *91 Karlsson* and with Torsten Bjarre's *Flygsoldat 113 Bom* ("Air Force Pvt. 113 No-hit") in the 1940s. There are some similarities to *91 Karlsson* because of the subject matter of the strip and Elworth was not at all convinced that it was a good idea to go up against a strip as well established as *91 Karlsson*, but the editors of *Lektyr* talked him into going ahead on the project.

With the success of the feature came the realization that he need not have worried. His anecdotal comic strip is modern in approach, with a cast of characters that fits in well with this comic strip sitcom. The character of Löken is more or less Elworth's alter ego. Kapten Kruth ("Captain Gunpowder") is based on Elworth's father, and most of the other characters are also based on real people. Elworth worked in an easy-going style, rarely ever using closeups. His style was in the tradition of Swedish comics as represented by Knut Stangenberg's *Fridolf Celinder* or Axel Bäckmann's *Påhittiga Johansson* ("Imaginative Johansson"), according to the Swedish fanzine *Thud*. Elworth created the strip *Thudor* for *Thud* and made good use of the man-stranded-on-an-island situation. With the discontinu-

ance of his strips in the 1980s he disappeared from the comics scene.

W.F.

EMBLETON, RONALD S. (1930-1988) British cartoonist, illustrator, and painter, born 1930 in London. He studied art at the South East Essex Technical College and School of Art under the painter David Bomberg. He entered a commercial art studio for six months, during which period he drew his first strips for Scion, a London publisher of one-shot comics. To their *Big* series he contributed dozens of two-page, 24-panel adventure strips, including *The Black Lion* (Africa) in *Big Noise*; *The Ranger* (Canada) in *Big Boy*; *Sahara* in *Big Idea*; *Litening* (superhero) in *Big Flame*; *Black Hawk* (Western) in *Big Win*; climaxing in a complete eight-page comic of his own, *Big Indian* (1949). His signature, "Ron," was a familiar one when his comic career was interrupted by national service in the British Army in Malaya, which meant he was unable to continue the character *Ray Regan* in the Modern Fiction comic book of the same title.

Returning to London in 1950, the comics scene had changed and the style was now the American type of comic book. Forming a team with cartoonists Terence Patrick and James Bleach, Embleton provided Scion with a sequence of sixpenny comic books: the *Gallant* series (*Gallant Adventure, Gallant Detective, Gallant Science, Gallant Western*), and while his style had improved he remained as prolific as ever, contributing to *Buffalo Bill, Five Star Western*, and the science fiction comics *Jet* and *Star-Rocket* (1953). He also advanced into the higher-quality comics published by Amalgamated Press, and drew the weekly serials *Forgotten City, Mohawk Trail*, and *Tom o' London* for *Comic Cuts* (1951-52); and *Black Dagger* and *Into Strange Lands* for *Wonder* (1952).

As the traditional British comic paper faded out, Embleton's interest in color work increased. And he became a member of the Royal Institute of Oil Painters in the 1950s, and of the National Society of Painters and Sculptors in the 1960s, eventually holding exhibitions in Australia, Canada, and the United States. His strip work moved out of the comics and into the adult field: he drew *Johnny Carey* for *Reveille* (weekly), and *The Life of Ben Hogan* for Beaverbrook Newspapers (daily).

In 1957 he combined his two techniques, painting and strips, by producing his first painted strip. This was *Wulf the Briton*, a serial saga in *Express Weekly*, printed full color gravure. His special interest in history continued to show in such superbly painted serials as *Wrath of the Gods* in *Boy's World* (1963) and the feature strips *Rogers' Rangers, Marco Polo*, etc. in *Look and Learn* magazine. Then came a reversal in his career, a switch to science fiction, adapting the television series *Stingray* and *Captain Scarlet* for *TV Century 21* (1967). Later he concentrated on historical paintings for books, prints, etc., but returned to strips with *Wicked Wanda*, an adult sex-cum-satire strip for *Penthouse* (1972). In 1978 he added the drawing of the science-fiction strip *Trigan Empire* to his workload. He died suddenly on February 13, 1988, in Bournemouth.

D.G.

ENGHOLM, KAJ (1906-   ) Kaj Engholm, a Danish comic and graphic artist, was born 1906 in Copenhagen, where he grew up and went to school. To his own surprise he made it through final exams at Copenhagen's commercial college, where he met his future wife. Having been interested in drawing since childhood, he paired his interest and education by working and drawing in the advertising business. He handled advertising campaigns for Carlsberg and Tuborg (oil) and C.W. Obel (tobacco) among others.

In 1942 Engholm's wife mailed some of the drawings he had done for fun to a contest in a Copenhagen newspaper. This led to the start of Engholm's comic strip *Gnidén* that same year. Mr. Gnidén was a miser; A symbolic skinflint representative of a human phenomenon usually occurring in well-to-do countries. This might help explain the fantastic success of *Gnidén* in Denmark and Sweden; the Dutch, however, did not see the humor of Mr. Gnidén's escapades.

During the war, Engholm introduced a character named W. Kirkehøj to the *Gnidén* comic strip. (W. Kirkehøj is a literal translation of Winston Churchill in Danish.) One episode showed Gnidén lamenting about the amount of postage due to send Kirkehøj a Christmas card. This resulted in lots of letters sent in by readers sending stamps for Gnidén's card to Kirkehøj, who was very popular with most readers, Germans excepted.

In 1947 Engholm started a second daily strip, *Far till fyra*, a domestic comedy strip. Nine movies based on this comic strip were produced. Of these, the first three starred Ib Schönberg as *Far* ("Father"). After this, Engholm added the weekly comic strip *Kon Rosa* to his two daily strips.

He is now retired.

W.F.

"Eric," Hans G. Kresse. © Marten Toonder.

ERIC DE NOORMAN (Netherlands) *Eric de Noorman* ("Eric the Norseman"), created by Hans G. Kresse, one of the big-three of Dutch comic artists, started in the Flemish newspaper *Het Laatste Nieuws* on June 6, 1946, and was picked up by Marten Toonder's weekly *Tom Poes Weekblad* in 1947. Some 66 episodes, at times written in collaboration with Dirk Huizinga, then Jan Walin Dijkstra, appeared until Kresse, in 1964, discontinued the strip, which at the time appeared in *Het Vaderland*. However, September 10, 1966, saw the return of the Norse hero in *Erwin*, a strip appearing in the weekly comics magazine and featuring the adventures of Eric's son.

When Kresse was accepted for work in the studio of Marten Toonder after submitting artwork at the age of 23, he had an idea about a Nordic comic hero named Leif. Toonder suggested that he rename the hero Eric, and he also suggested that Kresse draw a science fiction epic about Atlantis, based on a Toonder idea. Kresse felt ill-at-ease with Atlanteans and ray guns. Thus Atlantis was completely destroyed, with Eric and his wife, Winonah, the only ones to escape the holocaust. Kresse's art improved significantly when he changed from pens to brushes after the first few episodes. The stories also improved when, after a run-in with the Romans, Eric departed for his home country, there to depose the usurper who had assassinated Eric's father, Wogram, the rightful king. To achieve victory and revenge, Eric had to enlist the aid of a magician, who in turn wanted payment in gold. The victory was won and Eric departed for a seven years' journey taking him to South America, Australia, Hawaii, and China. Finally, Eric returned to Norway, the gold having been lost and recovered again on the way. He stayed in Norway for several episodes to reestablish peace before again roaming the world, the most famous of his quests being the search for the invincible sword of Tyrfing, stolen from him.

Taking on more and more work in addition to *Eric* resulted in Kresse having a nervous breakdown in 1954, but he soon was back on the job, sending his hero first to Britain, then to Iceland and North America. Finally, Eric passed his crown on to his grown son, Erwin, before going to Britain to help King Arthur fight the Saxons, and then encountering the Huns in Europe.

In 1964 Kresse abandoned *Eric* to work on other comic features. But in September 1966 his hero returned in *Erwin*, the story of Eric's son. When Erwin was accused of being a pirate, Eric began dominating the strip in order to clear his son. Like Prince Valiant, Eric also was aged enough by his creator to become one of the few heroes who are grandfathers. In 1972 Kresse's interest moved to doing a comic strip about the history of Native Americans.

While the Dutch version of the strip used narrative below the pictures up to 1964, foreign editions often were done in the more usual way of putting narration and dialogue in captions and speech balloons. *Erwin* is done in speech balloon version only, despite Kresse's preference for the more literary and original way. In *Eric* good writing and excellent art were merged into a quality strip that later enjoyed success in newspapers and strip reprints in the Netherlands, Belgium, and a number of other countries.

W.F.

"Ernie," Bud Grace. © King Features Syndicate.

ERNIE (U.S.) The zany, farcical and frenzied comic strip *Ernie* by Bud Grace was launched on February 1, 1988, by King Features Syndicate. Deemed "a comedy of low manners," it portrays the absurd doings of affable bachelor Ernie Floyd and a diverse cast of loony and expedient characters.

Ernie is an assistant manager at a repugnant squid restaurant, playing a benign foil to the grotesque cast fictitiously set in Bayonne, New Jersey. Doris Husselmeyer is his nebbish girlfriend, whose juvenile brother Spencer is better adjusted than his deranged guardians. Ernie's miscreant uncle Sid Fernwilter is the feature's most developed personality, a bamboozling con man and manager of the fraternal Piranha Club, whose cold-blooded mascot Earl would prefer to devour them all. Landlady Effie Munyon provides the leeching Sid with incredibly disgusting meals, while his friend Enos Pork operates an equally odious medical practice. Rounding out the primary company are the felonious Wurlitzer brothers and the lecherous yet simple-minded Arnold Arnoldski.

A former atomic physicist, Bud Grace began to draw magazine panel cartoons as a freelancer in 1979, and soon after left his research and teaching position at Florida State University. Noticeably influenced by underground cartoonists Robert Crumb and Kim Deitch, *Ernie* currently appears in over 200 domestic papers and in 25 countries. It is very popular in Scandinavia, and numerous book collections have appeared there, eclipsing the sales of the two paperbacks and the comic book released in the United States. Manic, uncouth, and humorously outrageous, the strip's highly developed troupe of characters were inspired by the cartoonist's divergent interests and anomalous associations, consequently raising the work above the usual syndicated fare.

On occasion Grace has caricatured himself into the strip, creating a rare and self-satirical portrayal not seen since Al Capp's cameos in *Li'l Abner*. Drawn in a solid, sketchy style, the comic was acclaimed as the "Best Newspaper Comic Strip" for 1993 by the National Cartoonists Society, and has received numerous international awards. Although not suited to everyone's taste, the well-defined humor and personalities in *Ernie* make it one of the finest examples of the contemporary style in comic strips.

B.J.

"Ernie Pike," Hugo Pratt. © Editrice Sgt. Kirk.

ERNIE PIKE (Argentina) Hector Oesterheld created *Ernie Pike* in 1957 in the magazine *Hora Cera* and entrusted the drawing to Hugo Pratt, who gave its protagonist the features of Oesterheld.

The figure of Ernie Pike was based on the real-life Ernie Pyle, an American war correspondent killed in Okinawa in 1945 and made into a legend by William Wellman's movie *The Story of G.I. Joe.* Burgess Meredith played the role of Pyle in the film with notable humility and patriotic fervor.

Hugo Pratt gave the character a different outlook, avoiding patriotic speeches to project only the image of a decent human being, lost amid the clamor of war, without regard to the cause for which it was fought. Resorting to a somber and austere drawing style, unpretentious and fast, Pratt succeeded in pushing the war heroics into the background to concentrate on the men struggling in the muck and mire of everyday military life. His Pike, in the company of photographer Tony Zardini (himself patterned after the real-life cameraman Robert Capa), moves from one theater of war to the next in order to tell the world of the tragedy of war.

The *Ernie Pike* episodes drawn by Hugo Pratt were widely reprinted in Italy, while in Argentina the feature had passed into the hands of Guzman, who drew it in the early 1960s. Years later, *Ernie Pike* was revived in the magazine *Top*, with the Vietnam War as the background this time: Oesterheld was still the scriptwriter, while the drawings were contributed by Nestor Olivera. In 1976 *Ernie Pike* was taken over by Francisco Solano Lopez, but the feature only lasted for a few more years.

L.G.

ERNST, KENNETH (1918-1985) American artist born in Illinois in 1918. Kenneth (Ken) Ernst studied at the Chicago Art Institute, but started his career as a magician. In 1936 he joined the "A" Chesler studio, and worked for a number of comic book publishers, including Western, for whom he did *Buck Jones* and *Clyde Beatty*, and National, where he drew *Larry Steele* (1939-40).

In 1940 Ken Ernst moved into the newspaper strip field as assistant on *Don Winslow of the Navy* before being asked by Publishers Syndicate to take over the drawing of *Mary Worth's Family* (1942). Together with writer Allen Saunders, Ken Ernst gave the feature (shortened to *Mary Worth*) the look it still retains.

Ernst was one of the more gifted practitioners of what had come to be called the "Caniff school." His drawings were elegant and uncluttered, and he always displayed in his layouts and compositions solid qualities of taste and craftsmanship. He continued working on *Mary Worth* until his death in Salem, Oregon, on August 6, 1985.

M.H.

ERNSTING, VOLKER (1941-   ) Volker Ernsting, German cartoonist and writer, was born in Bremen on May 4, 1941, the son of a bank clerk. He grew up, went to school and high school, and then went to the Hochschule für Gestaltung (college of design), all in Bremen. Ernsting's earliest work (1962) appeared in *Pardon*, a German monthly progressive satirical magazine. Ernsting contributed illustrations, political cartoons and cartoon portraits, and comics to *Pardon* in the 11 years he was closely associated with that magazine. The comic satire he produced for *Pardon* included a series of "pop classics" like "Don Giovanni" or "Odysseus," the latter appearing on the occasion of the military takeover in Greece. "Ballermann" was a satire on neo-Nazis. In 1970 he drew Jesus comics.

Also in *Pardon* were his *Köter & Co.* ("Cur & Co."), animal comics with topical contents, and illustrated fictitious reports about military maneuvers, sex, etc. Among the best of Ernsting's work for *Pardon* is an eight-page comics spoof done in the form of a comic supplement and poking fun at *Superman, Batman, Phantom, Rip Kirby, Tarzan,* and *Astèrix*. This satire, written by Gerhard Kromschröder, appeared in the October 1970 issue of *Pardon*. From 1966 to 1971, Ernsting had a regular column in *Pardon*, titled *MoPS*, which is short for M*onatlicher* P*resse* S*piegel* ("monthly review of the press"), and is at the same time a pun, as a *mops* (pug) is a dog.

Starting in 1966, some Ernsting cartoons appeared in book form: *Hals- und Beinbruch* (an equivalent of "Happy landings!" meaning literally "Break your neck and leg!" which is quite appropriate for doctor cartoons), *. . . und läuft und läuft und läuft* (a Volkswagen satire), *Goldrausch* ("Gold Rush," olympic cartoons). 1971 saw Ernsting's super production *Sherlock Holmes und das Geheimnis der blauen Erbse* ("Sherlock Holmes and the Secret of the Blue Pea"), a highly individual comic strip satire of television mystery programs fea-

turing far in excess of 100 TV personalities. Appropriately enough this comic strip satire appeared in *Hör Zu*, Germany's largest television weekly, before being published in book form. For many years, starting in 1972, Ernsting drew one *Mike Macke* story per year for *Hör Zu*. He also worked on ad campaigns for *Hör Zu* and for the city of Bremen. When *Mike Macke* was discontinued, Ernsting continued working in advertising and also did occasional cartoons.

W.F.

ERWIN, WILL   *see* Eisner, Will.

ESCHER, REINHOLD (1905-1994) Reinhold Escher, German artist and cartoonist, was born April 12, 1905, in Hamburg. At the age of 10 he drew his first picture stories—strips in the true sense of the word, as they were drawn on paper strips several yards in length. They came from rolls of silk and were provided by a milliner, a relative of the family. These early stories told of wars and Indian fights.

Escher grew up and went to school in Hamburg. There, he also studied painting and decorating at the Landeskunstschule (county art school). Following his studies, Escher did illustrations and cartoons. During an extended stay in Switzerland, he busied himself with rustic painting.

In the 1930s Escher first got a chance to draw full-page animal stories for the Sunday edition of the paper *Hamburger Anzeiger*. His first strip, *Peter mit dem Mikrophon* ("Peter with the Microphone"), appeared in the paper's insert *Der kleine Genossenschafter*. He also found employment with the renowned illustrated weekly *Hamburger Illustrierte*, for which he wrote and drew the strip *Hein Ei* ("Hennery Egg").

After World War II Escher first worked for Swiss magazines. Then, back in Hamburg, Escher illustrated several picture books, worked in advertising and for *Hör Zu* ("Listen In"), a large circulation radio and television weekly. Eduard Rhein, first editor-in-chief of *Hör Zu*, acquired the rights to *Mecki*, a cute hedgehog well known because of the films of the Diehl brothers. For *Hör Zu* the animated dolls of the Diehl films were transformed into a comic strip by Reinhold Escher. He created a number of additional characters, like Charly Pinguin or the Schrat (a troll), to widen the story potential beyond the rather domestic humor of the original animated films. *Mecki*, having the status of editorial talisman, occupied a full color page in all issues of *Hör Zu* from 1951 to 1972. Up to 1971 the stories used a running narrative within the picture frames, and in 1971 speech balloons were added to give the strip a more modern look. The strip, as conceived by Escher, was put on hiatus in 1978 when Hans Bluhm, second editor-in-chief of *Hör Zu*, was looking for new attractions.

Most of the stories of differing length and an innumerable number of single-page gags were written and drawn by Escher, with some of the writing done in cooperation with his wife. Escher was influenced by Wilhelm Busch, Lawson Wood, and the Disney productions, as well as by Buster Keaton, Charlie Chaplin, and Harold Lloyd. His stories had a warm, human quality, and there was a penchant toward adventure, especially in the continued stories. The success of the strip led to some 15 *Mecki* books published annually. They usually told a *Mecki* novel, with each page of text facing a page of art. Of these, only the first one was illustrated by Escher. Escher died in Switzerland on May 9, 1994.

W.F.

ESPIÈGLE LILI, L' (France) One of the longest running French comic strips, *L'Espiègle Lili* ("Mischevious Lili") saw first publication in the French weekly *Fillette* on October 21, 1909. It was the creation of Jo Valle for the text and Andre Vallet for the drawings.

Lili d'Orbois was a precocious seven-year-old girl whose tricks and escapades frustrated her parents. Sent to the boarding-school of the Poupinet sisters, she led her companions into innumerable scrapes and generally proved herself a worthy cousin of the Katzenjammers and Buster Brown.

Well before Frank King used the same device, Valle and Vallet had their heroine mature in the strip. During World War I Lili did her bit for the Allies, and in 1923 she married her aviator fiancé, bringing the strip to a temporary end.

In 1925 *Lili* came back, drawn by René Giffey. She was again the terrible little girl of her earlier life. Interrupted by World War II, the strip was revived in the late 1940s by Alexandre Gérard (who signed AL G). Gérard made Lili into a typical teenager with new friends, a family, a fiancé, etc. During its third life (which extended until 1972) the strip was first written by B. Hiéris, then by Paulette Blonay. Seemingly indestructible, the character was resurrected by Jacques Arbeau (signing his work Jacarbo) from 1978 to 1986.

L'Espiègle Lili enjoyed a solid success and was probably the most popular of European girl strips. A number of Lili's adventures were reprinted in book form and for a short while in the early 1920s she gave her name to an illustrated weekly, *Le Journal de Lili*.

M.H.

ETERNAUTA, EL (Argentina) The prolific Argentine scriptwriter Hector Oesterheld (author of the comic strip scenarios of *Ticonderoga*, *Verdugo Ranch*, *Bull Rocket*, *Indio Suarez*, and many others) created *El Eternauta* for the monthly magazine *Hora Cero* in 1957. The premise of the strip is one of the weirdest in the history of comics: a comic strip writer receives a visit from an extraterrestrial being who claims to be a 21st century philosopher, a navigator of time and traveler of eternity who had already lived over 100 lives. Tired of wandering and reincarnation, this "eternaut" came to Earth in order to take human form for the last time.

In the beginning, the feature was drawn by cartoonist Solano Lopez, and this version inspired an animated film produced by Hugo Gil and Mario Bertolini in 1968. But the strip took on added dimension when Alberto Breccia took over in the late 1960s and brought out the strip's potential. Breccia eschewed the conventional techniques of comic drawing to innovate on each page. He used an imaginative layout complemented by a very individual graphic style, and techniques in which he is a master: use of benday, scratch lines, chromatic experimentation, and other devices (unfortunately often lost in reproduction) in order to create an oneiric atmosphere which has contributed to making *El Eternauta* one of the most unusual comic strips of its time. This second version met only with incomprehension in Argentina, but was very successful in Europe, especially in Italy where a comics magazine in 1980 took the name *L'Eternauta* as a tribute to the pioneering

"Etta Kett," Paul Robinson. © King Features Syndicate.

series. Francisco Solana López is now turning out the series.

L.G.

ETTA KETT (U.S.) Cartoonist Paul Robinson produced *Etta Kett* for King Features Syndicate in 1925. It was initially intended as a panel for teaching good manners to teenagers (hence the pun on the word etiquette). It proved an impossible task, however, and *Etta Kett* soon turned into a typical teenage girl strip.

Etta Kett was a vivacious, curvaceous young lady who never got involved in anything more compromising than forgetting the money for the dress she had just bought or holding hands with some pimply boy in a soda parlor. Paul Robinson was very effective in keeping Etta and the other characters in the strip up-to-date on the latest fads and fashions, but the setting and psychology remained Squaresville, USA, in the 1940s. The fact that the strip survived until November 1974 is a testimonial to the endurance of the myth of American innocence right into the self-examining and cynical 1970s. As such, *Etta Kett* is probably more exemplary than other staples of the genre, such as Hilda Terry's *Teena* or Harry Haenigsen's *Penny*.

M.H.

EVANS, GEORGE (1920-   ) American comic book and comic strip artist born February 5, 1920 in Harwood, Pennsylvania. His first professional work appeared in pulp airplane magazines when he was 16. After studies at the Scranton Art School, Evans entered the army and served in World War II. He later enrolled in the Army Extension Correspondence Course. He began his comic art career in 1946 with the now-defunct Fiction House group, where he drew several of their minor features (*Air Heroes*, *Tigerman*, and others).

In 1949 he began working for the Fawcett group and drew strips such as *When Worlds Collide* and *Captain Video*. During this time he was also attending night classes at New York City's Art Students League. Evans joined E.C. Comics in 1953 and turned out superior work for all of the group's legendary horror, science fiction, war, and crime titles. But he did his greatest work in 1955 when he wrote and drew stories for the group's "New Directions" *Aces High* title. An avowed airplane fan, Evans' work on the short-lived (five issues) book's "flying" stories is among the best ever produced in comics. He also contributed artwork to E.C.'s abortive "Picto-Fiction" black and white magazines.

After E.C. folded in 1956, Evans began drawing for Gilberton's *Classic Comics*, illustrating the comic book adaptations of Shakespeare's *Romeo and Juliet* and *Julius Caesar*, Conrad's *Lord Jim*, Hugo's *Hunchback of Notre Dame*, Dumas's *Three Musketeers*, and other major literary works. He continued with Gilberton until 1962. During the early 1960s, Evans also worked for Western (Gold Key) and drew for such varied titles as *Twilight Zone* and *Hercules Unchained*. During 1964 and 1965 he contributed to Warren's *Creepy* and *Eerie* black and white magazines. In 1968 he began working for National Comics and contributed to their supernatural and humor books. He also drew for the war titles, illustrating an occasional "flying" story.

In 1960, Evans made his first foray into syndicated newspaper strips when he began ghosting George Wunder's *Terry and the Pirates*. Although he worked on the feature until 1972, he never received a byline. Throughout his career, (which has been highly influenced by the work of Alex Raymond and Hal Foster), Evans has done considerable advertising work. He is a member of the National Cartoonist Society. In 1980 he took over the syndicated *Secret Agent Corrigan* newspaper strip, which he drew until the feature's demise in 1996.

J.B.

EVERETT, BILL (1917-1973) American comic book artist and writer born May 18, 1917, in Cambridge, Massachusetts. After studies at the Vesper George School of Art in Boston, Everett went through a variety of commercial art jobs and finally landed with the Lloyd Jacquet Comic Shop in 1939.

Working under his own name and pseudonyms like "William Blake" and "Everett Blake," he created *Skyrocket Steele* and *Dirk the Demon* for Centaur. His best strip for that company was a unique superhero feature called *Amazing Man*. Between 1940 and 1942, he also produced a series of minor features for Novelty, including *Chameleon*, *Sub-Zero*, and *White Streak*.

Everett's greatest achievement came in 1939 when he invented *The Sub-Mariner*. Created out of the Jacquet shop, along with Carl Burgos' *Human Torch*, the character made his first appearance in *Marvel Comics* number one. Everett's undersea antihero quickly became a major success. And although his work was not technically perfect, it was highly stylized, and

Bill Everett, "The Sub-Mariner." © Marvel Comics Group.

Namor's triangular head and arched eyebrows became the character's trademark.

In 1940, Everett created an imitation of his character for Eastern Color and called it *Hydroman*. Back at Timely he created still another water hero called *The Fin*. During the early 1940s he also worked on features like *The Patriot* (Timely), *Conquerer* (Hillman), and *Music Master* (Eastern). After a stint in the armed forces, Everett returned to Timely in 1947. He began handling *Sub-Mariner* again and drew still another aquatic feature, *Namora*, in 1948. She was another spin-off of the Namor series. He later produced a large volume of horror material for Atlas (nee Timely) in the early 1950s.

After another stint on *Sub-Mariner* from 1953 to 1955, Everett left comics and worked in commercial art until 1964. He then returned to Marvel (the newest Timely name) and worked on most of their superhero strips. During this time, he made one final return to *Sub-Mariner*. After several contributions to the strip in the 1960s, he was reassigned to the feature in 1972 and immediately revitalized the series.

Just as the public was becoming reacquainted with Everett's material, the artist took ill and died February 27, 1973. He was so well-liked by his colleagues that the Academy of Comic Book Arts formed The Bill Everett Fund for Indigent Artists in his honor.

J.B.

FABULAS PANICAS (Mexico) Alexandro Jodorowski created his most personal work, *Fabulas Panicas* ("Panic Fables"), after completing his collaboration as scriptwriter of *Anibal 5*. Starting in 1967, this strip appeared in the form of a color page in "Heraldo Cultural," the Sunday supplement of the daily *El Heraldo de Mexico*. This time Jodorowski had complete control over the scenarios, the drawing, and the coloring. The author—founder with Juan Arrabal and Roland Topor of the "panic theater" movement—expressed in these simple pages, purportedly addressed to children, his own philosophy, inspired by his hippie-like attitude toward life. Jodorowski caricatured himself as the protagonist, with his kinky hair and tunic, who listened to or argued with the "Master," a kind of blonde god, bewhiskered and loving, who had two nearsighted and querulous children, a boy and a girl.

Jodorowski's style, informal and similar to the experiments of the American "underground," used color in a psychedelic fashion. The author utilized montages of old prints and caricatures, or hatchings, to narrate the questions put to the Master and his answers, or to have the fingers of one hand talk to one another. When the characters felt at a loss for words, or were too bored to talk, they employed blank balloons. At other times they limited themselves to groans, or to an exchange of onomatopeias. Sometimes machines would talk (foreshadowing the future world that Jodorowski would present years later in his movie *The Holy Mountain*), with meditations which lend consistency to these new fables.

L.G.

FABULOUS FURRY FREAK BROTHERS, THE (U.S.) Gilbert Shelton, whose cartooning career had begun with *Wonder Wart-Hog* in 1961, began his second series of outstanding material in 1967. Completely different in orientation from his superhero parodies in *Wonder Wart-Hog*, the *Freak Brothers* feature was a humorous look at what was then the emerging drug and youth culture of the 1960s. In truth, however, Shelton's stories were usually just exaggerations of real-life happenings among the youth of the time.

Shelton began *The Freak Brothers* for the *L.A. Free Press*, but its appeal was so universal that it soon began being syndicated to most of the underground newspapers beginning to flourish throughout the rest of the country. Along with Crumb's *Fritz the Cat* and *Mr. Natural*, *The Freak Brothers* became the best-known strip to emanate from the underground press. The feature made a smooth transition into underground comix book in 1968, in *Feds and Heads*. In their own title, which began in 1971, they became the most-read underground feature, with a circulation well over 100,000 copies.

Several factors account for the phenomenal success of *The Freak Brothers*: Shelton is generally regarded as the most professional of all the underground artists; the strip was meant to entertain more than to proselytize; and it was amazingly true to life and readers could identify with the antics of the three dope- and sex-hunting heroes. Perhaps most importantly, the characters were strong in themselves. Fat Freddy, Freewheelin' Franklin, and Phineas Freak were identifiable characters in the late 1960s. They were funny and crazy, and, occasionally, philosophical. In fact, Freewheelin' Franklin's utterance that "Dope will get you through times of no money better than no money will get you through times of no dope" became as widely quoted as Crumb's reintroduction of "Keep on Truckin'," and it was probably more germane to its readers.

On the artistic level, Shelton never allowed his position as chronicler of the times to interfere with his attempts to make the feature a showcase for the absurd. He parodied other strips—*Little Orphan Annie* became Little Orphan Amphetamine, the brothers' "favorite 14-year-old runaway"; *Dick Tracy* became Tricky Prickears, the "blind, deaf cop" who spouted enforcement codes in "Crimestompers Meinkampf"; and Mell Lazarus' Momma even made an appear-

"Fabulas Panicas," Alexandro Jodorowski. © El Heraldo de Mexico.

"The Fabulous Furry Freak Brothers," Gilbert Shelton. © Gilbert Shelton.

ance—and mercilessly exploded both the establishment and the counterculture's greatest myths.

As the strip developed, Shelton even borrowed a trick from George Herriman's book. Back in the 1910s, while Herriman devoted most of his time to *The Dingbat Family*, he ran *Krazy Kat* along the bottom of the daily strip. Shelton did likewise, and *Fat Freddy's Cat*, featuring an orange tomcat with a penchant for relieving himself in the most annoying places, began to appear at the bottom of the *Freak Brothers* pages. The strip-within-a-strip even developed its own characters: mice who constantly fought with Fat Freddy's Cat.

Since the brothers most consistently appeared in the *Free-Press*, most adventures are only a single tabloid-sized page long; however, there have been several longer stories drawn for the underground books. The best of these were collected in the 1974 *Best of Rip Off Press, Vol. II* anthology. The brothers have also appeared in a movie—something of a classic at comic conventions since it is too sex-oriented to be shown in regular theaters. In January 1975, they appeared in dazzling color in a multi-page story in *Playboy*.

J.B.

After Shelton left for Europe in the late 1970s, the brother's appearances in American comic books were more and more sporadic, despite the creator working in tandem with associate Paul Mavrides, who had remained in California. So scarce had the Freak Brothers made themselves that in 1985 the publisher of Rip-Off Press could announce only half-facetiously that the two cartoonists had set a record by managing to produce two issues of the title within the year.

M.H.

FACÉTIES DU SAPEUR CAMEMBER, LES (France)
Christophe's second masterpiece, *Les Facéties du Sapeur Camember* ("The Pranks of Sapper Camember"), appeared for the first time in 1890 in the pages of the weekly *Le Petit Français Illustré*.

Camember was an enlisted man in the French Army of the Second Empire. His simplicity and guilelessness made him an easy target for any sharpies in his outfit, and Camember would often end up in trouble with his sergeant or his officers as a result of his often self-defeating "pranks." The series ended in 1896 on a note of pathos: Camember took part in the Franco-Prussian War of 1870 and saw his colonel killed in front of him, but he wiped out the enemy platoon. Old and covered with decorations, he retired to his native village.

La Sapeur Camember, like *La Famille Fenouillard* before it, did not use speech balloons. Unlike *La Famille Fenouillard*, however, it did not contain weekly continuity (except in the very last episodes); it was a series of gag stories of military humor typical of the period. It gave rise to many other service comic strips, and can even be seen as a remote ancestor of *Beetle Bailey*.

Le Sapeur Camember has been kept in continuous print by Armand Colin, which issued many editions of Christophe's picture-story over the years; it has also been reprinted in paperback form by Hachette. In the 1960s it inspired a French television series that mixed animation and live action.

M.H.

FALK, LEE (1905-   ) American writer, born in 1905, in St. Louis, Missouri. From his days in high school, when he edited the school's paper, and throughout his adult life, Lee Falk felt a compulsion to write. He wrote stories, articles, and poems for his college newspaper and, after graduation from the University of Illinois, went to work as a copywriter for a St. Louis advertising agency. There he met artist and fellow Missourian Phil Davis, with whom he was to create *Mandrake the Magician*, his first attempt at comic strip writing.

After a stint as a producer-writer for a local radio station, Lee Falk went to New York to make the rounds of the syndicates, and in 1934 he succeeded in selling *Mandrake* to King Features. The success of the feature was such that two years later Lee Falk originated *The Phantom*, again for King.

In addition to writing the scripts for *Mandrake* and *The Phantom*, Lee Falk is the author of several theater plays; one of these, *Eris*, was staged in Paris in 1968, and revived in 1973 by a French repertory company. Since 1962 Lee Falk has been writing (or at least plotting) the *Phantom* paperback novels published by Avon Books. Falk received a special award for his work as a comic strip writer at the Lucca, Italy, Comics Conference in 1971. Now in his nineties, he is still actively writing the continuities of both *The Phantom* and *Mandrake*; in 1996 he was featured in a special on the A&E network celebrating the 60th anniversary of *The Phantom* and the theatrical release of the Phantom movie.

In a medium dominated by graphic artists, Lee Falk stands out as the creator of two successful features and as a fiction writer of great skill and imagination, whose characters and stories have been popular throughout the world for over six decades.

M.H.

FALLUTELLI (Argentina) The noted gag cartoonist Guillermo Divito, who had founded the humor magazine *Rico Tipo* in 1944, created *Fallutelli* the following year in the pages of his own magazine. Fallutelli is an Italianized version of a Buenos Aires slang word meaning "phony," and no other term can better define the protagonist of this humor strip.

Fallutelli is an office clerk; short, ridiculously attired with false and garish elegance, with bulging eyes and buck teeth, a fine moustache, and a narrow-brimmed hat. A servile flatterer of his superiors, scheming and pushy, capable of deceiving even his best friends in order to climb the social ladder, he displays his anxieties to little advantage and has remained in the same obscure position he occupied at the start. *Fallutelli* is a classic example of the Argentinian humor strip in which a simple and basic situation is milked to the limit, while succeeding in remaining fresh all the while.

When everyone else had abandoned him, Fallutelli would seek refuge in the house of his tall and attractive girlfriend Doris. To her alone he would confide his worst fear: that his coworker Escolasio would be promoted ahead of him. This typical obsession of the average bureaucrat would soon become reality, and Escolasio (who started initially as a secondary character on the strip) was to gain in time a more important position than Fallutelli. Escolasio, a womanizer, gambler, con artist, and professional survivor, became the star of the strip. The feature survived Divito's death in 1969 by more than a decade.

L.G.

FAMILIA BURRON, LA (Mexico) In 1937 the writer and cartoonist Gabriel Vargas created for the Mexican magazine *Pepin* a humor strip entitled *El Señor Burron o Vida de Perro* ("Mister Burron, or A Dog's Life"), which later became a color comic book under the definitive title of *La Familia Burron*.

The strip's direct antecedent was another series by the same author, *Los Superlocos* ("The Supercrazies"), in which he created the character Jilemon Metralla y Bomba. The Burron family has as its titular head Don Regino, the barber-owner of the "Golden Curl" beauty salon, a good-natured and meek little man incapable of standing up to his wife, the jovial Borola. A female counterpart of the above-mentioned Jilemon, Borola runs the household, leads the family—and soon becomes the real star of the strip. A female figure carved all of a piece, Borola is as bold as she is aggressive and assertive. She takes chances in all and every conceivable enterprise, ready to make use of every trick without scruple or remorse, sure as she is that every conceivable way for advancing the fortunes of her children must be good. Social status is her ultimate goal: thrifty, protective of her children, she thrives and prospers under all conditions. Nothing seems too good for her children, her son Reginito, her daughter Macuca (a much sought-after girl with two boyfriends), and her adopted son, Foforito, who reflects all the virtues that are conspicuous by their absence in her natural children.

This long-lived series' greatest merit lies not in the drawings of Vargas and his successors, Miguel Meji and Gutu (pseudonym of Agustin Vargas), but in its implicit social criticism, as valid today as it was in 1937. Regarded as the most famous Mexican humor strip, *La Familia Burron* is characterized by the colorful language spoken by the protagonists, sometimes derived from that used by street people, and sometimes invented, or even on occasion picked out of old dictionaries of obsolete idioms.

L.G.

FAMILIA ULISES, LA (Spain) Created in 1945 by cartoonist Benejam on the back cover of the Spanish children's weekly TBO with texts by Joaquin Buigas, *La Familia Ulises*, which depicts a typical Catalan family, is the best example of a satirical comedy of manners in the Spanish comic strip. Throughout its run it met with enormous success.

The author was able to narrate the events of more than 30 years as reflected in the doings of his family. Señor Ulises is an average man who has been successful enough to own his automobile, go for a vacation every year, and send his older son Lolin to a private college. He is a peaceful conformist. His wife is anxious to keep up with the times, his other children are too young to have a well-defined personality: the one who revolts is the grandmother, a cantankerous oldster who stubbornly refuses to enjoy the rewards of technology. She is a woman of the people, distrustful of newfangled inventions, who gets carsick, hates air conditioning, and spurns the good uses of the Spanish language to boot. Her conversation is filled with Catalan locutions and her most typical pose is that of the old woman with a black shawl over her shoulders sitting on a cane chair and nodding her head. So much does she shun reality (at least the social reality of post-Civil War Spain) that she still sleeps as in her youth, on a cot with a handkerchief fastened to her hair.

The success of the strip (written since 1949 by Carlos Bech) gave rise to a multitude of toys and dolls, as well as to a series of records. After the death in 1975 of Marino Benajam, the series was continued for some time by other hands; *La Familia Ulises* is no longer, but it lingers in memory through many reprints.

L.G.

"La Famille Fenouillard," Christophe (Georges Colomb). © Armand Colin.

FAMILLE FENOUILLARD, LA (France) Christophe (Georges Colomb) on August 31, 1889, published in the comic weekly *Le Petit Français Illustré* a short picture-story called *La Famille Fenouillard à l'Exposition* ("The Family Fenouillard at the Fair") on the occasion of the 1889 Paris World Exposition. The success was such that *Le Petit Francais Illustré* started issuing *La Famille Fenouillard* as a regular feature.

Agénor Fenouillard and his imposing spouse Léocadie are a couple of small-town shopkeepers, blessed with two quarrelsome daughters, Artémise and Cunégonde, and a pretension to culture and sophistication. Their consciousness having been raised by their experiences at the Fair, the whole family decides to leave their native Saint-Rémy-sur-Deule and see the world.

In a devastating parody of Jules Verne's *Around the World in Eighty Days*, the Fenouillards first find themselves by mistake aboard a ship bound for New York, and then in short order journey through the States on a train that is attacked by Sioux Indians. They cross the Bering Strait on an ice floe, are shipwrecked on a Pacific island where Agénor is made king, and go through a series of madcap adventures before finally reaching home.

La Famille Fenouillard (like all of Christophe's creations) did not make use of balloons but had the text running underneath the pictures. It was the first French comic feature to reach a wide public, and it introduced a variety of new themes and novel techniques into the formerly bloodless picture-story.

Armand Colin published *La Famille Fenouillard* in book form in 1893; the book has gone into countless reprints in hardcover and in paperback and has been in print ever since. In the 1960s a movie version of *La Famille Fenouillard* was directed by Yves Robert, with Jean Richard as Agénor and Sophie Desmarests as Léocadie.

M.H.

FAMILY UPSTAIRS, THE *see* Dingbat Family, The.

FANTASTIC FOUR (U.S.) When Atlas editor Stan Lee decided to reenter the superhero field, he renamed his company Marvel and together with artist Jack Kirby created the *Fantastic Four* in *Fantastic Four* number one (November 1961). Using themes that would constantly recur in all their future superhero features, Lee and Kirby gave birth to a group of four individuals endowed with superpowers who were constantly beset with personal difficulties while they fought crime. The title immediately became Marvel's keynote feature. There Lee and Kirby perfected the "superhero with problems" concept and introduced dozens of fascinating characters in their books. Lee and Kirby set what could be called the Marvel style, a style so different it revolutionized the comic book industry.

The Fantastic Four themselves are Reed (Mr. Fantastic) Richards, an intellectual scientist with stretching abilities; Sue (Invisible Girl) Richards, Reed's flighty wife with the powers of invisibility; Johnny (Human Torch) Storm, Sue's quick-tempered younger brother, who can burst into flame at will; and Ben (The Thing) Grimm, a tough but lovable man who became a monstrous orangy being with phenomenal strength. The quartet had endless flaws: Reed was often insensitive and oafish, Sue was immature, Johnny was simply too young, and Ben suffered tremendous insecurity because of his hideous looks. Together, the group fought epic villains while trying to keep their own lives from crumbling around them.

Writer-editor Stan Lee handled the feature for 11 years and juggled the characters' idiosyncrasies magnificently. His realistic and poignant characterizations stand out as possibly the most outstanding achievement of the 1960s in the comic book world. Artist Jack "King" Kirby turned the feature into a pleasing maze of exaggerated muscles, complicated gadgetry, and innovative and exciting layouts. Joe Sinnott began inking Kirby's pencils in 1965, and he made Kirby's work more subtle and cleaner than it had ever been. Both Lee and Kirby abandoned the strip in 1971, however, and despite the best efforts of talented creators like John Buscema, Roy Thomas, and John Romita, the strip faltered.

It would be impossible to catalog the many intriguing supporting characters Lee and Kirby developed in *Fantastic Four*, but Dr. Doom and the Silver Surfer rate particular attention. Doom is a schizophrenic eastern European monarch whose scientific powers surpass even those of Reed Richards. He wears an iron mask to hide a damaged face, and he is perhaps the most popular villain (or antihero) to develop in the 1960s. His complex psyche has fascinated scholars. On the other hand, the surfboard-riding Silver Surfer is a neo-Christ, a sort of perfect being chained to this imperfect and violent world. Many have called Lee's characterization of the Surfer the most mature and developed in comics.

Lee and Kirby produced the first 102 issues of *Fantastic Four*, and they are undoubtedly among the greatest group of commercial comic books ever assembled.

J.B.

A host of artists and writers have worked on *Fantastic Four*, since the departure of Lee and Kirby. Most notable have been John Byrne, who gave new life to the tired feature in 1980-84, and Walt Simonson, who was responsible for some enjoyable stories in 1990. Other artists of merit who have drawn the title include Art Adams, Barry Smith (for one issue), George Perez, and Paul Ryan. In recent years there have also been a number of spin-off comic books, such as *Fantastic Four*

Unlimited, Fantastic Four Unplugged, and *Fantastic Four 2099.*

M.H.

FANTOMAS (Mexico) At the initiative of Alfredo Cardona Peña, Editorial Novaro, on March 1, 1966, started the publication of the first *Fantomas* comic book, which bore the number 103 in the collection "Tesoro de Cuentos Clasicos." This series of full-color comic books has the same format and characteristics as American comic books, except that its illustrators and writers are all Mexican. The drawing of the first comic book was entrusted to Rubén Lara Romero, assisted by his brother, Jorge, who did the backgrounds.

This initial adaptation was quite conventional and followed an earlier version done by Alfredo Valdés in the Mexican magazine *Paquín* (1936-1937). Fantomas' dress was modeled after the covers of the first French edition: the master criminal created by French novelists Pierre Souvestre and Marcel Allain traditionally wore high tails and hat, a scarlet vest, white gloves and ample cape, and a walking stick. Lara Romero's graphic style, with his primitive look and coarseness of line, was in perfect keeping with dime novel illustration. This team was to produce a few more episodes of *Fantomas* until 1969, when the favorable reception the protagonist received from the public prompted the publisher to issue a twice-monthly *Fantomas* book, under its own title.

The new title was greeted with a tremendous popular response, and a team had to be set up to ensure the smooth functioning of the collection. Up till then Cardona Peña had closely supervised the scripts written by Guillermo Mendizabal; when Mendizabal left in 1969, Cardona Peña took over the writing, assisted by a number of collaborators. The drawings were signed "Equipo Estudio Rubens," which was composed of José S. Reyna, Fermin Marquez, and Agustin Martinez, with Luis Carlos Hernandez and Jorge Lara as background men.

In this second version, the character of Fantomas was considerably altered. He became a young man, athletic, powerful, full of vitality, who wore a white mask that showed only his eyes and ears. While he went on committing misdeeds and burglaries, his aims were altruistic, he proclaimed himself a supporter of universal brotherhood and progress, and in general he shunned the unwholesome characteristics of the ruthless antihero he had been in the original novels. He used the latest gadgets provided by science and was helped in his endeavors by Professor Semo and a whole army of secret agents. Fantomas lived surrounded by antiques and paintings, which contrasted with his taste for well-endowed and somewhat *déclassé* women.

It should also be noted here that *Fantomas* had enjoyed a much earlier comic strip adaptation in the short-lived French comic weekly *Gavroche* (1941).

L.G.

FATTY FINN (Australia) Originally called *Fat and his Friends,* this strip was launched by Syd Nicholls on September 16, 1923, in the *Sydney Sunday News*. It was created at the instigation of the managing editor, Sir Errol Knox, as a means of competing against *Us Fellers/ Ginger Meggs,* which had been running in the *Sunday Sun* for the previous two years. Fat was a corpulent, almost bald, nasty schoolboy after the style of *Billy Bunter* and was, more often than not, the butt of his friends' jokes. On August 10, 1924, the title was changed to *Fatty Finn,* and this heralded a gradual change in the strip's direction and the role of the main character. Over the next few years, Fatty lost considerable weight as well as gaining a Boy Scout uniform, a dog (Pal), a goat (Hector), and supporting characters such as Headlights Hogan, Lollylegs, and Mr. Claffey the policeman. Fatty adopted a more heroic role and the strip moved closer to the standard "kid" strip formula, with a distinct Australian flavor. In 1927, a motion picture called *Kid Stakes* was made with Fatty and Hector as the stars.

By the late 1920s, *Fatty Finn* had become the country's most visually pleasing strip. Nicholls' excellent draftsmanship and experimentation with long, sweeping frames and tall, column-like panels were complemented by vibrant coloring. In 1928, a new dimension was added when Nicholls introduced an adventure theme by involving Fatty in fanciful tales of pirates, cannibals, and highwaymen. While Fatty was still drawn in the traditional cartoon style, the other characters were depicted in a realistic manner—like a combination of animation and live-action films. Nicholls was, in fact, pioneering the adventure strip, which was to lead to his creation of *Middy Malone,* in 1929. That same year, the *News* merged with the *Guardian,* but when that paper merged again, with the *Sunday Sun* in 1931, *Fatty Finn* was dropped.

Fatty Finn emerged in May 1934 in its own tabloid-sized comic paper, *Fatty Finn's Weekly,* but faded by the

"Fantomas." © Editorial Novaro.

"Fatty Finn," Syd Nicholls. © Nicholls.

middle of 1935. From 1940 to 1945, it appeared in many of the comic books that were published by Nicholls, and from 1946 until 1950 Fatty appeared in his own monthly, *Fatty Finn's Comic.* He returned to the newspaper comic sections in October 1951, in the pages of the *Sydney Sunday Herald.* When that paper merged with the *Sunday Sun* (the paper that had originally dropped him) in October 1953, *Fatty* made a successful transition and continues to appear in the pages of the Sunday *Sun-Herald.* It now appears only episodically, however.

Although the passage of time has made *Fatty Finn* somewhat anachronistic, the strip is a constant reminder of the happier, less complicated childhood life of yesteryear. Fatty was the only serious rival to *Ginger Meggs,* but there was not a great deal of similarity between the two strips. *Ginger* was a humorous strip with a far greater appeal to adults looking back on their childhoods. *Fatty* tended to rely more on sight gags, was infinitely superior in art, and had a greater appeal for children. Had *Fatty Finn* not suffered so much editorial indifference over the years, it would have been Australia's longest-running comic strip that was created and drawn by the same artist.

J.R.

FAZEKAS, ATTILA (1948-   ) Hungarian cartoonist and writer, born July 25, 1948, in Keszthelyen, Hungary. After his final secondary-school examinations Attila Fazekas burst upon the Hungarian comics scene in the mid-1970s with his first strip, *Adventure in Ujvar,* which displayed a realistic, spectacular, detailed, and dynamic artistic presentation. As a result, by the 1980s he had become the most popular cartoonist in Hungary. His work appeared in the magazines *Pajtas* and *Fules* and in the daily political newspaper *Népszava.* He is equally at home working in science fiction and in humorous stories. He has turned out about 150 graphic novels and over 3,000 pages of comics. In addition, he has illustrated books, including 10 Tarzan novels, and has scripted an animated film.

The publishing of independent comic books was forbidden for a long time in Hungary. A breakthrough occurred when Fazekas was asked by a Hungarian publishing house to draw a comic-book adaptation of *Star Wars* in the late 1970s. After that he adapted many more films into comic-book form, including *Ben Hur* and *Alien.*

Fazekas was the first cartoonist to publish his own comic magazine, from 1988 to 1993, with all features drawn and written by himself. *Botond* was a humorous strip about a valiant warrior from the age of Hungarian conquests in the mold of Astérix who fought for truth in modern-day Hungary as well. His other major comic-strip character is Captain Perseus, who fights against robots and fantastic creatures in a distant future. (It is interesting to note that the artist drew himself as the hero.) He was also the first to publish a sex-comic magazine in Hungary: called *Szexi,* it features a buxom heroine named Tunde; and since 1989 his erotic illustrations have also become very popular.

K.R.

FEARLESS FOSDICK (U.S.) Al Capp's often hilarious strip-within-a-strip, *Fearless Fosdick* (an irregular continuity feature appearing sporadically in the *Li'l Abner* strip), is an affectionate parody of Chester Gould's *Dick Tracy.* It first appeared in the Sunday *Abner* episode of November 22, 1942, with a profile of Fosdick in a very Tracyesque pose in the *Abner* title logo (startling New York readers who found apparent Tracys looking at them from the covers of *both* of New York's highly competitive tabloid Sunday papers: the real Tracy on the *Sunday News,* and Fosdick on the *Sunday Mirror*). The initial *Fearless Fosdick* episode filled half of the *Abner* continuity. Fosdick, we learned, was not only Abner's favorite "comical paper" character, but also his heroic "ideel." (Fosdick, of course, hates women—to the despair of Daisy Mae.) In his first appearance, Fosdick does little but escape from a murder attempt in which he is tied to a quantity of high explosives with lit fuses; the kicker is that Pappy Yokum has torn part of the page away to smoke cornsilk behind the woodshed, and the torn part contains Fosdick's escape device. Abner is desperately trying to figure out how his hero got loose—and so has himself tied into the same trap by the agreeable Scragg Brothers. He, of course, can't escape and is blown up—to find out in another copy of the paper that Fosdick was having a bad dream and simply woke up. Weak as this gimmick was, the public liked the Fosdick concept, and Capp returned with the character on the Sunday page of May 30, 1943, this time as a full-length takeoff on *Dick Tracy,* complete with artist's byline (Lester Gooch) and eccentric adversaries (Bomb-Face, Stone-Face, etc.).

"Fearless Fosdick," Al Capp. © United Feature Syndicate.

"*Feiffer*," Jules Feiffer. © Jules Feiffer.

Gooch himself is introduced in the sequence as a small, bespectacled, moustached, mouse-like fellow, and there is much fun had with the Flattop-type of Gould villain.

By now, Capp was enjoying the Fosdick continuity as much as his readers (and presumably, Chester Gould), and he introduced a third, longer Fosdick narrative into the daily strip on June 16, 1944. The Fosdick character and continuity was in *Li'l Abner* to stay, and in a short time Capp had developed a separate cast of characters within *Fosdick*, such as Prudence Pimpleton, Fosdick's frustrated and aggressive girlfriend; Fosdick's sadistic Chief; and a superb array of comic villains, from Rattop (who sports the head of a snarling rodent) to Fosdick's archenemy, a brilliant and fiendish parrot named Sydney.

In later years there was little *Fosdick* in *Abner*, possibly for the reason cited above—or simply because Capp had so little real interest in or close supervision of the *Abner* continuity from his residence in London. But the dozens of *Fosdick* sequences printed remain an impressively funny body of work, and deserve reprinting in part. One *Fearless Fosdick* collection, with that title, was published in 1954.

B.B.

FEIFFER (U.S.) Jules Feiffer started a weekly series of comic strips satirizing current events for the *Village Voice* in 1956. Soon he branched out into a more general approach, relating his strips to each other and setting up a gallery of permanent characters. For lack of a better title he called his creation *Feiffer*. In 1958 several of the strips were published in book form under the title *Sick, sick, sick*; his work was then brought to the attention of Robert Hall, who started syndicating *Feiffer* that same year.

Feiffer's universe is the blackest and most depressing ever to be found in a comic strip. Spineless and craven men, neurotic and poisonous women occupy the center stage, pouring out plaintive accounts of their frustrations and misfortunes. A number of protagonists appear in the strip, but the most representative and

best known of these wretches is the abject Bernard Mergendeiler, a psychological wreck devoured by tics and complexes.

The atrocious repetition and the terrible banality of these confessions succeed in creating a vortex in which people, language, and concepts are swallowed up and destroyed. A parody of a bitter parody, *Feiffer* is not as much related to the classic comic strip as it is to the work of the "absurdist" playwrights, such as Adamov, Pinter, or Albee.

It is as a political strip that *Feiffer* is best known, however. It has lampooned every president since Eisenhower, although the author reserved his strongest venom for Nixon. After the collapse of the Soviet Union in 1991, the strip's Marxist undertones have become increasingly irrelevant; now distributed by Universal Press Syndicate to a very short list of newspapers (including the *Village Voice*, which is now a free sheet), it sounds as a distant echo of the 1960s, growing fainter with each passing week.

The *Feiffer* strips have been reprinted in both hardbound and paperback forms; following *Sick, sick, sick* there have been *The Explainers, Passionella, Feiffer's Marriage Manual,* and *The Unexpurgated Memoirs of Bernard Mergendeiler.* Feiffer's comic strip antiheroes also appeared in a play, *The Explainers,* staged at Chicago's Playwrights Cabaret in 1961.

M.H.

FEIFFER, JULES (1929-   ) American cartoonist and writer, born January 26, 1929, in the Bronx, New York. After a "miserable four years" at James Monroe High School, Jules Feiffer attended the Art Students League in New York. From 1947 to 1951 he studied at the Pratt Institute while working as an assistant on Will Eisner's *The Spirit*; in 1949 he created his first comic feature, *Clifford,* as part of the *Spirit* comic section.

In 1951 Feiffer was drafted into the Signal Corps doing animated cartoons. Returning to civilian life, he worked on different jobs before starting his long association with the *Village Voice* in 1956 with a weekly social and political commentary in comic strip form, which he simply called *Feiffer*. (Later *Feiffer* was to be syndicated by Publishers-Hall Syndicate.)

In addition to his work as a cartoonist, Feiffer has written a novel, *Harry the Rat with Women* (1963); a one-act play, *Crawling Arnold*, which was staged at Spoleto's Festival of Two Worlds in 1961; and a musical comedy, *Little Murders* (which was later adapted to the screen). He is the creator of *Munro*, an animated cartoon about a four-year-old mistakenly drafted into the army (which won an Academy Award in 1961), and the screenwriter of the award-winning film *Carnal Knowledge* (1971). Feiffer has also compiled an anthology of comic book stories, *The Great Comic Book Heroes*, published by Dial Press in 1965.

Jules Feiffer's work has been widely acclaimed and he has influenced many young cartoonists in both the comic strip and editorial cartoon fields. His sparse and desiccated style of drawing, so in tune with the times, has also given rise to numerous imitators. He wrote the script for the thoroughly unpleasant 1980 *Popeye* movie; and in 1986 he received the Pulitzer Prize for editorial cartooning.

M.H.

FEIGN, LARRY (1955-   ) Larry Feign was born in Buffalo, New York, in 1955 and grew up in California, where, contrary to his mother's plans, he dreamed of a cartooning career. He started a degree in folklore at the University of California-Berkeley, but quit after two years and hitchhiked across the country, working at menial jobs along the way. Later, he finished his degree at Goddard College, after which he went to Hawaii, drawing caricatures of tourists on the beach while pur-

suing a master's degree at the University of Hawaii. He returned to California after marrying a native of Hong Kong and worked briefly at DIC Studios, where he drew *Heathcliff the Cat* for television.

His career took a giant step forward when he settled in Hong Kong in 1985. His first work was a light-hearted introduction to the Cantonese language titled *Learn Cantonese the Hard Way*, which appeared in the *Hong Kong Standard*. Salvaging choice characters from this cartoon, Feign created *The World of Lily Wong* in November 1986, which for most of its life, ran six times a week in the *South China Morning Post*. The plot revolved around the sassy, self-confident, Hong Kong-born Lily, her gweilo (American) boyfriend Stuart Farnsworth, her lazy brother Rudy, her xenophobic father, and other characters. Originally, the strip emphasized Stuart's culture shock and experiences with the daily life of Hong Kong, but gradually, with a nudge from the *Post* management, the strip took on political nuances, becoming, in the eyes of some, one of the government's few critics in the press.

By the 1990s Feign had become the colony's most popular and controversial newspaper cartoonist. His strip won awards and was reprinted in at least six anthologies, in the daily *New Straits Times* of Malaysia, and on the Internet. At the same time, Feign increasingly used the strip to lash out at things that annoyed him—ineffectual bureaucrats; the British, who, in Feign's mind, sold Hong Kong down the river; the Hong Kong Legislative Council; and mainland China. In May 1995, at the peak of its popularity, *The World of Lily Wong* was dropped by the *Post*. The media throughout the world saw the move as a political

Larry Feign, "The World of Lily Wong." © Larry Feign.

maneuver on the part of the new *Post* owner, who had strong ties to the Chinese government in Beijing, and as an indication of what could be expected when Hong Kong reverted to Chinese rule in 1997. Feign remains in Hong Kong, although he has abandoned cartooning, disillusioned by his recent experiences.

J.A.L.

FEININGER, LYONEL (1871-1956) American painter and graphic artist, born July 17, 1871, in New York City. Lyonel Feininger's parents were both professional musicians and in 1886 they sent him to Germany to study music. Feininger soon shifted his interests toward art, and he studied in Hamburg, at the Berlin Art Academy, and at the Colarossi Academy in Paris. In 1894 Feininger started on a long and fruitful career as a cartoonist and illustrator for a number of German, French, and American magazines.

In 1906 James Keeley of the *Chicago Tribune* asked Feininger to create two strips for his newspaper, which appeared that same year under the signature "Your Uncle Feininger": *The Kin-der-Kids*, a fantastic round-the-world odyssey featuring an enterprising group of youngsters, and the wistful, lyrical *Wee Willie Winkie's World*. Following a dispute with his publishers, Feininger quit after a few months, and his two creations were left unfinished. The *Tribune* would have had trouble replacing Feininger, even if they had tried.

Feininger went on to a long and successful career as a painter and fine artist. His work was exhibited widely in Europe and the United States, and he taught at the famed *Bauhaus* school until it was closed down by the Nazis in 1933. In 1937 Feininger went back to the United States, teaching at Mills College in Oakland and exhibiting his paintings.

Although Feininger's career as a comic strip artist lasted for less than one year, his contribution to comic art is far from inconsequential. As Ernst Scheyer stated in his book *Lyonel Feininger: Caricature and Fantasy*, "Feininger's achievement as a cartoonist lies there like an erratic rock on the plains of the American comic strip."

Toward the end of his life Feininger would nostalgically go back to his comic creations. He carved small wooden figures of the *Kin-der-Kids* characters for his children and laid out the plans of a fantastic city ("the city at the edge of the world") directly out of *Wee Willie Winkie's World*. On several occasions Feininger expressed the desire to bring the *Kin-der-Kids* to conclusion. He died on January 13, 1956, before he could realize that dream.

M.H.

FELDSTEIN, ALBERT (1925-   ) American comic book artist, editor, and writer, born October 24, 1925, in Brooklyn, New York. After studies at the High School of Music and Art, the Art Students League, and Brooklyn College, Al Feldstein broke into the comics industry in 1941 with S. M. "Jerry" Iger's comic book shop. Working at the shop through 1946, he drew a multitude of strips for many companies, including Fiction House (*Sheena, Kayo Kirby*, and others), Quality (*Dollman* and others), Fox, and Aviation Press.

After a stint in the air force during World War II, Feldstein joined the E.C. group in 1947 and drew love, crime, and Western strips until the beginning of the "New Trend" in 1950. When the "New Trend" started, Feldstein quickly blossomed as an artist, writer,

and illustrator. But when he assumed the editorship of the line in late 1950, he almost totally abandoned his drawing board for the typewriter. Heavily affected by Bradbury and other contemporary writers, Feldstein produced almost all of the now-legendary E.C. crime, horror, science fiction, and suspense tales from 1951 through 1955. The first writer to utilize the O'Henry-like "snap ending" in comic strips, his scripts were among the most heavily worded and descriptive ever to appear in comic books.

Though he restricted himself to only an occasional science-fiction cover, his fine, clean renderings quickly became classics. His depiction of "static horror"—freezing a single action in time—has never been successfully duplicated in comics. After Harvey Kurtzman launched the fabulously successful *Mad* for E.C., managing editor-publisher Bill Gaines and Feldstein invented *Panic*, an imitation of their own title. Later, when the "New Trend" titles folded because of adverse public opinion and poor sales, Feldstein helped launch the short-lived "New Direction" series and the abortive "Picto-Fiction" black-and-white magazines.

When Kurtzman and Gaines parted company over the direction of *Mad* in 1956, it was Feldstein who was called in to edit the magazine. Having already made the transition from 10-cent color-comic to 25-cent magazine, *Mad* became an American institution with Feldstein at the controls. And while some critics complained that the magazine became more juvenile than it was when Kurtzman controlled it, circulation climbed to over two million copies per issue with Feldstein at the helm. After an almost 20-year absence from the comic-book scene, he came back in 1997 to draw covers for the newly minted comic-book series *Tomb Tales*, published by Cryptic Comics.

J.B.

FELIX (Denmark) *Felix*, a creation of Jan Lööf, is one of the highly individual comic strips to come out of Sweden in the 1960s and '70s. Having studied art in Stockholm, Lööf did his first picture book for children, *En trollkarl i Stockholm* ("A Wizard in Stockholm"), in 1965. This was followed by two more the following year. These books convinced the people of P.I.B., a press service based in Copenhagen, Denmark, that Lööf might be ideally suited to do a comic strip along the lines of his books. Jumping at the chance, Lööf came up with *FiffigeAlf* ("CunningAlf"), a 15-year-old boy falling from one adventure into another. By the time the first episode saw print in 1967 in *Politiken*, a newspaper in Copenhagen, Denmark, the strip had been rechristened *Felix*. Having moved to southern France at the time, Lööf worked ahead of schedule, assisted by his brother-in-law, Krister Broberg.

Felix is about a 15-year-old boy, bespectacled, five feet tall, who wears all kinds of different hats and caps. The fondness for hats has since worn off, but Felix still finds adventure wherever he turns. *Felix*, with its independent child-hero, is well in the tradition of *Tintin, Little Orphan Annie*, and a host of others. But *Felix* is more progressive than either of these, both in style and content. *Felix* is drawn in a seemingly simple, naïve style that is a cross between picture-book illustration and underground comix. Lööf makes good use of black and white in the composition of his art, which, despite its cartoon simplicity, comes alive with a feeling of three-dimensionality.

Albert Feldstein, comic book illustration. © E.C. Comics.

It is not only the art of *Felix* that appeals to young and older readers alike. The stories also appeal. The first episode has Felix help Captain Karlsson fight a power-crazed Latin dictator named Lurifaxus. Closer inspection of this seeming stereotype shows that Lööf never fails to add a new twist, testing the reader's

memory. In fact, Lööf spices adventure with satire. Felix meets with heroes and crooks of radio, television, films, and comics, while also commenting on politics.

Returning to Sweden, Lööf produced *Felix* animated cartoons for television, finally abandoning *Felix* in 1972. The strip, which had been picked up by 20 Euro-

"*Felix,*" Jan Lööf. © PIB.

"*Felix the Cat,*" Pat Sullivan. © King Features Syndicate.

pean newspapers, was continued by Danish artist Werner Wejp-Olsen, whose first work had been a humorous detective series, *Peter og Perle* ("Peter and Perle"), in 1966. Continuing *Felix* was his breakthrough into the comics world. Wejp-Olsen toned down the political and socially critical elements of *Felix*. He stayed with the feature until 1976. It was then handed over to other writers and artists, among them Ole Munk Rasmussen and Per Sanderhage. The strip ceased publication in 1987.

W.F.

FELIX THE CAT (U.S.) Australian-born cartoonist Pat Sullivan created the character Felix the Cat in an animated cartoon produced in 1917. Its success was so great that Sullivan was to produce over 100 more animated cartoons of Felix before his death in 1933 (including the first sound cartoon and the first televised cartoon, in the historic NBC broadcast of 1930). In 1923 King Features Syndicate approached Pat Sullivan with an offer to adapt the character into a comic strip. Thus *Felix the Cat* made its debut as a Sunday page on August 14, 1923, and a daily strip followed on May 9, 1927.

Although the *Felix* strips were signed Pat Sullivan for a long time (at his death in February 1933, the original Pat Sullivan was succeeded by a nephew also named Pat), it is doubtful whether Sullivan, uncle or nephew, ever did any of them. There have been many conjectures and conflicting claims as to *Felix's* actual authorship (Bill Holman is alleged to have ghosted the strip from 1932 to 1935, for instance), but it is likely that Otto Messmer (who was an early collaborator of Sullivan's and who signed his name to the strip starting in 1935) had been drawing—or at least directing—*Felix*

from its inception until he relinquished it to Joe Oriolo in 1954. The strip was then done by a variety of ghosts working for Joe Oriolo Productions (which also produced *Felix the Cat* animated cartoons for TV).

Felix is said to have been inspired by Rudyard Kipling's "cat who walks by himself." The little black feline is one of the great creations of comic art: his loneliness, his sense of alienation, and his obstinate fight against fate, the elements, hunger, cold, and an uncaring and callous humankind, mark him as an early hero of the absurd in animal guise. Under Messmer's inspired pen, Felix was to live his most memorable adventures—in the land of Mother Goose, in a mechanized civilization of the future, on the planets of the solar system, among the savages of Africa—drenched in a fantastic mood hovering midway between daydream and fantasy. And always the star-crossed Felix found himself on the outside, spurned by his love light Phyllis, kicked out of his master's house, or pursued by unrelenting enemies. Messmer also experimented with the formal contents of the comic medium, probably reflecting his training as an animator: having Felix use his speech balloon (after having blown away all the lettering inside) to parachute down to earth from Mars, for instance; or providing his hero with a weapon in the form of the exclamation mark suspended over his head.

In the 1920s and 1930s *Felix* displayed a poetry and a lyricism not unworthy of that other legendary cat strip, *Krazy Kat*. *Felix* has always been better known and appreciated in Europe than in the United States. In 1954 French Academician Marcel Brion wrote in a famous essay: "Felix is not a cat; he is the Cat. Or better to say yet, he is a supercat, because he does not fit in any of the categories of the animal kingdom."

Many of the *Felix* episodes were reprinted in Popular Comics; Felix also had his own comic book published by Toby in the 1940s and 1950s (some of the original stories were done by Messmer, but most were the product of uninspired hacks). And, of course, Felix lived on bravely on the television screen.

Indeed it was the durability of the screen Felix that induced King Features to bring back the little feline, along with his screen contemporary Betty Boop, in a newspaper strip called *Betty Boop and Felix*. The new feature was done by the Walker brothers (Neal, Morgan, Brian, and Greg, sons of Mort) and only lasted from November 1984 to the summer of 1987 (Betty lingered a little while longer).

M.H.

FENG ZIKAI (1898-1975) A well-established writer, literature critic, art teacher, calligrapher, and translator, Feng Zikai was also considered the founder of modern cartoons in China after his *Zi Kai Man Hua* ("Cartoons of Zikai") was published in 1924. Since then the term "Man Hua" is used to describe modern cartoons by Chinese cartoonists.

Feng's numerous published cartoons fall into four categories: children's cartoons based on his own children's behavior; cartoons displaying a deep love of the beauty of nature; cartoons showing a hatred of the dark side of society; and cartoons demonstrating his profound knowledge of classical literature, especially poems, which were often found in Feng's cartoons.

Feng graduated from the First Zhejiang Normal College in 1919 and studied music and art in Japan in 1921. While teaching high school a year later, Feng began his cartooning. His typically Chinese traditional style, characterized by its simplicity, was heavily influenced by a Japanese artist named Takehisa. After the People's Republic of China was founded, Feng was made a board member of the Chinese National Artist Association, chair of the Shanghai Chinese Artist Association, and president of Shanghai Chinese Art Academy.

Hu Sheng Hua Ji ("Collections of Drawing on Life Protection") were created between 1927 and 1973 during his 50-year-long career as an artist. The six collections reflect the deep friendship between Feng and artist Li Shuong (1880-1942). Li was a famous artist, teacher, and pioneer for his introduction of Western culture—music, opera, arts—to contemporary China. Feng was Li's best student at the Normal College during the 1910s. In 1918, Li unexpectedly became a monk, and in 1927, Li proclaimed Feng a Buddhist in a ceremony during the same period they decided to create *Hu Sheng Hua Ji* with the purpose of "advocating humanitarianism in art form."

All the creations in the collections followed Feng's style, and each picture was accompanied by a poem written by Feng in collections one, two, and six. In collections three, four, and five, the poems were copied by Ye Gongzhuo, Zhu Youlan, and Yu, respectively. The collections contained a total of 450 drawings, and although each was treated independently, the theme of "protecting life" was clearly evident in each drawing.

The first volume, completed in 1928, contained 50 works of art celebrating Li's 50th birthday. Thus, every 10 years thereafter, the number of art pieces in each volume increased in accordance with Li's age. Li died in 1942 at the age of 62, but Feng continued this practice until the final volume contained 100 pieces of artwork.

During the Cultural Revolution (1966-76) all cartoon drawing was curtailed by the government. Along with most of the other Chinese intellectuals and artists, Feng was accused of subversive activity; he was labeled one of the "Shanghai ten most important targets for criticism," so it was very dangerous for Feng to openly paint or draw. He kept his promise to Li and secretly continued working on the collection, however, with the last volume completed in 1973, two years before Feng's death. Long after he died, after the Cultural Revolution was over, collections of Feng's essays and cartoons have been republished and are still popular with the Chinese public.

H.Y.L.L.

FERD'NAND (Denmark) *Ferd'nand*, a comic strip that came out of Denmark, fits in with the kind of Scandinavian comic strips traditionally exported to the United States. Created in 1937 by Danish artist H. Dahl Mikkelsen, *Ferd'nand* followed a European form of pantomime comic strips that is easily understandable the world over. Like *Adamson*, by Swedish artist Oscar Jacobsson, and *Alfredo*, by Danish artists Jørgen Mogensen and Cosper Cornelius, *Ferd'nand* is a strip of universal appeal, combining European and American ideas in a calm, quietly humorous family strip.

Ferd'nand is published in newspapers all over the world in daily comic strip and Sunday-page versions. Reprints have appeared in a number of comic magazines, books, and annual albums. This does not come as a surprise, considering the constant quality of this pantomime strip. To a degree, pantomime strips are more difficult to do than strips incorporating speech balloons because the point to be made is put across by illustration alone. "Reading" *Ferd'nand* is like watching a silent movie. The full meaning is arrived at by watching action, gestures, and facial expressions. While no word is spoken, writing on signs, for example, "To trains," appears whenever necessary to identify a certain location. And, of course, onomatopoeic words are used when the need arises.

The "hero" of this humorous strip is Ferd'nand, a round-headed, big-nosed, wide-eyed, somewhat plump, middle-aged, middle-class husband. He usually sports a cone-shaped hat to hide the bald spot on his pate. Even his little son (of kindergarten age) is never

"Ferd'nand," H. Dahl Mikkelsen (Mik). © PIB.

seen without similar headgear. Neither father nor son seems to have a mouth but, in the case of the elder Ferd'nand, the mouth might be hiding behind his tiny, black mustache. Ferd'nand's wife is nearly as tall and wide as her husband. The Ferd'nand family has a shaggy dog for a pet.

Ferd'nand depicts all kinds of humorous situations that might happen to a middle-class family living in the suburbs of American or European cities. Mikkelsen has a knack for evoking smiles with the little things of life. This is one aspect of *Ferd'nand* that explains the strip's success. Another is Mikkelsen's admirably clear and expressive style.

W.F.

FERD'NAND (U.S.) The American distribution of Henning Dahl Mikkelsen's 1936 creation, *Ferd'nand*, was begun by United Feature Syndicate on November 10, 1947, in dailies and on April 4, 1948, for the Sunday page. Already an established favorite in Europe, Mik's silent little man caught on quickly in the Western Hemisphere and still remains a favorite.

The hero of this pantomime strip wears a Tyrolean hat and is whatever occupation a particular gag requires. Ferd'nand has a wife and son who have never needed the names they don't have, and the hero has no surname.

Mik lived in his native Denmark during World War II, when the German occupation government let *Ferd'nand* continue happily in the Danish press. Later he moved to California, where he engaged in several lucrative real estate deals.

Since late 1970 veteran cartoonist Al Plastino (*Hap Hooper, Barry Noble, Abbie an' Slats,* much D.C. work) has been drawing *Ferd'nand* with the same delightful, cozy style and humor. He signs his work "Al Mik." In 1993 Henrik Rehr took over the feature, which is now closing in on the half-century mark of publication in American newspapers.

R.M.

FERNANDEZ, FERNANDO (1940-   ) Spanish cartoonist and illustrator, born February 7, 1940, in Barcelona. Immediately following his high-school studies Fernandez embarked on an artistic career by drawing science-fiction stories for a French comic-book publisher and romance and war comics for a British publisher from 1956 to 1965. He later veered away from purely commercial considerations; since 1972 he has imparted a spirit of poetry and humanism that immeasurably adds to the visual spectacle of his compositions.

His stories in black and white, which were published between 1972 and 1975 in the American magazine *Vampirella*, are rich in lyrical expression that transcends the simple graphic lines. In *L'Uomo di Cuba*, for the Italian publisher Sergio Bonelli, the beauty of the illustrations overwhelms the narrative thread of the comic. With great literary and artistic conviction Fernandez undertook *Zora* (1980-81), a series first published in the Spanish magazine *1984* and later translated in the United States in the pages of *Heavy Metal*. In *Zora* the artist brought out the full panoply of his graphic, narrative, and illustrative talents in a vast display of spectacular effects.

In 1982 Fernandez, who had already used color in *Zora*, produced a pictorial version of Bram Stoker's novel *Dracula*. "Fernandez's most personal expression

Fernando Fernandez, an extract from one of his science-fiction stories. © Fernando Fernandez.

in *Dracula* resides in his composition, his sense of line, and his use of color," Maurice Horn wrote in his preface to the book. "The painter's touch is apparent at every step, and the painter's eye recognizable in each frame." At the same time he was using his skills as a painter, Fernandez, however, was reverting back to a more traditional method of storytelling, with his use of a grid consisting of rectangular panels, in contrast to the curvilinear structure of *Zora*. The story was thus told in predominantly cinematic terms, and the color tones all had a deep narrative function. More than any other Spanish comics artist perhaps, Fernandez realizes how much the intelligent staging of narrative sequences can contribute to the art of the comics.

Fernandez's next comic series, *La leyenda de los cuatro sombras* ("The Legend of the Four Shadows," 1983), based on a script by the Argentine writer Carlos Trillo, was a fantasy on a medieval theme. In the early 1990s he turned out a science-fantasy series titled *Lucky Starr*. Since that time he has alternated drawing for comics and working as a highly prized illustrator.

J.C.

FERRIER, ARTHUR (1891-1973) Arthur Ferrier was a British cartoonist and painter, who was born in Scotland in 1891 and died on May 27, 1973, at 82. The son of an organist, he qualified as an analytical chemist, and while working in Glasgow he freelanced cartoons to the *Daily Record*. When the editor, William McWhirter, came south to London as editor of the *Sun-*

Arthur Ferrier, "Spotlight on Sally." © News of the World.

day Pictorial, he sent for Ferrier to redraw the topical strip cartoons by their aged staff artist, G. M. Payne.

Once in London, Ferrier began to draw joke cartoons for Punch (April 1918), London Opinion, The Humorist, Passing Show, and other weekly magazines. By the 1920s his cartoons were appearing in five Sunday newspapers, and Sir William Carr offered him an exclusive contract for his News of the World. Always interested in show business, Ferrier began a weekly composite cartoon feature devoted to whatever show or play had opened that week, and this panel ran from 1922 to the 1950s. As his contract allowed him to continue to draw for magazines, he started a similar showbiz spot in Everybody's Weekly in the 1930s, quickly augmenting this with Ferrier's World Searchlight, a similar composite featuring topical gags, and his first weekly strip, Film Fannie.

Fannie, although not the first "glamour girl" strip (q.v. Jane), was Ferrier's first. He was the pioneer of the glamour girl cartoon in Britain, and his leggy lovelies, stripping off over some forgettable wisecrack, were star attractions in magazines through the 1930s and, especially, the war-torn 1940s, when the armed forces magazine Blighty regularly ran his pinup fun.

When his newspaper contract ended, he created another regular girl, a panel spot called Our Dumb Blonde (1939), in his old home paper, Sunday Pictorial. This ran for seven years until the News of the World once again signed him exclusively. George Davies took over the Dumb Blonde, and Ferrier started a new strip, Spotlight on Sally (1945). His only attempt at a daily strip, Eve, ran in the Daily Sketch from November 23, 1953, to January 21, 1956. Over the years the models for Ferrier girls included Anna Neagle, Lillian Bond, Mirian Jordan, Renee Gadd, Elsie Randolph, and Dodo Watts; all became film stars. His oil portraits of celebrities are collectors' items. His books include Arthur Ferrier's Dumb Blonde (1946).

D.G.

FIGHTING YANK (U.S.) Fighting Yank was created by writer Richard Hughes and artist Jon Blummer and made its first appearance in Nedor's Startling number

10 in September 1941. The character quickly became popular and was appearing in his own title by September of the next year.

The Fighting Yank was really Bruce Carter III, a rather mild-mannered young man who happened to stumble upon his ancestor's bulletproof cloak. Somehow, the cloak also gave him great strength, and Carter set out to save America from crime. Billed as "America's Greatest Defender," the Fighting Yank sported a costume in the colonial motif: three-sided hat, an American flag chest emblem, and square-buckled boots. Additionally, whenever he needed that little bit of extra inspiration to defeat an enemy, the spirit of old Bruce Carter I would appear to instill the needed bits of confidence and, of course, patriotism.

The strip was never particularly well written, although Fighting Yank did boast some exceptional artists during its run. Jack Binder (1942-43) is the most remembered illustrator, but Alex Schomburg (1943-49), Jerry Robinson (1947-48), and Mort Meskin (1948-49) all worked on the feature.

While most of Fighting Yank's superheroic competitors were felled by the end of the war, the character held on in Startling until the 48th issue (January 1949). His own magazine even lasted until August 1949's 29th issue, and he also appeared in America's Best from April 1944 until February 1948.

J.B.

FIGUERAS, ALFONSO (1922-   ) A Spanish cartoonist born near Barcelona on October 15, 1922, Alfonso Figueras started his apprenticeship with the printing plant of Editorial Bruguera in 1939, working as a letterer and a layout man. From there he graduated to cartoonist on the magazines Chicos, Nicolas, Leyendas Infantiles, Cubilete, Paseo Infantil, and others published by Editorial Bruguera.

A man of ample culture and an expert on American humor strips, as well as dime novels, science fiction, and the horror film, he has devoted his professional life to the production of such humor strips as Dedalito, Hércules Paput (about a comical private eye), Loony, and Patoflor (whose hero seems to be a relative of Chico Marx's), all for Nicolas. For Cubilete Figueras has drawn Rubin Rut and Tonty. He is also the creator of Rody, Aspirino y Colodíon, Mysto, and the daily newspaper strips Don Placído and Topolino. His latter creations have included Don Terrible Banuelos and El bon Jan ("Good John"); beginning in the early 1980s he published his reminiscences of the Spanish comics scene in a number of magazines and fanzines.

Figueras's dozens of comic creations are bathed in a sentimental and preposterous humor that marks him as a master of nonsense.

L.G.

FILS DE CHINE (France) Fils de Chine ("Son of China") saw the light of print in the Communist-controlled French comic weekly Vaillant on October 8, 1950, at a time when China was still within the fold of orthodox communism (and, not coincidentally, about to strike in Korea). The feature was written by Vaillant's chief scribe, Roger Lécureux, and drawn by the talented Paul Gillon.

Set at the time of the Long March, the strip re-created the hardships, vicissitudes, and ultimate triumph of the Communist troops in their struggle against the forces of Chiang Kai-shek. The story revolved around Tao, a young farmer who joined the Communists through a mixture of idealism and class conviction. Although heavy on political propagandizing at times (especially in the beginning), the strip made an effort at historical accuracy while telescoping events of many years into a few months. The Communist leaders made a few discreet appearances, but their contributions were usually played down. The strip finally ended in March 1962, at a time when China was about to be written out of the world Communist movement.

Fils de Chine is worthy of study on at least two counts. From an artistic viewpoint it remains one of Gillon's best contributions (far superior to the daily *13 rue de l'Espoir* strip, which he was doing at the same time for *France-Soir*); a few pages were drawn by Pierre Legoff and Pierre Dubois, but Gillon's rendition remains supreme, with a number of images of sheer lyric beauty. The strip also provides an ironic footnote to the history of international communism in recent times.

M.H.

FINE, LOUIS (1914-1971) American comic book artist, born in 1914 in New York City. His major art training was from New York's Grand Central Art School, but he also studied briefly at the Art Students League and Pratt Institute. He joined the Eisner-Iger comic book shop in 1938 and quickly became, with Eisner himself and Reed Crandall, one of the shop's best artists.

Producing a horde of comic strips under house names like "Jack Cortez" and "Basil Berold," Lou Fine won immediate praise for his excellent draftsmanship and tremendous knowledge of the human anatomy in motion. For the Eisner-Iger shop he drew parts of *Jumbo* and *Sheena* comics (Fiction House) and also produced several adventures of *The Flame* (Fox) and later *Rocketman* and *Master Key* for Harry Chesler's Dynamic Comics group.

Fine's most prolific and creative comic book period was from 1939 through 1943, when he was the major artist for "Busy" Arnold's Quality Comics group. He produced *Black Condor* for *Smash Comics*, *Stormy Foster* for *Hit Comics*, and various adventures of *Uncle Sam*, *Quicksilver*, and other Quality features. He also drew an outstanding array of covers for Quality comics like *Hit*, *Smash*, *National*, *Uncle Sam*, *Police*, and *Blackhawk*. Fine also ghosted a substantial portion of *The Spirit* newspaper strip when Will Eisner joined the armed forces.

One particular feature, however, was to make Lou Fine a major force in the comic book field. Looking for a new feature for *Smash*, Arnold assigned Fine to create a strip, and he developed *The Ray* (*Smash* number fourteen, September 1941). *The Ray* had all the prerequisites for a superhero strip: a hero with an offbeat origin, a colorful costume, an alter ego, a gimmick, and even a sidekick named Bud. But it was Fine's spectacular renderings that made the strip a success. Although he drew only about half the feature's 26 stories, his work contained some of the most impressive and stylized material in the comics. Despite the fact that all strips of *The Ray* are signed by "E. Lectron," Fine's work is easily recognizable—his heroes were classically featured, and his backgrounds were highly detailed with cross-hatches, stipples, and every conceivable comic technique. As drawn by Fine, *The Ray* became a

minor classic, and much of it has been reprinted in *Special Edition Comics* number two (Alan Light, 1974).

Fine left the comic book industry in 1944 and concentrated for most of the next 25 years on commercial art and magazine illustrating, most notably his material for the now-defunct *Liberty*. He made several minor attempts at comic strips, the best of which, *Peter Scratch* (1965), was highly acclaimed but short-lived. Lou Fine died of a heart attack on July 24, 1971, and was eulogized by Will Eisner in *Graphic Story World*: "Lou Fine was one of the greatest draftsmen I have ever known," he said. "His consummate skill may never be equalled. What can one say at the death of a giant?"

J.B.

FINGER, BILL (1917-1974) American comic book writer, born February 8, 1914, in New York City. After studies at De Witt Clinton High School in Manhattan, he and artist Bob Kane created two minor adventure strips for National Comics in 1938: *Rusty and His Pals* and *Clip Carson*.

But Finger's greatest achievement was his collaboration with Kane on *The Batman*, the quintessential costumed mystery feature in comic books. Premiering in the 27th issue of National's *Detective Comics* (May 1939), the strip became fabulously successful and spawned many less inventive imitations. Although Finger was instrumental in the design of the character and his costume, only Kane's name went on the strip. He never signed his stories either. Consequently, it is only recently that Finger has been receiving recognition for his integral part in the *Batman* legend.

Finger's *Batman* scripts were far and away the best of the character's "golden age" period of 1940 through 1947. His stories were always moody, mysterious, and somber, and when the strip became more gimmick-oriented, Finger's scripts were always the most inventive. He is considered the definitive writer of *Batman*, despite a horde of talented successors.

Although Finger produced some material for the Timely, Fawcett, and Quality groups in the mid 1940s, most of his scripts were done for National. During the period between 1938 and 1967, he produced hundreds of stories for every genre of National comic—superhero, mystery, crime, adventure, science fiction.

He died in February 1974, and when National reprinted the first *Batman* comic book later that year, publisher Carmine Infantino dedicated the book to Finger's memory.

J.B.

FISHER, HAMMOND EDWARD (1901-1955) The tragically vain creator of *Joe Palooka*, Hammond Edward Fisher was born in Wilkes-Barre, Pennsylvania, in the fall of 1900, the son of a middle-class businessman. Fascinated by comic strips from the age of five, Fisher worked every spare moment at his cartooning ability through high school, then skipped college to enlist in the army during World War I, just in time for the armistice. Back in Wilkes-Barre, he landed his first job on the local *Herald* as editorial and sports cartoonist in 1919, then moved on to the *Wilkes-Barre Times-Leader* a year later in the same capacity. Going into local politics, he stayed with his newspaper work in order to keep cartooning. As early as 1920, however, Fisher had drawn his first *Joe Palooka* episodes, and tried them out on every syndicate in the business—to no avail. In 1925, Fisher started his own newspaper in

INSTEAD OF A SELF PORTRAIT I HAD PALOOKA DRAW ME!
HAM FISHER.

Ham Fisher.

Wilkes-Barre, until a minor depression wiped out his capital and forced him to fall back on his *Palooka* idea again. Going to New York in 1927, he took a temporary job with the advertising department of the *New York Daily News* and started around the syndicate circle once more. This time he found real interest in Charles V. McAdam, general manager of the McNaught syndicate, who took on *Palooka* for a 1928 release.

Fisher decided to promote the strip himself, going on the road to visit a number of large newspapers around the country and taking the promotional material for another new McNaught strip, *Show Girl* (later *Dixie Dugan*) with him. Emphasizing *Show Girl* first, Fisher placed the strip with some 30 papers in 40 days, a syndicate record. Tackling his own *Palooka* next, Fisher sold it to 20 papers in three weeks, and returned to New York to find McAdam almost more interested in making Fisher the McNaught sales manager than in publishing *Palooka*. Fisher, however, true to his early ambition, stuck with the strip.

Fisher promptly used his sales technique to acquire sharper artistry for his strip, and he beat the Manhattan bushes for young talent on its way up. Among the first such cartoonist he signed up was Al Capp, who later berated Fisher for the fast talk and low pay (plus hard work) Fisher gave him. (After Capp, Moe Leff did the bulk of the work on the strip.)

Fisher's real contribution to his own strip was the story line. The *Palooka* readership had gone into the tens of millions by World War II, and Fisher's early plunging of Joe into the war sent the circulation soaring even higher. For a time Fisher was on the top of the comic strip world. Then came the first slow, and finally precipitous, collapse.

Fisher was fundamentally concerned with his public image as a great cartoonist and princely fellow. Al Capp, his old ghost, began to erode that image—at least in Fisher's eyes. Capp wrote articles for *The Atlantic Monthly* in the late 1940s (one was called "I Remember Monster") in which he excoriated Fisher, though not in name, for his treatment of the young artist a decade before, and he pilloried him in the *Li'l Abner* strip as a savagely vicious strip artist. Fisher grew increasingly paranoid, until he destroyed himself by going to court to accuse Capp of public obscenity, using faked examples of the *Li'l Abner* strip he had prepared himself. It took Capp no time at all to disprove the charge (he simply showed copies of newspapers carrying the actually printed episodes), and the dis-

gusted members of the National Cartoonists Society expelled Fisher from membership. As a result, Fisher committed suicide at the New York studio of a friend on December 27, 1955. It was a petty, tragic, unnecessary end for a man who had started out so adroitly and risen so high with such good reason. His strip continued in Moe Leff's hands, but the spirit was gone forever.

B.B.

FISHER, HARRY CONWAY (1885-1954) Harry Conway Fisher, who was to draw the world-famed *Mutt and Jeff* strip as "Bud" Fisher, was born on April 3, 1885, in a Chicago rebuilding from its great fire. Precociously talented, Fisher had left the University of Chicago in his third year to take a job as a triple-threat cartoonist (theater, sports, and general news) on the *San Francisco Chronicle* in 1905. Here, in the wake of the San Francisco fire, he persuaded the sports editor to let him draw a page-wide daily comic strip, imitative of Clare Briggs' *A. Piker Clerk*, to be called *A. Mutt*, and (like the Briggs work) to deal with a chronic horseplayer's hunches, wins, and losses. Drawn like Briggs' chinless Clerk, Mutt was simpler and funnier and made a great hit with San Francisco pony players. He also sold papers—so many that the *Chronicle*'s rival, Hearst's *San Francisco Examiner*, hired Fisher for more money a few weeks later. Here Fisher's star met his short pal, Jeff, the two going into national circulation when Fisher was shunted to Hearst's *New York American* in 1909. A Sunday page was added around the time the strip got its permanent title, *Mutt and Jeff*, but Fisher wanted greener pastures and took the strip to the Wheeler Syn-

BUD FISHER
AS SEEN BY HIMSELF

H. C. (Bud) Fisher and friends.

dicate at the close of his Hearst contract in 1915, receiving $1,000 a week for just six strips. (Later a Sunday page was added by Wheeler, for more money.)

By now Fisher was established as the richest and most famed strip cartoonist in America. He had proven that readers would buy a daily paper for an outstanding strip, but only if they were sure it would be there every day. By the time he transferred to the Bell Syndicate in 1921, he was well on his way to making his top salary of $4,600 a week. He now owned a string of racehorses himself, including a number of outstanding winners, loved the racing life and the international set, and grew less and less interested in the daily mechanics of drawing *Mutt and Jeff*. Accordingly, he hired Billy Liverpool to do most of the drawing on the strip. Liverpool was a talented Hearst cartoonist originally assigned to draw *Mutt and Jeff* for Hearst after Fisher's departure in 1915, until Fisher won a lawsuit for the rights to his own characters.

This freed Fisher to follow the life of a bon vivant as he wished. Loving well but unwisely (his marital squabbles with two wives gave the still-rancorous Hearst papers good scandal copy), Fisher often made more newspaper copy than his actor and writer friends of the 1920s and 1930s. But he was never far from his creations in mind, and timely gag and continuity ideas reached Liverpool's drawing board from Fisher and made the strip arrive at its peak of art and wit between 1919 and 1934. But then Liverpool left the strip, and a new aide, Al Smith, took over. Then, for some reason, much of the old fantasy and high jinks drained out of the strip, and it became little more than a routine gag strip, as it is today.

Aside from his apparent loss of interest in the strip after 1934, Fisher continued to enjoy life but managed to squander most of the wealth *Mutt and Jeff* had made him before his death on September 7, 1954.

B.B.

FIVE FIFTEEN, THE *see* Sappo.

FIX UND FOXI (Germany) *Fix und Foxi* ("Fix and Foxi") started out as a feature in Rolf Kauka's comic book *Eulenspiegel*, which began early in 1952. At the time Kauka probably didn't know he would soon have one of the hottest comic properties in Germany, second only to Walt Disney's *Micky Maus* ("Mickey Mouse"). With issue No. 10 of *Eulenspiegel*, Fix and Foxi became the stars of the book. Fix and Foxi, two clever little foxes, characters that could be found in German fairy tales and fables, started out as relatively naturalistic anthropomorphic animals but, in time, the art became more stylized so changes of artist would not be too apparent. Over the decades the art on *Fix und Foxi* has been handled by artists Werner Hierl, Ludwig Fischer, Walter Neugebauer, Branco Karabajic, Vlado Magdič, Ricardo Rinaldi, V. Kostanjsek, Franz Roscher, and Florian Julino.

Fix and Foxi eventually got their supporting cast of Lupo, the roguish wolf, Grandma Eusebia, Uncle Fax, Cousin Lupinchen, and Professor Knox, the absent-minded inventor.

In 1953-54 expansion set in after a setback over the initial press run had occurred. The *Fix und Foxi* comic book always had a policy of including backup features. Thus comics like *Hops und Stops; Tom und Klein Biberherz* ("Tom and Little Beaverheart"), later retitled *Tom & Biber; Mischa* (Mike); and *Pauli*. The latter started in

"Fix und Foxi," Rolf Kauka. © Rolf Kauka.

1954 and since 1963 was done almost exclusively by Branco Karabajic. Despite a loyal following, *Pauli*, a mole, never got his own book. As some of the animal characters were defined more clearly, they stopped crossing over into each other's series. Funnies featuring human characters like *Tom und Biber* (a Western) or *Mischa* (science fiction) did not lend themselves to crossovers anyway.

Fix and Foxi stories, in general, are either sitcoms or comedy-adventures. The artistic style has been largely influenced by Walter Neugebauer, who, as art director, also drew style sheets that had to be adhered to by other artists. Neugebauer's style, influenced by his Yugoslav experience, has become exemplary for a new "German" style of comics.

If anything, Rolf Kauka and his writers have bent over backwards to represent a humorous intact world. Allegations of reactionary or nationalistic tendencies have never been proved for the bulk of the Kauka comic books but have been inferred after the *Asterix* fiasco in *Lupo*.

Fix und Foxi and their supporting cast have seen quite a commercial success. Besides the weekly comic book there have been specials, annuals, digest-sized comics, and some 18 comic books with accompanying record. There have also been dolls, puppets, cups, puzzles, games, bubble gum cards, iron-ons, stick-ons, rub-offs, coloring books, cut-outs, calendars, T-shirts, wallpaper, some 10 records, etc. In 1972, Fix and Foxi appeared in a first cartoon short, "Synfonie in Müll" (Symphony in Trash), taking up the ecology theme. It was presented together with Kauka's feature-length animated cartoon of the fairy tale "Maria d'Oro."

By 1970 Kauka's artists grew restless, with some leaving to return later. In 1972 Walter Neugebauer broke with Rolf Kauka over copyright and financial arrangements that had been smoldering since production of *Maria d'Oro*. This did not hurt the Kauka magazines, however. In fact, Kauka enlarged his operations by collaborating with a British company and with

Springer Verlag. In a series of shrewd deals, Kauka sold his company but retained copyrights to his features.

In his deals, he usually kept the *Fix und Foxi* comic book as a separate entity. But, ultimately, he sold out on his creations and retired to the United States. In the 1990s the magazine's sales stagnated, and when the magazine's editors decided to include editorial matter aimed at teenagers in 1994, Kauka was so appalled that, out of retirement, he used his copyright ownership to suspend publication of the magazine until the decision was rescinded. In October 1994 the magazine ceased publication after more than four decades on the market. The characters remain popular in numerous reprints, as a merchandising property, and in advertising.

W.F.

FLAMINGO (U.S.) *Flamingo* was one in the line of daily comic strips fielded by S.M. "Jerry" Iger's newly created Phoenix Features in February 1952 (others were George Thatcher and Jack Kamen's *Inspector Dayton*, Thorne Stevenson's *South Sea Girl*, Rod Maxwell and R.H. Webb's *The Hawk*, and Iger's own *Bobby* and *Pee Wee*). *Flamingo*'s scripts were written by Ruth Roche, and the artwork was supplied by Matt Baker.

Flamingo was a dark-haired, full-bodied, and sexy Gypsy dancer who got involved in all kinds of romantic and dangerous adventures while traveling the European roads with her caravan. When danger lurked she was always ready to lend a hand, whether to foil the plot of some scheming impostor bent on talking an innocent lad out of his inheritance, or to rescue the kidnapped heir to a throne. She was vigorously assisted in her endeavors by her tribe of fellow Gypsies led by her grandfather, Old Pepo the mask-maker. Most of the men who crossed Flamingo's path fell madly in love with her, although the alluring Gypsy remained fiercely faithful to her boyfriend, Joe, an American.

The story line sounds conventional, but the strip came to life under the expert handling of Matt Baker, who displayed superior draftsmanship and a sense of mood and composition. The action moved at a fast pace, punctuated by large, detailed panels in which the fiery figure of Flamingo burned bright. Following Baker's untimely death at age 33, John Thornton took over the daily strip on July 3, 1952 (a Sunday feature was added a few weeks later). A competent craftsman, Thornton had little of Baker's brilliance and vibrancy, and the strip steadily lost most of its appeal. It was finally discontinued on March 21, 1953; the last strip ended with Flamingo's wedding to Joe.

Despite the brevity of its run, *Flamingo* created a strong impression on its readers (especially the episodes drawn by Matt Baker). Had Baker not died so soon after the strip's inception, it may have gone on to become a success. (Baker had also prepared two stories for a planned *Flamingo* comic book before he died. They were never published).

M.H.

FLANDERS, CHARLES (1907-1973) American comic strip artist, born in 1907 in Mayville, New York. Flanders' father was a painter and encouraged his son's early artistic efforts. While attending high school, Flanders spent all of his spare time drawing and studying art. After graduation, he took a job in the art department of a silk-screen company in Buffalo and at the same time attended classes at the Allbright Art School. Later he became an instructor in another Buffalo art school.

In 1928 he came to New York, where he worked as a freelance artist, an assistant art director in an advertising agency, and a magazine illustrator before joining the staff of King Features Syndicate in 1932. There he served his apprenticeship by working on any strip that came his way, from *Tim Tyler's Luck* to *Bringing Up*

"Flamingo," Matt Baker. © S. M. Iger.

Father. In 1935 Flanders got his big chance at KFS when he was asked to draw the only feature he ever created, *Robin Hood*, a Sunday page depicting the adventures of the legendary outlaw of Sherwood Forest. The strip was not a success and was retired from circulation after only three months.

This setback did not discourage either Flanders or the editors at King Features. When, later that same year, Alex Raymond abandoned *Secret Agent X-9*, the strip was turned over to Flanders, who was to draw it until April of 1938. In addition, early in 1936, Flanders took over the Sunday page of *King of the Royal Mounted*; in April 1938, Flanders became sole artist on *King*, drawing both the Sunday and the dailies until one year later, when he was assigned to draw *The Lone Ranger*, a Western strip created by Fran Striker.

With *The Lone Ranger*, Flanders had finally found his niche and his style, and he was to draw the feature until the syndicate decided to discontinue it in December 1971. On January 10, 1973, Charles Flanders died in Palma-de-Mallorca, where he had retired.

Flanders was never a remarkable artist. Unlike some of his more gifted colleagues, he had to overcome obscurity by sheer effort, hard work, and staying power. He always managed to do a creditable, if unexalted, job, with a solid, craftsmanlike, and earnest attention to the task at hand. In his love for the comic strip medium, Flanders represents the quintessence of the journeyman strip artist.

M.H.

FLASH (U.S.) *Flash* was created by writer Gardner Fox and first illustrated by Harry Lampert in January 1940. It made its first appearance in National Comics' *Flash* number one. The Flash was really Jay Garrick, who, when bathed in the fumes of hard water, became the fastest man alive. He adopted a red, blue, and yellow costume, boots, and wing-adorned steel helmet.

The character was never handled as imaginatively as he could have been. He spent most of the time running or catching bullets, and the most enjoyable parts of the *Flash* were the inventive and offbeat villains. The best of this evil lot was The Fiddler, who often plagued the speed monarch. Looking like a virtuoso conductor gone astray, The Fiddler had a magical Stradivarius that could force others to do his bidding. One of the best-known villains of the comic book's golden age, he was one of the first to be revived in the 1960s.

Artistically, E. E. Hibbard drew the bulk of *Flash* from 1940 to 1949, although his material was always too linear and static for such an action-oriented character. Many of the later artists, including Lee Elias, Joe Kubert, and especially Carmine Infantino, handled the feature with considerably more style and verve.

Flash appeared in all 104 issues of *Flash* until its demise in February 1940. The character also appeared in all 32 issues of *All-Flash* from Summer 1941 to January 1949, and also made appearances in *All-Star* and *Comic Cavalcade*.

The revival of the Flash in October 1956's *Showcase* number four is officially regarded as the beginning of the second "golden age" of superheroic comics. This time Flash was police scientist Barry Allen, who became the super speedster after being doused by chemicals. Unlike his predecessor, this new Flash wore a more standard superhero costume—a skin-tight red and yellow suit and cowl, which sprung to full size from a special ring.

"The Flash." © *National Periodical Publications.*

The Flash was eventually reinstated in his own title in March 1959, and the book began with number 105. The definitive creators of this Flash were two veteran *Flash* artisans, writer John Broome and artist Carmine Infantino. Broom's scripts were fast-paced and tightly organized, and Infantino's pencils, aided by inkers Joe Greene and Joe Giella, set the pattern for the illustration of super-speed characters. Over the years, Broome created a rogues' gallery of exciting villains, including Grodd, a super-gorilla; Mirror Master, a felon with a reflection fetish; and Captain Cold, who controlled ice and frost with a cold gun. Broome and Infantino made *Flash* the quintessential superhero strip of the 1960s.

At the same time, Gardner Fox was using *Flash* to develop his Earth-one and Earth-two theory, which conveniently allowed National to revive all their old 1940s characters by claiming that they existed on Earth-two. In short, while Broome was using *Flash* for character development, Fox was using *Flash* for character revival.

Flash fell on hard times late in 1967. Infantino left to become a National executive, and his artistic replacements did not match up to his outstanding achievements. Both Broome and Fox began to falter, and both were gone by the end of 1969. Since then the strip has been handled by many people, none of whom were able to recapture the Fox-Broome and Infantino-Greene-Giella magic.

J.B.

In 1982 Infantino returned in an attempt to bolster the character's faltering fortunes. He was unsuccessful, as were Rich Buckler, Frank Robbins, and Mike Grell, who were among the artists who succeeded Infantino. The Flash was killed off in 1985, but he was resurrected in a different guise in a new *Flash* comic book (June 1987) that continues to this day.

M.H.

FLASH GORDON (U.S.) Alex Raymond created *Flash Gordon* on January 7, 1934, as a Sunday page (with *Jungle Jim* as its top) for King Features Syndicate. In the opening sequence (inspired by Philip Wylie and Edwin Balmer's novel *When Worlds Collide*) three earthlings, Flash Gordon, "renowned polo player and Yale graduate," his female companion Dale Arden, and a scientist, Dr. Hans Zarkov, set out in Zarkov's spaceship to the alien planet Mongo, which threatened to destroy Earth. In the strange world they entered, Flash and his companions found themselves locked in a death struggle with Ming the Merciless, the dreaded emperor of Mongo. Amid the grandiose landscapes, in the futuristic cities and the forsaken regions of the planet (Queen Undina's undersea kingdom, the land of the tuskmen, Queen Fria's ice kingdom), Flash, the defender of justice, helped by Ming's daughter Aura and her husband Barin, the king of Arboria, clashed swords with Ming until final victory and the liberation of Mongo (June 1941).

After a brief return to Earth, Flash again returned to Mongo in 1942 (along with Dale and Zarkov), but his fight against the tyrant Brazor no longer had the same dash as his earlier exploits. In February 1944 Raymond joined the Marines and abandoned his creation (his last page appeared on April 30, 1944).

In the meantime a daily *Flash Gordon* strip had appeared (May 27, 1940), drawn by Raymond's former assistant Austin Briggs. Thus Briggs was the logical choice to succeed Raymond on the Sunday page, and he did a creditable job in sustaining the epic inspiration and the grandiose imagery of his predecessor.

After Briggs (who left *Flash Gordon* in July 1948) there came Mac Raboy (1948-67), succeeded by Dan Barry, who took over the Sunday page, with the help of a number of assistants (his brother Sy, Al Williamson, Frank Frazetta, Ray Krenkel, Ric Estrada, and others) beginning December 31, 1967. The daily strip, meanwhile, had been discontinued from June 1944 to

November 1951, but was revived by the same Barry who left it to his former assistant Ric Estrada in 1967. In the hands of Barry and Estrada, Flash became just another space adventurer working for an intergalactic police force of the future. After Barry left the strip in 1990, he was followed by a bewildering array of artists, including Ralph Reese, Gray Morrow, and Tom Warkentin. The daily strip was discontinued in 1993, while the Sunday is now being done by Jim Keefe.

The first episodes of *Flash Gordon* were written by Raymond himself, but he soon had to call upon Don Moore to relieve him of the writing burden. Moore proved a skillful scriptwriter and was to work on *Flash Gordon* until the late 1940s, when he was replaced by a succession of staff writers, Fred Dickenson notable among them.

Flash Gordon met with immediate success, establishing itself as the supreme science-fiction strip (over *Buck Rogers*). Alex Raymond's style, imagery, and composition were widely imitated (but never equaled), and the strip has been held ever since as the epitome of the adventure story. In 1936 an original novel, *Flash Gordon in the Caverns of Mongo*, credited to Alex Raymond (who, in all probability, did not write it), was published by Grosset & Dunlap. That same year, a memorable movie serial, with Buster Crabbe as Flash and Charles Middleton as Ming, was made of *Flash Gordon*, followed by *Flash Gordon's Trip to Mars* (1938) and *Flash Gordon Conquers the Universe* (1940), both with the same cast. *Flash Gordon* was also made into a radio program in the 1930s and 1940s, and into a television series in 1953-54. A new version of *Flash Gordon* was produced by Dino de Laurentiis in 1980, with Sam Jones in the title role, and with Ornella Muti, Max von Sydow, and Topol in supporting roles. There has also been a *Flash Gordon* telefilm in 1982, as well as a series of animated cartoons, also in the 1980s.

Flash Gordon had a number of comic books from 1930-70 variously published by King, Harvey, Charlton, and others. Among its many contributing artists, mention should be made of Paul Norris, John Lehti, Reed Crandall, and especially Al Williamson (1966-67), Alex Raymond's most faithful imitator. Raymond's early episodes have been reprinted by Nostalgia Press in two hardbound volumes: *Flash Gordon—In the Ice*

"Flash Gordon," Alex Raymond. © King Features Syndicate.

Kingdom of Mongo (1967) and *Flash Gordon—Into the Water World of Mongo* (1971).

M.H.

FLEISCHER, MAX (1885?-1972) An American cartoonist and animator born in Vienna, Austria, in 1885 (other sources say 1888), Max Fleischer was taken to the United States at the age of four. After studies at the New York Evening High School, the Mechanics' and Tradesmen's School, the Art Students League, and the Cooper Union, he finally got a job as photo-engraver on the *Brooklyn Eagle*. In 1915 he started doing research in animation, turning out the first *Ko-Ko the Clown* cartoon with his brother Dave.

After seeing service in World War I, Max and Dave Fleischer worked for pioneer animator J. R. Bray before forming their own partnership in 1921 called Out-of-the-Inkwell Films, Inc. During the 1920s the Fleischer brothers turned out many cartoon films. Their fame came with the advent of sound, however: in 1931 the first full-fledged *Betty Boop* cartoon was released. The success was immediate; more Betty cartoons followed, and in 1933 the Fleischer brothers scored an even bigger hit with the animation of Segar's *Popeye the Sailor*. In 1934 King Features, which syndicated *Popeye*, adapted *Betty Boop* to comic strip form.

In 1937, Max Fleischer decided to move his studios from New York to Miami. There he produced several feature-length cartoons and the acclaimed *Superman* series. But financial success did not follow, and Fleischer had to sell his studios to Paramount in 1942. After several tries at a comeback in motion pictures and TV, Max Fleischer finally retired in the 1960s. He died on November 12, 1972.

Max Fleischer is mentioned here not only for his creation of *Betty Boop*, but also for his contribution to the mythography of two of the most legendary comic characters—Popeye and Superman.

M.H.

FLETCHER, FRANK (1919-   ) American artist, born in St. Louis, Missouri, on November 26, 1919. Fletcher's early interests were drafting, engineering,

Max Fleischer.

and aviation, and his first artwork appeared in the newsletters of a local power and light company. At the University of Missouri, Fletcher earned spare money through commercial art when his studies permitted. After graduating with a degree in engineering, Fletcher joined the air force in late 1940 and served in combat intelligence, once again employing drafting talents.

After the war, Fletcher went to New York City as an art director with the Hearst organization and served as art director on two newspaper magazine supplements, *Pictorial Review* and *Saturday Home*. From there he transferred to King Features' "tragic art"—as opposed to comic art—department, and did staff and promotional work for five years.

An opening in King Features' comic art department and Fletcher's budding talents in that area led to a drawing board assignment, alongside the other artists who worked under Frank Cilino there: incomplete strips were finished, benday laid in, Sunday pages reworked for format changes, and special artwork drawn to order.

In 1954 George McManus died, and Fletcher, who had shown a special feeling for McManus's techniques, was given a shot at the *Bringing Up Father* Sunday page. He won the assignment, and Vern Greene drew the dailies. Bill Kavanaugh wrote, and continues to write, the gags for *Father*.

Fletcher's background in the engineering arts and drafting boards served him well in an unusual way when the *Father* assignment came along, for Fletcher draws with a pen in one hand and a straightedge in the other; very few of his lines, including those for clothing, are drawn freehand. Thus Fletcher succeeded in capturing McManus's precision and restrained exactitude.

Likewise the characteristic architectural backgrounds of McManus's fancy were approximated by Fletcher. He strove, consciously, for the combination of the comic and the illustrative that he sensed in McManus.

The drawing in the latter-day *Bringing Up Father* has definitely continued close to McManus's style; if the zip has left the strip, it too can be traced to the continuum, for McManus's later work had lost much of its earlier genius and life. Fletcher retired from the strip in the late 1980s.

R.M.

FLINDERS, EVELYN (1910-   ) One of the few female strip cartoonists, Evelyn Flinders was another of the British artists who were forbidden by their publishers to sign their names to their work. Nevertheless, her style was recognized by her many loyal fans, who particularly adored her long-running serials about *The Silent Three*, three very ladylike public school girls, Joan, Peggy, and the Unknown Number One, who attended St. Kit's and donned masked cloaks to right the wrongs of the world that cropped up with surprising regularity. The trio were the front-page stars of *School Friend*, one of the earliest comics designed solely for circulation among schoolgirls, which first appeared on May 20, 1950. For its first two years, *The Silent Three* was the most popular feature among *School Friend*'s readers, and was consistently popular for a run of more than 370 weeks, ending in 1957.

Evelyn Flinders was born in London in 1910. She demonstrated unusual artistic promise and was permitted to enter Hornsey Art School at the early age of 15. She studied there for over three years, then met an art agent who gave her a children's story to illustrate. Flinders' goal was to work for the Amalgamated Press, the London-based publishers of almost every comic and story-paper for children. "I just kept badgering them and worrying them," she later said. "I can't think how I dared!" Her first break came with *Schooldays*, a new weekly that began with promise in 1928. The two female editors gave Flinders "little nick-knacks to copy for articles." The weekly was not a success and was incorporated into another, more popular paper, *Schoolgirl*.

By the time she was 21 years old, Flinders was illustrating stories for virtually all the A.P.'s girls' weeklies and also the Christmas annuals. The advent of World War II brought paper shortages to England, and *Schoolgirls' Weekly* folded in 1939, and soon only the *Girls' Crystal* was left. Flinders was given a serial to illustrate, and the occasional cover drawing for the monthly *Schoolgirls' Own Library*, but this was not enough to live on. She took a job making shell cases in a munitions factory for four years. After the war, Flinders was back in the A.P. family, illustrating annuals, libraries, and the new *School Friend*. A total of 15 picture serials came from her pen before she retired in 1959. There were six serials of *The Silent Three*, plus such titles as *Rivals at the Alpine School*, *The Riding Mystery at Moorland School*, *The Masked Ballerina*, and *Rozana, Schoolgirl of Mystery*. In retirement she continued to illustrate books for girls, including several stories by Constance White, and various girls' books for Dean Publishers.

D.G.

FLOOK (G.B.) Originally titled *Rufus* after its redheaded hero, a boy in search of a pet, renamed *Rufus and Flook* as the pet's part grew in proportion, and finally renamed *Flook* in honor of his takeover, this strip started on April 25, 1949. It celebrated its silver jubilee in 1974, and shows no sign of flagging. This is partly due to a changing line of celebrated scriptwriters who keep a highly contemporary line of social comment running throughout their plots, but mainly due to the excellent and individual artwork of its cartoonist.

The man who signs himself "Trog" is actually Canadian-born Wally Fawkes, jazz bandleader and clarinetist, who took his pseudonym from one of his groups, The Troglodytes. Trog's artwork has remained consistent, while his writers have changed around him. Douglas Mount created the strip on instructions from the editor of the *Daily Mail*, who wanted a children's strip in the style of the popular American strip *Barnaby*. Robert Raymond took over and was followed by Sir Compton Mackenzie, for a sequence set in Scotland, then Humphrey Lyttelton (another jazz-man-turned-cartoonist), George Melly (a writer-turned-jazz-singer), Barry Norman (a television personality), and radio writer and panel game chairman from *Sounds Familiar*, Barry Took.

Rufus, who lived with an oppressive Victorian uncle, met Flook during a prehistoric dream. He and Flook fell out of the dream balloon and into reality in strip number 21. Flook (so called because, originally, he could say nothing but that sound) was a magical creature able to turn himself into whatever might be required, but gradually he lost that convenient ability. The friends' earliest opponent was Moses Maggot, abductor of Sir Cloggy Bile's daughter Ermine. The voyage to Volcano Island was fraught with peril: pirates turned out to be actors for a film directed by Orson Kaart!

"Flook," Trog (Wally Fawkes). © Associated Newspapers Ltd.

Then there was Lucius Phiz, Shakespearean ham, and a sojourn at Blackwoods Academy under Dr. Beebe and the introduction of the memorable Bully Bodger and his sister, Lucretia, who was exposed as a witch! Both reappear from time to time, but not so frequently as Sir Montagu Ffolly, Bart. Then there was another upper-class twit, Scoop, of "Instant Sludge" fame. But the cast list is endless. In 1999 Flook will celebrate his golden jubilee.

Reprints of the strip in paperback form include: *The Amazing Adventures of Rufus & Flook*; *Rufus & Flook v. Moses Maggot*; *Rufus & Flook at School*; *Flook by Trog*. There is also an "autobiography": *I, Flook* (1962).

D.G.

FLORITA (Spain) In 1949 cartoonist Vincent Roso created *Florita* as the standard-bearer of the Spanish girls' magazine of the same name.

Florita is a young girl with an abundant mane of hair who wears dresses more appropriate for an older woman. But Florita plays at being adult because she was conceived as an example to be followed by the readers. If the other characters of the magazine could be cheeky and mischievous, Florita always showed contrition after her rare strayings from strict morality. She would offer advice to her readers not only in her comic strip, but also in other parts of the publication as well, where she recited verses and gave lessons in crafts, cooking, and etiquette. One of her comic sequences, "Andanzas de Florita revoltosa" (The Wanderings of Florita the Mischievous) was discontinued because it might have tarnished her image. Florita's closest friend was the blonde Gildita, much shorter but of equal priggishness. Her boyfriends were named

Oscar and Fredy, and they would escort her on her shopping trips and her excursions to the beach. Weak, sugar-sweet and sad-looking, they set a pitiful example for Spanish boys to emulate. The scripts, anonymous with the exception of a few signed by Sebi, were written in a florid language whose extreme correction was itself a manual of good manners.

Florita was the last "good girl" to appear in Spanish comics, the heiress to a long tradition of children's literature and a cousin to the legendary Nino Juanito. After Roso left the magazine, *Florita* was drawn by anonymous cartoonists, among whom Perez Fajardo is the only one to stand out. In France, *Florita* was published by the indefatigable Marijac, and, under the new name of *Mireille*, the strip was to enjoy even greater success than in Spain. A relic from the Franco era, *Florita* managed to survive into the 1980s.

L.G.

FLUTTERS, THE (G.B.) The Flutters, Mr. and Mrs., lived at "The Fluttercote" on the back, or sports page, of the *Daily Mirror,* and as their name and station might indicate, they were interested in a gamble. Their lodger, Bert Cert, not only spoke in rhyme ("My name is Bert, though I lost my shirt, I hope and pray that later today, my shirt's back and wid me, protectin' my kidney!") but also had a talking shirt that lisped! ("I wesisted till he bwoke my buttons!")

To add to this wacky whimsy, the Flutters later adopted the milkman's horse (it talked, of course) and trained it to race in the Whalemeat Stakes. Bert rode Incognito ("Sire Unknown, Dam Doubtful") to win, and the strip was a winner too, once it whittled away the more outrageous fantasies of writer Ian Gammidge. (A cartoonist himself, he drew the weekly *Gammidge's Bargain Basement* for the *Sunday Pictorial.*) The artist was "L.G." in the 24 years of the strip's life.

The strip started as a thrice-weekly serial on July 7, 1947, then went daily, and eventually ended happily with a marriage for Bert Cert and the overweight

"The Flutters," Len Gamblin. © Daily Mirror Newspapers Ltd.

Brenda on February 27, 1971. *The Flutters* were replaced by another family strip, this time from the North: *The Fosdyke Saga.*

D.G.

FLYIN' JENNY (U.S.) Aviation features were in full flower in 1939 when veteran cartoonist Russell Keaton (who was still drawing the *Skyroads* strip at the time) proposed the idea of an aviatrix as the heroine of a new series; Bell Syndicate liked the notion and bought the feature, called *Flyin' Jenny* (the name was inspired by the JN-40 training plane of World War I). It started as both a daily and a Sunday page in October 1939.

Jenny Dare was a blonde and sexy bombshell who flew all kinds of planes in all kinds of weather. Like her male counterparts, she was always fighting one menace or another when she did not take part in hair-raising air competitions. She also met a number of eligible bachelors who invariably fell in love with her, but she professed not to notice. To her friend (and rival) Wanda—who once wistfully observed, "You really are a beautiful brat, Jenny! I can't say I blame Rick for being crazy about you!"—Jenny demurely replied, "Tut! He admires my flying ability! I taught him, you know!"

At first Keaton both wrote and drew the strip. Later he turned to former navy pilot and Hollywood scriptwriter Frank Wead for the text. In 1941 Wead was recalled to service and Glen Chaffin (former scriptwriter of *Tailspin Tommy*) succeeded him. In 1943 Keaton himself became a flying instructor, and he turned over the drawing of the Sunday page to his assistant, Marc Swayze; when Keaton died of a sudden illness in 1945 Swayze took charge of the daily as well.

Flyin' Jenny was a winsome strip, beautifully drawn and entertainingly written by a much-improved Chaffin. Chaffin and Swayze kept on turning out the strip for a dwindling number of newpapers until it finally ended with a whimper in 1952.

M.H.

FOOTROT FLATS (New Zealand) Murray Ball, a farmer and amateur cartoonist, had been living and working on his ranch near Gisborne on the eastern coast of New Zealand's North Island for some time when it occurred to him that he might use his experiences as the basis of a comic strip. He sent samples of his proposed feature to local publications. In 1976 the strip, called *Footrot Flats*, made its appearance in several New Zealand newspapers, where it was seen by Sol Shifrin of Inter Continental Features, resulting in wide syndication in Australia, beginning in 1977.

As befits a feature set in the outback, *Footrot Flats* has a limited cast of characters. Wallace (Wal) Footrot, from whom the strip derives its name, is an unmarried sheep rancher of dubious abilities who lives on a secluded farm with his redoubtable Aunt Dolly, an old spinster with strict morals. (She once washed Wal's mouth out with soap after hearing him call his dog's inamorata a no-good bitch.) His closest neighbor is Cooch Windgrass, a dirt farmer and animal lover extraordinaire. His lady love is Cheeky Hobson, a buxom blonde working as a beautician in a nearby town.

Animals play a large part in the goings-on in Footrot Flats. Wal's sheepdog, variously going by the names "Dog" and "the Big Black Brute," herds sheep by

"Footrot Flats," Murray Ball. © Murray Ball.

throwing them over the fence. His pet peeves are Major, Cooch's hunting dog, and Prince Charles, Aunt Dolly's pampered corgi; and his nemesis is a colossal cat called "Horse" whose greatest delight is grabbing the hapless dog by the neck and throwing him out of the house.

Australian comics historian John Ryan characterized the strip as "mirroring the humorous side of farm life in New Zealand." So far the barnyard humor has included jokes about golf balls lost in cow dung, humans finding themselves in bed with goats, birds dropping on Aunt Dolly's wash, dogs in heat, and, of course, footrot. Reasonably well drawn and written in a colorful vernacular, *Footrot Flats* is an amusing, if not quite delightful, strip.

M.H.

FOR BETTER OR FOR WORSE (U.S.) Canadian-born Lynn Johnston has been drawing her comic strip, in which she mixes humor and drama, since September 9, 1979. It is internationally distributed by Universal Press Syndicate to about 1,700 newspapers.

Using her own family as models, Johnston presents the relationships among the fictional members of the Patterson household, while she shares with her readers the ups and downs, trials and tribulations, joys and sorrows of everyday life in and out of the family circle. The family of five includes John Patterson, a dentist by profession, who in a welcome change from other domestic humor entries is not the usually harried father and henpecked husband. Neither is Elly, the wife and mother, a harebrained and cutely silly woman. In fact,

an early strip shows her vacuuming in her old robe and curlers while she hears a song on the radio advising housewives to be beautiful and perky when their husbands come home after a hard day at work. Her reaction is a very modern one: she smashes the radio to bits.

The Patterson children are Michael, a college student; his sister Elizabeth, a high schooler; and April, the youngest, a first grader. The Pattersons had a dog, Farley, who, unhappily, died in 1995 shortly after he rescued April from drowning. Edgar, a lovable mutt, has recently been introduced and has his own share of typical (mis)adventures. The strip's main focus is on how the Pattersons interact with one another and with extended family members and friends. Whether April is testing her mother by saying vulgar words, or Michael is regurgitating little-understood Freudian theories, or Elizabeth is interfering with Mike's phone call with the current love of his life by posing—loudly—as his girlfriend ("That's for all the times you've called me 'Lizardbreath' "), it is all acutely depicted, as is the relationship between husband and wife ("for better or for worse"). In the end, one knows of course that they all love and respect each other.

Like the Wallets in Frank King's *Gasoline Alley*, Johnston's characters are allowed to age, albeit in comic-strip time. This not only gives the strip a realistic feel but also provides for discussions of contemporary, even controversial, topics. The March 26-April 24, 1993, episode concerning Lawrence, the son of Elly's friend, was an example of this. The sequence dealt poignantly with the teenager's revelation that he was

"For Better or For Worse," Lynn Johnston. © Universal Press Syndicate.

gay; although a number of newspapers decided not to run it, it elicited a wide positive response from readers who appreciated the honesty, sensitivity, and complete absence of moralizing in Johnston's work.

For Better or For Worse is drawn in an easy, illustrative style (after art school in Vancouver, Johnston had worked in animation and medical illustration), with special emphasis on the treatment of the protagonists' hair, which adds to their liveliness and recognition. Regularly reprinted in paperback collections and the subject of a number of animated TV cartoons, the strip received the Reuben Award from the National Cartoonists Society in 1986. Additionally, in recognition of her work, Lynn Johnston was elected the Society's first woman president (1988) and in 1997 was the first woman to be inducted into the International Museum of Cartoon's Hall of Fame in Boca Raton, Florida.

M.B.C.

FOREST, JEAN-CLAUDE (1930-   ) French comic strip artist and illustrator, born in 1930 in Le Perreux, a suburb of Paris. At 17, while still at l'Ecole des Arts et Métiers in Paris, J. C. Forest produced his first comic strip, *La Flèche Noire* ("The Black Arrow"), adapted from R. L. Stevenson. In 1952 he joined the staff of the French weekly *Vaillant*, for which he contributed two comic strip creations: *Pour la Horde* ("For the Horde"), a tale set in prehistoric times; and *Copyright*, about a fantastic animal.

In 1955 Forest's career really took off. He started designing magazine covers, took over the new version of *Bicot* (*Bicot* had been the French title of Branner's *Winnie Winkle*) and re-created *Charlot* (one of the countless comic strips based on the famous Charlie Chaplin tramp character), both for Offenstadt. In 1959 he contributed a number of comic strip serializations to the daily *France-Soir*. Forest's most famous creation, *Barbarella*, appeared in 1962 in the quarterly *V-Magazine*. He conceived the adventures of the scantily dressed female space explorer as a kind of *divertissement,* and he was taken aback by the strip's unprecedented success. (*Barbarella* was reprinted in hardbound form in 1964, and in 1968 it was made into a movie, which Forest himself designed.)

In 1964 Forest was asked to edit the newly created (and short-lived) comic magazine *Chouchou*, in whose pages he created *Bebe Cyanure* ("Baby Cyanide"), a girl strip, and for which he wrote (under the pseudonym Jean Valherbe) *Les Naufragés du Temps* ("The Shipwrecked Men of Time"), a science-fiction strip. In 1965 he created a series of animated cartoons for French television, *Marie Math*, a toned-down teenage version of *Barbarella*.

Since the mid-1960s Forest's career has been mostly downhill. He exhibited his paintings and illustrations in various French galleries without much success. In 1969 he tried (again unsuccessfully) to revive *Barbarella*. Discouraged, he went back to illustration before trying his hand again at a comic strip, *Mystérieuse Matin, Midi et Soir* ("Mysterious Morning, Noon and Night") using once more the well-worn formula of adventure with sex. *Mystérieuse* first appeared in *France-Soir* before winding up in *Pilote*. Other strips of interest created by Forest have been *Contes de la Barque Saoule* ("Tales of the Drunken Boat," 1977), *La Déchéance du Professeur Adamus* ("Professor Adamus's Downfall," 1979), *La Jonque Fantome Vue de l'Orchestre* ("The Ghost Junk Seen from the Orchestra," 1980), and *Enfants, c'Est l'Hydragon Qui Passe* ("Children, Here Comes the Hydragon," 1982). In recent years he has mostly confined himself to writing scripts illustrated by others, including one last Barbarella story.

Jean-Claude Forest deserves to be remembered for more than *Barbarella's succèss de scandale.* As it happened, however, Forest could not maintain the self-discipline and integrity required by any serious artist, and he chose instead to succumb to facility and formula, trying to repeat endlessly (and futilely) the success of *Barbarella*. He is the classic example of a great talent gone to waste due to a lack of direction or purpose.

M.H.

FORTON, LOUIS (1879-1934) French cartoonist, born March 14, 1879, in Sées, a small town in Normandy. Forton's life reads like the scenario of one of his own strips. The son of a horse trader, he was "almost born on horseback." He never received a formal education or learned to draw but was successively stable-boy, jockey, and racetrack tout. Fittingly enough, he met his future publishers, the brothers Offenstadt, at the racetrack in Vincennes. The Offenstadts owned a string of magazines, and Forton soon started contributing to most of them, under his own name or various pseudonyms. Drawing from his own experiences, he created *Les Aventures de Seraphin Laricot* ("The Adventures of Seraphin Laricot") about a bum he once knew, in 1907, and *Les Exploits d'Isidore MacAron and Anatole Fricotard*, relating the escapades of two con artists, in 1908. That same year Forton's most famous creation appeared: *La Bande des Pieds-Nickelés* ("The Nickel-Plated-Feet Gang"), depicting the unsavory doings of a trio of unredeemable rogues. The success of the new series was immediate and overwhelming, and Forton was to draw and write it (with minor and major interruptions) until his death.

Forton is also the creator of a number of other comic strips of note: *La Carrière Militaire d'Onésime Baluchon* ("The Military Career of Onesime Baluchon"), which in 1909 anticipated *Beetle Bailey* by some 40 years; *Les Cent Vingt-Six Métiers de Caramel* ("The 126 Jobs of Caramel"), about a born loser in 1920; and, in 1924, his

J. C. Forest, "Mystérieuse Matin, Midi et Soir." © J. C. Forest.

second most popular strip, *Bibi Fricotin*, a nostalgic look at his childhood.

Forton retained his interest in horses throughout his life; he was also a dandy, an inveterate gambler, a pillar of café society, a convivial host and bon vivant—all of which left him scant time for drawing. (This explains why *Les Pieds-Nickelés* was interrupted for months and sometimes years at a clip.) On February 15, 1934, Forton died at 55 of cirrhosis of the liver.

Forton is most famed as a writer and creator of types (he has been compared to Francois Villon, LeSage, and Balzac). As a cartoonist he was no innovator. He inserted a printed narrative underneath the pictures and used the balloon only sparingly. The success and popularity that he enjoyed stimulated many cartoonists around him and contributed to making France a major center of comic strip creation, second only to the United States.

M.H.

47:AN LÖKEN (Sweden) *47:an Löken* (literally, "The 47 Onion"; freely translated, "Soldier 47, Chowderhead") was created in 1967 by Swedish comic artist and illustrator Lennart Elworth for the newspaper *Lektyr*. The strip stands in a Swedish tradition of humorous army strips, which was started in 1932 by Rudolf Petersson with *91 Karlsson* and continued in the 1940s by Torsten Bjarre with *Flygsoldat 113 Bom* ("Air Force Pvt. 113 No-hit"). Elworth had not quite liked the idea of entering the comic strip ring with a feature that would have to stand up against something as well established and popular as *91 Karlsson* (also known as *91:an* in the comic book version). But the editors of *Lektyr* talked him into it, and Elworth never rued the day he signed his contract.

The army being a kind of society within society with a certain set of rules and rank, it does not come as a surprise that there should be some parallels

"47:an Löken," Lennart Elworth.

between *47:an Löken* and *91 Karlsson*. Both soldiers have their costars: 47:an's best friend is 69:an, and 91 Karlsson has 87 Axelsson for a friend and sometimes antagonist. Karlsson and Axelsson fight each other to win the favor of Captain Berån's buxom daughter Elvira. Löken and friend have an eye out for the shapely WACs frequenting their garrison's sauna and bathing facilities. Finally, there are generals and other officers to be made fun of and, of course, the privates' efforts to avoid having to go on cross-country hikes.

The anecdotal episodes of *47:an Löken* are in a way Elworth's memories of his own time in the army. Or rather they are an amalgam of having to bow to the necessities of army life and trying to make the best of it by not succumbing to a military outlook on life. The humor and the stereotypes are one way of taking the sting out of military life. The stereotypes, characterized by their names, have their roots in real persons. Thus, Kapten Kruth ("Captain Gunpowder") has certain of Elworth's father's character traits.

47:an is played strictly for the fun of it. The strip is modern in approach, makes use of some very fresh humor, and is drawn in a zesty, flowing style. The comics are now drawn by various artists.

W.F.

FORZA JOHN (Italy) In recent years it has become a trendy gimmick to insert a cheap gadget within the pages of comic magazines in order to attract the younger readership. The practice, however, is not so new. At the end of World War II Cino and Domenico Del Duca resorted to the same idea of giving out something for nothing by enclosing a small comic book (of the kind that sold for 10 or 15 lire on the newsstands) within the pages of their comic magazine, *L'Intrepido*. They succeeded in increasing their circulation and gave birth to two worthwhile features to boot: *Forza John* and *Rocky Rider*.

Forza John (that could be translated as "Come On John") first appeared in late 1949, became self-selling and, starting with issue number 100 on August 28, 1951, enjoyed its own weekly comic book until April 14, 1953, when it was transferred to the pages of the comic weekly *Il Monello*; there it remained for over 10 years, winning the appreciation of a wide public.

Forza John, written in the beginning by Luigi Grecchi and drawn by Erio Nivolo (later replaced by Lino Jeva), had as its leading character a strapping, fair-haired, blue-eyed air cadet named John Graham. He was cast in the youngish heroic mold of many of the boy-heroes of the time (Capitan Miki, Piccolo Sceriffo, Sciuscià, etc.). After accomplishing several suicide war missions, John worked as a secret agent, battling outlaws, drug smugglers, saboteurs, and spies. His adventures, often very involved, made up a picaresque novel filled with interesting characterizations. There was Linda, a typical Italian girl, faithful and family-loving, who joined the WACs in order to be beside her fiancé, John; other characters included the wise and loyal Dr. Sam; the athletic and shrewd Captain Conterios and his wife; the scrawny and nearsighted newspaperman, Palissandro Giacinto Livingston, nicknamed "Pal"; and the thinking parrot, Geremia, who added a touch of welcome slapstick to the stories.

G.B.

FOSDYKE SAGA, THE (G.B.) "A kind, cussed, but totally endearing family, name of Fosdyke (raised in

Lancashire, weaned on tripe), will be moving, lock, stock and black pudding, into the *Daily Mirror*, starting Monday." With these words, a full-page article by Donald Zee, *Mirror* columnist, introduced the new daily strip, *The Fosdyke Saga*. It began on Monday, March 2, 1971, with an epic scene. Josiah Fosdyke, a coal miner from Insanitary Cottages, Griddlesbury, a grimy mining town in Lancashire, is caught in a cave-in in No. 3 shaft. Brought up alive, just able to walk, he is promptly chucked out of town, coal nuggets raining on his bald head, for blacklegging his mates: "Strike Now for Tuppence a Week." To keep his family ("We need luxuries like bread and dripping") Jos goes cap-in-hand to his wife Rebecca's rich brother, Bloody Tod Olroyd of the Black Pudding Factory. "Lend us two shillin's for train fare to Manchester. I'll have my solicitors draw up a contract with the children as security!" (Jos and Becky had three offspring, Tom, Victoria, and Albert, plus Little Tim, brought on by the mine hooter!) and so the saga was under way. As of 1997 it was still going strong.

The strip was treated by Bill Tidy (born 1932), a big Northerner from Southport, as his low-class answer to the middle-class Galsworthy serial, then running on BBC Television: "When I saw *The Forsyte Saga* I thought the working classes ought to have their own. Their lives, thoughts and dreams have been neglected for years. I hope the Fosdykes will fill the gap." Helping them to fill it were their prominent noses, a Tidy trademark: "I believe in the Duke of Wellington's dictum that strong characters go with big hooters."

Tidy, a postwar phenomenon in British cartooning, was a major provider of "singles," or one-gag drawings, to *Punch* and other periodicals, before taking to strips. His weekly strips include *Grimbledon Down* (1970) in *New Scientist* and *The Cloggies* (1969), the saga of an everyday Northern clog-dancing team, in *Private Eye*.

The Fosdyke Saga has been reprinted in annual paperback collections since 1972. Bill Tidy has become a television personality with his appearances on *Quick On the Draw* and other shows, and he was named Cartoonist of the Year in 1974.

D.G.

FOSTER, HAROLD (1892-1982) American artist, born August 16, 1892, in Halifax, Nova Scotia. In 1906 Harold R. Foster moved with his family to Winnipeg, Manitoba. At age 18 he quit school to support his family, trying his hand as a prizefighter, a guide in the wilds of Manitoba, and a gold prospector. In 1921 Foster travelled to Chicago on a bicycle to attend classes at the Art Institute. From there he went to the National Academy of Design and the Chicago Academy of Fine Arts.

After his studies Foster worked as an illustrator and advertising artist and soon gained a solid professional reputation for his illustration and poster work. In 1928 Joseph H. Neebe, a literary agent who had acquired the rights to adapt Edgar Rice Burroughs' *Tarzan* into comic strip form, approached Foster (after J. Allen St. John had turned him down) and asked him to take the job. Foster agreed to draw only the first *Tarzan* episode (January-March, 1929), then went back to advertising. In September 1931 he did finally come back, and then only to draw the *Tarzan* Sunday page.

In 1937, tired of illustrating someone else's stories, Foster created *Prince Valiant*, the tumultuous saga of a knight in King Arthur's court. In 1944-45 Foster gave *Prince Valiant* a companion strip, *The Medieval Castle*, another tale of the Middle Ages; he also found time to do some illustration work. But the main object of his attentions remained *Prince Valiant*, on which he worked as much as 50 hours a week. In the 1960s the overworked and aging Foster left more and more of the work to his assistants, and in 1971 he finally ceased drawing *Prince Valiant*, while continuing to submit pencil layouts to his successor, John Cullen Murphy, until 1980. He also wrote most of the story lines at least until the mid-1970s, and he kept his interest in his creation up to the time of his death on July 25, 1982, in Florida, where he had retired.

Harold Foster's reputation as one of the foremost artists of the comics is secure. He never made use of balloons but instead enclosed his text within the frame of the image (a throwback to earlier European usage), but as an illustrator rather than a cartoonist he brought to the comic strip a number of new techniques as well as a knowledge of anatomy and a sense of space. As Coulton Waugh wrote in 1947, "Foster possesses also the true illustrator's passion for periods and authentic detail. He is a remarkable figure among comic artists and his place in strip history is unique."

Foster has exercised a decisive influence on the following generation of comic strip artists, from Clarence Gray and Alex Raymond to his successor on *Tarzan*, Burne Hogarth. He was also the recipient of a number of cartooning awards (the Reuben among them), but in view of his achievements, these seem rather trivial.

M.H.

FOX AND THE CROW, THE (U.S.) *The Fox and the Crow* was created by Frank Tashlin, who directed the first *Fox and Crow* cartoon for Screen Gems, a division of Columbia Pictures, in 1941. This cartoon, *The Fox and the Grapes*, inspired by Aesop's fable "The Crow and the Fox," introduced the two friendly enemies who later made their comic book debut in *Real Screen Funnies* number one (Spring 1945) published by National. The magazine, renamed *Real Screen Comics* in the second issue and changed to *T.V.-Screen Comics* shortly before its demise in 1960, featured characters licensed from Columbia. These included *Tito and His Burrito* and *Flippity and Flop*.

Despite the mild success of the animated films and Columbia closing down its cartoon operation in 1948, bringing the *Fox and Crow* cartoons to a halt, the characters remained popular in comic books. In 1948, *Comic Cavalcade*, a National comic that had previously featured superheroes, converted to the "funny animal" material and lasted until 1955, featuring *The Fox and the Crow* in the lead spot. In April 1950, *The Fox and the Crow* was awarded its own comic book of the same name and continued for 108 consecutive issues until 1968.

At first, the stories and artwork for the Columbia-licensed comic books were done by an art "shop" composed of men from the animation studio, including Jim Davis, Bob Wickersham, Howard Swift, Paul Sommer, Hubert Karp, Warren Foster, and Cal Dalton. Wickersham was the primary artist on early *Fox and Crow* stories. In 1948, he decided to concentrate on the *Kilroys* comic for the American Comics Group, so Jim Davis began drawing *Fox and Crow* and working directly for National. Davis employed a former story man and animator from Columbia and Disney, Cecil Beard, to help with some of the inking. Hubert Karp, also a Disney alumnus, supplied the stories and refined the format. Most stories involved only two characters—Fauntleroy F. Fox and Crawford C. Crow—and the untiring efforts of the latter to cheat the former out of food, money, and/or personal dignity. The Crow employed an array of costumes and schemes, usually appealing to the Fox's incurable vanity.

In 1953, Karp died, and the stories were handled for a time by Davis and Beard, until Beard finally took over the entire writing chore with the help of his wife, Alpine Harper. Except for brief art fill-ins by Owen Fitzgerald and Karran Wright, Davis handled the artwork until the end. Many covers were done by Mort Drucker.

In 1968, a backup feature entitled *Stanley and His Monster* took over the *Fox and Crow* comic book, bringing to an end a series that had spanned 20 years and over 500 stories. Seven issues later, *Stanley and His Monster* was canceled. It resurfaced briefly in 1993 in a four-issue miniseries.

M.E.

FOX, FONTAINE TALBOT, JR. (1884-1964) Born March 3, 1884, in Louisville, Kentucky, Fontaine Talbot Fox Jr. drew from his grammar school days, kept it up through high school, and then went to work in the *Louisville Herald* as a reporter and part-time cartoonist. Among the local subjects he caricatured was the Brook Street trolley line, noted in Fox's youth for its haphazard schedule and prolonged nonappearance in rain or snow. His cartoons were popular with readers, and when Fox made enough to go to the University of Indiana, the paper asked him to draw them a cartoon a day on current subjects while away. The strain of studies and cartoon work proved too much after two years, however, and Fox dropped out to follow his obvious profession. Now the *Louisville Times* wanted him for more money, so Fox carried on his daily gag miscellany for them, and then for the *Chicago Post*, until the Wheeler Syndicate gave him national distribution in 1915.

For several years, Fox developed his small-town characters (it is not recorded when he first hit on the town name of Toonerville), basing many of them on people he had known in suburban-rural Louisville. His own father was the source of the Terrible-Tempered Mr. Bang, for example. At first, he used the Toonerville Trolley and its Skipper (based on his memories of the Brook Street line and another in Pelham Manor, New York, which he saw while visiting a friend), and its popularity grew, the avalanches of letters letting him and the syndicate know they had a hit. Thereafter, the Trolley was in at least once a week.

A Sunday page was added in 1918, where the Trolley appeared with increasing frequency. In 1920, he went to the McNaught Syndicate, then after a few years to Bell, finally gaining contractual control of his own work, which he retained to his death.

Fox, an accomplished golfer, won various tournaments, belonged to over six golf and art associations, and was the author of several books and articles, including one series that ran in many papers based on his narrow escape in 1939 from war-torn Europe. During the war, he was a member of the Division of Pictorial Publicity.

In February 1953, Fox (aware of the replacement of trolley lines by buses) converted a wrecked Tooner-ville Trolley into a new Toonerville Bus, still driven by the Skipper. But he relented three months before he retired, in November 1954, and restored the Trolley to service. He formally retired in February 1955 and folded his strip and characters away for good. He died in Greenwich, Connecticut, on August 10, 1964.

B.B.

FOX, GARDNER (1911-1986) American comic book writer, born in May 1911 in Brooklyn, New York. Scripting more than 50 million words in his career, Fox is considered the quintessential superhero and science-fiction comic book writer.

After securing a law degree from St. John's University, Fox opted for writing short stories for pulp magazines. He moved to National Comics in 1937 and produced a horde of noncostumed adventure features like *Steve Malone*. From there he went on to write literally dozens of National superhero strips, including *Starman, Zatara, Dr. Fate, Batman, Spectre, Flash, Hawkman*, and others. He also produced a line of minor strips for Columbia in 1940 and 1941, most notably *Skyman*.

But Fox's greatest achievement during the 1940s was his stories for the *Justice Society of America*, a National superhero group feature that appeared in the pages of *All-Star Comics*. Populating his stories with offbeat villains and well-researched scientific information, Fox's scripts were always among the best-handled in the comics' golden age. The adventures of the Justice Society, which at one time or another featured about 25 heroes, remain among the most-sought-after comics from the 1940s.

As the emphasis shifted away from superheroes during the late 1940s and early 1950s, Fox changed too. After producing material for ME, Avon, and EC, he returned to National and began churning out an exciting series of science-fiction tales for books like *Strange Adventures* and *Tales of the Unexpected*. Fox's scientific bent made the stories believable. One of these science-fiction titles, *Mystery in Space*, showcased what many believe to be Fox's greatest effort, *Adam Strange*. An earth-bound scientist, Strange was struck by a strange beam and transported to the planet Rann. Falling in love with a Rann woman and the Rann civilization, Adam Strange eventually became a permanent resident and the planet's greatest defender. Aided by Carmine Infantino's outstanding artwork and Fox's most fantastic flights of scientific fancy, the strip became a phenomenal success and lasted from 1959 to 1965.

When superhero comics took a new upturn in early 1960, Fox and John Broome became editor Julie Schwartz's mainstays, and Fox turned out a string of fine superheroic stories for *Hawkman, Atom, Green Lantern, Flash*, and several others. He was instrumental in reviving many of the golden age heroes and making the 1960s the "second golden age." His finest work in the period was done on a superhero group strip, this time called *Justice League of America*. Fox turned the feature into a showcase for his scientific knowledge and tight scripting. Several of his human interest stories, including "Riddle of the Robot Justice League," "Man, Thy Name Is Brother," and "Indestructible Creatures of Nightmare Island," predated the "relevance" craze of the early 1970s. He died in Princeton, New Jersey, on December 24, 1986.

Despite his fantastic comic book success, Fox also found time to write over 100 novels in all fields under the pen names "Jefferson Cooper" and "Bart Sommers." He also scripted a popular series of fantasy titles under his own name.

J.B.

FOXWELL, HERBERT (1890-1943) One of the best "nursery school" artists to work in British comics, Herbert Foxwell was famous for taking over two characters created earlier by other cartoonists and making them almost immortal. The first was *Tiger Time*, created by Julius Stafford Baker, and the second was *Teddy Tail*, created by Charles Folkard. Foxwell was also famous because he insisted on signing his strips, first with his initials, "H.S.F.," and later simply as "Foxwell"; he was one of the few British comic strip artists granted this privilege.

Herbert Sydney Foxwell was born in Camberwell, South London, in 1890. Although virtually nothing is known about his early years, he arrived on the children's comic paper scene in 1912 when he was 22 years old. His first known strip was entitled *Jumbo and Jim* and appeared in *The Penny Wonder*, an Amalgamated Press publication. He would stay with this prolific publisher until 1933, when he was their top juvenile artist and was lured away to draw the front pages of two newspaper comic supplements, *The Boys and Girls Daily Mail* and *Jolly Jack's Weekly*, the supplement to the *Sunday Dispatch*.

His early work involved adult characters such as Harold Hazbean in *Comic Cuts* (1913), Artie Artichoke in *The Favorite Comic* (1913), and others. In 1914, Foxwell began to work for *The Rainbow*, a nursery comic edited by William Fisher. First he drew *Sam the Skipper*, a jolly old seadog, and then *The Dolliwogs' Dolls' House*, an unusual strip depicting the inhabitants of a three-story dollhouse. His success led to an offer to take over the front-page heroes *Tiger Tim and the Bruin Boys* from Julius Stafford Baker, whose style was considered too cartoony for juvenile consumption. Foxwell introduced his highly decorative style to the series, and especially wonderful were his "specials," such as the Seaside Holiday Numbers, Christmas Numbers, Grand Boat Race Numbers, and Fireworks Numbers.

The popularity of Foxwell's work among both the children readers and their parents who were buying the comics soon shot *The Rainbow* into the top sellers list, and legend has it that one copy was delivered to the Royal Family inside the daily copy of the king's *Times*. This legend was noted in one issue's headline, "The Comic for Home and Palace!" New series of publications followed, *Tiger Tim's Tales* (1919) with *Pauline and Patsy* by Foxwell, whose title changed the following year to *Tiger Tim's Weekly*, to which Foxwell contributed *Goldilocks, Tinklebell Tree,* and *The Tiny Toy Boys*. Soon he was also drawing the front color page of *Bubbles* (1921) and *Mrs. Bunty's Boarding House*, which featured humans for a change, but it was back to animals when *The Playbox* began in 1925. Foxwell created clones of the entire Tiger Tim brood. Throughout this prolific output of comics, which included a real-life strip, the adventures of Hollywood star Lloyd Hamilton in *Kinema Comic* (1920), plus *Merry Merlin* in *Children's Fairy* (1919) and *Mr. Croc's School* in *Bubbles*, never once did Foxwell's line falter or any picture or page seem slapdash.

In 1933, when the boom in free comic supplements for younger readers began in the British press, Associated Newspapers—once part of but now a rival to the Amalgamated Press—lured Foxwell away to illustrate their *Boys and Girls* section, best remembered as the *Teddy Tail Comic*. Foxwell also drew *Rollicking Rollo*, a pirate, *The Gay Goblins*, and *The Happy Family* (1935), as well as *Chubby and Lulu, Professor Simple, Toby and Tinker,* and the cover characters for *Jolly Jack's Weekly* for the *Sunday Dispatch*.

This prolific period was all too short. Foxwell joined the army during World War II. He was made a captain in the Royal Army Service Corps and was killed in action in 1943. No one ever replaced him, despite the attempts of several cartoonists to revive Teddy Tail after the war.

D.G.

FOXY GRANDPA (U.S.) The least-rewarding of the great classic titles from the early days of comic strips, C. E. Schultze's *Foxy Grandpa* opened the 20th century by first appearing on the front page of the *New York Herald* Sunday comic section on January 7, 1900. The charming, simply rendered art of the new strip, together with its easy, unelaborated switch on *The Katzenjammer Kids* theme—in which the kid-plagued parent cleverly turns the tables on the trick-playing kids (two 10-year-old boys, blonde and brunette, never named)—captivated the public of the time and made the strip an overnight success.

Soon after joining Hearst's *New York American* for its 1902 Sunday section, Schultze continued *Foxy Grandpa* as a half-page, second-fiddle strip inside a four-page color section opened and closed by Opper, Dirks, and Swinnerton full pages. Public interest in the dully repetitive strip swiftly waned, however, so Hearst's editors omitted *Foxy Grandpa* entirely from the comic section within a few years, running it only when space permitted on the back of the Sunday *American Weekly* magazine section. Since other subscribing papers outside the Hearst group were few, *Foxy Grandpa's* renown faded. Only a few readers noticed or cared when the strip left Hearst at the end of the decade and moved to the *New York Press*, where it continued sporadically as a full page once again until 1918, when *Press* owner Frank Munsey's repeated amalgamations of the paper with other New York dailies squeezed it into oblivion.

Within a few years, Schultze revived Foxy Grandpa as the narrator of a daily series of animal and nature narratives for children, each accompanied by a small drawing of Grandpa and a younger boy named Bobby observing the subject of the day's 500-word piece. Titled *Foxy Grandpa's Stories* and distributed by Newspaper Feature Service, the series ran in many papers in the early 1920s, without any specific opening or closing date (they were sold in yearly sets), but generally dropped from sight by 1929. Published in several book collections of the Sunday strip in the early 1900s (*Foxy Grandpa and the Boys, Foxy Grandpa's Surprises*, etc.), the feature has had no other publication in any form (aside from examples in texts) since 1930.

B.B.

FRANKENSTEIN (U.S.) The most successful attempt to put Mary Shelley's Frankenstein Monster into a regularly scheduled comic book feature was made by artist and writer Dick Briefer. Combining aspects of Shelley's 1818 novel and some popular features of contemporary horror movies, Briefer premiered the *New Adventures of Frankenstein* in Feature's *Prize* number

André Franquin, "Modeste et Pompon." © Editions du Lombard.

seven for December 1940. Briefer's version, done under the name "Frank N. Stein," had Victor Frankenstein creating his monstrosity in 1940 Manhattan. He immediately saw his creation begin a crusade against humanity; meanwhile, the repentant Dr. Frankenstein cared for a boy named Denny, whose family had been killed by the monster. The youth subsequently became "Bulldog Denny" and set out after the monster. The creature is eventually caught and put in the care of Dr. Carrol for "rehabilitation."

This was the turning point of the series. Briefer's art, which had always been loose and comical, was quickly becoming a lampoon. His monster was now more whimsical than horrifying. By the end of 1943, the strip was simply being called *Frankenstein* and played strictly for laughs. The monster was even given a home in "Mippyville." This comical Frankenstein got his own book in 1945, and Briefer's humor was appealing; the humorous interpretation became extremely popular in the mid-1940s, but the string eventually ran out. Already having been dropped from *Prize* after March 1948's 68th issue, the humorous series ended with the publication of February 1949's *Frankenstein* number 17.

When horror made an upswing in the early 1950s, Briefer was called in to revive the *Frankenstein* title. Beginning with March 1952's 18th issue, Briefer again resurrected the character, but this time he was once more the snarling, raging monster of the earlier years. This third interpretation was Briefer's weakest, however. His forte was not serious material, he was obviously bored, and he relied heavily on stories rewritten from old plots. This series ended in Frankenstein number 33 (November 1954).

Between Briefer's humorous monster and the 1952 reincarnation, the ACG group published the lackluster *Spirit of Frankenstein* series in *Adventures Into the Unknown*. Appearing only sporadically between June 1949 and February 1951, the stories totally ignored the Shelley novel.

After a 1963 adaptation of the 1931 Universal film, Dell comics introduced a new *Frankenstein*: a superhero with a red costume, a crewcut, and the secret identity of Frank Stone. It was a financial and artistic disaster and made only three appearances between September 1966 and March 1967.

Tom Sutton (under the name Sean Todd) began a series called *Frankenstein Book II* in the third issue of Skywald's black-and-white *Psycho* magazine in May 1971. The series began where the Shelley novel left off, but Sutton's weak writing doomed the series after three appearances.

In January 1973, Marvel comics began publishing another series set in 1898. Originally drawn by Mike Ploog, the strip bears little resemblance to recognized Frankenstein lore.

Early in 1973, National introduced the *Spawn of Frankenstein* series, a backup feature in *Phantom Stranger*. Set in the present, the strip boasted artwork by Mike Kaluta and Bernard Baily, but folded in April 1974 after eight appearances.

Additionally, the Frankenstein monster has appeared as a character (usually a villain) in hundreds of stories from many publishers; these one-shot appearances rarely had anything to do with the cast of characters in the original novel. There was also a chapter on Frankenstein in comic books in *The Comic-Book Book*, published in 1974 by Arlington House.

J.B.

Mary Shelley's monster was brought back to life again (and again) in *Frankenstein, or The Modern Prometheus*, a one-shot published in 1994 by Caliber Press, and in 1995 he was confronted by Bram Stoker's vampire in Topps Comics' *The Frankenstein/Dracula War*. Mention should also be made of Berni Wrightson's lavishly illustrated version of the 1980s.

M.H.

FRANQUIN, ANDRÉ (1924-1997) Belgian cartoonist, born in 1924 in Brussels. After high school André Franquin studied art at the Académie St. Luc near Brussels for only one year. In 1945 he was, along with Jijé, Morris, and Peyo, one of the animators in a cartooning studio that closed down the following year. Franquin then joined the staff of the comic weekly *Spirou*, where in 1946 he succeeded Jijé on the drawing of the title strip. Franquin was to draw *Spirou* until 1969, and he is universally regarded as the definitive artist on the strip as well as its most innovative contributor.

In 1948, along with his inseparable companions Morris and Jijé, Franquin left for a long journey of discovery to the United States and Mexico. Upon his return to Belgium in 1955, and following a contractual dispute with his publisher, Franquin created for *Tintin* a new strip, *Modeste et Pompon*, about a boy and a girl and their (nonromantic) adventures, which he drew until 1959. Meanwhile he had settled with his publishers and resumed drawing *Spirou* in 1956—one of the rare cases of a European cartoonist working for two rival publications at once, without benefit of a pseudonym.

Within the framework of the *Spirou* strip, Franquin created a number of secondary characters, two of whom were to gain strips of their own: Gaston Lagaffe, a befuddled, blundering copyboy; and the fantastic animal known as the Marsupilami. (*Gaston* debuted as a strip in 1957, and *Le Marsupilami* in 1968). Beginning in 1969 Franquin devoted most of his time to these two features. He occasionally found time, however, for outside projects. He wrote a few episodes of Will's *Isabelle* in the 1970s; and in 1978 he wrote *Ernest Ringard*, a satirical strip drawn by Frederic Jannin. His last attempt at an original creation, *La Chroniqu des Tifous* ("The Chronicle of the Li'l Imps," 1989) met with scant success and lasted only a few months. He died on January 5, 1997.

André Franquin was one of the foremost European cartoonists, the head of what has come to be called the "Marcinelle school" (from the city where *Spirou* magazine is published) and the inspiration of scores of comic strip artists. One of his colleagues defined him as "a realistic draftsman among humor cartoonists." Indeed Franquin's style, in the attention paid to details, and verisimilitude, is a far cry from the broad "big foot" traditions of the gag cartoon. Franquin was honored with a number of awards and distinctions in the course of his long career, not only in his native Belgium, but in most European countries and in the United States as well.

M.H.

FRAZETTA, FRANK (1928-   ) American comic book and comic strip artist, born February 9, 1928, in Brooklyn, New York. After studies at Brooklyn's Academy of Fine Arts under the Italian artist Michael Falanga, "Fritz" began his career at age 16 as the assistant to science-fiction artist John Giunta. His first comic book work, a character called Snowman, appeared in Baily Comics' *Tally Ho* number one (December 1944).

Throughout the rest of the 1940s, Frazetta drew a multitude of minor characters for many comic houses, including Toby, Pines, Fawcett (notably *Golden Arrow* in 1949), Prize, Fiction House, Standard, and Avon. His first major assignment came in 1949 when he began

drawing the *Shining Knight* feature for National's *Adventure Comics*.

Frazetta was later praised for *Ghost Rider* and *Tim Holt* comics of the M.E. group, and in April 1952, he produced what many critics consider his best comic book work, M.E.'s *Thun'da* number one. Written by Gardner Fox, the book contained four flawlessly drawn jungle tales. The book was so popular that it was reproduced as a 10-dollar, limited collector's edition (Russ Cochran, 1973). Also during the early 1950s, Frazetta produced other superb comic book work. His Buck Rogers covers for *Famous Funnies* are among the best-loved and most-reproduced pieces of comic book work ever published. During 1953 and 1954, Frazetta drew some particularly excellent material for comics like *Personal Love*. The stories were mediocre at best, but Frazetta's artwork, especially where the female figure was concerned, reached great heights. He also contributed a small amount of steller cover and interior work for E.C.'s "New Trend" books, mostly in collaboration with Al Williamson. "Squeeze Play," his only solo story (*Shock SuspenStories* number 13, March 1954), was so well drawn that it appeared in the *E.C. Horror Library* (Nostalgia Press, 1972). It was this material that solidified Frazetta's reputation as one of the best illustrators in the field.

Frazetta made his first foray into syndicated strips in 1952 when he drew a short-lived feature called *Johnny Comet* (later titled *Ace McCoy*). When this was dropped in 1953, Frazetta spent several weeks ghosting Dan Barry's *Flash Gordon* and then joined Al Capp's *L'il Abner* staff. He left Capp nine years later to begin a career as a freelance illustrator.

Although he started slowly (most of his early work was done for "girlie" publications), he soon blossomed as one of the most-sought-after cover artists in the book field. After creating a memorable series of covers for Ace's *Tarzan*, he illustrated several outstanding *Conan* covers for Lancer. In recognition of his superlative work in the science-fiction and fantasy field, Frazetta was awarded sci-fi's highest honor, The Hugo Award, in 1966.

Preferring to spend his time drawing more lucrative assignments (like book covers and movie posters), Frazetta has produced little recently in the way of comic art. He contributed several drawings to Kurtzman and Elder's *Little Annie Fanny*, but his only sub-

Frank Frazetta, "White Indian." © Frank Frazetta.

"Freckles and his Friends," Merrill Blosser. © NEA Service.

stantial work has been an occasional cover painting for Warren's black-and-white magazines. His material was so impressive, however, that publisher James Warren named a corporate award in his honor—and then bestowed several of them upon him.

Although Frazetta has chosen to concentrate on fields outside the comic book and comic strip, and even though his volume of work is meager in comparison to workhorses like Gil Kane and Jack Kirby, his work has always been so outstanding and visually excellent that he is considered one of the major artists ever to work in comics. Many successful artists—Jeff Jones, Berni Wrightson, Mike Kaluta, and others—began by imitating Frazetta's unique style.

J.B.

FRECKLES AND HIS FRIENDS (U.S.) Merrill Blosser's classic boyhood strip, *Freckles and His Friends*, one of the earliest continuing daily strips circulated by NEA Syndicate, first appeared in most newspapers in mid-1915. A Sunday page was added in the early 1920s. Like Frank King's Skeezix, Freckles McGoosey was a comic strip boy who grew up, although much less smoothly and logically than Skeezix (a freckle-faced, buck-toothed eight-year-old in 1915, Freckles was the same age, minus the buck teeth, in 1927). Initially introduced with an older sister and younger brother (Elsie and Tagalong), as well as a small spotted dog, Jumbo, Freckles had lost Elsie by the early 1920s but added four new boy pals, Alek, Slim, and a pair of twins named Ray and Jay. By the end of the 1920s, only two other major kid characters had been added to Freckles' gang: Oscar, with his huge bow tie engulfing his mouth, and Patricia Penelope Fitts, a plain neighbor girl who plagued Freckles and the boys.

In the 1930s, however, Freckles shot up into young adolescence and acquired a whole new troupe of bud-

dies and girlfriends, such as June Wayman, his best girl; Lard Smith, his closest friend; Nutty Cook, boy inventor; Hilda Grubble, Lard's girl; Hector, Hilda's obnoxious kid brother; and other assorted kids such as Pepper, Fuzzy, and Kenny. Tag, Freckles' brother, had grown to Freckles 1920's size in the meantime, while Freckles' old buddy Oscar had not aged at all, and became Tag's friend. Oddly enough, all of this worked in the context of the strip, and since one only glimpses at certain of the characters before and after Freckles' worldwide adventures and travels (he left his hometown, Shadyside, about once a year on some junket or other), their growth or lack of it was not too noticeable.

During World War II, Blosser defied the nearly universal trend elsewhere in the strips and ignored the war almost altogether. Freckles did not surge to age 18 and enlist; he stayed sanely 16 and kept on with his adolescent activities and buddies. The result was a refreshing consistency of content through the 1940s. In the 1950s and 1960s, too, Freckles remained the same age and retained the same crowd of friends, although the wilder sort of 1930s adventuring involving plane crashes in the wilderness, ship mutinies, African safaris, etc., largely disappeared from the strip. Beginning in the mid-1960s the strip was ghosted, and signed, by Henry Formhals under Blosser's supervision, with considerable thematic and graphic similarity to the Blosser original. *Freckles and His Friends* ended its long run in 1973.

B.B.

FRED BASSET (G.B.) Alex Graham was drawing basset hounds in his joke cartoons for some years before it occurred to him to transfer the dog to strip cartoons. The result, *Fred Basset*, started in the *Daily Mail* on July 9, 1963, and managed to stay ahead (hold his lead, one might say) despite the heavy cartoon canine opposition: *Snoopy* appears in the same newspaper!

Fred, subtitled "the hound that's almost human," cannot talk—aloud, that is. But he can think, and it is his very human thoughts that make the fun, floating out of his head in traditional "thought balloons," such as the time he smilingly studies his master posing for a seaside snap. As his mistress lowers the camera, Fred thinks: "You can relax. Stop pulling in your stomach!" Many of his comments are addressed directly to the reader, with a smile or a quizzical pucker over the outward-looking eyes. Fred's little world is highly domesticated suburbia: home, car, pub, and golf club, the latter venue reflecting his Scots creator's private mania.

Alex Graham, born in Glasgow in 1915, won portrait painting prizes at the Glasgow School of Art and started submitting "singles" (gag cartoons) to the Scots papers of D. C. Thomson. His first strip was *Wee Hughie* in the *Weekly News*, followed by *Our Bill* (1946) and *Willy Nilly* in *Sunday Graphic* (1947). He raised his sights to the society weekly *Tatler* with *Briggs the Butler* (1949), who served tea, scones, and jokes for 17 years! Later came *Graham's Golf Club* in *Punch*.

Reprints of *Fred Basset* in paperback collections were published regularly, having reached 17 volumes by 1974. Other strips appeared among the gags reprinted in his many collections, of which *Oh Sidney Not the Walnut Tree* (1966) was the first. Graham was such a great professional that after his sudden death on December 3, 1991, his newspaper had so many unpublished *Fred Basset* strips in hand that the series continued with new gags for more than a year. (It is now done by anonymous staffers.)

D.G.

FREDERICKS, HAROLD (1929-   ) American comic book and comic strip artist, born in Atlantic City, New Jersey, on August 9, 1929. Harold (Fred) Fredericks was educated at the Atlantic City Friends School, where he was art editor of the school paper. From 1947 to 1949 he worked for the *Atlantic City Press*. After joining the Marine Corps in 1950, Fredericks became a cartoonist on the *Camp Lejeune Globe*, where he drew *Salty Ranks*, a military comic strip. Discharged in 1953, Fredericks attended classes at the School of Visual Arts and drew a number of historical strips and panels, including *New Jersey's Patriots* (syndicated throughout the state from 1957 to 1960), *The Late Late War*, and *Under the Stars and Bars* (the latter two originated in 1960.)

In 1960, Fredericks started his career as a comic book artist with Dell and Gold Key, working on such titles as *Daniel Boone*, *The Munsters*, *Mister Ed*, *King Leonardo*, and *The Blue Phantom*. His work attracted the attention of Lee Falk, who was looking for an artist to succeed Phil Davis on *Mandrake the Magician* after Davis's death in 1964. Fredericks tried for the job and was accepted by the syndicate. His work on the *Mandrake* Sunday page and daily strip started appearing in 1965. Since that time he has devoted most of his career to drawing the feature, aside from a brief foray back into comic books in the late 1980s, inking such Marvel titles as *The Hulk* and *Captain America*.

While his illustrations for *Mandrake* cannot compare with those of Davis, Fred Fredericks has nonetheless remained faithful to the spirit of the strip. Ironically, his competent but hardly innovative artwork seems as

"Freelance," Ted McCall and Ed Furness. © Anglo-American Publishing Co.

well suited to the dull *Mandrake* of today as Davis's stirring pen line was to the golden *Mandrake* of yesteryear.

M.H.

FREELANCE (Canada) Written by Ted McCall and illustrated by Ed Furness, Freelance, a daring guerrilla battling the Axis powers, appeared during the war years in his own black-and-white comic book published by Anglo-American Publishing Company of Toronto. During a wartime embargo on the importation of American comic books, Anglo-American offered black-and-white versions of such Fawcett heroes as Captain Marvel, Bulletman, Captain Marvel Jr., Spy Smasher, and Commando Yank. Sometimes the original American artwork, *sans* color, was used, but for much of the time, the strips were redrawn by Canadian artists. Along with these reprints such Canadian creations as *Freelance*, *The Crusaders*, *Commander Steel*, *Dr. Destine*, and *Sooper Dooper, Mighty Man of Yesterday* appeared. Head and shoulders above them all stood *Freelance*.

Furness's initial artwork on *Freelance* can only be described as crude, but issue by issue he evolved a dramatic style to suit McCall's well-rounded scripts, which, within context, were relatively sophisticated for the time and generally took a realistic approach to war. True, Freelance always won out against the Axis, but it was often at great cost and physical and mental effort. An example of one such endeavor centered on Allied attempts to sink a heavily defended German battleship while it was tied up for repairs. Using a high-explosive mine dropped by an RAF bomber, Freelance, with the assistance of his powerful aide Big John Collins, managed to fasten it to the side of the battleship and set it off under cover of a diversionary air raid. The Nazis believed the battleship's destruction was due to a powerful new type of bomb dropped by the British and therefore did not take reprisals against French civilians for an act of sabotage.

In his book-length adventures, Freelance operated all over the map—in France, Italy, Yugoslavia, Belgium, Portugal, Switzerland, North Africa, and Southeast Asia—giving the Axis all kinds of problems and always leaving his trademark, a tiny stick figure jauntily waving from its perch on a flying lance, a symbol similar to that of Leslie Charteris's The Saint. Freelance's nationality was never clearly established in any of the stories, although in issue number 2 (July-August 1941) he is described as a "valiant champion of freedom's cause who fights alone for Britain—and doomed by fate to hide his true self from his own people."

Of all the Canadian wartime comic books, the Anglo-American titles were the most cheaply produced. The covers were newsprint, printed in black and white and one other basic color and, the interior pages, of course, were black and white throughout. But, when Anglo-American converted to full color at the end of the war, its product became thoroughly professional in appearance. However, U.S. competition was too tough, and within two years, Freelance had disappeared. With him went any hope for a viable Canadian comic book industry.

P.H.

FREYSE, BILL (1898-1969) One of the most skillful and enthusiastic imitators of a major strip artist's feature characters, Bill Freyse has been equaled in this difficult art only by F. O. Alexander (who continued Kahles' *Hairbreadth Harry*), Leslie Turner (Crane's *Captain Easy*), Paul Fung (Young's *Dumb Dora*), and a bare half-dozen others, out of the many who have tried. Freyse's task was to continue Gene Ahern's widely read *Our Boarding House* for NEA after Ahern decamped to King Features in 1936. Born in 1898 in Detroit, Freyse graduated from Detroit's Central High School and took his youthful talent to the *Detroit Journal*, where he did editorial cartoons until the *Detroit Times* took him on as entertainment page cartoonist. From there he went into commercial cartooning, doing advertisements, billboards, etc., until he went to work for NEA in the 1930s. His big break came when NEA turned Ahern's pompous Major Hoople and his rooming-house ménage over for daily and Sunday continuation. Freyse saw no point in tampering with Ahern's perfect formula for the strip, nor with his effective style, and he closely followed both in going forward with the strip. Freyse's comic inventiveness was the equal of Ahern's, and there was no perceptible difference in the art or content of the strip from the time Ahern left it until Freyse's death in 1969, after which the strip was continued by NEA in new and notably less adept hands. Freyse lived in Tucson, Arizona, for most of his active career with NEA. His *Our Boarding House* moves as briskly and hilariously from panel to panel as did Ahern's, and would make a fine series of reprints in book form.

B.B.

FRIDAY FOSTER (U.S.) *Friday Foster* made its debut on January 18, 1970. Written by Jim Lawrence and drawn by the Spanish artist Jorge Longaron, it was distributed by the News-Tribune Syndicate.

Friday Foster is a black American woman, beautiful and sophisticated, who comes to New York to start a professional career as a photographer. Her assignments for agencies and newspapers bring her into contact with many diverse characters, both glamorous and shady. From New York to Hong Kong she always maintains her cool and her remarkable qualities of understanding and good humor.

The scripts, frequently devoted to Friday's sentimental complications, sometimes lightly delve into racial problems. It is evident from the reading of the strip that Lawrence (or his editors) tried hard not to offend anyone (in the most hallowed tradition of syndicate editors) and thus defeated the stated purpose of the strip.

Longaron's remarkable artwork could not compensate for the blandness and aseptic quality of the scripts. *Friday Foster* started floundering after the first few years. At the beginning of 1974 Longaron left the strip, to be succeeded by Gray Morrow, who was unable to stem the downward slide, and *Friday Foster* finally expired in May of the same year.

Friday Foster is worthy of interest purely on an artistic level and as another example of a doomed collaboration between American scriptwriter and foreign artist, a combination that has never proved successful in the history of the American comic strip.

M.H.

FRISE, JAMES LLEWELLYN (1891-1948) A self-taught Canadian cartoonist-illustrator born on a farm on Scugog Island, Ontario, in 1891, Jimmie Frise created one of the enduring institutions of the Canadian popular arts—*Birdseye Center*, a weekly black-and-white strip that was the comic realization of everyone's dream of small-town life, but with a gentle touch of satire and slapstick humor. Until the age of 19, Frise helped out on his father's farm and then, in 1910, headed for Toronto to pursue a career in drawing. He got a job with an engraving company, Rolph, Clark, Stone, ruling squares on Canadian Pacific Railway immigrant-settlement maps of Saskatchewan. Six months later, when the map project was completed, Frise was let go and almost immediately, on the strength of a cartoon submitted on speculation, was hired by the *Toronto Star*'s art department.

In 1916, Frise moved to Montreal to work for another engraving firm, but after a few months left that job to enlist in the Canadian Field Artillery. During overseas service, he lost part of his left hand (not his drawing hand) when an enemy shell landed so close to him that it killed two packhorses he was using to deliver ammunition to his battery. After the war, Frise returned to the *Toronto Star* and, in a few months, was a full-time cartoonist-illustrator for the *Star Weekly*, the *Star*'s separate weekend publication that included features, fiction, comics, and rotogravure sections.

In 1921 Frise began a weekly panel called *Life's Little Comedies*, which, by 1922, evolved into *Birdseye Center*. Regular characters developed over the next 25 years, including Pig-Skin Peters, Archie, Eli and Ruby, Big Jack the Giant Jackrabbit, Hector the Pup, the Police Chief, and the Captain of the Noazark, a tiny lake steamer.

"Friday Foster," Jorge Longaron. © News-Tribune Syndicate.

Frise left the *Star Weekly* in 1947 to join the *Montreal Standard*, which offered him the opportunity of doing the strip in color. The *Star Weekly* retained the *Birdseye Center* title, so Frise's strip became *Juniper Junction* in the *Standard*, which began syndicating it to the U.S., initially in Pennsylvania and New Jersey. Frise's death 18 months later cut short his promising new career.

In 1965, a hardcover collection of Frise's *Birdseye Center* panels was published by McClelland & Stewart Ltd., Toronto, and in 1972 the 43rd Battery Association published a collection of his wartime drawings.

P.H.

FRITZ THE CAT (U.S.) Perhaps the best-known of the "underground comix" features is writer/artist Robert Crumb's *Fritz The Cat*. Paradoxically, however, only the last Fritz story was created with the underground comic book market in mind, all the others being drawn for Crumb's own amusement. Even more ironic was the fact that although *Fritz The Cat* didn't begin to reach the public eye in significant quantities until 1968 and 1969, all but two of the stories were drawn before 1965.

The definitive Fritz the Cat character—complete with human dress, human foibles, wiseacre dialogue, and upright posture—was apparently first drawn for one of Crumb's numerous one-copy comics, *Crumb Brothers Almanac*, which Robert and brother Charles Crumb produced and dated October 15, 1959. This book—which, like all the other Crumb brothers books

before it, did not call the character Fritz by name, and which featured a more feline Fritz prototype—was meant only for Crumb's friends and relatives. From then on, Robert Crumb produced many pencil and pen-and-ink Fritz stories, almost none of them being publicly presented. In fact, the first general-public appearance that Fritz made was in the "Fred the Teenage Girl Pigeon" strip in *Help!* magazine in 1965. In this James Warren-published, Harvey Kurtzman-edited magazine, Fritz is not called by name, but the escaping rock star that eventually eats the girl pigeon groupie is definitely Fritz. Another story done around this time, which recounts Fritz's journey around the world and his return to seduce his sister, finally appeared in 1969, in a pamphlet entitled *R. Crumb's Comics and Stories*.

Most of the 1959-1965 stories that Crumb produced were lost, but the dozen or so stories that eventually surfaced produced a mass of publicity for Crumb and the character. *Head Comix*, an outsized paperback book published by Viking Press in 1968, showcased some of the finest Fritz material. Again, all of this work was first done in 1960-65 and was just being published. In 1969, two more old *Fritz The Cat* stories were published for the first time by Ballantine. A third story, *Fritz the No-Good*, was drawn specially by Crumb for the book in 1968, almost three years since his last Fritz effort, and he has said that he produced it simply to fill out the book.

Fritz The Cat is essentially a phony, and the fact that he is a cat is arbitrary. He is quite human, in fact more human than many of the people Crumb was to draw later in his career. He is a con man, a sex maniac, and totally incorrigible. Artistically Crumb handled the strip with a fixed "camera" angle: there were no innovative storytelling approaches, most of the panels consisting of simple, medium-range shots. And generally, Crumb's work here is more sexually subdued than his later, more explicit material. Some critics contend that the bulk of the Fritz material was Crumb's "wish fulfillment": Fritz was glib, Crumb was not; Fritz was a ladies' man, and Crumb did not see himself as such. Crumb denies such a relationship, but in any event, he dropped the character in 1965. His original Ballantine strip, as mentioned, was done only to fulfill a commitment.

His only other strip done after 1965 was drawn in 1972, and he did it simply to kill off Fritz the Cat. Crumb was moved to do this new strip—which was the only one prepared expressly for underground comic books and appeared in *People's Comics*—because of the forthcoming *Fritz The Cat* animated motion picture. In 1969, Crumb met with Ralph Bakshi and Steve Krantz to discuss a possible *Fritz The Cat* motion picture. Crumb says he never "really" agreed to the film, but production went on haltingly and the X-rated film was released in 1972. Crumb hated it, took the producers to court to have his name removed from the film, and drew the story that eventually appeared in *People's Comics*. In the story, Crumb showed a new Fritz: a playboy movie star who is becoming a "fatcat" establishment type along with cohorts "Stevie" and "Ralphie." Crumb kills Fritz by having a rejected female ostrich split his skull with an icepick. In this way, the enigmatic Crumb rids himself of a character he had outgrown years before it ever appeared publicly, and also disassociated himself from any further Fritz movies.

A second Fritz movie, *The Nine Lives of Fritz The Cat*, was produced in 1974 without Crumb or Bakshi, and unlike its predecessor, this film was both financially and artistically a disaster.

J.B.

FUCHS, ERIKA (1906-   ) German writer, translator, and editor, born in Rostock, Macklenburg. Erika Fuchs, née Petri, was the only girl to attend the boys' secondary school emphasizing the study of Latin and Greek in Belgard an der Passante, in Pomerania. Intending to become an art dealer, she studied the history of art, archaeology, and ancient history at the Universities of Lausanne, London, and Munich from 1926 to 1931. She received her PhD—magna cum laude—for her dissertation "Johann Michael Feichtmayr—a Contribution to the History of the Rococo." In 1932 she married Günter Fuchs, an engineer and inventor.

Living in her husband's native Schwarzenbach/Saale after World War II, she freelanced, translating articles for the German edition of *Reader's Digest* in Stuttgart. While visiting there, she met a representative of Walt Disney Productions who was looking for four Germans who would collaborate on a German edition of *Mickey Mouse*. Her husband's arguments that there were some pedagogical aspects to the job contributed to her decision to become editor-in-chief of *Micky Maus*.

The first issue of *Micky Maus* appeared in September 1951 and was a smash success, no little thanks to Mrs. Fuchs, whose linguistic artistry enhanced the success of Carl Barks' *Donald Duck* and of the other Disney features in the comic book that was made up of material from *Walt Disney's Comics and Stories*. At first, *Micky Maus* was published monthly, then specials were added on a monthly basis until the book turned to biweekly. Finally, in December 1957, *Micky Maus* turned weekly.

The day Mrs. Fuchs accepted her editorial job on *Micky Maus* was a very lucky one indeed for German children. This brought them not only the wit of the likes of Carl Barks and Paul Murry but also the wit and witticism of a highly literate lady (with a penchant for the works of Jane Austen, George Eliot, and Henry James) whose translations have a flavor all their own that, in its creativity, has yet to be surpassed by other writers. Despite allusions to literature, her dialogues are never bookish, and those who have grown up with

"Fritz the Cat," Robert Crumb. © Robert Crumb.

"Fuku-chan," Ryūichi Yokoyama. © Asahi.

her version of Disney comics fondly cherish the gems of her genial wit.

Erika Fuchs met Carl Barks for the first time in 1992. While she retired from her position as editor-in-chief of the *Mickey Maus* comic long ago, at age 90 she is still at work translating Barks's stories that have not yet been published in Germany. Fuchs has probably been the strongest influence on the German language in the past four decades. Her lines are quoted like those of the literary geniuses of the past and Internet-speak abounds in her vernacular.

W.F.

FUKU-CHAN (Japan) On January 25, 1936, Ryūichi Yokoyama created *Edokko Ken-chan* ("Ken from Eddo") for the *Daily Asahi*. Fuku-chan was only a secondary character, but, as often happens in comic strips, his popularity soon grew larger than that of Ken-chan, the titular hero, and as of October 1, 1939, the strip's title was changed to *Fuku-chan*. From this time, and for the next 35 years, Fuku-chan became the hero, and his popularity remained constant through the years, not only in newspapers, but also in magazines. On January 1, 1956, the strip transferred to the *Daily Mainichi*, where it appeared until its demise on May 31, 1971.

Fukuichi Fukuyama, alias Fuku-chan, was a five-year-old boy, bright and lovable, always wearing a college cap, wooden clogs, and a short kimono. His name was derived from that of a cartoonist friend of Yokoyama's, Fukujirō Yokoi, as were the names of most of the others characters in the strip: Konkichi Shimizu, alias Kon-chan (inspired by cartoonist Kon Shimizu); Kiyoshi Shimizu, alias Kiyo-chan; and Namiko Shimizu, all little friends of Fuku-chan. There were also Arakuma the moocher (whose name came from a comic book) and Fuku-chan's grandfather Fukutarō Fukuyama. (The latter two were the most famous characters in the strip, after Fuku-chan himself.)

The stories, genteel and simple, retraced the daily adventures of the little hero, his friends, and his family. At one time *Fuku-chan* was as popular in Japan as *Blondie* was in the United States. (Their humor was not that dissimilar.) It remains the longest-running daily strip in the history of Japanese comic art.

The masterpiece of Ryūichi Yokoyama, *Fuku-chan* has been beloved by intellectuals as well as by the general public. It has also influenced many cartoonists. Fuku-chan himself has become the mascot of Waseda University during their yearly baseball match with the rival Keiō University.

H.K.

FULLER, RALPH BRIGGS (1890-1963) An American artist born in Michigan in 1890, R. B. Fuller's first work in a major market was a drawing sold to *Life* magazine in 1910. It was incredibly crude and out of place in that journal, but editor J. A. Mitchell obviously had a sixth sense about latent talent: Charles Dana Gibson's first drawing for *Life* in 1886 was also embarrassingly crude.

In short order Fuller was the most published cartoonist in American magazines. His panel cartoons filled the pages of *Puck*, *Life*, and *Judge*, as well as *Collier's*, *Harper's*, and, later, *Liberty*, *Ballyhoo*, *College Humor*, and occasionally the *New Yorker*.

His work was so popular that in the early 1920s *Judge* devoted a standing feature—*Fuller Humor*—to his work, an honor afforded few others.

The early cartoons, even when Fuller was published everywhere, were always slightly crude and stiff, just as was the work of his contemporary, Percy Crosby. Just after the war, however, Fuller's work matured and he mastered anatomy and his tools; the inevitable pen-and-ink cross-hatching gave way to a handsome use of washes. Unlike many of his fellows, he wrote all his own gags and was one of the funniest of the breed that launched *Ballyhoo* and brought lunacy to *Judge* magazine in the mid-1920s.

With cartoon markets drying up in the Depression years, Fuller turned his creative talents to the strip form and sold *Oaky Doaks* to Associated Press Newsfeatures. It debuted in October 1935. Into this strip, one of the classic historical comedies in all of stripdom, Fuller poured his long experience, excellent artistic capabilities, and a pleasantly surprising knack for writing continuities. He immediately adapted to the strip format; *Oaky Doaks* has some of the greatest inane adventures in comics. His funny characterizations of sappy men and brassy women were inimitable.

Fuller was bitter when the AP folded its comic operation in 1961. His strip was appearing in few papers then, but was still witty and stood far above its few fellow survivors in the AP stable, such as the poorly drawn *Scorchy Smith* by John Milt Morris. Fuller reluctantly laid down his pen, for he enjoyed drawing the strip.

An accomplished watercolorist, Fuller lived for years in the artists' colony around Tenafly and Leonia, New Jersey. He died on August 16, 1963, while vacationing in Boothbay Harbor, Maine.

R.M.

FULTON *see* Lazarus, Mel.

FÜNF SCHRECKENSTEINER, DIE (Germany) *Die Fünf Schreckensteiner* ("The Five Schreckensteiners"), by the artist Barlog, graced the pages of the *Berliner Illustrirte* (Berlin Illustrated) from 1939 to 1940. The *Berliner Illustrirte* had already had experience with the comics medium in the form of the very successful *Vater und Sohn*. The five Schreckensteiners are the ancestors of the modern-day owners of Castle Schreckenstein (which might be translated as Scarystone). They are depicted on three paintings hanging on the castle's walls. A large rectangular one shows the three early seventh-century gentlemen, the brothers Schreckenstein. A smaller oval painting holds the ancestress in

Restoration dress. A small square picture with a little boy is there, too. At the stroke of midnight the five Schreckensteiners step out of their paintings to haunt the castle for one hour. They are very playful ghosts whose pranks never fail to leave butler Johann or the castle's owner with open-mouthed consternation. One very cold night they step out of their paintings shivering with cold. They step over to the fireplace to warm up. Finally, at the stroke of one A.M., the butler is flabbergasted to see that the paintings have moved from their wall to a spot above the fireplace.

The *Schreckensteiners* were done with a kind of humorous realism that looks a bit like cute picture-book illustrations. They used speech balloons sparingly. In one 1940 episode they commented on the war effort, admonishing their offspring not to hoard. Apart from that they remained true to their prankish nature and kept out of politics during their run of 51 episodes, 46 of which were reprinted in book form at the end of 1940.

Artist Barlog, before doing the Schreckensteiners, had already been known for his comic strip work in *Der heitere Fridolin* ("Cheerful Fridolin"), a biweekly children's magazine that was started in 1921. For it Barlog had drawn *Laatsch and Bommel*, a Mutt-and-Jeff-type pair, and *Professor Pechmann* ("Professor Badluck"). Some of Pechmann's inventions, like TV, have since become reality. *Pechmann* combined pictures and verse much like the traditional Bilderbogen. *Der heitere Fridolin* also featured *Benjamin Pampe* by Schafer-Ast, who put his hero on a new job in every episode. There was also *Onkel Toldi* ("Uncle Toldi") with his dog Schlupp. They are practically forgotten nowadays, and their tradition, by and large, has been replaced by the traditions imported (and reimported) with foreign comics.

W.F.

FUNG, PAUL (1897-1944) Born in 1897 in Seattle into the family of a Baptist minister of Chinese origin named Fung Chak, Paul Fung started school in Portland, Oregon, and was then sent by the Reverend Fung to secondary school in China, where he studied art in the traditional Chinese mode. His father, however, sent him the American Sunday comic sections in packages from home every month, and the young Fung, more excited by these than by the fan painting of his instructors, developed an expert comic strip style—to the dismay of his conservatively raised classmates and teachers. Back in Seattle, the boy finished Franklin High School and prepared for Stanford (from which his father had been an honorary graduate). The unexpected death of his father left Fung on his own, and the boy managed to get a position on the *Seattle Post-Intelligencer* as a sports and news cartoonist in 1916. There, on March 1, his first comic strip, *Innocent Hing* (about a young Chinese boy in traditional clothes facing problems in an American city) appeared, but was short-lived, as the editors obviously preferred Fung's talents in sports commentary.

In the early 1920s, the *Post-Intelligencer* became a Hearst newspaper, and Fung a Hearst employee. His talents caught the eye of his new boss, and before long Fung was turning out such popular Hearst strips and panels as *A Guy from Grand Rapids*, *Bughouse Fables*, and others. When Chic Young left *Dumb Dora* in April 1930 to start *Blondie*, Fung was assigned to continue the popular strip both daily and on Sunday, which he did in fine style. He then went to work as assistant to the

great Cliff Sterrett on *Polly and Her Pals* later in the 1930s. Fung died on October 16, 1944, and was survived by his talented cartoonist son, Paul Fung Jr., whose active career in comedy began as a six-year-old Warner Brothers film star named One Long Hop (the name being his father's invention). Highly skilled, Paul Fung Jr. has drawn the *Blondie* comic book for many years and today lives in Greenwich, New York, on a "116-acre chop suey farm."

B.B.

FUNKY WINKERBEAN (U.S.) Appearing in some 400 newspapers, Tom Batiuk's strip was syndicated in 1972, first by Publishers-Hall, then by Field Enterprises, and now by North America Syndicate. It takes place in and around Westview High School and presents the goings-on of the students and their teachers in mildly amusing fashion.

As a high school student, Funky Winkerbean is an average teenager, more interested in girls than in trigonometry. Other characters in the strip include Bull Bushka, the gridiron star, whose low football scores match his IQ; the bespectacled Les Moore, a nerd as inept at sports (he was once a bowling goalie) as with pretty coeds. Grown-ups, mostly teachers and coaches, are not any smarter or more dedicated than the students. Mr. Dinkle, the band director, always in his glittering uniform, is apt to lead his charges down the field in a freezing rain, compose some silly ditty for Earth Day assembly, push yet another candy sale fund-raiser on an unwilling student body, or celebrate the first anniversary of the Rock and Roll Hall of Fame by playing "A Hundred Bottles of Beer on the Wall . . ." on the sax.

Besides the talking computer or the copying machine with an attitude, the strip's other personnel include Cliff the security guard, who enjoys Sundays, since the students are not in attendance; Dr. Schoentell, a superintendent who lacks vision for the future, in contrast to Westview's principal, who cannot wait for the 21st century so he can *finally* retire. With a team named the Scapegoats, Coach can only be the losingest man in the school's football history.

As the pizza-parlor proprietor, Tony Montoni is the only adult who understands and empathizes with the kids. Never one to lecture, he teaches his young clients by example and by the genuineness of his concern for them.

Over the last few years, many of these students have graduated: Les is now an English teacher, a soon-to-be published author (he wrote a novel on the murder of talk-show host John Darling), and the husband of perky Lisa Crawford (wedding reception *chez* Montoni and honeymoon in Niagara Falls); he seems to have taken over the entire strip, even if Funky appears every so often as a worker in Tony's pizzeria. Following Coach's final humiliating defeat and subsequent retirement, Bull takes over at the helm of the Scapegoats, although the team probably won't win soon under his direction either.

During all of this character development, Batiuk has dealt with some important social and adolescent problems, ranging from underfunding of schools to teenage smoking and drug abuse. A June 1995 sequence, for instance, showed in a compassionate manner how Susan Smith, an A+ student and a lovely girl, had attempted suicide over her unrequited love for Les, her English teacher.

FUNKY WINKERBEAN

"Funky Winkerbeam," Tom Batiuk. © Batom Inc.

The anecdotes are drawn in a pleasant, unencumbered style suitable to the daily happenings at good old Westview High.

P.L.H.

FURIO ALMIRANTE (Italy) The comic weekly *L'Audace* was purchased in the early months of 1940 by Casa Editrice Idea of Gianluigi Bonelli, who transformed it completely in content as well as in format. He called in the most able Italian writers and artists of the period, and after a few months he changed the magazine (which until then had published a whole series of continuing strips) into a comic book featuring a complete story devoted to a different character each issue, foreshadowing the postwar editorial trend.

Among the most successful characters, there was Furio Almirante, conceived by Bonelli himself with illustrations by Carlo Cossio. Furio's psychology was very close to that of Cossio's very popular Dick Fulmine, and Furio was soon nicknamed "the steel-fisted man" for his great ability in the ring. First called *X-1 il Pugile Misterioso* ("X-1 the Mysterious Prizefighter"), the strip was soon rechristened *Furio Almirante*. In February 1941 Carlo Cossio turned over the feature to his brother Vittorio.

Furio had thick, raven-black, curly hair and was exceptionally strong; he exterminated the hoodlums who tried to muscle in on the boxing business as well as the racketeers who preyed on the poor Italian immigrants of whom Furio became the defender. Thanks to his job, which took him from Africa to Central America and from Australia to Canada, Furio was able to help a host of expatriate Italians victimized by unscrupulous foreigners.

In 1942, when the war propaganda was at its peak among comic strip heroes, Furio (whose adventures were now produced by Franco Donatelli and Enrico Bagnoli) did his duty in a number of battles in every conceivable theater of war. When the speech balloons were later abolished from the strip, *Furio* looked more like a propaganda tract than a story meant to entertain.

After the war, the strip was revived with appropriate modifications and was presented in a new version drawn by Franco Bignot: it was met with indifference, however, and lasted but a few months.

G.B.

FURTINGER, ZVONIMIR (1912-   ) A Yugoslav writer, journalist, radio editor, good historian, expert technician, passionate sailor, constant researcher—in short, a man who is interested in everything and who knows about everything—Zvonimir Furtinger was born in Zagreb on November 12, 1912. The world crisis of 1929 interrupted his schooling, and he had to take care of his mother and himself. Furtinger worked as a gravedigger, magician, musician, singer, clerk, and technician and studied military science, history, and linguistics. His life's wish was to be a naval officer. However, today he sails only his own yacht. He has published several science-fiction novels and monographs on Schliemann and Karl May.

In the 1950s Furtinger started writing for comics. His first product was a science-fiction strip drawn by Walter Neugebauer and titled *Neznanac iz svemira* ("An Unknown from the Universe"). After that he met Jules Radilović, and they collaborated on many comic strip series together. The most popular ones were *Herlock Sholmes, Kroz minula stoljeća* ("Through the Past Centuries"), and *Afričke pustolovine* ("The African Adventures"), which they produced for *Plavi Vjesnik* magazine in Zagreb, and later for *Strip Art*, Sarajevo.

Furtinger also collaborated with Žarko Beker and Zdenko Svirčić, also cartoonists of the *Plavi Vjesnik* group. Furtinger is now an editor at Zagreb Radio Station and the author of several radio and TV dramas.

E.R.

FUSCO BROTHERS, THE (U.S.) The innovative and wacky strip *The Fusco Brothers* was developed by J.C. Duffy for Lew Little Enterprises and began distribution by Universal Press Syndicate in August 1989.

An illustrator as well as cartoonist, J.C. Duffy attended Temple University's Tyler School of Art and contributes drawings to the Philadelphia *Daily News*. His drawings have appeared in such publications as *Esquire* and *TV Guide*. He has designed greeting cards distributed by Recycled Paper Greetings since the early 1980s.

His strip depicts the lives of Rolf, Al, Lars, and Lance Fusco, who live in Newark, New Jersey, with their pet dog Axel. Axel, who thinks of himself as a wolverine, uses word balloons, not thought balloons, to speak with the other characters. In essence, he is the fifth brother, sharing the family physical trait of a large nose. Occasionally Ma Fusco visits the brothers. She leaves the impression that the never-seen Pa Fusco is a career criminal. Asked why she now lives in Nebraska, Ma responds that she wants to be close to Mr. Fusco, who used to make license plates in New Jersey and now makes them in Nebraska.

While each brother has a distinct personality, it is difficult to tell them apart. This may be the reason why

THE FUSCO BROTHERS

LARS, WHY DON'T WE HAVE A LITTLE CONTEST...LET'S SEE HOW LONG IT TAKES ME TO GET A DATE. THEN LET'S SEE HOW LONG IT TAKES YOU TO GET A DATE.

MAYBE WE SHOULD SYNCHRONIZE OUR WATCHES.

MAYBE YOU SHOULD SYNCHRONIZE YOUR CALENDARS.

"The Fusco Brothers," J.C. Duffy. © Universal Press Syndicate.

Duffy often has the brothers address each other by name. Although they are all in the strip together quite often, the four do not equally share the spotlight. It is usually Lance and family dog Axel who carry the strip. Al is the easily contented, not-too-bright optimist. Lars is quiet, and Rolf considers himself a classy individualist, although others consider him neither. Lance has a live-in girlfriend named Gloria, but he shirks from commitment. Gloria often bests Lance with rapier comebacks to his comments. While reading *Gray's Anatomy*, Lance grabs Gloria's arm and bites her elbow. "I'm trying to keep the humerus in the relationship," he explains. "A little knowledge is a terrible thing," Gloria retorts, inspecting her bleeding elbow.

Theirs is a strange love, but *The Fusco Brothers* is a strange strip and therein lies its charm. Even though the strip has no action drawings, Duffy has fun with his artwork. In one daily, "Al has an out-of-drawing experience," only Al's feet and his shadow on the floor are seen in the frame as his word balloon shouts "Help!" Rolf looks up from reading the newspaper to comment to Axel, "Gosh, You don't see this kind of thing in *Beetle Bailey*." Axel, with martini in hand, responds, "With good reason, perhaps." *The Fusco Brothers* have been called "nerds for the nineties." Duffy blends wild, hip writing with artwork that uses strong cross-hatching and dots, and solid black areas to keep the strip varied and visually interesting.

B.C.

FUSHIGINA KUNI NO PUTCHĀ (Japan) Fukijiro Yokoi's *Fushigina Kuni no Putchā* ("Putchā in Wonder World") made its first appearance in the Japanese monthly *Shōnen Kurabu* in 1947.

Putchā, the son of a Japanese scientist, and his companion, the robot Perii, met Dr. Banbarun, who had invented an electric wave that allowed people to levitate in the skies. Dr. Bunbarun tried out his invention on Perii, and it worked; Perii, however, was spirited away by Bunbarun's arch-rival, Torahige, in his black plane. After many chases and adventures, Putchā, with the help of Dr. Banbarun, rescued his robot companion.

After this episode, Dr. Banbarun, Putchā, and Perii started a long journey through the universe in the year 2047. They discovered a new element, X-nium, capable of neutralizing atomic power (a big concern in Japan at the time) on the moon, then traveled to Mars, where they met with the Martian president who, gave them a seven-color light wand with supernatural powers.

The feature was a blend of comic strip and illustrated story, using both balloons and narrative under the pictures. After Fukijiro's death on December 5, 1948, the strip was taken over by Tetsuo Ogawa. It lasted only for a short time longer.

Fushigina Kuni no Putchā was the star strip of its time, and it is credited for the renewed interest in science fiction as a source for comic art in Japan.

H.K.

FŪTEN (Japan) Created by Shinji Nagashima, *Fūten* made its first appearance in the April 1967 issue of the monthly magazine *COM*. It related the doings of those young boys and girls who had dropped out of general society (they were called "fūten" and were the Japanese equivalents of the American hippies). *Fūten* soon became a favorite of young people, and Nagashima's

"Fūten," Shinji Nagashima. © Shinji Nagashima.

most famous creation, along with *Mangaka Zankoku Monogatari* ("The Cruel Story of a Cartoonist").

There was no one hero in the strip. The main characters were Hinji Nagahima (a cartoonist, and the creator's alter ego), Coat-san (a clever fūten who always wore a coat), Minori (a vagabond fūten), Akira (a former trumpet player), and Sanchi. Midorikawa, the only one of the little band holding down a job, and Shachō, a company president turned fūten after he had met Nagahima and his companions, were also in the strip.

Nagashima graphically depicted the reasons why all these people had dropped out of society, and he pictured their lives filled with decadence and suffering, but also with joy and fulfillment. The creator tried to answer the questions: "What is life?" and "What is the meaning of youth?", drawing on his own experience as a fūten.

The strip was the second in a trilogy titled *Kiiroi Namida* ("Yellow Tears"); the first had been *Mangaka Zankoku Monogatari* (1961), and the third was *Usura Retsuden* (1971). *Fūten* last appeared in June 1970 in the twice-monthly magazine *Play Comic*.

Fūten has been reprinted twice in book form—first as a large-run paperback, and second as a deluxe limited edition.

H.K.

FUTUROPOLIS (France) In 1937 the readers of the French comics weekly *Junior* were treated to a new series of hitherto unprecedented violence (at least in a French comic strip): *Futuropolis* by René Pellos.

Futuropolis is a subterranean city of the remote future dominated by a tightly knit oligarchy—"the Sages"—who rule their subjects with the help of a heartless technology and an arid science. The masters of Futuropolis, upon learning that on the earth's surface there still remains a race of men that have gone back to the Stone Age, decide to send one of their henchmen, Rao, and his female companion, Maia, to destroy the "barbarians." Rao, however, befriends the primitive but honest and loyal stone-men and leads a revolt against the masters of Futuropolis. The struggle soon involves not only what remains of mankind but also the animal and vegetable kingdoms, and even the primeval forces of nature, all uniting in a final Götterdämmerung that engulfs the whole planet.

In *Futuropolis* the text (there are no balloons) is tightly enclosed in the surrounding images. Pellos's style, an epitome of kinetic tension and restless motion, prefigures Hogarth's. His compositions, chaotic and forceful, sweep away all semblance of normality in a whirlwind of jarring images and distorted perspectives. The characters, tense with excitement or braced for danger, never seem to know peace and are in constant turmoil.

Futuropolis is at once an outstanding example of comic art at its most powerful, and an almost desperate cry against the civilization of the machine (a theme dear to the French science-fiction writers of the time). It is now justly regarded as a classic comic, on a par with *Buck Rogers* and *Flash Gordon*.

M.H.